The Holyrood Inquiry

D1586730

A Report by the Rt Hon Lord Fraser of Carmyllie QC on his Inquiry into the Holyrood Building Project

This report, presented to the First Minister, Rt Hon Jack McConnell MSP and the Presiding Officer, Rt Hon George Reid MSP, is laid before the Scottish Parliament by the Rt Hon Lord Fraser of Carmyllie QC and is published by the Clerk of the Scottish Parliament under the authority of the Parliament in accordance with a resolution of the Parliament of 24 June 2004.

WITHDRAWN

15 September 2004

SP Paper No. 205   Session 2 (2004)

Acknowledgements

The conclusion of my Report could not have been achieved without the masterful work of Derek Bearhop as Secretary to the Inquiry. As this Report will reveal, I am not uncritical of the performance of a number of public servants from which criticism Derek is wholly excepted. Scotland should be proud that it has in Derek Bearhop such a fearlessly independent public servant with a keen eye for detail, unswerving objectivity and a preparedness for hard work.

Diane Barr from the Scottish Parliament has, to my advantage, demonstrated her high intelligence and her incomparable capacity for hard work. She and Derek were central to the task and I acknowledge, with the greatest respect, their contributions.

Lauren Drummond was irrepressibly charming and helpful and if she had not already achieved her ambition of joining a Ministerial Private Office, that would have been one clear recommendation I would willingly have offered the First Minister.

Jonathan Elliott was a quiet but thoroughly effective member of the Team and valued by all.

John Campbell, Counsel to the Inquiry, is now, with cause, after the brilliance of his questioning throughout the Inquiry probably the most famous QC in Scotland. He could not have achieved that immense reputation without the tireless and assiduous work of Douglas Tullis assisting him. Lawyers do not come better than Douglas.

Jim Cassidy and Archie Mackay of Media2k have been invaluable with their shrewd and skilled media advice.

We were all working on the principles of openness and transparency. Neither could have been achieved without the contributions of this small Team. The mould of past inquiries in Scotland has been broken and their workings will never again be allowed to become remote or opaque.

ISBN 1-4061-0013-7

© Scottish Parliamentary Corporate Body 2004.

All photographs © of the Scottish Parliamentary Corporate Body, except the photograph of the Rt Hon Lord Fraser of Carmyllie which is © of Media2k.

Contents

Contents

Introduction

I was invited by the First Minister, the Rt Hon Jack McConnell MSP and the Presiding Officer of the Scottish Parliament, the Rt Hon George Reid MSP to undertake an inquiry into the cost over-run and the delays in the construction of the Scottish Parliament building. My agreed terms of reference were:

"To review the policy decisions in relation to the Holyrood Project taken prior to its transfer to the Scottish Parliamentary Corporate Body on 1st June 1999 and subsequently.

To build on the Auditor General's existing findings in respect of procurement strategy and cost control, contractual and project management arrangements and to extend the consideration of these issues to cover the subsequent stages of the project.

All with a view to producing a full account of the key decisions and factors which have determined the costs and value of the Parliament throughout the life of the project and the processes involved in reaching those decisions and to identifying the lessons to be learned for the procurement or construction of major buildings in the future; and to report to the Parliament and the Scottish Executive as soon as reasonably practicable, taking account of the Auditor General's intention to examine the economy, efficiency and effectiveness with which resources have been used at all stages of the Scottish Parliament building project."

There are a number of features of this remit to be highlighted. I am invited to "build on" the work of the Auditor General for Scotland and I have sought to do that utilising his Report of September 2000 and more recently his Report of June 2004. Apart from an opening Press Conference and a preliminary hearing we have not sat together but we have maintained regular contact with a view to avoiding unnecessary duplication and to ensuring no relevant issue was overlooked by both of us. In addition there has been regular and useful contacts between our respective Teams.

I am not invited to offer any observation on the aesthetics or architectural value of the buildings. If I had been invited to do so, I would have declined. That assessment is not for me but for this and future generations of Scots. Prior to 1997 I was Sponsor Minister for the North East of England and I received regular entreaties to intervene to prevent the erection of the Angel of the North. I did not do so as I could not see what I could have done even if I had wanted to. Once it had been erected, it immediately became one of the best-loved pieces of public art anywhere. In similar fashion once the Scottish Parliament building has been stripped of all cranes and scaffolding and all construction activity has ceased, the Scottish public can make up its own mind on the architectural merits of the buildings.

Nor was I invited to comment on the workability of the building as a Parliament and rightly so. That assessment is properly and exclusively for MSPs, their staff and the staff of the Scottish Parliament itself.

Donald Dewar harboured an aspiration to be "the most important patron of the architecture of government for 300 years" and it is not difficult to understand why he was so enthused by what Enric Miralles presented to him in concept. The eloquent and perceptive Miss Joan O'Connor put it thus:

"His heart was in developing a contemporary icon. He wanted to make a landmark building that would identify that particular moment in Scotland's history."

Sadly, at the present time my measured consideration is that the quality of what he sought to achieve has been mired in never-ending complaints of spiralling costs and ever-extending delays.

With the honourable exception of Sir David Steel on behalf of the SPCB accepting some responsibility for increased costs, the ancient walls of the Canongate have echoed only to the cry of "It wis'nae me". That has made my task more difficult. Ian Rankin has written a cunning Rebus novel with the Holyrood site at its core but in my book there is no single villain of the piece. Rather there has been a series of systemic failures and an unwillingness of those involved in the Project to call a halt and demand a re-appraisal. The few that tried were quickly shown the door.

It is a matter of dismay to me (and I understand this view to be shared by the First Minister and Presiding Officer) that the BBC and/or Wark Clements Ltd have declined to allow me other than the most restricted access to tapes accumulated for a proposed programme "The Gathering Place" to be shown publicly in one or more episodes in late 2004 or early 2005. I repeatedly made it clear that if my request put anyone's life at risk, I would immediately desist. However, no such risk has been claimed. All I wanted was access to tapes to be shown to the public at some point in the future, to allow me to be confident that no stone had been left unturned and that there was no contradiction on tape, from the late Donald Dewar or the late Enric Miralles or other primary players which would cause me to re-consider the conclusions of this Report.

I was first told that contractual agreements with those filmed precluded any showing of the tapes. However the evidence before the Inquiry did not support that. For example, John Home Robertson MSP (Convener of the HPG) told the Inquiry that he had been filmed repeatedly. He had neither signed nor had he required any agreement to be signed to the effect urged by the BBC. It is true that some of those interviewed did require no disclosure prior to the showing of "The Gathering Place" and declined to give any waiver and I would have respected that, however unwarranted I regarded it. However that option was never offered to me.

Having voiced this dismay and criticism of the BBC and having been unable with an application to the Courts to require that the tapes be handed over, I am bound to say that I remain nevertheless doubtful whether anything relevant to the Inquiry will be revealed in "The Gathering Place" beyond that already before the Inquiry. However, for the greater caution, I have to advise the First Minister and the Presiding Officer that I cannot formally close this Inquiry until I have seen the programme(s).

It causes me particular discomfort to level this criticism against BBC Scotland as I have nothing but unstinting praise for the manner in which Val Atkinson and her Team covered the Inquiry. It was done in ground-breaking fashion and I received not a single complaint that the coverage was intrusive or unacceptable. On the contrary across Scotland the coverage has been lauded. For the early evening news Brian Taylor was unerring in his assessment of the significance of the evidence on any particular day and I concur with *The Scotsman's* observation that the analysis on Newsnight Scotland of the Holyrood Inquiry was "unmissable". That is rightly quoted with pride within BBC Scotland's Annual Report.

I have seen it alleged that my criticism of Sir Muir Russell will be muted on account of the fact he was once my Private Secretary when I was the Junior Minister for Agriculture and Fisheries in Scotland. While in time he did head up Agriculture, Environment and Fisheries in Scotland, I was never a Minister with these responsibilities and he was never my Private Secretary. He had been known to me from his time as Principal Private Secretary to the late George Younger in the 1980's and it would not have been difficult then to predict his rise to the top of the Scottish Office but I do not hold back from personal criticism on account of a familiarity 20 years ago.

In my view he was unwise to write the report set out in Annex B to the Auditor General's Report of September 200 but as Permanent Secretary of the Scottish Executive he possibly had no option. He would not appear to have been engaged in the calculation that led to the non-reporting of the cost-consultants risk estimates to the late Donald Dewar and was not personally to blame. Nevertheless he fell on his sword and attracted the criticism of the Audit Committee that if as Accountable Officer at the Scottish Office he was not given information on cost estimates from the earliest stages, he should have done more to seek it out. That led the Committee to conclude that he was "semi-detached from the process".

I heard no new criticism during the course of the Inquiry and note only that he bristled with righteous indignation that words like "illegality" and "impropriety" had been used, albeit not in evidence, in relation to the selection of Bovis as Construction Manager, but he declined to offer a judgment on that selection in the light of the later decision in <u>Harmon</u> and the advice from the Comptroller and Auditor General. He cannot be criticised for that, but it would have been interesting to have heard the views of a former Permanent Secretary.

There have also been accusations made that the Holyrood Inquiry has resulted in an increase in costs and had an adverse effect on the programme. For example, John Home Robertson MSP made the claim that having key people preparing the Inquiry was causing costs to rise and delays to the Project and asked that it be put on record that Mr Brian Stewart had attended the Inquiry from October through to December 2003 and that: "His absence did give rise to some difficulties."

Mr Stewart gave evidence for half a day on 3 December 2003 and was timetabled to give evidence in March 2004 on a date convenient to him. Mr Stewart's attendance during 2003 had therefore been, with one exception, entirely a matter of personal choice. Mr Stewart in turn claimed that the client's decision to appoint the Inquiry at this time had caused delays and cost increases:

"The point is respectfully made that the decision to appoint the Inquiry – to sit in the very months when completion by July 2004 was to be such a 'drop dead' objective for all concerned – is in itself evidential of the at times contradictory nature of the client's demands."

Mr Home Robertson was requested to provide information to the Inquiry Team of any delay to the project occasioned by the Inquiry. To date no information confirming this has been received from either Mr Home Robertson or any other party.

I conclude that although the timing of the Inquiry may not have been ideal given the deadline for completion, I have received no evidence of it having contributed in any significant way to the cost of, or delay to the Project.

The revelation during the course of the Inquiry that MSPs on the Holyrood Progress Group were being asked to choose between a linoleum floor cover at £75/sq m or oak at £100/sq m for their Block has given rise to the impression that the whole Project was nothing but a surfeit of extravagance and self-indulgence. As I trust my analysis reveals, that is nothing like the whole story.

In my view at relatively early stages a number of decisions were taken which were fundamentally wrong or wholly misleading. It is the consequences of those decisions which have caused the massive increases in costs and delays. Coupled with that the situation was admirably summed up in a curt handwritten note by Mr Ian McAndie, a partner at Davis, Langdon & Everest as far back as March 1999:

"Nobody tells Enric to think about economy with any seriousness."

Little in this Report improves on that early astute observation.

Finally, this Report is delivered by its due date and within budget.

The Rt Hon Lord Fraser of Carmyllie QC

Chapter 1

Events Prior to 1 May 1997

The 1979 Referendum

1.1   Earlier proposals for a Scottish Assembly nearly came to fruition in 1979 when the UK administration held a referendum to offer this constitutional change to the Scottish electorate. The outcome of the March 1979 vote was controversial; not least because a clause had been inserted during the Parliamentary proceedings of the Scotland Act on the initiative of a Labour backbencher, George Cunningham MP. This clause provided that unless 40% of all those entitled to vote voted in favour the Government had to lay an Order before Parliament which, if passed, would repeal the Act.

1.2   The referendum saw a narrow majority of those who voted in favour of the devolution proposals but some parts of Scotland voted against and, with a turnout of only 62.9%, the 'Yes' vote fell considerably short of the required 40% of the electorate. The Labour Government accordingly tabled an Order repealing the Scotland Act 1978 although Parliament did not vote on the Order until after the change of Government in May 1979. The experience of 1979 may have played some part in the subsequent determination of the incoming Labour administration in 1997 to ensure that its devolution proposals, including a building for the Parliament, were irreversibly established. This has been asserted as being the reasoning behind the Secretary of State's swift move to secure a site for the Parliament so quickly after the success of the

1997 referendum. So far as I am aware there is no written record of a conclusion to this effect by Donald Dewar. If, however, this did influence his thinking it was erroneous.[1] The Conservative Party in Scotland recognised immediately after the 1997 referendum that a Scottish Parliament was going to be set up and ceased its hostility towards it. Furthermore, the Conservative Party in the United Kingdom had privately appreciated that it had virtually no prospect of winning the General Election after 1997 and had no plans to repeal the Scotland Act 1998. If he had so chosen, Donald Dewar could have proceeded in a more leisurely fashion with the selection of a site for the Scottish Parliament without putting the Government's devolution proposals in their entirety at risk.

Scottish Constitutional Convention

1.3 In the period following the 1979 referendum a number of pressure groups were formed which were influential in keeping the issue of constitutional change in front of the public and the political parties during the period of the Conservative administrations. One such group was the Campaign for a Scottish Assembly. This "gathering of notables"[2] produced a report in 1988 *A Claim of Right for Scotland* which asserted the right of the people of Scotland to decide on their own constitution. A key recommendation of the report was that a convention should be brought into being to draw up a blueprint for a Scottish Assembly or parliamentary body.

1.4 Accordingly, a body calling itself the Scottish Constitutional Convention was set up and held its first meeting in March 1989. Although the Conservatives and the Scottish National Party declined to participate, the Convention included members of the other main political parties, local authorities, trade unions, churches and other organisations. The joint chairs of the Convention were Lord Ewing of Kirkford and Sir David Steel, and its Executive was chaired by Canon Kenyon Wright. The Convention's final report, *Scotland's Parliament, Scotland's Right*, was presented on St Andrew's Day 1995.

1.5 The report proposed the key elements of the constitutional changes that would form the backbone of the subsequent White Paper. The proposals were for a Parliament of 129 members, elected under an additional member system; a power to vary the basic rate of income tax by up to 3p in the pound; and substantial devolution of legislative and executive functions to a Scottish Parliament and an Executive formed from it. The report made only one reference to the accommodation that might be required by the proposed legislature. Under a chapter headed "What price accountability?" the Convention's report stated:

---

[1] Evidence of Mr Kenneth Thomson on 3 February 2004, Par 85
[2] Himsworth C (The Scotland Act 1998) (2nd Edition) W Green & Son 2000

'The cost of Scottish democracy will certainly be no more than the current cost of government in Scotland. A building is waiting ready on Edinburgh's Calton Hill. The Parliament will have the power to set about replacing many of the undemocratic, accountable and expensive quangos which blight Scottish political life.'[3]

1.6 Convention confirmed that in its deliberations there had been little concern attached to the ultimate home for the proposed Parliament.[4] Some assumptions had, however, been made from the beginning; such as that the Parliament would be located in the capital city, Edinburgh, and that being so, the Old Royal High School (which had been earmarked to accommodate the Assembly had the 1979 referendum been successful) would provide a suitable location. It was stated to the Inquiry that the Old Royal High School building had been part of "the journey of devolution".[5] In his evidence Mr Henry McLeish, Minister of State for Home Affairs and Devolution, also suggested that, against some of the other daunting priorities at that time, the Parliament building itself was not a major consideration prior to 1997.

Labour's 1997 Manifesto

1.7 The Labour Party manifesto for the 1997 General Election included a pledge to enact as soon as possible after the election legislation to allow the people of Scotland and Wales to vote in referendums on devolution proposals to be set out in White Papers. Those referendums were to take place not later than the autumn of 1997. For Scotland the manifesto proposed the "creation of a parliament with law-making powers, firmly based on the agreement reached in the Scottish Constitutional Convention". There was a further manifesto commitment, subject to the outcome of the referendum, to introduce in the first year of the (UK) Parliament legislation on the substantive devolution proposals.[6] The White Paper that would set out the detail of these proposals would require to be a wide ranging document addressing those matters to be reserved to Westminster, the structure of government in Scotland, relations within the UK and with the European Union, local government, as well as tax raising powers, financial, electoral and parliamentary arrangements.[7]

1.8 As with the Convention's proposals, in the scheme of the Labour party manifesto the accommodation arrangements for the new Parliament was not mentioned at all.

---

[3] *Scotland's Parliament, Scotland's Right*, Page 17
[4] Evidence of Sam Galbraith on 28 October 2003, Para 100
[5] Evidence of Henry McLeish on 29 October 2003, Para 23
[6] *"New Labour: Because Britain Deserves Better"*, The 1997 Labour Party Manifesto
[7] White Paper - http://www.scotland.gov.uk/government/devolution/scpa-00.asp

Briefing for Incoming Ministers

1.9   The Inquiry had it confirmed that it has been the long-standing practice of the Civil Service to anticipate the various potential outcomes of General Elections and to undertake a detailed scrutiny of political manifestos with a view to identifying how parties' policies could be implemented. The Permanent Under Secretary of the Scottish Office at the time, Sir Russell Hillhouse, spoke of the tasks and pressures facing officials in evidence to the Inquiry:

> "What always happens when an election is declared is that, throughout the government machine, senior civil servants get together and prepare briefing for incoming Ministers of both main parties. In fact, usually these days, work is done for other parties as well. This normally takes the form of a fairly lengthy incoming brief, divided into subjects, which picks up all the main points in the manifesto, and which also briefs them on all the running issues which they will encounter as soon as they step in the door, or which may turn up in the first two or three weeks.
>
> In the case of Labour in 1997... we did have this very, very major commitment which would affect the Scottish Office, and which had very acute time constraints. Therefore, for devolution in 1997, we made rather special efforts and we did identify, in good time, small teams of capable officials whom we could put together as soon as the election campaign began in earnest, and who would have to work up quite detailed papers in order to get early decisions from our Ministers, which they could then try to work through the Cabinet process, since it was clear to us that one would have to produce a White Paper, fully cleared, explaining the Government's plans for a Scottish Parliament, well in advance of a referendum date. The referendum, in turn, would have to take place in time to clear the way for the introduction of a Bill — assuming the referendum was won — and all that meant a very tight timetable indeed."[8]

1.10   On taking office on 2 May 1997 the incoming Labour Ministers were presented with such a briefing which had been prepared under the direction of Mr Robert Gordon, who was then Head of Constitution Group. One part of that briefing addressed the accommodation needs of the Scottish Parliament and stated:

> "New Parliament House (the former Old Royal High School) is available under the City of Edinburgh Council's ownership and we assume that Ministers will want that to be the Parliament building. While the Debating Chamber appears to be suitable the condition of the structure is unknown and the building's interior is very inflexible. However, use of the building would avoid a potentially difficult debate about alternative sites and it is likely, in the short term at least, to be cheaper than purpose built new accommodation." [9]

---

[8] Evidence of Sir Russell Hillhouse on 30 October 2003, Para 236-237
[9] SE/2/169-180 – Briefing from Mr Robert Gordon for Incoming Ministers, May 1997

1.11   Mr Gordon suggested to the Inquiry that the content of the briefing on these matters would have involved contributions from staff in Accommodation Division, Estate Services and possibly the Building Directorate. He also assumed that the City of Edinburgh Council might have been consulted in connection with references to New Parliament House.[10] The Inquiry has uncovered no evidence, either in documentation or in oral testimony, to suggest that Scottish Office officials had any expectation prior to May 1997 that an incoming Labour Government would do other than consider the Old Royal High School building as the preferred home for the proposed Scottish Parliament.

---

[10] Evidence of Mr Robert Gordon on 4 November 2003, Para 29

Chapter 2

White Paper to the Passing of the Scotland Act 1998

The Ministerial Team

2.1.   On 2 May 1997, after election with a landslide majority of 179 in the House of Commons, Tony Blair appointed Donald Dewar as his Secretary of State for Scotland. Donald Dewar had been the Labour Party Chief Whip while in opposition. His appointment came as a surprise to many. The Ministers of State at the Scottish Office were Henry McLeish and Brian Wilson, and the junior ministers included Sam Galbraith and Lord Sewel. All four gave evidence to the Inquiry. Mr Dewar appointed Ms Wendy Alexander and Mr Murray Elder (later Lord Elder) as his Special Advisers, both of whom also gave evidence.

The Civil Service Team

2.2.   The Scottish Office Constitution Group, headed by a senior civil servant, Mr Robert Gordon, was charged with delivery of the manifesto commitment on devolution for Scotland. The Group comprised four teams:

- The Constitutional Policy Team, led by Ms Isabelle Low with responsibility for co-ordination and editorial control of the White Paper and later for development of constitutional policy and electoral aspects of the Scotland Bill;
- The Powers and Functions Team, with responsibility for the functions of the Parliament and Executive, involving co-ordination across the entire Scottish Office and extensive negotiation with most Whitehall Departments to settle the

extent of the proposed Parliament's legislative powers and the responsibilities of the proposed Scottish Executive;

- The Referendum, Legislation and Implementation Team, led by Mr Paul Grice with responsibility for the Referendum Bill and the conduct of the Referendum, co-ordination of the Scotland Bill and making the staffing and other preparations to allow the Parliament to become operational in May 1999;

- The Legal Advisers Team, with responsibility for providing legal advice, instructing legislation and drafting subordinate legislation.[11]

2.3. At that time Mr Gordon reported to Mr Muir (later Sir Muir) Russell, then Head of the Scottish Office Agriculture, Environment and Fisheries Department. Mr Russell, who had retained a particular responsibility for constitutional affairs since working in the Cabinet Office in 1992,[12] in turn reported to Sir Russell Hillhouse, the Permanent Secretary. The Scottish Office structure at that time is set out by Mr Gordon in a diagram which he presented to the Inquiry

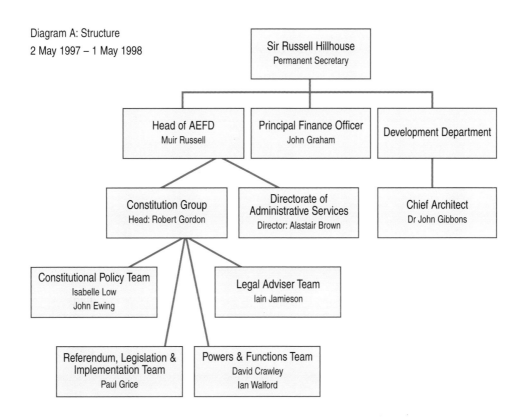

Diagram A: Structure
2 May 1997 – 1 May 1998

2.4. Working closely with Mr Gordon's team was the Directorate of Administrative Services, the responsibilities of which included accommodation planning and services, and which was headed by Mr Alistair Brown who also reported to Mr Russell. Mrs Barbara Doig, then the Head of Accommodation Division, reported to Mr Brown. Similarly involved in consideration of accommodation for any new Parliament was Dr John Gibbons who held the position of Chief

[11] WS/18/001–010 – Mr Robert Gordon's First Witness Statement, 4 November 2003
[12] Evidence of Sir Muir Russell on 5 February 2004, Para 13

Architect and Director of Building.[13] In this capacity he was head of a multi-disciplinary group known as the Building Directorate which provided advice and support on building matters to all the Departments of the Scottish Office. He was also head of the Construction and Building Control Group which formed part of the Scottish Office Development Department and consisted of two separate Divisions, one of which, headed by the Chief Quantity Surveyor, Mr Alastair Wyllie, had responsibility for building procurement and project and programme advice.

2.5.   On 1 May 1998 Sir Russell Hillhouse retired and was replaced as Permanent Secretary by Mr Russell. Mr Gordon continued as Head of the Constitution Group reporting directly to Mr Russell. Mr Gordon thereafter had managerial responsibility for the Directorate of Administrative Services, still headed by Mr Brown,[14] in addition to the four teams previously reporting to him.

2.6.   Donald Dewar's private office was then headed by Mr Michael Lugton, his Principal Private Secretary, who was succeeded by Mr Kenneth Thomson on 8 September 1997.

Drafting the White Paper – Site Selection

2.7   The Inquiry learned that, in anticipation of a Labour electoral success, civil servants had undertaken some rough drafting of a possible White Paper prior to the election.[15] On 3, 4 and 5 May 1997 Mr Gordon took part in lengthy discussions with Donald Dewar, Murray Elder and Wendy Alexander on the tactics of giving effect to the manifesto commitment to legislate quickly for a Scottish Parliament.[16] Thereafter officials undertook further work on draft chapters which were to be cleared with Scottish Office Ministers. Ms Low circulated a draft White Paper among civil servants on 7 May 1997, section 11.1 of which said:

> 'It is expected that the New Parliament House (the former Old Royal High School) and its ancillary buildings will, after purchase from the City of Edinburgh Council, house the Chamber, Committee Rooms and main offices of the Scottish Parliament. The refurbishment will need to be extensive to bring the building up to a standard appropriate for modern parliamentary use.'[17]

2.8   As more fully set out in paragraph 4.1, on 30 May 1997 Donald Dewar paid a visit to the Old Royal High School (ORHS) and expressed serious reservations about its suitability. From that time the presumption that had previously existed in favour of the ORHS site was displaced and it was accepted that a range of sites should be identified and evaluated; a situation which was

---

[13] WS/17/001-015 - Dr John Gibbons' First Witness Statement, Para 3, 24 November 2003
[14] SE/2/1496 – Organisation Chart dated 1 May 1998 to 23 December 1998
[15] SE/1/087-092 – Minutes from Mr Paul Grice to Ms Isabelle Low, 16 April 1997
[16] WS/18/001–010 – Mr Robert Gordon's First Witness Statement, 4 November 2003, Para 12
[17] SE/1/073-075 – Minute from Ms Isabelle Low, Draft White Paper, 7 May 1997

reflected in subsequent drafts of the White Paper. As Mr Gordon put it in his first written statement to the Inquiry: 'This was the point at which our previous assumption that the Parliament would be in ORHS was first questioned seriously'.[18]

2.9 Throughout June and July 1997 work continued on the White Paper. A new draft was produced on 4 July 1997 which included a passage as follows:

'*A home fit for the Scottish Parliament*

10.2 The building the Scottish Parliament occupies must be of such a quality, durability and civic importance as to reflect the Parliament's status and operational needs; it must be secure but also accessible to all including people with special needs; it must promote modern and efficient ways of working and good environmental practice.

10.3 It will be an important symbol for Scotland. It should pay tribute to the country's past achievements and signal its future aspirations. It must be flexible enough to accommodate changes over time in operational requirements. Quality and value for money are also key considerations.

10.4 The accommodation must allow Scottish Parliamentarians and their staff to work efficiently harnessing the best of modern technology. People must be able to see and meet their elected representatives and to watch the Scottish Parliament in operation. Provision needs to be made to permit easy reporting and broadcasting of Parliamentary proceedings so that people throughout Scotland can be aware of its work and decisions.

10.5 Scotland's Parliament will be in its capital city. Edinburgh is the natural centre of government in Scotland. The bulk of the staff who will transfer to the Scottish Executive and be answerable to the Scottish Parliament already work there.

10.6 The Government are looking carefully at options available in Edinburgh which can best meet the criteria set out above. These will include new buildings as well as the conversion of existing ones. One of the options will be the Old Royal High School on Calton Hill. It is an existing building which has been widely regarded as the inevitable choice for the Parliament since it was prepared for this purpose in the 1970s. There are, however, serious disadvantages associated with the Old Royal High School. Public accessibility is poor - particularly for people with disabilities; there is little suitable space within the main building for people to meet their representatives; space is so limited that MSPs and their support staff would need to

---

[18] WS/18/001–010 – Mr Robert Gordon's First Witness Statement, 4 November 2003, Para 17

have their offices elsewhere; and there is an inherent lack of flexibility in the accommodation.'[19]

2.10   This wording represented the final format for the White Paper which was published on 24 July 1997.

Cost Estimates in the White Paper

2.11   The earliest cost estimate in relation to which evidence has been produced to the Inquiry was put before a pre-election meeting of Scottish Office officials on 11 March 1997 The minute of that meeting, which does not confirm who was present, records:

'... there will be inevitable significant costs in capital for administration and additional running costs (the table attached contains the costings we put together in November 1995 in response to a *Scotsman* article .....on the eve of the Constitutional Convention's proposals)...'.[20]

2.12   An article in *The Scotsman* of 29 November 1995[21] had postulated costs of around £10.5 million for the acquisition and reconstruction of the Old Royal High School.   The table[22] annexed to the note of the 11 March meeting gave figures as follows:

Capital Items	Costs	Notes
Parliament building	£12m	Purchase (£2m) and refurbishment (£10m) of Old Royal High School; listed building requires substantial expenditure to make wind and watertight and bring up to a standard appropriate for modern Parliamentary use
Offices for MSPs plus support staff	£10m	Assume that SAH used; **that major refurbishment is not included;** but that the building is fitted out to a standard comparable to other Parliamentary buildings; that meeting and media facilities in line with Convention's proposals are provided; and facilities for MPs at Westminster
Parliamentary staff offices	Inc in figs above	Assume most of Parliament's staff will have to be located in SAH; some in ORHS (eg Speakers Department)
Additional offices for Scottish Office	£14m	Assume that Parliament requires all of SAH; 800 staff displaced and space required for additional staff (750 assumed in 1979 scheme); assume that new building(s) is/are leased rather than purchased outright; capital costs of fit out only.
Total	£36m	

---

[19] SE/1/049-051 – Minute from Ms Isabelle Low to PS/Secretary of State, 4 July 1997
[20] SE/1/138-140 – Minute of Meeting on Infrastructure Issues, 11 March 1997
[21] SE/1/141 – *The Scotsman* article "Adding up parliamentary bills", 29 November 1995
[22] SE/1/138-140 - Minute of Meeting on Infrastructure Issues, 11 March 1997

2.14 The identity of the originator of those figures was not the subject of evidence before the Inquiry and could not be clarified in correspondence with the Scottish Executive. The figures would seem likely to have come from within the former Scottish Office but there was in evidence the suggestion of an input from the City of Edinburgh Council, see paragraph 2.20 below. In the absence of clear evidence it is not for me to speculate as to their precise source.

2.15 The early drafts of the White Paper put together by civil servants in April 1997 prior to the election referred to costs in only the most general way. The draft of 16 April 1997 simply stated:

> 'There will be initial capital costs in establishing the Scottish Parliament and with the refurbishment of both New Parliament House and St Andrews House accounting for a large percentage of the capital costs'.[23]

2.16 The first draft of the White Paper produced to the Inquiry which included actual estimated figures for capital expenditure was that dated 21 April 1997, Section 11.6 of which stated:

> 'Overall the capital costs of establishing the Scottish Parliament – purchasing and refitting the New Parliament House and other buildings – are estimated to be between £24.5 and £34 million...............Detailed estimates are set out in Annex D'.[24]

2.17 No copy of Annex D to that draft of the White Paper had been retained and it was not available to the Inquiry. The range of figures between £24.5 and £34 million is the same as that provided in the briefing to incoming Ministers[25] which included a table in the following terms:

Function	Notes	Minimum cost	Maximum cost
Parliament Building	Purchase (£2-3m) from the City of Edinburgh Council and refurbishment (£8-10m) of New Parliament House: listed building assume substantial expenditure to make wind and watertight and to bring up to a standard appropriate for modern parliamentary use	£10m∗	£13m∗
Offices for MSPs' support staff	Assume that SAH used; that major upgrading is not included; but building is fitted out to a standard comparable to other Parliamentary buildings; that members' accommodation, meeting and media facilities in line with Convention's proposals are provided and are similar to those at Westminster	£8m	£12m
Parliamentary staff offices	Assume that most will be located in SAH with some in NPH	Included in above figures	

---

[23] SE/1/085-087 – Minute from Mr Fergus Cochrane to Ms Isabelle Low, 16 April 1997
[24] SE/1/078-081 - Minute from Mr Fergus Cochrane to Mrs Barbara Doig, 21 April 1997
[25] SE/2/169-180 - Briefing from Mr Robert Gordon for Incoming Ministers, May 1997

Offices for Executive (displaced from SAH plus additional staff)	Assumes between 250 - 500 additional staff required in Departments and a net displacement of up to 300 due to use of SAH for MSPs and support staff, more intensive use of existing buildings and min. new acquisition of leased building(s), capital costs of fit out only, temporary decant only	£6m	£8m
Offices for residual SofS staff	Assumes between 25-50 staff in separate self contained building in suitable locations	£0.5m	£1m
Total		**£24.5m**	**£34m**

∗ Note these figures are very tentative estimates which require to be refined by more defined work.

2.18 This range of figures was confirmed, but without further information as to their source, in a minute from Mr John Graham, the Principal Finance Officer, to Donald Dewar of 13 May 1997.[26] In a minute of 20 May 1997[27] from Mr Brown to Ministers he put forward estimated overall costs of £19 to £28 million for the acquisition and refurbishment of ORHS and the fitting out of St Andrew's House and of £36.5 to £48 million to include additional works to St Andrew's House. He had not at that stage examined the costs of possible sites other than ORHS. The subsequent draft of the White Paper of 6 June 1997[28] referred in section 13.2 to the range of between £24.5 and £34 million as set out in Annex E,[29] the terms of which bear close resemblance to the table contained in the briefing to Ministers.[30] It is not clear why the figures given in Mr Brown's minute were not used at that time.

2.18 The draft of 13 June 1997[31] restated in section 10.15 the range of £25 to 34 million under reference to an Annex C in the same terms[32] and was the last draft to express figures in such terms. Further discussions as to the appropriate way for cost estimates to be expressed continued culminating in a minute dated 27 June 1997 from Ms Low to the Secretary of State's Private Secretary enclosing a briefing paper for Donald Dewar's use at the Devolution for Scotland, Wales and the Regions (DSWR) Cabinet Sub-Committee meeting on 1 July. In relation to costs Ms Low advised:

- 'We are currently working up our best estimates for capital and running cost expenditure. These are likely to be expressed as ranges.

---

[26] SE/1/030-032 - Minute from Mr John Graham to PS/Secretary of State, 13 May 1997
[27] SE/2/156-163 - Minute from Mr Alistair Brown to PS/Henry McLeish and PS/Secretary of State, 20 May 1997
[28] SE/1/009-011 – Minute from Ms Isabelle Low to PS/Secretary of State, 6 June 1997
[29] SE/1/011 - Annex E of Minute from Ms Isabelle Low to PS/Secretary of State, 6 June 1997
[30] SE/2/169-180 - Briefing from Mr Robert Gordon for Incoming Ministers, May 1997
[31] SE/1/016-19 - Minute from Ms Isabelle Low to PS/Secretary of State, 13 June 1997
[32] SE/1/019 - Annex C of Minute from Ms Isabelle Low to PS/Secretary of State, 13 June 1997

- We are inclined to drop Annex C to the current draft as a table of this nature might give the impression of spurious accuracy.' [33]

2.19 The next draft of this chapter of the White Paper to appear became available on 2 July 1997, paragraph 10.17 of which was in the following terms:

> "**Costs**
>
> It is not possible to say precisely how much the accommodation would cost until a final decision is made on where to locate and how to build or refurbish the Parliament building and on the most suitable funding option. **However the capital costs of establishing the Parliament are estimated to be between £10 million and £40 million..."**[34]

In a further draft circulated by Ms Low on 4 July 1997 this passage had been revised to read:

> 'It is not possible to say precisely how much the accommodation would cost until a final decision is made on where to locate and how to build or refurbish the Scottish Parliament building and on the most suitable funding option. Because of the range of sites under consideration and the variety of funding methods potentially available it is necessary to express the cost as a range of between £10m and £40m.'[35]

This was the format which eventually found its way into section 10.7 of the final version of the White Paper which was published on 24 July 1997.[36] In other words, although an earlier minimum of £24.5 million had been identified, for the purpose of the White Paper the minimum cost was reduced to £10 million.

The Origins of the £24.5 to £34 million Range

2.20 There was an absence of conclusive evidence before the Inquiry as to who had responsibility for the £24.5/£25 to £34 million range quoted in the annexes to the sequence of drafts prepared between 21 April and 13 June 1997. Mr Wyllie was asked in relation to Annex E of the draft of 6 June 1997[37] if he recognised the format as something for which he had responsibility.[38] He confirmed that he "had no involvement in the compiling of that set of figures" and that they "did not come from the Building Directorate". He went on to suggest that they may have emanated from the City of Edinburgh Council or from The Edinburgh Development & Investment Limited (now known as The EDI Group Limited), the Council-

---

[33] SE/1/052-053 - DSWR Briefing Paper from MS Isabelle Low to PS/Secretary of State, 27 June 1997

[34] SE/1/087A-092- - Minute from Mr Paul Grice to Ms Isabelle Low, 2 July 1997

[35] SE/1/048-051 – Minute from Ms Isabelle to PS/Secretary of State, 4 July 1997

[36] White Paper http://www.scotland.gov.uk/government/devolution/scpa-13.asp

[37] SE/1/007-011 – Minute from Ms Isabelle Low to PS/Secretary of State, 6 June 1997

[38] Evidence of Mr Alastair Wyllie on 4 November 2003, Paras 98 *et seq*

owned property development company.[39] He thought that the costs related to St Andrew's House might have come from Accommodation Division. Support for the view that these figures might have emanated from the City Council is to be found in the written statement provided by Mr Brown prior to his evidence on 6 November 2003 in which he said:

> "The source of the costings associated with the ORHS option in the submission of 20 May was the pre-election briefing prepared for incoming Ministers, which indicated that work to prepare a debating chamber and ancillary services would cost in the range of £8 million to £10 million. This estimate was prepared before I moved into the (*Directorate of Administrative Services*) post. However I believe that it would have been based on a condition survey of the ORHS buildings carried out a few years earlier on behalf of City of Edinburgh Council. Costs associated with the work on SAH would have been based on detailed assessments of the condition of SAH carried out by professional firms engaged by (*Accommodation Division*), who had in 1995 or 1996 prepared detailed, costed options for refurbishing the building and replacing building systems."[40]

The Origins of the £10 million Figure

2.21 The evidence is inconclusive as to what the £10 million figure was intended to cover or as to the origins of that figure. A possible explanation for the figure is to be found in the evidence of Mr Wyllie who, when questioned about its origins, said:

> "I do not know precisely; the only possible clue I have had subsequently is through reading other papers since the event. Clearly, at the time the new Administration was coming in, there was information from the City of Edinburgh Council and their consultants that it might cost around — I think £8 million to £10 million is the figure I recall...... — possibly around £10 million to refurbish the Royal High School building. So there is a figure of £10 million. Now whether it was that figure that was used or not, I do not know, but of course that was simply a minimum figure to refurbish the Royal High School. There would be additional costs on top of that for refurbishing St Andrew's House and adding whatever office accommodation was needed. That could be the £10 million, but I have no way of knowing."[41]

2.22 In his evidence Mr Brown suggested that the £10 million figure might have represented "whatever incidental one-off costs would have been associated with establishing a Parliament in a building which was provided by a developer and leased or rented or some such arrangement".[42] Mr Grice thought that the figures had been produced by colleagues from

---

[39] Evidence of Mr Alastair Wyllie on 4 November 2003, Para 108 *et seq*
[40] WS/15/001-013 – Mr Alistair Brown's Witness Statement, Para 2.4, 6 November 2003
[41] Evidence of Mr Alastair Wyllie on 4 November 2003, Para 224
[42] Evidence of Mr Alistair Brown on 6 November 2003, Para 256

"building/accommodation",[43] which I understood to be a reference to the Building Directorate and/or the Accommodation Division. In the written statement given prior to his evidence on 4 November 2003, Mr Gordon referred to "the wide range of possible outcomes still under discussion at that stage including minimal work on ORHS/St Andrew's House and/or private funding at the lower end of the range...".[44]

2.23 On the evidence before me it is clear that, whatever may have been its source, the £10 million figure was intended to cover no more than a minimal refurbishment of the Old Royal High School. As such it would only have been sufficient to provide temporary accommodation for the Scottish Parliament and not a permanent home. Perhaps it could have been intended to cover the incidental costs associated with a leased building or one acquired by PFI/PPP or by some means other than conventional funding. As was confirmed by Sir Muir Russell in a letter of 24 October 2000 to David McLetchie,[45] the bottom end of the range of £10 to £40 million was effectively eliminated in October 1997 when it was decided to pursue options involving extensive building work. It thereafter became an irrelevance although the extent to which the Scottish public could have been expected to grasp this is unclear.

The Origins of the £40 million Figure

2.24 The evidence before the Inquiry is reasonably clear that this figure originally came from Mr Wyllie. On 10 June 1997 he minuted Mrs Doig with his costing of the option of constructing a new building on a greenfield site. Assuming a building with an area of 15,000m² gross (11,250m² net – a net to gross ratio of 25%) including 1,000m² for the Chamber, 3,000m² for Committees and Ministers and 11,000m² for the remainder, he put forward figures "in the order of £35-40 million".[46] His minute made it clear that the figures included professional fees, fit out, furniture and VAT although the position in this respect contrasts with his written precognition[47] in which he said that his figures had "excluded site works, fit out, professional fees and VAT". In a further minute of the same date to Dr Gibbons he elaborated on that range of figures as follows:

---

[43] WS/22/001-005 – Mr Paul Grice's First Witness Statement and Evidence of Mr Grice on 5 November 2003, Paras 55 and 56

[44] WS/18/001–010 – Mr Robert Gordon's First Witness Statement, 4 November 2003, Para 18

[45] SE/1/039 – Letter from Sir Muir Russell to David McLetchie, 24 October 2000

[46] SE/2/1547-1548 – Minute from Mr Alastair Wyllie to Mrs Barbara Doig, 10 June 1997

[47] WS/23/001-012 – Mr Alastair Wyllie's First Witness Statement, Para 12, 4 November 2003

"Option 3 – New Building on Greenfield Site

Building Cost (inc siteworks, carpets + fees)			£m
Chamber etc	$1,000m^2$ x £2,200av	=	2.2
Committee/Ministers	$3,000m^2$ x £2,200av	=	6.6
Office Space	$11,000m^2$ x £1,500av	=	16.5
Total	$15,000m^2$ x [£1,687av.]	=	25.3
Add VAT @ 17.5%			4.5
Total Shell Cost			29.8
Fit Out and furnishing (inc.VAT)			
As VQ allow 28% of net shell cost			7.1
			£36.9m

Therefore Likely Cost (exclusive of land) in the order of £35-40m" [48]

2.25 Mr Wyllie's figures were expressed as subject to a number of caveats.[49] In particular he explained that the "building costs are based on unrated (Victoria Quay) shell costs for the basic accommodation and a 47% loading for the higher quality Chamber and Committee space (equivalent to recent Court building costs)". As explained in his evidence, Mr Wyllie had proceeded by "using very broad assumptions about the likely cost required for different types of accommodation, and assuming a gross floor area that might be appropriate for a Parliament complex".[50] Mr Wyllie's purpose in putting forward these figures was as part of the exercise then in hand of evaluating the costs of the various potential sites then under consideration as described in Chapter 3.

2.26 In his written precognition Mr Brown said that in his minute to Ministers of 12 June 1997 he had advised that a new building on a greenfield site in Edinburgh would cost an estimated £35 to £40 million.[51] From his earlier note to Ministers of 6 June[52] it was clear that this estimate related to a building of about 120,000 square feet. I note that this equates to $11,148m^2$ and is close to Mr Wyllie's net figure of $11,250m^2$. He said that the £35 to £40 million figure for a 120,000 square feet building on a greenfield site at Leith was prepared at his request by Construction and Building Control Group colleagues, which I take to be a reference to Mr Wyllie. He recollected that the figure of 120,000 square feet represented the area of the Old Royal High School building (around 30,000 square feet) plus half of the net area of St Andrew's House (approximately 90,000 square feet). This was not an attempt to make an assessment of the likely accommodation needs of a new Parliament but his intention was to show that the estimated cost of the greenfield option was broadly comparable in terms of floor space to the Old Royal High School/St Andrew's House option, which at that stage assumed

---

[48] SE/2/1549–1551 – Minute from Mr Alastair Wyllie to Dr John Gibbons, 10 June 1997
[49] SE/2/1550 - Annex A of Minute from Mr Alastair Wyllie to Dr John Gibbons, 10 June 1997
[50] Evidence of Mr Alastair Wyllie on 4 November 2003, Para 158
[51] SE/2/092–100 - Minute from Mr Alistair Brown to PS/Henry McLeish and PS/Secretary of State, 12 June 1997
[52] SE/2/141–145a – Minute from Mr Alistair Brown to PS/Henry McLeish and PS/Secretary of State, 6 June 1997

that around half of St Andrew's House would continue to be available for Scottish Executive use. He believed that Construction and Building Control Group had used a costing ready reckoner to derive an overall building cost from the floor area, treating the Debating Chamber as very high quality (High Court) standard, with the remainder of the space costed as office space. In his oral evidence to the Inquiry Mr Brown confirmed that he was "practically certain" that the estimate of £35 million to £40 million which "found an echo" in the White Paper, was an estimated cost drawn up by Construction and Building Control Group. [53]

2.27   In her evidence Wendy Alexander confirmed her understanding that the £40 million figure had emanated from the two minutes of 6 and 16 June 1997 referred to by Mr Brown.[54]

2.28   By contrast Mr Mark Batho, Head of one of the Scottish Office Finance Divisions, said in his evidence to the Inquiry:

> "While the £40 million figure reflected an initial new build at Leith ....the figures had been rebased to a 1998 figure from a 1995 figure that had underpinned the White Paper £40 million figure."[55]

His comments suggest that there might have been little in the way of fresh input apart from the rebasing of the 1995 figure referred to above, but it is unclear whether he was aware of Mr Wyllie's input.

2.29   Mr Wyllie himself did not think that the £10 to £40 million range of figures had emanated from Building Division and was "surprised" that his figures might have found their way into the White Paper.[56]

2.30   The origins of the £10 to £40 million range were the subject of correspondence in 2000 between David McLetchie and Sir Muir Russell following the report of Mr Robert Black, the Auditor General for Scotland on the Project and the appearance of Sir Muir before the Audit Committee of the Scottish Parliament. In David McLetchie's letter of 27 September 2000[57] he posed two questions. The first proceeded on the basis that as the Permanent Secretary of the Scottish Office he had presumably cleared the publication of the White Paper and asked if it was intended that the published estimate in paragraph 10.7 should be for construction costs only as this fact was not clearly stated. The second was as to when the £10 million estimate

---

[53] Evidence of Mr Alistair Brown on 6 November 2003, Para 244
[54] Evidence of Wendy Alexander on 29 October 2003, Paras 259 to 261
[55] Evidence of Mr Mark Batho on 30 November 2003, Para 397
[56] Evidence of Mr Alastair Wyllie on 4 November 2003, Paras 222 to 225; WS/23/001-012 First Witness Statement, Para 12
[57] SE/1/040-041 - Letter from David McLetchie to Sir Muir Russell, 27 September 2000

was "eliminated as unrealistic by Ministers". In his reply of 24 October 2000,[58] although not taking the point that his personal appointment as Permanent Secretary was not until 1 May 1998, Sir Muir clarified firstly that the £40 million was inclusive not only of construction costs but also fees, fitting out, furniture and land acquisition. In fact Mr Wyllie's estimate of £35-£40 million was stated to be exclusive of the cost of land acquisition. Secondly, and in relation to the £10 million figure, Sir Muir made the point referred to above.

2.31 I have little difficulty in coming to the conclusion that, whatever may have been Mr Wyllie's understanding as to the use to which his figures were to be put, it was the range of costs put forward by him in his minute of 10 June 1997 which informed the figure of £40 million which appeared in the White Paper.

Was the Figure of £40 million Realistic?

2.32 In Mr Wyllie's minute of 10 June 1997 to Mrs Doig he clarified that he was proceeding on a very general assumption that the hypothetical Parliament building of 15,000m² would, for general office space, have standards of shell and fit out comparable to Victoria Quay.[59] A "significantly higher" standard was assumed for the Debating Chamber and Committee rooms. In his minute to Dr Gibbons of the same date he had pointed out that his figures had been "very much ball park estimates".[60] Mr Wyllie did not elaborate further in evidence as to the sort of building he had in mind. There was no evidence before the Inquiry to suggest that Mr Wyllie's figures, nor the caveats to which they were subject, received any scrutiny before the decision was taken to include an upper figure of £40 million in the White Paper.

2.33 Although having no personal responsibility for Mr Wyllie's figures, when it was put to Mr Brown that the £10 million to £40 million range which appeared in the White Paper were for what was described by one witness as "a bog standard new building"[61] he responded that the £40 million related "to a building that is a reasonably simple building in architectural terms" but which he would not describe as "bog standard".[62]

2.34 It is instructive to compare the £40 million figure with the more detailed costings obtained by the Scottish Office from independent quantity surveyors as part of the site selection exercise later in 1997. In August and September Doig & Smith, Chartered Surveyors, were commissioned by the Scottish Office Construction and Building Control Group to produce various costings of the range of sites then under consideration. Their advice was contained in

---

[58] SE/1/039 - Letter from Sir Muir Russell to David McLetchie, 24 October 2000
[59] SE/2/1547-1548 - Minute from Mr Alastair Wyllie to Mrs Barbara Doig, 10 June 1997
[60] SE/2/1549-1551 – Minute from Mr Alastair Wyllie to Dr John Gibbons, 10 June 1997
[61] Evidence of Sam Galbraith on 28 October 2003, Para 193
[62] Evidence of Mr Alistair Brown on 6 November 2003, Paras 283 to 285

a report dated 30 September 1997.[63] Of those sites, Leith and Haymarket would both have involved "new builds" which might relevantly be compared with Mr Wyllie's "new building on a greenfield site". Doig & Smith were proceeding however on the basis of a new building of 20,000m², including 3,600m² of car parking, as opposed to Mr Wyllie's 15,000m² building. On 30 September 1997 Doig & Smith produced "indicative estimates" for a new build on the Leith site of £54.225 to £56.95 million and for Haymarket of £67.8 to £71.2 million. In both cases fees and VAT were included but there was no reference to site acquisition costs.

2.35 While I am not in a position to challenge the validity of the calculation put forward by Mr Wyllie or the assumptions upon which it was based, it is clear to me that the £40 million figure could never have been a realistic estimate for anything other than the most basic of new Parliament buildings. However, what can be stated clearly is that at the time £40 million was included in the White Paper, there was no clear understanding whether that was a total cost including professional fees or only a construction cost. It was certainly not explained to the Scottish public what the figure was anticipated to cover.

Funding from the Scottish Block

2.36 One of the issues requiring to be addressed in the White Paper was as to whether the funding for any new Parliament was to be met out of the assigned budget or "Scottish Block" or whether it would be separately funded by the UK Government. The briefing presented to incoming Ministers pointed out that "The key question which the Government is going to have to decide is whether the capital costs of establishing the Scottish Parliament should be met from within existing Scottish resources or should be regarded as a new burden and funded by the provision of additional resources from the centre (i.e. Treasury)".[64]

2.37 The question was focused in a minute of 13 May 1997[65] from Mr Graham who sought guidance from Donald Dewar as to whether the costs of setting up and running the new Parliament should be met from within existing Scottish resources or whether a case should be argued for United Kingdom funding. The tenor of Mr Graham's advice was that Donald Dewar would "face an uphill struggle" in arguing for access to UK funds. He was concerned that to do so might provoke a wider review of Scottish funding arrangements. By 13 June 1997 it was being reported by Mr Batho[66] that the Secretary of State recognised that the prospects of getting extra money out of the Treasury were slight. No decision had been taken on the issue by 20 June 1997 when the Treasury indicated in a letter from Mr Mark Neale, Head of the Scotland,

---

[63] SE/2/1672-1685 – Fax from Doig & Smith to Mr Harry Watson, 30 September 1997
[64] SE/2/169-180 - Briefing from Mr Robert Gordon for Incoming Ministers, May 1997
[65] SE/1/030-032 – Minute from Mr John Graham to PS/Secretary of State, 13 May 1997
[66] SE/2/131 – Minute from Mr Mark Batho to Mr Henderson, 13 June 1997

Wales and Northern Ireland Team, that it considered that the costs of establishing and running the new Parliament should fall on the Scottish Block.[67] His view was that the point should be explicitly covered in the White Paper. The point had not been conceded by Donald Dewar as at 25 June 1997 when in a minute from Mr Grice it was confirmed that the Secretary of State for Wales was bidding for extra resources.[68] The Treasury view was confirmed in a letter of 30 June 1997 from Alistair Darling, Chief Secretary to the Treasury, to Donald Dewar in which he said:

'... I think it would be better to say explicitly that the setting up costs and the running costs of the Parliament will be met from the block budget.'[69]

2.38 Acceptance of the position in this respect appears to have been a matter of inevitability. When asked about the matter when giving evidence before the Inquiry, Sir Russell Hillhouse, himself a former Principal Finance Officer, said:

"He (Donald Dewar) was tempted to wonder if he should try to make an issue of it. As a former Principal Finance Officer of the Scottish Office who spent five years operating the block system, I have to say I didn't think he had a snowball's chance in hell of getting anywhere with it. The one thing that Treasury officials were interested in in this section of chapter 10 was whether we were going to try to make a bid for any special deal, and they were making it very clear to us that that would not be acceptable and, indeed, they would probably have liked us to say something more explicit about the way the block would work. So, after a good deal of thought, and perhaps a little bit of sounding out particularly, Donald Dewar decided that this was not one of the battles he was going to enter into. There were more important things he wanted to win than that. He didn't, of course, know how much it would end up costing".[70]

2.39 Discussions took place on 3 July 1997 involving Donald Dewar at which it was agreed to accept the position in this respect as confirmed in a minute from Ms Low of 4 July 1997.[71] The agreed redraft of section 10 of the White Paper provided for both start up and running costs to be met from the assigned budget, or the "Scottish Block". The final position was accepted in terms of section 10.17 of the White Paper as published which confirmed that these costs would indeed be met from the assigned budget.

PFI/PPP – Funding

2.40 Public Private Partnerships ("PPP") embrace a wide range of co-operative ventures between the public and private sector which include the Private Finance Initiative ("PFI") which was a

---

[67] SE/1/033-034(R) - Letter from Mr Mark Neale to Mr Kenneth Mackenzie, 20 June 1997
[68] SE/1/024-027 - Minute from Mr Paul Grice to PS/Secretary of State, 25 June 1997
[69] SE/1/035-038(R) – Letter from Alistair Darling to the Secretary of State, 30 June 1997
[70] Evidence of Sir Russell Hillhouse on 30 October 2003, Para 305
[71] SE/1/048-051 - Minute from Ms Isabelle Low to PS/Secretary of State, 4 July 1997

creation of the early 1990s. Under a PFI scheme, rather than procuring a capital asset directly, the public sector purchases services from private sector businesses which create and own the assets needed to provide them. Payments are then made for the services provided. The advantages of PFI include the transference of risks to the private sector but a high degree of certainty about a project is usually necessary before a private sector PFI provider is prepared to take on those risks.

2.41   The briefing for incoming Ministers did not make any reference to the alternative methods of funding potentially available but funding options were raised in Mr Brown's minute to Ministers of 20 May 1997.[72] He raised in general terms the possibility of Millennium or lottery funding as well as PFI and pointed out in relation to the latter that it would be unlikely to deliver the Old Royal High School buildings in usable form by the dates then in mind of having a debating chamber available for the spring of 1999 and a completed building by April 2000.

2.42   By the time of Mr Brown's next minute of 6 June 1997[73] investigations had been carried out into the possibility of Millennium or lottery funding which had revealed significant difficulties in that area. The possibility of PFI funding was further raised in a minute from Mr Batho of 13 June 1997[74] to his colleague Mr John Henderson of the Private Finance Unit from whom a discussion paper was requested. The Inquiry heard evidence from Wendy Alexander that Donald Dewar had on a number of occasions asked for advice on both PFI and indeed on the involvement of a private developer.[75]

2.43   On 16 June 1997 Mr David Rogers of the Private Finance Unit circulated a minute on the subject highlighting the requirement under PFI rules for a sufficiently significant transfer of risk to achieve "off balance sheet" accounting and for there to be demonstrably better value for money.[76] A draft paper was circulated by Mr Henderson on 20 June 1997 in terms of which he set out at length the perceived advantages and possible disadvantages of PFI.[77] He concluded that a well managed PFI procurement could well take 18 months from a Ministerial decision on the preferred option and procurement route to contract signature which, allowing for a construction period of a further 18 months, would leave the Parliament in temporary accommodation until 2000. Commenting on Mr Henderson's draft in a minute of 23 June 1997, Mr Wyllie raised some concerns as to the appropriateness of a PFI approach and made the valid point that the benefit of less delay after starting in comparison with traditional

---

[72] SE/2/156-163 - Minute from Mr Alistair Brown to PS/Henry McLeish and PS/Secretary of State, 20 May 1997
[73] SE/2/141-145a - Minute from Mr Alistair Brown to PS/Henry McLeish and PS/Secretary of State, 6 June 1997
[74] SE/2/131 – Minute from Mr Mark Batho to Mr Henderson, 13 June 1997
[75] Evidence of Wendy Alexander on 29 October 2003, Para 375
[76] SE/2/1541-1544 – Minute from Mr David Rogers to Mr Henderson, 16 June 1997
[77] SE/2/1521-1528 – Minute from Mr Henderson to Mr Grice, 20 June 1997

procurement did not make up for the long lead in time which he thought might have been understated by Mr Henderson.[78] It was the general thinking of civil servants at that time that a PFI approach would be incompatible with the very high priority attached by Ministers to the building being available very quickly.[79] The matter was discussed at a meeting on 27 June 1997 with Ministers.[80] Wendy Alexander is noted as having suggested that the range of possible figures then under consideration for insertion in the White Paper might be "very wide indeed if consideration was given to the use of a private developer". Henry McLeish felt that it should be stated in the White Paper that this was one of the options under consideration and this was the approach eventually adopted.

2.44 Section 10.17 of the White Paper as finally published left all bets open by saying:

'As part of the evaluation of sites for the Parliament, the Government are considering a range of funding options. The objective will be to secure suitable accommodation at a reasonable cost. The options include traditional funding, under which the capital costs would be met from public funds; using the Private Finance Initiative, under which responsibility for building the Parliament would be passed to the private sector; or some other form of joint public/private sector venture where the Scottish Parliament building itself would be publicly owned but where private sector partners would offset some of the costs of the Project'.[81]

2.45 The matter of potential funding methods does not seem to have received any further active consideration until 29 December 1997 when Mr Graham and other civil servants met to discuss the pros and cons of procuring the Scottish Parliament through PFI. After that meeting Mr Graham, circulated for comment a draft minute for Ministers.[82] The thinking of the civil servants was that there was a lack of experience of coping with PFI where design quality was critical and that an initial design competition, committing the PFI contractor to the winning entry, would be less likely to produce value for money.

2.46 After the finalisation of Mr Graham's draft a lengthy and detailed minute went up to Ministers on 6 January 1998[83] in the name of Mr Gordon, who was at that time the Accounting Officer for the Project. The minute explored the key issues such as the implications for timetable, the difficulties of specifying in advance the precise services to be provided by a PFI contractor and

---

[78] SE/2/1519-1520 - Minute from Mr Alastair Wyllie to Dr John Gibbons, 23 June 1997
[79] SE/5/027-034 – Minute from Mr Robert Gordon to PS/Henry McLeish and PS/Secretary of State, 6 January 1998
[80] SE/1/028-209 - Minute from Mr Michael Lugton to Mr Paul Grice, 27 June 1997
[81] White Paper http://www.scotland.gov.uk/government/devolution/scpa-13.asp
[82] SE/5/009, and SE/5/010-018 – Minute from Mr John Graham to Mr Robert Gordon and Draft Minute from Mr Robert Gordon to PS/Secretary of State and PS/Henry McLeish, 31 December 1997
[83] SE/5/043-050 – Minute from Mr Robert Gordon to PS/Henry McLeish and PS/Secretary of State, 6 January 1998

the possible difficulties of accommodating a design competition within a PFI procurement exercise. It also raised questions specific to the St Andrew's House and Holyrood sites as well as political issues. The minute commented on the political or "Parliament on tick" objections and pointed out that civil servants had been unable to identify any other Parliament which has its main facilities in accommodation it did not own. After looking at funding and value for money considerations, Mr Gordon felt that he did not have any conclusive evidence as to whether PFI was likely to offer better value than conventional procurement.

2.47   In a prescient passage Mr Gordon said:

> 'This project has many of the characteristics (one-off, high public interest in design, brownfield site, influential clients, time pressures) which have been associated with cost overruns on some public sector construction projects in the past. Although we would obviously put great effort into managing the Project effectively under conventional procurement and can point to a recent success in Victoria Quay, the risks under conventional procurement are real.'[84]

2.48   Mr Gordon's conclusion was that it would be difficult to rule out further exploration of PFI on value for money grounds. However a key consideration, as ever with this project, was that of programme. Mr Gordon pointed out that on policy grounds Ministers might "conclude that delaying the operation of the Parliament in its permanent home by what seems likely to be a further 6 to 12 months or so is not acceptable". He also advised:

> 'Ministers could also conclude that in principle it was wrong for the Parliament building to be privately owned and operated. This may not be very logical, but it would be a robust basis for defending a decision not to explore PFI.'[85]

2.49   Mr Gordon invited the views of Ministers and clarified that in the event of Ministers concluding that conventional procurement was the preferred route officials would advertise the design competitions immediacy. If Ministers wanted PFI to be explored further the next step would be to draw up a formal public service comparator, including an assessment of the risks involved in conventional procurement and to explore informally the likely interest among potential bidders. At the end of this process which, it was estimated, might take two months, a final decision could be taken.

2.50   Mr Gordon's minute was discussed at a meeting on 14 January attended by Donald Dewar, Henry McLeish and senior civil servants at which the decision was taken to opt for

---

[84] SE/5/048 Minute from Mr Robert Gordon to PS/Henry McLeish and PS/Secretary of State, 6 January 1998, Para 21
[85] *ibid*, Para 26

conventional procurement. That decision is recorded in a minute from Mr Thomson of 23 January 1998 in which he said that Ministers had taken into account:

'the fact that the PFI option would lengthen the timetable for the Parliament building. Ministers remain committed to having the Parliament building ready by the autumn of 2001 and concluded that this would not be possible under PFI;

the PFI option would mean specifying and entering into fairly long term agreements for services which, to judge from the Westminster experience, MSPs would regard as those which should be under the direct control and management of the Parliament, rather than a third party facilities manager;

the fact that PFI would be a novel procurement method for a Parliament building. Although PFI was relatively well developed as procurement methodology for other buildings, the Parliament would be (obviously) a one-off with very distinctive features in its design, use and operation. Experience suggested that PFI procurement was a learning process in which the first project so procured had to identify and solve problems which might well produce delay over and above that which could be foreseen.'[86]

2.51 The decision to adopt conventional procurement was the subject of consideration by the Auditor General in his report on the management of the Holyrood project published in September 2000.[87] The Auditor General made the valid point that the procurement strategy adopted at the outset should have included a more considered analysis of the different procurement options and the risks associated with each such option. While that is a view with which I strongly agree, I am unable to conclude that the decision to adopt conventional funding, rather than resorting to PFI procurement, was wrong and was the cause of the delay and cost which has plagued this Project. I cannot say with the same confidence that the later decision to follow a construction management route, a decision not put to Ministers, was without cost and delay consequences. I shall examine that in more detail later.

Referendum and the Scotland Act

2.52 The Referendums (Scotland and Wales) Act 1997, the Bill for which had been introduced in May, received Royal Assent on 31 July 1997. In the ensuing referendum which took place on 11 September substantial majorities voted in favour of the setting up of a Scottish Parliament with tax varying powers. The Scotland Bill was published on 17 December 1997 and after a relatively uneventful passage through both Houses of Parliament the Scotland Act 1998

---

[86] SE/5/025 - Minute from Mr Kenneth Thomson to Mr Robert Gordon, 23 January 1998
[87] Auditor General for Scotland's Report of September 2000, Paras 1.4, 3.16-3.19 (inc Exhibit 13)

received Royal Assent on 19 November 1998. The Act contained no specific provision in relation to the arrangements for the accommodation of the new Parliament. It did however, in section 21, make provision for the setting up of the Scottish Parliamentary Corporate Body ("SPCB"). The SPCB, with a membership to consist of the Presiding Officer and four MSPs to be appointed in accordance with Standing Orders, was to be charged with the provision of the property, staff and services required for the Parliament's purposes. In terms of the Transfer of Property etc. (Scottish Parliamentary Corporate Body) Order 1999[88] made under the Act, provision was made for the transfer to the SPCB on 1 June 1999 of all rights and liabilities belonging to a former Minister of the Crown or government department in so far as relating to the new Parliament. This was the mechanism by which the contracts with architects, cost consultants and others entered into by the former Secretary of State in relation to the Project were legally transferred to the Scottish Parliament.

---

[88] S.I. 1999 No 1106 - Transfer of Property etc. (Scottish Parliamentary Corporate Body) Order 1999

Chapter 3

Selection of the Holyrood Site

Feasibility of the Old Royal High School Site

3.1   A submission about the accommodation aspects of a Scottish Parliament was put to Ministers by Mr Brown as early as 20 May 1997.[89] The speed with which this was presented to the new Ministerial team demonstrates the importance which officials attached to making early progress with the accommodation issue and meeting the demanding timetable set by Ministers. The submission sought Ministers' views on whether they wished to pursue the 'Scottish Constitutional Convention's proposal' that the Scottish Parliament should be located on the Regent Road site incorporating the Old Royal High School building. The submission also aired the possibility of alternative accommodation options, but stressed that alternatives would require additional time and would require temporary accommodation to be identified for the first two years or so of the Parliament's life.

3.2   Mr Brown's analysis in this significant document concluded that the decision of Ministers should rest upon their assessment of the political arguments for adopting the Old Royal High School site or seeking an alternative. He suggested that selection of the Old Royal High School would save considerable time and reduce uncertainty and scope for controversy. If

---

[89] SE/2/156-163 – Minute from Mr Alistair Brown to PS/Secretary of State and PS/Henry McLeish, 20 May 1997

however, Ministers did not consider 'political considerations' to be overwhelming and were prepared to accept uncertainty about when a new Parliament building might be ready, then alternatives could be explored. The costs of alternatives were not estimated in the submission although it was speculated that alternative solutions might be cheaper than the Regent Road option, notwithstanding the need to identify temporary accommodation for the early life of the new institution. Even at this early stage, officials appeared to be aware that a decision to locate the new Parliament on a site other than on Calton Hill could be controversial and politically charged.

3.3   Upon receipt of this submission, as previously noted Donald Dewar undertook a formal visit to the Old Royal High School with a small group of officials and advisers on 30 May. This visit turned out to be a key event in the process of site selection. From the recollections of those who accompanied him, it was evident that the visit confirmed his doubts as to the suitability of the building to house the new Parliament. Lord Elder gave his impressions of the visit in evidence:

> "I hadn't, until I went there, realised the complexity of the site: the number of separate buildings; the range of historic buildings, which there were reasons to keep; and thoroughly unhistoric buildings, which were not obviously useful. I do remember it being remarked that the main teaching block was a state of the art 19th century boys' school and it was not entirely obvious what the usefulness of that would be. I remember particularly as we were being taken round, we were being told what the plan had been in the 1970s; and as Donald, as I said to you, had been Chief Whip in the run up to the election, and was used to being able to see what was happening in the Chamber, walk out his door, be in Members' Lobby and get a grip on things in 15 seconds, the prospect of finding that the proposed place for the Whips' Office were the two little sub-temples at the far outreach from the main building. I'm afraid Donald did rather take a dim view of what it would be like going from there into the main building on a wet February morning to see what was going on. There were a lot of issues about unconnected buildings, with no pathways between them. None of them were particularly suitable certainly for disabled access; and the Chamber itself, whether you liked it or not, had remarkably little room immediately adjacent to it, which is really one of the requirements, I think, of a parliamentary building."[90]

3.4   Dr Gibbons confirmed the negative impact that the site visit had upon Donald Dewar:

> **"Dr Gibbons:** He was also concerned about accessibility. He took us to the public gallery at the first-floor level, and showed how limited the sight-lines were down to see people speaking.
>
> **Mr Campbell QC:** I wonder if you formed a view as to whether or not it would have lent itself to adaptation to accommodate the sort of apprehensions that the Secretary of State had?

---

[90] Evidence of Lord Elder on 29 October 2003, Para 69

Dr Gibbons: Yes, it would have been very difficult to have dealt easily with the sight-line and access problems, because it was a very fine group of buildings, particularly the buildings that housed the Chamber. That certainly was going to be very difficult. The overriding difficulty that was in my mind at the start of the visit was that we knew from the drawings and the condition survey that it was something like 5,400 sq m, which is not a very large building.

The other difficulty with the configuration of the building was that it was a configuration of some very grand and some very large rooms, which would not have led easily to subdivision. Now we did not know at that stage the precise nature of what a Parliament was going to be, but it was clear that there was going to be administrative accommodation that was linked with it. That would have been difficult to have done within that range of buildings. I remember very clearly a discussion with Donald Dewar about dividing the building horizontally and the difficulties that that would have meant — aesthetic problems; problems in convincing Historic Scotland that that was an acceptable thing to do."[91]

3.5   Following the visit, Donald Dewar commissioned further work by suggesting that, notwithstanding the 'formidable difficulties about an alternative location', Ministers would find it helpful to have a paper appraising various accommodation alternatives, to include the Old Royal High School site and a location in Leith near the Scottish Office building at Victoria Quay.[92]

Four Site Options Considered

3.6   Mr Brown put forward further advice to Ministers in June 1997 in response to Donald Dewar's request. The first of these submissions on 6 June[93] proposed four possible options for consideration. They covered a range of possibilities, from utilising the Old Royal High School or St Andrew's House, to a site near Victoria Quay or a new-build on a greenfield site. It did not at that stage offer any estimates of the comparative costs of the various options. As Mr Brown explained,[94] the purpose of that exchange was to see if Ministers were interested in particular options that could possibly have been taken forward within buildings or on land which the Scottish Office either owned or controlled. Had they been, then officials took the view that it would have been possible to proceed in that direction without the delay of further detailed option appraisal work. A second substantial submission was put to Ministers by Mr Brown on 12 June.[95] This submission elaborated on each of the four options and suggested some initial general estimates of costs for each. These ranged from £27 million for an option based upon the adaptation and refurbishment of St Andrew's House, to up to £43.5 million for a new-build solution in Leith.

---

[91] Evidence of Dr John Gibbons on 24 November 2003, Para 67 *et seq*
[92] SE/2/151 - Minute from Mr Michael Lugton to Mr Alistair Brown, 2 June 1997
[93] SE/2/141–145A – Minute from Mr Alistair Brown to PS/Henry McLeish and PS/Secretary of State,6 June 1997
[94] Evidence of Mr Alistair Brown on 6 November 2003, Paras 182 - 183
[95] SE/2/132-140 - Minute from Mr Alistair Brown to PS/Henry McLeish and PS/Secretary of State, 12 June 1997

3.7 Henry McLeish responded to Mr Brown's first submission with perceptive comments, noted in a minute from his Private Secretary.[96] He considered that it might be sensible to proceed on the basis of 'minimum expenditure on the Old Royal High School option, making a virtue out of that; and to leave open the possibility of the new Parliament deciding its own future'. He also observed that had the timescale and political costs been more favourable, he would have preferred the bold option of a greenfield site.

3.8 Henry McLeish suggested in his evidence to the Inquiry that he was concerned, firstly, that the accommodation arrangements for the new Parliament were not a priority among the many competing issues at the time but appeared gargantuan in terms of the time and consideration required[97] and, secondly, at the prospect of a "disconnect" between the Scottish Office Ministers and the ultimate users of any new Parliament building.[98] As he put it:

> ".......I did believe that the scale of the task was so significant that that should have been a warning to all of us that we maybe needed to proceed more cautiously and at the end of it give some kind of sharing of ownership to the Parliament".[99]

3.9 The same point was raised at a later stage by the former Lord Advocate, Lord Mackay of Drumadoon QC, in a debate in the House of Lords on 12 November 1997 when he said:

> "If a decision were to be taken as to location and design, I understand that it would not be possible to have the building complete and fully operational by the date when it is anticipated that the new Scottish Parliament will start its work. For that reason, some temporary accommodation will be necessary and that will need to be fitted out to allow for a parliamentary chamber, committee rooms and all the ancillary offices required by a parliamentary assembly. I hope that the Minister will be in a position to confirm in his reply that that is likely to be the situation. If it is, I venture to suggest that another option ought to be considered; namely, to wait until the Parliament is up and running before any final decisions are taken, certainly so far as concerns the overall design of the building."[100]

3.10 There is no contemporaneous record to suggest that any serious consideration was given to either of Henry McLeish's proposals at the time. Henry McLeish told the Inquiry in his evidence that "*they* didn't think that was a runner"[101] by which he meant both Ministers and officials.[102] In relation to this proposal Sam Galbraith told the Inquiry that he had never heard it

---

[96] SE/2/146 - Minute from Mr Alan Johnston to PS/Secretary of State, 11 June 1997
[97] Evidence of Henry McLeish on 29 October 2003, Para 161
[98] *ibid*, Paras 162 & 190
[99] *ibid*, Para 177
[100] House of Lords Hansard, Vol. 583, Col 218 (http://www.parliament.the-stationery-office.co.uk/pa/ld199798/ldhansrd/vo971112/text/71112-09.htm)
[101] Evidence of Henry McLeish on 20 October 2003, Para 177
[102] *ibid*, Paras 183 to 185

considered, and did not think Henry McLeish had ever mentioned it to him.[103] When questioned about the minute of 11 June 1997 Mr Grice said:

> "I am not aware of... a follow-up. In my experience in the Civil Service, it would not be uncommon in other circumstances for such a memo to trigger a response from the Secretary of State saying: "Great idea, run with it", or, "I am not interested". I have not been able to find anything on the file which conveys a view one way or the other, and in the absence of that, I think you would not normally expect work to be triggered by such a memo." [104]

3.11 Sir Russell Hillhouse indicated to the Inquiry that he had put the point in a private conversation with Donald Dewar in late July. According to Sir Russell, his thinking on the matter was:

> "I ... did actually take the opportunity of a private informal conversation with Donald Dewar to put a very similar point to him because it was clear that there would be some controversy about the site if we didn't go to the Royal High School, and that there would certainly be likelihood that parliamentarians would turn up and have rather different views as to where it was they were, and what it was they were going to get. So I said to him, "Wouldn't it be better to go for a temporary solution and let the Parliament decide?" He said "Well" — I'm paraphrasing — "that, of course, is correct in principle, but my fear is that, unless we get ahead and do something now, the Parliament will find it extremely difficult to get round to it. There will always be something else that has higher priority for them, and I think it is my duty to endow them" — that was the word he used – "to endow them with really a good building which will be fit for purpose, and which will enable them to operate effectively."[105]

3.12 The suggestion that a temporary location be identified and the permanent solution left to the incoming Parliament was a fundamental issue that did not appear to have been aired before this point. The evidence suggests that the requirement for a temporary solution did not carry any weight with Donald Dewar, who was insistent that progress should be made towards the delivery of a building for the new Parliament at the earliest possible opportunity. In my opinion, this was a matter for his judgment and a decision he was entitled to take at that time. The Inquiry has sought to identify the circumstances under which other new legislatures have secured their accommodation; whether by inheritance or by their own hand.[106] Unfortunately no directly comparable legislatures were identified in the study although it is notable that in relation to the Welsh Assembly, the decision on the site for the new Debating Chamber was taken by the Secretary of State for Wales in advance of the political 'handover' to the devolved Assembly.

---

[103] Evidence of Sam Galbraith on 28 October 2003, Para 334
[104] Evidence of Mr Paul Grice on 5 November 2003, Para 123
[105] Evidence of Sir Russell Hillhouse on 30 October 2003, Para 269
[106] Study by DTZ PIEDA Consulting for the Holyrood Inquiry. Details available on Inquiry website.

3.13 Donald Dewar discussed these matters at a meeting with officials on 13 June 1997. Although he was aware that a detailed option appraisal of alternative sites would take time,[107] he was not satisfied with any of the options presented to him at that stage and wished further appraisals to be undertaken. Donald Dewar's reservations about the Old Royal High School were well aired at this meeting,[108] yet he did not wish to see it excluded from consideration.

3.14 It is legitimate to question why Donald Dewar wished to retain the Old Royal High School site as a potential candidate when he so clearly had major reservations about its suitability for purpose. In response to questioning on this point, Sir Russell Hillhouse proposed a rationale for Donald Dewar's position:

> **"Sir Russell Hillhouse:** I don't think the Secretary of State or any of us could be at all sure that we'd get a better site, a better solution. Secondly, and it's quite explicit this from the papers I've been rereading, the Secretary of State was extremely conscious that a lot of people in Scotland had the idea that this was where it was going to be, this was the place it should be. And while this wasn't perhaps wholly logical because it was a matter of some chance that this had been fixed on in (*the 1970s)* when it had been refurbished in order to form the home of the Scottish Assembly that never happened, but there it was; it had become a kind of emblem for people of the aspiration for an Assembly or a Parliament.

> **Mr Campbell QC:** But nevertheless, Sir Russell, we have the former members of the Scottish Grand Committee and Select Committee sitting there and grumbling about it. We have Lord Mackay of Drumadoon later on talking about his experiences, we have the Secretary of State's own visit and, no doubt, internal knowledge as well within officialdom about the limitations on the building. You go to the country, as it were, with a White Paper which puts it there in the front line.

> **Sir Russell Hillhouse:** I think the reason the Secretary of State felt it was necessary to mention this, and he explicitly (*said*) it should be mentioned, was that he just didn't feel it could be ignored or dismissed. In fact, what he did at the meetings that took place in June, ... and I think this was all fresh thinking on his part at that time, ... was to set out the criteria which he thought ought to be used in selecting a site, and, indeed, going for an ultimate design, I suppose, and setting these out in the White Paper, and they came first in that part of the White Paper. And then he said "I would like you to remind people about the existence of the Royal High School site, but assess it against those criteria." This was his way of trying gently to persuade people that maybe the Old Royal High School wasn't such a good idea after all, that there might be something better, and we would look and see if we could find something that might be better."[109]

3.15 Some other key issues were discussed at the meeting on 13 June. It is recorded that Donald Dewar felt that 'a new building would help to symbolise the new approach which was being

---

[107] Evidence of Mr Alistair Brown on 6 November 2003, Para 184
[108] SE/2/126-128 - Minute from Mr Alistair Brown to Ms Thea Teale, 16 June 1997
[109] Evidence of Sir Russell Hillhouse on 30 October 2003, Paras 260-263

taken to Government in Scotland'. He also accepted that the Parliament would meet initially in temporary accommodation but permanent accommodation should be ready by Spring 2000 if at all possible. To meet this timetable he accepted that quick decisions would be required from all involved and there should be no substantive changes to specifications and designs once agreed. It was agreed that the White Paper should make clear that an assessment of sites in addition to the Old Royal High School was underway.[110] The Secretary of State hoped that a decision on the site for the Parliament could be taken before the referendum in September.

Short-list of Three Potential Sites

3.16   The assistance of the City of Edinburgh Council was enlisted in the search for suitable alternative sites. By August 1997 an initial long list[111] had been whittled down to three short-listed areas with the potential to accommodate the Parliamentary complex. The Inquiry learned that the Holyrood Brewery site had been included on the long list but was dismissed as being too constrained. There was no realisation at that stage that the adjacent Queensberry House might be available for development as part of the site. The short list comprised the Regent Road/Calton Hill site, a site at Haymarket on Morrison Street and a site in Leith adjacent to Victoria Quay. Working to a set of criteria identified by the Scottish Office, the City Council provided further detailed information about each of the short-listed sites for more thorough consideration.

3.17   Mr Brown put forward further submissions to Ministers on 25 August and 4 September 1997 providing them with the information to assist them in reaching a decision on the preferred site for the Parliament. In the first of those submissions he advised against making a site announcement in advance of the referendum on 11 September (on the basis that to do so could compromise negotiations with private sector interests to achieve best value for money) and warned that the spring 2000 timetable was very tight. He offered the following prescient comment:

> 'Having more time to plan the Project properly and timetable in at least some of the possible hitches would reduce the risk of the initial specification having to be changed and of contractors holding us to ransom.'[112]

3.18   The 4 September submission presented the accommodation options in a balanced way to Ministers, without making a specific recommendation. The final choice of a location was seen as being dependent upon the weight which Ministers wished to give to a range of factors,

---

[110] SE/3/207-208 - Press Release, 'Design Competition for New Parliament', 16 July 1997
[111] SE/2/343-344 – Annex C of Minute from Robert Gordon to Mr Alistair Brown, 4 September 1997
[112] SE/2/309–313 - Minute from Mr Alistair Brown to PS/ Henry McLeish and PS/ Secretary of State, 25 August 1997

among which financial considerations were important but not necessarily paramount. Mr Brown concluded:

> "We believe that a choice of either Regent Road or Leith could be justified on the basis of the information available. The choice comes down to an essentially political judgment of whether public accessibility and visibility, combined with the re-use of existing buildings and the symbolism of building on public administrative tradition, is to be preferred over internal efficiency, lower running costs, and the symbolism of a new start and directions".[113]

3.19   Donald Dewar and Henry McLeish met officials on 5 September 1997 to discuss these key submissions (with the referendum looming large only six days away). The meeting reached no firm conclusion but did commission further advice on the comparative costs of Regent Road and Leith from Doig & Smith. The meeting seems to have been the first indication that the Haymarket site was not a frontrunner in the Secretary of State's mind. As Mr Grice put it in evidence to the Inquiry:

> 'Haymarket was seen as perhaps the best of both worlds and perhaps turned out to be the worst of both worlds. It just did not quite cut it.'[114]

3.20   During the following weeks there was considerable public speculation about the proposed site and Scottish Office officials were lobbied by the representatives of various interested parties. Following competitive tender, the Scottish Office appointed Jones Lang Wootton, Chartered Surveyors, on 23 September to assist in assessing the acquisition costs and potential difficulties of the candidate sites from a commercial perspective. Assessments of traffic and environmental issues were also undertaken at this time.

3.21   It is apparent from the evidence that Donald Dewar took a close personal interest in all these matters; not just through the official papers that he was seeing but in informal conversations with the officials who were driving the site selection process. His Private Secretary, Mr Thomson, indicated to the Inquiry that Donald Dewar felt that he had to deliver the full devolution package, including the building, as he was well aware that devolution had floundered previously in the 1970s despite having had both a White Paper and an Act of Parliament in place. The drive of Donald Dewar seems to have impressed all those who worked with him. He had an undoubted ability to grasp the minutiae of the issues of the Parliament Project while simultaneously keeping abreast of the wider political priorities of his new administration.

---

[113] SE/2/302-308 - Minute from Mr Alistair Brown to PS/ Henry McLeish and PS/ Secretary of State, 4 September 1997
[114] Evidence of Mr Paul Grice on 5 November 2003, Para 182

3.22   Mr Brown put forward yet more advice on 8 and 15 October in advance of formal presentations to Donald Dewar from Forth Ports Authority and EDI in relation to the Leith and Regent Road sites. Donald Dewar accepted advice to postpone a decision on the site selection issue until the end of the year to allow design feasibility studies, environmental, and traffic impact studies of the three site options to be completed and for more information to be collected on 'the likely costs to the public purse of providing accommodation for the Parliament'.[115] He recognised that this timetable could push occupation of the new building back into 2001, depending upon the eventual option chosen. In the press announcement at the time, the Secretary of State spoke of the importance of making the right choice rather than taking a quick decision.

3.23   Different architectural practices were chosen to undertake the feasibility studies which were carried out during October and November in advance of presentations on each of the options to the Secretary of State planned for 15 December 1997. The Inquiry has seen all those feasibility studies. It is important to understand that they assessed only architectural feasibility, and were costed in only general terms, using standard rates for standard buildings. By no stretch of the imagination could the studies or the tentative costings be described as in any way definitive, and indeed the costings themselves are expressly stated to be indicative.

Inclusion of the Holyrood Site on the Short-list

3.24   On 3 October 1997 Dr Gibbons received a letter from DM Hall, Chartered Surveyors, on behalf of Scottish & Newcastle plc drawing attention to the availability of the Holyrood site, including Queensberry House.[116] This approach, the Inquiry was told, resulted from Mr John Clement of that firm having engaged in a discussion with civil servants on a train returning from Glasgow about their frustration in locating a suitable site for the Parliament. Mr Anthony Andrew, Chief Estates Officer, was one of those civil servants and confirmed these events to the Inquiry. When the DM Hall letter was received there was initially some uncertainty as to whether the site had been considered previously as part of the long list proposed by the City Council. When it was established that the addition of Queensberry House made the size of the whole site potentially viable, work was taken forward speedily.

3.25   Mr Andrew's initial assessment of the new entrant from Mr Brown was unenthusiastic:

> 'It is not really attractive unless Calton Hill and Leith fail, in which case you could pitch this site — poor communications, good ambience, against Haymarket — good

---

[115]SE/2/605–619 – Minute from Mr Alistair Brown to PS/Secretary of State and PS/Henry McLeish, 8 October 1997
[116] SE/2/590-590a – Letter from Mr John Clement to Dr John Gibbons 3 October 1997

communication and poor ambience. ... The short answer is no, it is not a contender at present.'[117]

3.26 It has not been established exactly when Donald Dewar was first informed of the emergence of a possible fourth contender, but it is understood that he may have taken an early informal visit to the site to establish for himself whether it could be a serious candidate. Although his initial reaction to the Holyrood site was apparently not that it was ideal or "trumped all the others",[118] Mr Thomson articulated how the Secretary of State later perceived its benefits:

> "He later thought that it offered in some ways the best of both worlds in that it offered the chance of a modern building on a city-centre site, those being two of the criteria that he was quite attracted to in looking at the two, then three, then four sites. He was attracted by it partly because of the symbolism of the Parliament being juxtaposed with the Crown in the shape of Holyrood Palace, and partly also the symbolism of the Parliament being next to a mountain and open country. Around this time Ministers were developing their proposals for land reform and the idea that Scotland is all like the middle of Edinburgh, or that the Parliament should be a classical temple, were certainly not things that he thought. Those two things were the attraction of the site. He recognised also its constraints, the fact that it was in the middle of a cluster of new buildings or building sites, the fact that there were traffic issues around it, the fact that the site would be less predictable and controllable in terms of costs because of unknown ground conditions, things of that sort. I am trying to think of his early thinking on the site before the later investigations had been done."[119]

3.27 Other Ministers saw the emergence of the Holyrood site as a potential solution to the perceived inadequacies of the other contenders. In evidence, Lord Sewel spoke of it as "an answer to all our prayers".[120] Work continued throughout October and November towards producing final reports on the three principal sites and officials worked on building up an informed view on the suitability of the Holyrood site in comparison to the other three candidates. It was not until 8 December 1997, however, that an announcement was made that Holyrood would be added to the short-list and design and cost feasibility studies undertaken. Consideration of the Holyrood site had been kept out of the public domain because of the commercial risk to the site owners (Scottish & Newcastle) in securing an alternative site for their headquarters, should an intention to dispose of it become widely known. Others did not see it that way but I have seen or heard no evidence to suggest that there was some covert arrangement between Donald Dewar and Scottish & Newcastle nor that Donald Dewar had reached an early conclusion favouring Holyrood before its candidacy was announced. In response to Alex Salmond's

---

[117] SE/2/592 - Annotated comments from Mr Anthony Andrew to Mr Alistair Brown, 8 October 1997
[118] Evidence of Mr Kenneth Thomson on 3 February 2004, Para 137
[119] Evidence of Mr Kenneth Thomson on 3 February 2004, Para 167
[120] Evidence of Lord Sewel on 30 October 2003, Para 150

accusation that "you do not include a new candidate site unless you want it to win", Mr Thomson commented:

> "I think you do not include a candidate site unless you think it has a chance of being a winner, and therefore, it is worth doing the work. If you thought it was definitely going to win, then why have the process of examining the other sites? I am clear from my recollection of Mr Dewar and his views at the time that what he was doing was adding a runner to the race, not declaring that the race was over".[121]

3.28 On the assertion that the Secretary of State had decided upon Holyrood before the public announcement, he had this to say:

> "Certainly all the dealings that I had with him suggested to me that Mr Dewar regarded the decision that was eventually taken on 6 January as being a decision among four sites. By January 1998 I think he had narrowed it down in his mind to two sites — Regent Road and Holyrood. I distinctly recall in this period of late 1997 that he was genuinely torn between the Regent Road site as worked up by Page & Park and the potential at Holyrood. If he had made some earlier commitment to Holyrood, he was going well out of his way to disguise it from me, for whom there was little purpose in him doing that. I find it really quite hard to believe that that was the case".[122]

3.29 It is true that the Secretary of State was very careful to keep the options open but it is difficult not to conclude that he and his political advisers did not like the Old Royal High School in isolation or in association with St Andrew's House. As Wendy Alexander pointed out, Donald Dewar wanted the executive arm of Government separated from the parliamentary arm.[123] Hence, perhaps, his unwillingness to see St Andrew's House used for both functions. Dr Gibbons provided an interesting insight into Mr Dewar's thinking, telling the Inquiry Mr Dewar did not like the architecture of St Andrew's House which he thought "somewhat fascist."[124]

3.30 Haymarket was never a runner and he correctly sensed there was a real hostility in Edinburgh to the Parliament being located anywhere other than centrally, thus eliminating Leith. As Alex Salmond correctly predicted, against this background the selection of Holyrood was obvious.

3.31 The Inquiry learned that RMJM Ltd (who had earlier been commissioned to undertake the design feasibility study of the Haymarket site) were given (at most) one week to conduct a feasibility study of the Holyrood site. The case was presented to me that RMJM Ltd had a running start in that they were familiar with the content of the Building User Brief from their Haymarket experience. I am of the view that the Holyrood feasibility study was only marginally less detailed and of no significant qualitative difference from the studies for the

---

[121] Evidence of Mr Kenneth Thomson on 3 February 2004, Para 179
[122] *ibid*, Para 149
[123] Evidence of Wendy Alexander on 29 October 2003, Para 302
[124] Evidence of Dr John Gibbons on 24 November 2003, Para 714

other site options. However, the merits of these studies as a tool for comparative decision-taking must be questioned. Although operating to a standard design brief, three different architectural practices interpreted that brief in different ways. I am unconvinced that the cost studies of their work provided a meaningful basis by themselves for Ministers to reach decisions. Nor have I been persuaded that the costings for these schematic designs were a sound basis from which to derive a realistic budget for the eventual Parliament building. As speed was regarded as being of the essence, it was probably inevitable that three different practices would be involved, but it was as difficult then, as it is now, to be confident that like was being compared with like.

3.32   Ministers received presentations on the design feasibility and estimated construction costs of the four site options on 15 December 1997. The presentations were informed by a compendium submission from Mr Brown summarising the results of the comparative studies.[125] Leaving aside the cost of staff relocation, the construction cost for the Regent Road/St Andrew's House site was calculated at £65 million plus fees and VAT; Leith was costed at £59 million plus fees and VAT; Haymarket was costed at £53 million plus fees and VAT, together with site acquisition costs of £6 million, whilst Holyrood, excluding Queensberry House, was costed at £49.5 million plus fees and VAT, together with site acquisition costs of £5 million. All these estimated costs were significantly greater than the figures contained in the White Paper published only five months earlier.

3.33   At a meeting on 15 December 1997 Donald Dewar felt unable to reach a final view, although the note of the discussion[126] suggests that he had narrowed the options down to a choice between Regent Road and Holyrood. Cost considerations do not appear to have featured in the discussion, which focused primarily on issues of feasibility and potential public reaction. To assist him with that final decision, he requested that further information on some specific aspects of the Holyrood site be presented to him in the New Year. By that stage a target had been set to make a site announcement before the key political milestone of the Second Reading of the Scotland Bill which was scheduled for 12 January 1998.[127] Mr Gordon proposed that there was a wish to avoid the wider devolution debate being distracted by the site issue.

3.34   The Inquiry heard various pieces of evidence arising from a press item that appeared in *The Herald* at this time.[128] The article maintained that Donald Dewar was of the view that Calton Hill was a "nationalist shibboleth" and on that basis he would be dismissing it as the preferred

---

[125] SE/2/1071-1080 – Minute Mr Alistair Brown to PS/Secretary of State and PS/Henry McLeish, 12 December 1997
[126] SE/2/1253-1255 - Minute from Mr Kenneth Thomson to Mr Alistair Brown, 16 January 1998
[127] Evidence of Mr Robert Gordon on 4 November 2003, Paras 170 - 172
[128] Article in *The Herald* by Mr Murray Ritchie and Ms Catherine McLeod, 7 January 1998

site for the Parliament. Although several witnesses were asked about this colourful phrase, no-one could confirm either its origins or whether it had ever been uttered by Donald Dewar himself. The issue went some considerable way towards souring the consensual relationship that had been developing between Donald Dewar and Alex Salmond during the referendum campaign and the relationship was to positively curdle when Alex Salmond was informed that Holyrood had been selected as the location.

3.35   In early January, Donald Dewar was presented with the final pieces of information with which to make his decision. Central to these was a cost report[129] by DLE on each of the earlier feasibility studies. As noted above DLE, assessing construction cost only, costed the option at St Andrew's House/Regent Road at £64.8 million and the option at Holyrood at £49.5 million. The report stated carefully that these figures were based only on indicative build costs. Their conclusion, based on the feasibility studies, was that a realistic budget for a 'conventional' building of about $16,000m^2$, using conventional and contemporary construction costs, would be between £50 and £55 million at March 1998 rates. In light of later developments, one has to wonder at the usefulness of such an estimate. Officials and Ministers might reasonably have anticipated an unconventional solution from the designer competition they already had in mind. The political balance may well have been between a budget which was sufficiently realistic, having regard to professional advice, yet sufficiently low to allow for its political acceptability.

3.36   It is to be noted that the DLE costings were based upon a building at Holyrood totalling $20,070m^2$ while that for Regent Road/St Andrew's House totalled $24,806m^2$. As, fundamentally, area was the key determinant in the DLE costings, a disparity between the costs for these two sites was perhaps inevitable. Given the later increases in the space requirements of the new Parliament, it is tempting to speculate on how these increases might have been accommodated on a different site - but I shall with hesitation desist from so doing. In presenting the comparative costings of the two sites to Ministers, Mr Brown's eve of decision submission of 6 January 1998 contained the following annex: [130]

---

[129] SE/2/1349-1494 – DLE Feasibility Report and Site Feasibility Estimates, 12 December 1997
[130] SE/2/1316 Submission from Alistair Brown to Ministers, 6 January 1998

	Regent Road	Holyrood
Site Cost	£0 million	£4.5 million
Estimate building cost	£65 million	£50 – 55 million
VAT and fees	£26 million	£17.5 - 19 million
Building running cost (20 years)	£106 million	£91 million
Consequential estate costs (capital)	£5 million (inc First Minister's Office)	£15 – 20 million (1)
Consequential estate running costs (20 years)	Reduction of £14m	Reduction of between £14m and £23m (2)
Total (20 years)	£188 million	£155 – 175.5 million

(1) Assumes SAH is refurbished for civil service use at a cost of £15m-£20m and would provide accommodation for the First Minister and their Office; costs of Queensberry House conversion not included.
(2) Depends on what office buildings are retained by The Scottish Office estate; assumes SAH is retained.

3.37   The Inquiry heard detailed evidence on the validity of this cost comparison, specifically from Mr Gordon. While Mr Gordon's oral evidence on this point left me in some doubt,[131] he subsequently provided a supplementary statement which explained matters much more fully.[132] At this stage it appears that a decision remained to be taken on whether a refurbished Queensberry House would be required as part of the Parliamentary complex, should Holyrood be the preferred site. Ministers had been informed that the cost of restoring Queensberry House up to a fully adequate standard was likely to require up to £6.9 million including VAT and fees. It was suggested that this figure was excluded from the cost comparison in view of the uncertainty. Mr Gordon confirmed that under the Holyrood option as it was envisaged at that stage the First Minister's accommodation would have been in St Andrew's House. This would undoubtedly have had knock-on cost implications for the public purse but was presented to the Inquiry as a separate decision relating to the civil service estate. I see it as a further cost of the new Parliamentary building (on whatever site) that was not clearly and explicitly declared at the time of the site announcement.

3.38   In reaching the decision announced on 9 January 1998[133] to proceed with the Holyrood site Donald Dewar also had in front of him a report by Simpson & Brown, Architects, on Queensberry House, prepared in a week over Christmas and New Year, and providing cost estimates *inclusive* of fees and other extraordinary items, and a detailed transport assessment completed by Scott Wilson Kirkpatrick.

3.39   It was suggested to the Inquiry by Mr David Black that Donald Dewar may have been subjected to influence from senior members of the UK Labour Party, specifically from Peter

---

[131] Evidence of Mr Robert Gordon on 4 November 2003, Paras 396 to 440
[132] WS/19/001-004 – Mr Robert Gordon's Second Witness Statement
[133] SE/3/011-012 - News Release, 'Scottish Parliament to be Built at Holyrood', 9 January 1998

Mandelson, in reaching his decision on a preferred site.[134] The Inquiry found no evidence to substantiate this claim. The Inquiry has received an assurance from Mr Mandelson that he 'played no role and exerted no influence in relation to the siting of the Scottish Parliament.'[135] All the other evidence leads me to accept his assurance.

3.40 Although I have some reservations about the value of the cost information presented to Ministers, it was certainly comprehensive. Furthermore, under the constitutional arrangements that existed at the time, I am in no doubt as to Donald Dewar's right to come to his decision. Alex Salmond acknowledged this point in his evidence:

> **"Mr Campbell QC:** Well, would you agree with me .... then that what he did was legitimate in all the circumstances, since it is the job of the Secretary of State, ultimately, to take a decision?
>
> **Mr Salmond:** Under the terms of the Secretary of State, he was entitled to take that decision. Even the peremptory consultation that we had on this issue was greater than consultation on many other social and economic and political issues in Scotland. However, in the atmosphere of Scotland having regained its first Parliament for 300 years, in the atmosphere of a consensus established in the referendum campaign, and in the atmosphere of consensus that was being built about how the Parliament should be run in terms of its Standing Orders, then it was not the correct decision to make that decision as Secretary of State, because it cut against that grain of democracy and consensus."[136]

3.41 Donald Dewar undoubtedly led the site selection process personally from the front. Mr Brown again:

> "It was really Mr Dewar who was the captain of the ship. We absolutely realised that the devolution project, in political terms, was clearly his. And, both in theory and in fact, we were there to make sure that what he wanted done was done. If there were insuperable obstacles or problems with that, it was up to us to come and tell him that and provide advice."[137]

3.42 I do not propose to comment on the merits of the Holyrood site in comparison with those of the other site contenders, as these are matters outwith my remit. I do not have the benefit of detailed comparative evidence in relation to the other sites to enable me to make this judgment. My investigation of the subsequent events gives me no cause to disagree with Mr John Spencely[138] that the delays and cost rises that befell the Project at a later stage were not directly attributable to the Holyrood location.

---

[134] Evidence of Mr David Black on 5 December 2003, Paras 549 to 570
[135] MS/27/002 - Letter from Peter Mandelson to the Holyrood Inquiry, 2 March 2004
[136] Evidence of Alex Salmond on 13 November 2003, Paras 289 to 290
[137] Evidence of Mr Alistair Brown on 6 November 2003, Para 75
[138] Mr Spencely's Report, Section 6.6.1 'Changing the Site'

3.43   Throughout the site selection process, the Inquiry has heard of the requirement at every turn to take decisions promptly, so that subsequent stages could be embarked upon and the Parliament Building could become a physical reality. There is an abundance of documentary evidence of officials warning Ministers of the consequences of over-hasty decisions. It is perhaps easy at this distance to underestimate the political momentum that had been generated in the wake of the 1997 General Election. I conclude that Donald Dewar was entitled to take the decision on the Holyrood site and to take the political risk of alienating a number of prominent politicians in Scotland, including Alex Salmond, Margo MacDonald and Donald Gorrie, who considered the Calton Hill site was a preferable one or who took the principled view that this was a decision for MSPs to take. Whether he was wise to do so is open to question. As I understand it, apart from the other considerations already mentioned, Donald Dewar did not want the new Parliament to spend its early years squabbling over the location or cost of a permanent home. If that was his worthy ambition, by following the course he did, he has patently failed.

Chapter 4

Appointment of the Architect

The Decision to Hold a Designer Competition

4.1   When Donald Dewar visited the Old Royal High School on 30 May 1997, Dr Gibbons recalled that he discussed the use of an architectural competition as a means of procuring the new Parliament Building. Dr Gibbons thought that was a "courageous" step for Government, since the process was "obviously not the safest of routes to procure a building".[139] He went on to point out that there was a long history of difficulty with architectural competitions, which was well known and well documented. In his evidence,[140] Dr Gibbons made it clear that Donald Dewar was keen to keep control of the appointment process, and that he took heed of the difficulties which had emerged with competitions in the past. Dr Gibbons described the competitive selection process as having, in his view, a "higher probability" of delivering a successful Parliament building on time and on budget. In evidence, he recognised that these aspirations should all be tempered by experience, and that significant cost and time risks attached to the process however it was tackled.

4.2   Mr Brown's comprehensive minute of 12 June 1997 on accommodation options for a Scottish Parliament went through a number of revisions in its preparation but did not mention any

---

[139] Evidence of Dr John Gibbons on 24 November 2003, Para 91
[140] Evidence of Dr John Gibbons on 24 November 2003, Para 191

competition for the selection of an architect. It noted that "...any publicly funded project of this kind should be subject to a value for money appraisal before a favoured option is identified."[141] While the need for such an appraisal had been identified, it is also clear that at that stage only the most basic estimates of likely cost had been attempted.[142]

4.3   At a meeting of 16 June 1997 Donald Dewar indicated a preference for a "new build" solution, as helping "to symbolise the new approach" and left others at the meeting with his understanding that once a design had been procured, no substantive changes to specification and design should be permitted.[143] Officials recognised that a design brief would inform any competition and its eventual results and, even before the publication of the White Paper, they were being contacted by developers keen to advance their own proposals.[144] It is quite clear and not surprising that officials were taken up with the issues of site selection long before considering how the building might be designed, and that the political pressure upon them was significant, and unusually heavy.

4.4   On 16 July 1997 Donald Dewar announced that a competition would be held to select "...the best design for a new Scottish Parliament."[145]   He emphasised architectural quality, accessibility, value for money, cost-saving efforts and a design "worthy of the hopes and aspirations of the Scottish people". He stated his reservations about the ORHS, and indicated that it would be considered as one of a number of options. The time frame which he wished was clear, and the demand was for a designer to be in place early in 1998 and for the building to be completed for the new millennium. The Press release said "We want value for money as well as quality. We will be looking at ways in which the cost of the Parliament can be kept to a minimum." That was the architectural equivalent of motherhood and apple pie. Who would not want all these desirable architectural and economic virtues? It appears to me that Scottish Office officials were not slow in understanding their task. What they were to struggle with was where the priority lay: Quality? Cost? Or speed of the completion of the building? As events unfolded it appears to me that they understood their task to be one of trying to achieve early delivery of the new Parliament building, whilst maintaining quality. In my opinion that meant inevitably that whatever lip-service was paid to it, the cost of the building took a back seat.

4.5   On 24 July 1997 *The Architect's Journal* headlined the dissatisfaction of the Royal Incorporation of Architects in Scotland (RIAS) with the announcement of a competition. This view of events was, however, soon contradicted when Mr Sebastian Tombs, the Secretary and

---

[141] SE/2/092-100 – Minute from Mr Alistair Brown to PS/Henry McLeish and PS/Secretary of State, 12 June 1997
[142] SE/2/1547-1548 – Minute from Mr Alastair Wyllie to Mrs Barbara Doig, 10 June 1997
[143] SE/2/126-128 - Minute from Mr Alistair Brown to Ms Thea Teale, 16 June 1997
[144] SE/2/081 - Minute from Mrs Barbara Doig to Mr Anthony Andrew and Mr Graeme Purves, 23 July 1997
[145] SE/3/207-208 - Press Release – 'Design Competition for New Parliament', 16 July 1997

Chief Executive of the RIAS wrote to the Scottish Office underlining the willingness of the RIAS to assist with the conduct of a competition and pointed to its experience with architectural competitions. His first detailed letter[146] on the subject was far-thinking, in that he appeared to fully understand and expressed well the complexities of competition management, procurement of such a competition within Europe, and the necessary timescales. He sounded a very clear note about timing, the importance of the accuracy and precision of a brief, the uses of internal spaces, the significance of public consultation, and above all the need to take the necessary time to 'get it right'. The letter also covers the different types of competition (open and closed), the need for development of the brief, and the avoidance of unwarranted assumptions about the final needs of the users. This was a perceptive letter addressed to Dr Gibbons, which in my opinion should have remained in the forefront of his mind. This advice was repeated a number of times by the RIAS[147] both in meetings[148] and in subsequent correspondence.[149] [150]

4.6   On 12 August 1997 Mr Brian Peddie, an official in one of the Scottish Office Finance Divisions, noted in dialogue with HM Treasury Donald Dewar's intention to hold an architectural competition, to be held "within the explicit constraint of a stated building cost budget, which has yet to be set."[151] It might be argued that this assertion was fulfilled, but it is another question as to whether or not a realistic budget was set. A progress report by Mr Brown[152] submitted on 25 August 1997 underlined officials' understanding that there would be a competition, but that its type and scope had not yet been decided, and would be a matter for Ministers.

4.7   On 1 October 1997 Mr William (Bill) Armstrong, then in post as a consultant Project Manager, produced a highly ambitious draft timetable for a design competition running from 31 October 1997[153] to 30 March 1998.[154] [155] This programme, acknowledged by its author to be controversial, only allowed eight weeks for the preparation of proposals (between 19 December and 14 February 1998.) On any but the most optimistic view it should, in my opinion, have been regarded immediately as unworkable, as only three weeks later he was to produce a very different timetable. In part this might have been occasioned by the emergence, for the first time, of the Holyrood site as a candidate.

---

[146] RI/1/029-031 - Letter from Mr Sebastian Tombs to Dr John Gibbons, 21 July 1997
[147] RI/1/034-035 - Letter from Mr Sebastian Tombs to Dr John Gibbons, 6 August 1997
[148] RI/1/036-038 – Mr Sebastian Tombs' notes from Meeting of 1 October 1997
[149] RI/1/042-043 - Letter from Mr George Wren to Donald Dewar, 1 December 1997
[150] RI/1/044-045 – Letter from Mr George Wren to Donald Dewar, 8 December 1997
[151] SE/2/472-474 - Letter Mr Brian Peddie to Mr Barry Coidan, 12 August 1997
[152] SE/2/309 - Minute from Mr Alistair Brown to PS/Henry McLeish and PS/Secretary of State, 25 August 1997
[153] The date of the Advertisement in the Official Journal of the European Communities ('the OJEC Notice')
[154] The expected date for the announcement of the winner
[155] SE/2/735-736 - Minute from Mr William Armstrong to Dr John Gibbons, 1 October 1997

4.8 Mr Armstrong's note of 21 October 1997[156] substantially revised his earlier timetable and he envisaged completion of the appointment of a designer by July 1998, Stage D – Scheme Design of the RIBA Work Stages by October 1998, and a site start on 1 April 1999. Mr Brown had the good sense to see the force of this advice, which he appears to have accepted as being realistic.

4.9 The press release of 9 January 1998,[157] announcing the selection of Holyrood as the site for the Scottish Parliament, stated that the Parliament "will be the subject of an architectural design competition. The way is now clear for detailed consideration to be given to the precise form that the competition might take."[158] It explained the two types of competition and indicated that the objective would be to choose the type of competition "that is most appropriate in the circumstances, and that gives the greatest certainty of delivering a building of high quality and civic importance, but at the same time is built to our cost budget and completed on time". It concluded that "these criteria (pointed) to a designer competition with opportunities to the public to see options as they are developed".

Form of the Competition and its Announcement

4.10 In an earlier submission to Ministers dated 6 January 1998[159] Dr Gibbons had set out the options for the design competition. He suggested that a decision was required urgently as it was "essential to move ahead quickly to keep up momentum." He went on to comment that design competitions as a procurement process had a long history but enjoyed a somewhat mixed reputation. He pointed out that such well-known buildings as the Houses of Parliament, Sydney Opera House, the Tate Modern and the new Museum of Scotland had all been the subject of design competitions and stood as testament to what could be achieved. He also noted that in recent times design competitions had been used to procure the Australian Parliament building in Canberra, the Saxony State Parliament in Dresden, the Dutch Second Chamber in The Hague and the re-modelled Reichstag in Berlin.

4.11 In the same submission he had explained the different types of design competition:

> 'There are fundamentally two types of design competition:
>
> Those competitions which are held in order to find a **design**, and
>
> Those competitions which are held to find a **designer**. These competitions are more accurately known as **competitive selection** procedures.

---

[156] SE/2/995 - Minute from Mr William Armstrong to Mr Alistair Brown, 21 October 1997

[157] SE/3/011-12 - 'Dewar Opts for New Building in Historic Heart of Edinburgh', 9 January 1998

[158] SE/2/1262- 1270 – Briefing Note from Mr Paul Grice to PS/Secretary of State , 8 January 1998

[159] SE/3/003-006 – Minute from Dr John Gibbons to PS/Henry McLeish and PS/Secretary of State, 6 January 1998

In short the advantage of the classic design competition is that it is a very transparent process which can explore widely differing design philosophies. It can also easily be used to allow public consultation and debate about alternative proposals. The advantages of the competitive selection process, intended to find a designer rather than a design, are that it is quicker and cheaper than a classic design competition and that it allows a creative dialogue to take place between architect and client at a much earlier stage in the process. This method is also less likely to be subjected to external influence as the selection process is more clearly in the hands of the client.'[160]

and concluded with his recommendations:

'The choice lies between design competition, with the opportunity to attract very high quality architectural talent to the job of designing a Scottish Parliament building, but with a significant risk that the job will take longer and cost more than presently estimated; and a competitive selection process which would have a rather narrower focus, would come across as being less ambitious and exciting, but would have a higher probability of delivering a successful Parliament building on time and to budget.

On balance, officials would recommend the choice of the competitive selection route, with full advantage being taken of every opportunity for public participation through exhibition and through ensuring as far as possible that a wide range of architectural talent joined in the designer competition. We would be grateful for Ministers' views, and would of course be happy to discuss further.'[161]

4.12 The advice given by Dr Gibbons was very much in line with guidance set out in the Department of the Environment handbook "Architectural Competitions - A handbook for promoters"[162] which had been published as recently as 1996. In evidence, Dr Gibbons explained that there had been discussion about the handbook with those at the RIBA with experience of architectural competitions and that it represented "by and large" the model that was followed when it was later decided to proceed by way of a competitive interview to select a designer rather that by way of a design competition.

4.13 The minute of the meeting held on 6 January 1998[163] at which the Holyrood site was selected[164] discloses that the features of a competition were also discussed. Dr Gibbons again outlined the main characteristics of competitions to choose a design and competitions to choose a designer. He offered the suggestion that a designer competition would be quicker and offer "closer control". There was a clear emphasis that time was a priority and that control over the process was required. Ministers agreed that there should be a designer competition (or "competitive interview process", as it was sometimes referred to). Donald Dewar sought to achieve wider political acceptance by expressing a wish to involve the Royal Fine Art

---

[160] *ibid*

[161] SE/3/006 - Minute from Dr John Gibbons to PS/Henry McLeish and PS/Secretary of State, 6 January 1998

[162] RI/1/001-028 – 'Architectural Competitions – a Handbook for Promoters', by the Department of Environment, 1996

[163] SE/3/007-010 - Minute from Mr Kenneth Thomson to Mr Robert Gordon, 23 January 1998

[164] Evidence of Mr Kenneth Thomson on 3 February 2004, Para 226

Commission for Scotland (RFACS) and the RIAS. The RIAS was said to prefer an open design competition but it was believed that it would "go along with the proposals provided they were given their place".[165]

4.14 Notwithstanding the decision taken on 6 January 1998, at a meeting with Ministers on 14 January 1998[166] the RIAS emphasised the importance of timescales, noted the tight selection criteria proposed by Dr Gibbons and suggested the appointment of an eminent architect to assist the Scottish Office through the process. Interestingly Dr Gibbons, who was present, appears to have highlighted the difficulties which could arise from the use of foreign "name" architects forming local marriages with Scottish practices.

4.15 In a Position Report for the RIAS Council Meeting held on 21 January 1998 Donald Dewar is quoted as having said that "he had a mandate to act as the most important patron of the architecture of government for 300 years".[167] The mechanics of the competition were explained to officials of the RIAS and RFACS at a meeting on 22 January 1998[168] attended by Mr Gordon, Mr Grice and Mr Wyllie of the Scottish Office and Mr Armstrong. Once again, emphasis was laid upon the "highly accelerated programmes set by Donald Dewar".

4.16 The RIAS was so concerned about what it saw as the undue haste with which the process overall was proceeding that its President, Mr George Wren, wrote on 23 January 1998 to Donald Dewar, drawing his attention in particular to the concern shared amongst many in the profession.[169] "Speed", he wrote, "had two inevitable consequences". Firstly, there was the reduction in the availability of design time. The need for quick methods of construction, combined with the truncation of sufficient time to "work through" a design and refine it, both impacted on the subtlety and elegance of the design solution itself, and influenced the design towards increased levels of prefabrication and standardisation. He was also concerned that the competition would create an ambiguous bias in favour of the larger practices, given the scale of the Project, and he repeated his plea for a design competition, rather than one for a designer. This disappointment was repeated in an RIAS press release issued on 26 January 1998, in which it publicly warned that the Scottish architectural community considered that the process was being "unduly rushed."[170]

4.17 Following a submission by Mr Grice on 22 January 1998 Ministers agreed the terms of a press release formally announcing the competition. Mr Grice set out the procedure devised within

---

[165] SE/3/013(R)-017 – Minute from Mr Paul Grice to PS/Henry McLeish and PS/Secretary of State, 22 January 1998
[166] RI/1/050-054 – Minutes of Holyrood Parliament Building Meeting of 14 January 1998
[167] RI/1/057-062 – RIAS Scottish Parliament Position Report, 21 January 1998
[168] RI/1/063064(R) – RIAS Note of Meeting on Designer Selection Procedure, 22 January 1988
[169] RI/1/137-138 – Letter from Mr George Wren to Donald Dewar, 23 January 1998
[170] RI/1/139 – 'Architects Disappointed at Secretary of State's Decision', 26 January 1998

the Scottish Office to select the architectural design team and the panel, or jury.[171] The minute dealt in detail with media arrangements and also with the proposed membership of the panel, which, it was suggested should appropriately have between five and seven members. It was, at that time, envisaged that it would be chaired by Henry McLeish and would include both Dr Gibbons and Mr Gordon. The question was posed "if we want to be sure of having a majority … that would mean having another Scottish Office person on the panel." The proposition was put that it was important to keep the Scottish Office membership in the majority to ensure that "we could not be outvoted" but, with the participation of an independent architect who was considered by officials to be "utterly reliable",[172] there appears to have been confidence that further independent membership could be limited to two. Mr Grice went on to suggest the appointment of a lady journalist to redress the gender balance and to introduce a perception of representation of the public interest. Names were suggested, including that of Ms Kirsty Wark.[173] Having heard her evidence, I am quite satisfied that Ms Wark agreed to join the panel in the public interest. I cannot but wonder whether she would have been so accommodating had she known that within the Scottish Office plans were afoot to ensure that the Scottish Office nominees on the panel "could not be outvoted."

Conduct of the Competition

4.18 The competition itself was duly launched with a press release on 26 January 1998.[174] The OJEC notice[175] of the same date described the commission, giving the Project cost as being in the region of £50 million excluding VAT and the gross floor area of the accommodation as approximately 17,000m² (excluding car parking).

4.19 Pre Qualification Questionnaires[176] to elicit information about would-be competitors had been designed by Mr Eric Kinsey, Member of the Project Team, and were to be returned by 2 March 1998. They included a requirement for information on the following:

- business organisation and principles;
- evidence of the ability to provide relevant professional indemnity insurance of at least £5 million for each and every claim;
- numbers of suitably qualified staff specialising in the services to which the contract relates, including principals and their professional qualifications;
- a list of clients for whom comparable services had been provided in the past three years with the contract sums, dates and recipients of the services provided;
- relevant experience in conversion and refurbishment of listed buildings; and

---

[171] SE/3/013-017(R) – Minute from Mr Paul Grice to PS/Henry McLeish and PS/Secretary of State, 22 January 1998
[172] *ibid*, Para 13
[173] SE/3/013-017(R) – Minute from Mr Paul Grice to PS/Henry McLeish and PS/Secretary of State, 22 January 1998, Para 15
[174] SE/3/029 - 'Secretary of State Gets Design for Scottish Parliament Underway', 26 January 1998
[175] SE/3/031-033 - OJEC Advertisement for the Architectural Design Services, 26 January 1998
[176] SE/3/040-053 – Minute from Mr Eric Kinsey on Design Services Appointment, 30 January 1998

- the availability of ongoing interface with the client; a description of measures for insuring quality control; for example certification to BS5750/ISO9000/EN29000.

4.20 The form of PQQ, like the OJEC notice, left open the legal question of how a team might be formed to carry out the commission.

4.21 The award criteria (other than price) were stated in the OJEC notice to be the "economically most advantageous tender, relevant experience and design ability". European Procurement Rules[177] are designed to ensure fair competition and transparent procedures for candidates throughout the European Union, and will normally apply where the promoter is a 'contracting authority' and the value of the contract is likely to exceed 130,000 Special Drawing Rights.[178]

The Appointment of the Selection Panel

4.22 As previously noted, the original proposal was that the selection panel would be chaired by Henry McLeish.[179] However, a decision appears to have been made on 6 February 1998[180] by Donald Dewar that he would chair the panel himself. Membership of the panel was finally settled on 27 February 1998.[181] In addition to Donald Dewar it comprised Dr Gibbons, Mr Gordon, Ms Wark, Professor Andrew MacMillan, formerly Professor of Architecture in Glasgow University and Head of the Mackintosh School of Architecture in Glasgow, and Miss Joan O'Connor, a former President of the Royal Incorporation of Architects in Ireland.

Evaluation of Pre-Qualification Questionnaires

4.23 The OJEC Notice resulted in the submission of 70 Pre-Qualification Questionnaires,[182] including separate submissions by the firms of Enric Miralles y Moya of Barcelona[183] and by RMJM (Scotland) Ltd[184] of Edinburgh. An evaluation of the 70 PQQs was undertaken by Mr Armstrong[185] adopting a scoring system[186] that he had agreed with Dr Gibbons and which was intended to establish the capacity of the various contenders to undertake the Project. In Mr Armstrong's analysis, Snr Miralles' practice was assessed as 44th out of the 70 PQQs on the basis of the adequacy of the practice's resources and Snr Miralles' extensive teaching commitments. He did not recommend that it be included in the initial long list of 20 for consideration by the panel.

---

[177] Directive 92/50/EEC UK implementation by Public Services Contracts Regulations 1993 (SI 1993 No. 3228)

[178] The threshold at the time, equivalent to just over £100,000

[179] SE/4/007-009 - Minute of Building Steering Group Meeting of 15 January 1998

[180] SE/3/058-059(R) – Minute from Mr Paul Grice to PS/Secretary of State, 9 February 1998

[181] SE/3/068-074(R) – Minute from Mr Paul Grice to PS/Secretary of State, 27 February 1998

[182] SE/3/087-088 - List from Mr William Armstrong of Returned PQQs, March 1998

[183] CB//1/137-195(R) – Enric Miralles y Moya Pre-Qualification Questionnaire, 2 March 1998

[184] CB/1/087-136 - RMJM Scotland Limited Pre-Qualification Questionnaire, 2 March 1998

[185] Evidence of Mr Armstrong on 2 December 2003, Para 526 *et seq*

[186] MS/5/004-007 - Blank Scoring Sheet , the sheets scored by Mr Armstrong have not been produced for reasons of confidentiality

4.24 The Inquiry also heard that Mr Armstrong had overlooked an apparent shortcoming in Snr Miralles' PQQ in relation to Professional Indemnity Insurance.[187] The PQQ required applicants to demonstrate evidence of ability to provide PII cover. It was only in the course of this Inquiry that it was identified that Snr Miralles had provided an out of date certificate of insurance and one that did not provide the required level of cover. It was Mr Armstrong's view that had this been picked up at the time he would have consigned the application to the bottom of his ranked list, notwithstanding that the matter only merited 10% of the marks under his scoring system. I do not consider this to have been a fatal flaw in the application although it does demonstrate a lack of clarity in what was actually being sought in response to the OJEC notice. I am aware that appropriate PII cover was eventually arranged through the offices of RMJM Ltd on behalf of the eventual joint venture company.

The Short-listing Process

4.25 The selection panel first met on 23 March 1998[188] in Glasgow. In a minute advising Donald Dewar of the arrangements, Dr Gibbons records that he had previously held a number of "bilateral" meetings with individual panel members. He stated "we have thoroughly examined all 70 of the submissions, as have some panel members…" and that consensus had begun to emerge amongst panel members that there were 20 submissions which commanded more or less their universal support. A systematic approach was not adopted towards the handling of the PQQs by panel members. All members appear to have been issued with copies of the PQQs although no instructions seem to have been given that would ensure a methodical approach to shortlisting. Some panel members adopted their own scoring systems; some members scrutinised the PQQs in Victoria Quay, others did it independently; and Donald Dewar was taken through the applicants in a long session with Dr Gibbons. Mr Armstrong's scoring matrix was not shared with all the panel members. Nevertheless, the meeting on 23 March did succeed in identifying a long list of 17 candidates, each of which was considered in detail before the panel reduced the number to 12. The identities of the 12 were publicised on 27 March 1998 although the record of how this was achieved is rather threadbare. Notably, Enric Miralles y Moya's entry succeeded in making the final 12 but RMJM Ltd did not. The Inquiry heard of the strong support within the panel for Snr Miralles, particularly from Professor MacMillan.[189]

4.26 The Inquiry learned that visits were undertaken by members of the selection panel and, in some cases, officials to the premises of most but not all 12 of the shortlisted candidates.[190]

---

[187] Evidence of Mr Armstrong on 2 December 2003, Paras 688 to 719
[188] SE/3/089-091 - Minute from Dr John Gibbons to PS/ Secretary of State, 20 March 1998
[189] Evidence of Mr William Armstrong on 2 December 2003, Para 653
[190] Evidence of Mr Laurence Bain on 26 November 2003, Para 745

The visits were intended to verify the information contained in the applicants' PQQs by inspecting the previous work of the competitors, meeting individuals to be assigned to the Project and exploring the basis of joint submissions. Oral accounts of the visits were made to the panel who, it was suggested, were able in many instances to supplement this with their own personal knowledge of output from the practices. There was however no consistency in the personnel undertaking these visits, no written reports of the visits and no evidence of any structured assessment of the candidates against a fixed set of criteria. This rather haphazard arrangement does not strike me as an exemplar for a competition process and, in exposing individual members of the selection panel to candidates in a random way, could even be considered as irregular. I do not question the integrity of those involved but I cannot see this as other than an expensive distraction which, in the way it was conducted, added little to the panel's ultimate ability to select the most appropriate candidate and may possibly have given rise to a perception of unfairness by some.

4.27 The panel reconvened from 3 May to 5 May and interviewed all 12 of the long-listed candidates. All members of the panel participated in all of these interviews which were fashioned around Donald Dewar's schedule. No formal minute of this part of the process was kept and again there does not appear to have been a systematic approach to the assessment for each candidate. A scoring system was proposed but apparently was abandoned in the course of the interviews.[191] Five clear front runners emerged from these interviews including Enric Miralles, who impressed as "an inspirational architect of stature".[192]

4.28 The final five design teams named on 7 May 1998, were as follows:
- Rafael Vinoly
- Michael Wilford
- Richard Meier with Keppie Design
- Enric Miralles y Moya
- Glass Murray & Denton Corker Marshall International.

Public Display of Concept Designs

4.29 Before final interviews the five shortlisted candidates were required to submit concept designs which were sent on public exhibition around Scotland. There was a clear view from the panel[193] as to the importance of making these designs as visible to the public as possible across Scotland. Importantly it was made clear that the exhibition was not to be regarded as a public consultation exercise and was to be treated simply as an opportunity for the public to express their views. The responses of the public were tabulated.[194] From 4,480 responses,

---

[191] WS/12/001-007 - Miss Joan O'Connor's Witness Statement, 25 November 2003
[192] *ibid*
[193] SE/3/097-102 – Minute from Mr Paul Grice to PS/Secretary of State, 23 April 1998
[194] SE/3/077F-J – Interim Report: Results of Public Information/Consultation Exercise, 19 June 1998

the Vinoly and Miralles concepts were evidently preferred, but all received some degree of negative comment. The analysis seems a sensible one and was plainly and clearly set out.

EMBT/RMJM Ltd Joint Venture and Contractual Arrangements

4.30　On 5 June 1998 a press release from the Scottish Office[195] disclosed that the identity of the fourth competitor had changed and was now to be described as Enric Miralles y Moya and RMJM (Scotland) Limited. While the evidence is not clear, it appears that during the visit of Dr Gibbons and Professor MacMillan to the studio of Snr Miralles in Barcelona there was some discussion about the possibility of a link up with a Scottish practice. Of those mentioned, RMJM was one.

4.31　When Enric Miralles and RMJM subsequently emerged as the selected architects after the final round of interviews on 22 June, no formal or legal arrangements had been put in place with regard to the constitution of the proposed joint venture. The Inquiry has ascertained that Randotte (No 452) Ltd, a shelf company, was incorporated on 17 February 1998, and a resolution to change its name to EMBT/RMJM Ltd passed on 13 August 1998. The company had a share capital of £100 divided into 100 ordinary shares of £1 each, of which two shares were issued and fully paid. A Certificate of Incorporation on Change of Name was issued by the Registrar of Companies on 9 September 1998. In other words, until that date there was no company registered under the Companies Act having the name "EMBT/RMJM Ltd". The initial Minute of Agreement dated 7 August with the Secretary of State for Scotland signed by Enric Miralles purportedly on behalf of EMBT/RMJM Ltd was without contractual validity.

4.32　After this inauspicious start and good legal advice, a new Minute of Agreement was agreed on 4 November 1998 after the Registrar of Companies had granted a Certificate of Incorporation on Change of Name. Prior to the signing of this Minute of Agreement, some work had already been done by the two constituent parts of the joint venture for which invoices were charged to the Scottish Office[196] without there being in existence any valid contract.

4.33　It is a matter of surprise to me that so little inquiry was made of the joint venture and how it was to operate. The architectural commission for the new Scottish Parliament building was let to a company with a nominal share capital of £100 and only £2 issued and fully paid up. I would have expected a rigorous process of due diligence to have been undertaken and collateral warranties to have been obtained from both RMJM Ltd and EMBT. None was sought; none was obtained and this major and expensive project moved forward with a breathtaking degree of informality and an almost non-existent legal framework. I have since learned that in early

---

[195] SE/3/105-106 – 'Visions for Holyrood Parliament Go On Show', 5 June 1998
[196] RM/6/168-169 – Letter from Mr William Armstrong to Mr Brian Stewart, 15 October 1998

2004 RMJM Ltd has offered to subscribe to an undertaking by which it will formally bind itself as accountable for the past, present, and future performance of the architect. In other words, it has offered a form of collateral warranty. I consider this to be commendable, but to reinforce the point which I have made above.

4.34 Miss O'Connor told the Inquiry that she had assumed that the Scottish Office had "lawyered" the link up between Snr Miralles and RMJM Ltd but conceded that the link up was seen as an administrative solution to a problem.[197] That problem was seen as the relatively light weight of Snr Miralles' office, in terms of staff and other logistics and resources, whilst RMJM was able to provide efficiency, international reach, a range of professional services, and of course their well-established Scottish contacts. In my opinion that was a reasonable assumption on her behalf and possibly of the remainder of the lay members of the panel.

4.35 I am very critical of this episode. It appears to me to have been sloppy, unprofessional and fraught with danger. However, in the event the Architect has not sought to take advantage of the lack of definition in the legal relationships and I am slow to suggest that this incomplete legal framework caused delay or expense, although it set an unhappy precedent in the history of the Project.

External Advice to the Selection Panel

4.36 Mr John Hume, the former Chief Inspector of Historic Buildings with Historic Scotland, had submitted a commentary on the long listed candidates separately on the concept designs of the five short-listed candidates.[198] He described the approach of the ultimate winner as "radical ... but very thoughtful and considerate. The involvement of RMJM is still an unknown quantity." He endorsed the ability of EMBT and RMJM to deliver, although he did not make clear how he was aware that that was the case. The ultimate winner was ranked first by Mr Hume,[199] who offered the view that "Enric Miralles' vision might require modification to achieve a workable and acceptable building, but the combination of that vision with the practical approach of RMJM could deliver an inspiring but operationally satisfactory outcome".

4.37 Mr Armstrong, by now appointed as Project Manager, offered his views on 11 June 1998. He regarded Snr Miralles as a "serious contender" but underlined that "whoever is appointed (before it is formalised or announced) will have to be told the home truth, that there are three priorities – budget, programme and design, and they must all be achieved to an equal degree". With perception he advised: "I should think none of these proposals could be built within the

---

[197] Evidence of Miss Joan O'Connor on 25 November 2003, Para 905
[198] SE/3/107-110(R) - Paper by Mr John Hume, Selection of Design Team, 8 June 1998
[199] ibid

budget."[200] He also emphasised his doubts on the EMBT/RMJM marriage. He would have disqualified each of the candidates for ignoring the brief; EMBT/RMJM specifically for presenting concept drawings that extended outwith the site boundary. He cautioned further that "all our previous questions on RMJM's abilities, which took them out at the first sift, are liable to be overlooked".

Costing of Concept Designs

4.38 DLE, who had by this time been appointed as quantity surveyors for the Project, undertook a cost commentary on the design entries,[201] carefully making the points that any figures should be treated with caution at this stage, that a comparative exercise was inappropriate and that a like for like comparison was not possible. The area in the Building User Brief schedule of accommodation at that stage totalled $20,740m^2$ (gross, including car-parking). DLE applied uniform cost allowances for demolition and archaeology, highways work, fit-out and repairs to Queensberry House and costed the schemes as follows:

COMPETITOR	ESTIMATED COST (Budget £50 million)	AREA m² (User Brief – 20,740m²)
Glass Murray/Denton Corker Marshall	£57.89 million	23,620
Richard Meier/Keppie	£43.00 million	Impossible to tabulate
EMBT/RMJM	£62.60 million	27,610
Rafael Vinoly/Reiach & Hall	£89.60 million	38,700
Michael Wilford & Partners	£73.40 million	39,885

4.39 At this stage DLE also reported a figure of £1.4 million in connection with work to the existing roads and pavements adjacent to the site. Their conclusion was that the five entries were each indicative of a "style of approach" rather than a specific design solution which made cost assessments rather academic. Importantly, they also concluded that "the variety of approach taken by the individual teams is confirmation of the vital necessity for the selected design team (which DLE will join) to establish a meaningful financial framework within which design development can proceed. This must be achieved very early in the process. The brief must be understood and adhered to in order that the risks inherent in undertaking such a project within an extremely tight timescale and a finite budget and be properly managed." They added: "The cost commentary forms part of the first stage of the process. Its use is informing a basis on which to proceed with the stated architect/design team and as a pointer towards the very detailed cost management that must accompany the design development of this challenging project."

---

[200] SE/3/114-117(R) – Minute from Mr William Armstrong to Dr John Gibbons, 11 June 1998
[201] SE/3/118-129(R) – DLE Architectural Selection Process - Cost Commentary, 10 June 1998

4.40 The importance of these passages is that it is clear that none of the finalists adhered either to the User Brief or the budget. Yet the panel felt confident that it could proceed to the selection of a winner without any of theses discrepancies being highlighted and without querying whether these significant variations placed the competition outwith the EU procurement rules and OJEC advertisement requirements. I have my reservations about the legitimacy of this, but if necessary, it will be for a court of law to reach a determination on this and not me. Of more immediate interest is why, if the earliest assessments revealed in almost every bid that a significant cost over-run was expected, no fee-tapering or other incentive to keep costs down was in contemplation. So far as I can ascertain it was never in mind until much, much later and never implemented until the present Presiding Officer, George Reid, stamped his foot and required it.

Final Selection Interview and Decision

4.41 The final interviews of the 5 short listed candidates took place in Glasgow on 22 June 1998. The candidates gave presentations to the panel illustrating their concepts using design boards and models. The evidence suggests that Enric Miralles and his EMBT/RMJM colleagues gave a significantly superior presentation to that of the other candidates. Panel members were particularly impressed by Snr Miralles' sensitivity to the location of the Holyrood site and its juxtaposition with Holyrood Palace and the Royal Park. His vision of a parliament building which "sits in the land because it belongs in the land" appears to have struck a chord with Donald Dewar and his colleagues.

4.42 In her written evidence, Miss O'Connor suggested that the panel were aware that the selection of EMBT/RMJM carried some risk but it was their assessment that the risk was worth it. She said:

> 'We unanimously took the decision in favour of EMBT/RMJM at the end of the meeting on 22 June. .. Miralles' presentation and concept were unquestionably head and shoulders above the others and by consensus he came out top. In deciding on EMBT/RMJM we were alert to an element of risk arising from the personality of Enric Miralles and the working methods of the design studio. We were alert to potential problems in the relationship between EMBT and RMJM but were assured by both that difficulties were not expected and that such minor problems as might arise would not be insuperable. My note (*of the interviews*) records the panel asking itself whether Miralles was "controllable". As per my note we all identified this as a significant risk but a risk that was worth taking. I should say that I am myself normally risk averse.'[202]

---

[202] WS/12/001-007 Miss Joan O'Connor's Witness Statement, 25 November 2003

4.43   Ms Wark too hinted of the panel's awareness that the choice carried some risk:

> "Even Donald Dewar, who I had initially thought of as normally a cautious man, was clearly in favour of Miralles."[203]

4.44   Prior to the final interviews the panel had been shown the DLE cost commentary on each of the five finalists' concepts.[204] Miss O'Connor had noted that none of the concepts proposed by the five finalists could be delivered within the £50 million target. She did not see that as being a concern for the panel:

> 'I was of the view, which was generally shared by the panel, that the object of the exercise was to choose a winner on the basis of design intent and that it would be for the architect to complete the design in accordance with a final brief and agreed cost constraints. It seemed likely that the brief would change and that as a result the costs would also do so.'[205]

4.45   That cost was not a consideration in the decision to appoint EMBT/RMJM was graphically illustrated in a revealing exchange between Counsel to the Inquiry and Ms Wark:

> **"Mr Campbell QC**: Can I suggest to you perhaps that, without knowledge of the competing fee rates, it is difficult for a panel to make a decision about the economically most advantageous tender?
>
> **Ms Wark:** That is certainly the case, but there was no way that we were making a decision on economically the most advantageous tender; you would have ended up with a shed.
>
> **Mr Campbell QC:** Why so?
>
> **Ms Wark:** Because, that was not what it was about. It was getting a building which was the most exciting, innovative building — a modern building — so therefore the most advantageous tender as the very, very first thing you were looking at is not right. I mean all three taken together, the design ability, relative experience, fine; but we would never have begun simply with the most... I mean you would not have gone through all that process to rely on envelopes."[206]

4.46   I did not need to learn at this Inquiry that both Ms Kirsty Wark and Miss Joan O'Connor were persons of steely will, independence of mind and a keen appreciation of architecture. Both acquitted themselves in their evidence with distinction and were unswerving in their conclusion that ultimately the unanimous selection of the team led by Enric Miralles was correct. I cannot and do not challenge the aesthetic judgment of any of the panel members.

---

[203] WS/13/001-008 Ms Kirsty Wark's Witness Statement, 26 November 2003
[204] SE/3/118-129(R) – Architectural Selection Process – DLE Cost Commentary, 10 June 1998
[205] WS/12/001-007 Miss Joan O'Connor's Witness Statement, 25 November 2003
[206] Evidence of Ms Kirsty Wark on 26 November 2003, Para 395

The Tender Opening Process

4.47　The opening of the tender of the preferred Design Team took place on 26 June 1998.[207] Donald Dewar agreed that the Design Team proposed by Enric Miralles and RMJM Ltd be appointed for the design of the Scottish Parliament at Holyrood. There is a curious hybridity in this which was later to bedevil progress on the Project. The panel had selected a designer, namely Snr Miralles, and had undoubtedly been unanimous in that selection, albeit with some misgivings over the organisational capacities of his 'atelier' practice. Now, though, the appointment was to be awarded to EMBT/RMJM (Scotland) Ltd. Leaving aside the propriety of that change at this late stage in the designer competition process in terms of EU Procurement Rules, there is a further problem over these Rules. Within the United Kingdom the procedure has been to identify a preferred tenderer on non-cost grounds, to estimate an acceptable fee and, if that preferred candidate's tender came within the acceptable range previously fixed, to accept it <u>without</u> opening other rejected candidate tenders. There is a clear logic in following such a course, but it is not what EU Rules require. As I understand it, they allow for a first stage preference to be expressed comparable to past UK practice but require <u>all</u> tender letters to be opened – not in the first place just the tender of the preferred bidder to determine whether it falls within an acceptable range.

4.48　The EU logic is, again as I understand it, that if one who has not been otherwise preferred comes up with such an interestingly low tender on fee rate, then that might lead to a re-assessment overall of what is on offer. This essential change in practice required under EU Rules does not appear to have been grasped at this stage. As I have already indicated I am not a court of law and if challenge is to be made of the then Scottish Office procedures, it will be for the Courts to decide and I do not seek to usurp their function. I only observe that in the Harmon case[208] which related to Portcullis House, a new Parliamentary building in Whitehall, and which was not appealed, the Court found against the authorities. That decision was later at the centre of very useful advice from the Comptroller and Auditor General. The DoE guidelines on Architectural Competitions[209] explicitly states: "Where the two envelope system is used all fee proposals must be considered before a selection is finalised".[210]

4.49　The press release announcing the success of Snr Miralles in the competition confirmed his intention to team up with RMJM and his intention to postpone many of his international commitments and base himself in Edinburgh during the design and construction stage of the

---

[207] SE/3/186-187 - Tender Opening Record, signed by Dr John Gibbons and Mr Robert Gordon, 26 June 1998
[208] Harmon CFEM Facades (UK) Ltd v. The Corporate Officer of the House of Commons [1999] EWHC Technology 199 (28th October, 1999)
[209] RI/1/001-028 – 'Architectural Competitions – A Handbook for Promoters', Department of Environment, 1996
[210] ibid, RI/1/023

Parliament Building.[211] The panel's decision to select Snr Miralles had been unanimous. The levels of each candidate's fee were kept confidential, but the briefing material used by Ministers at the press conference stated the budget to be £50 million excluding VAT and fees. This has to be contrasted with DLE's estimate of £62.6 million for the winning entry. As I have said, it is of concern to me that the so-called budget, which never had any basis in reality, was not at this stage set against even the most tentative of cost estimates.

4.50 Dr Gibbons wrote to Snr Miralles on 3 July 1998 confirming his appointment, and advised him that he had been selected in association with RMJM (Scotland) Limited to be the architect and lead consultant for the new parliament building. The commission was offered on the basis of the information that had been provided and the fee proposal, which was accepted.[212]

4.51 Reliance was certainly placed on the assertions by the architectural joint venture at interview that the Project could be delivered within the £50 million budget and adapted to bring about additional cost improvements.[213] It is difficult to see how that assertion could have been given conscientiously or taken seriously, given the embryonic state of the designs.

4.52 The competition process that was followed was in general a sound one. All of the surviving members of the selection panel gave evidence to the Inquiry and I was impressed by the obvious commitment they had applied to their task. The diversity of the panel contributed to its strength and I have no reason to question their unanimous conclusion as to the eventual winner. Some parts of the process were, however, less systematic than they should have been. In particular I point to the obvious uncertainty as to how the PQQs were to be evaluated and the almost whimsical series of visits undertaken to some candidates. I do no more than query that a member of the jury, Dr Gibbons, should also play such a prominent role in the administration of the process. I also have to highlight the absence of a meaningful record of many aspects of the conduct of the competition; somewhat unusual in the civil service culture. In effect there is not an audit trail of the designer competition and it has only been through this Inquiry that much of the process has been explored for the first time.

---

[211] SE/3/134 – Press Release – 'Architect Chosen to Design Scottish Parliament', 3 July 1998
[212] SE/3/178-179 – Letter from Dr John Gibbons to Snr Enric Miralles, 3 July 1998
[213] See also Para 8.8

Chapter 5

Evolution of the Building User Brief

Purpose of the Brief

5.1   Treasury Guidance at the time[214] indicated the purpose of a project or building brief as follows:

> 'The project brief is a comprehensive statement of the department's requirements for the project. Tender documents for professional services should include either a complete project brief or a draft version requiring the successful tenderer's input to its completion. This should enable the construction professionals to understand the scope and extent of the project and the department's quality requirements'.

5.2   Treasury Guidance[215] also referred to the Construction Industry Board report "Briefing the team" published in June 1997, the introduction to which says:

> 'Briefing is the process by which a client informs others of his or her needs, aspirations and desires.....
> The outcome of any project relies on the quality of the briefing provided.
> ...

---

[214] SE/5/421-448 – HM Treasury Procurement Guidance Note No 3 'Appointment of Consultants and Contractors', December 1997, Para B6

[215] SE/5/399-420 - HM Treasury Procurement Guidance Note No 2 "Value for Money in Construction Procurement, 1997

Effective briefing is essential throughout the project. **However, perhaps the most important element is the time spent at the outset.** Many construction projects suffer from poor definition due to inadequate time and thought being given at an early stage. This is often because there is a sense of urgency fuelled by the desire for an immediate solution.

Investing time at the beginning of a project in developing a complete definition taking account of all the requirements will reduce the likelihood of changes later. The later that changes are made in a project, the more likely they are to cost in both direct and knock on effects'.[216]

5.3 The Inquiry heard evidence from Mr Tombs, Secretary of the RIAS, who confirmed that the Brief is "critical" to how architects work.[217] Dr Gibbons in his evidence said: "one of the critical issues, in terms of how the building works, is the clarity of the Brief".[218] When asked why such clarity was important he said it was "to avoid change in the process of building. ...The amount of time you can invest before you start to build is very important in the efficiency of the process that follows on".[219] He went on to say: "Change has to be avoided at all costs, for obvious reasons."[220]

5.4 It was pointed out in the September 2000 report of the Auditor General for Scotland that the Scottish Office did not issue separate strategic and detailed project Briefs for the new Parliament building[221] as a first stage which the Construction Industry Board would regard as desirable, and as was also recommended in Scottish Office Guidance.[222] The guidance sets out with great clarity the need for clear definition of the cost and timetable criteria for any large project. In fact Project Management issued a composite Building User Brief which appeared in various versions. It seems to me that the Auditor General intended this as a criticism but this is not a matter on which there was specific evidence before the Inquiry. It is however my view that the decision to construct a new Parliament was a given factor so far as those with responsibility for the Brief were concerned.

5.5 Accordingly many of the questions which might, in terms of the guidance,[223] have been addressed in developing any strategic brief were redundant. If there is a criticism of the fact that no separate strategic brief was prepared, it would be subsumed within any broader

---

[216] MS/28/001-020 - Construction Industry Board Report "Briefing the Team", June 1997
[217] Evidence of Mr Sebastian Tombs on 2 December 2003, Para 50
[218] Evidence of Dr John Gibbons on 24 November 2003, Para 126
[219] *ibid*, Para 142
[220] *ibid*, Para 152
[221] Auditor General for Scotland Report of September 2000, Para 3.23
[222] SE/5/621–644 – Building Directorate Practice Note 5 'Consultant Selection & Fee Tendering', Page 627
[223] MS/28/001-020 - Construction Industry Board Report "Briefing the Team", June 1997, Page 13

criticism of the decision to press ahead with a new Parliament building instead of leaving it to the Parliament itself.

The Appointment of Mr Bill Armstrong

5.6   From an early stage the preparation of a brief was seen as an urgent and important task. After a first start towards identification of the requirements of any new parliament by civil servants in June 1997[224] it was decided to employ the services of a consultant, and during that month Mr William (Bill) Armstrong was engaged for the specific task of developing a brief for a Parliament Building.[225] Mr Armstrong was an experienced architect and project manager. While employed by Project Management International he had worked as project adviser to the Scottish Office in relation to the construction of Victoria Quay and had acted as project manager for the fit out. As a result he was well known to Mr Gordon, Mrs Doig and other civil servants with whom he had worked successfully. Mr Armstrong's appointment as a consultant did not follow a formal competitive recruitment process of any kind but I have no doubts as to his competence to carry out this role.

Early Development of the Brief

5.7   Mr Armstrong set in hand a process of consultation and, in the company of either Dr Gibbons or Mrs Doig, made fact-finding visits to Westminster and to the Parliaments in Dublin, The Hague (the Tweede Kamer or Second Chamber), Berlin (both the Reichstag and the Berlin State Parliament), Oslo and Dresden.[226] Dr Gibbons told the Inquiry that the Brief was heavily based on the Dresden building, the State Parliament in Saxony, which had almost exactly the same number of members as the 129 foreseen for the Scottish Parliament.[227]

5.8   Drafts of sections of a brief were circulated among civil servants and assistance was sought from external consultants in relation to areas such as traffic, environment and structure and mechanical and electrical services. On 5 September 1997 Mr Kinsey circulated four draft sections of the Brief relating to (1) Planning and Functions, (2) Space Requirements and Uses, (3) Schedule of Accommodation and (4) Building Fabric.[228] Views were sought from Ministers on a range of issues such as the shape, size and layout of the main chamber, the numbers of committee rooms, MSP accommodation and catering arrangements.[229] By 3 November 1997 Mr Armstrong was in a position to circulate a further draft[230] making the point in his covering

---

[224] SE/7/006-016 – Minute from Mrs Barbara Doig, 18 June 1997

[225] MS/6/001-002 - Letter from Dr John Gibbons to Mr William Armstrong, 12 July 1997

[226] MS/6/046-071 – Mr William Armstrong's Witness Statement, Para 3.1 and Evidence on 2 December 2003, Para 169 *et seq*

[227] Evidence of Dr John Gibbons on 3 February 2004, Para 195

[228] SE/7/084-090 – Minute from Mr Eric Kinsey to Dr John Gibbons and Mr Alistair Brown, 5 September 1997

[229] SE/7/091-097, SE/7/098-10 and, SE/7/103106 – Minutes from of 10 and 17 September 1997, E-mail: Parliament Specification, 25 September 1997

[230] SE/7/107a-115 – Minute from Mr William Armstrong, 3 November 1997

minute that if the selection of the architect was to be by competition the Brief would need to be finalised by the end of that month to enable publication of the necessary notice in OJEC by the end of 1997 to keep the current programme on course. At that time there was no formal programme as such but since a meeting on 13 June 1997 the Secretary of State's declared objective had been to have permanent accommodation available, if at all possible, by the spring of 2000.

5.9   It is not clear to me that the Brief in fact required to be finalised before the OJEC advertisement or before conduct of the competition. In connection with the competition there was evidence before the Inquiry to suggest that the version of the Brief then available was considerably more detailed than was appropriate.[231] Greater detail meant greater inflexibility and although the Auditor General was broadly and correctly complimentary about the success of the User Brief in presenting a "clear vision of the requirements of the new Parliament", he noted that it did not address the potential for conflict between the various dimensions of area, cost, time and quality. Nor did it recognise that client needs might evolve.[232] I find myself in agreement with the Auditor General's comments. A further version of the Brief was made publicly available in January 1998 when a copy was placed in the House of Commons library.

5.10   On 5 February 1998 officials met with Ministers to discuss various matters including the Brief, in relation to which agreement was sought on design specification in relation to the Chamber, MSP accommodation, media and catering facilities.[233] It was confirmed at that meeting that the whole of Queensberry House should be used for offices which represented a departure from the previous position that only the basement would be used for parliamentary purposes.

Scottish Parliament Building Steering Group and the Consultative Steering Group

5.11   Mr Armstrong was principally directed in his preparation of the Brief by the Scottish Parliament Building Steering Group which was set up in August 1997. After selection of the site, this group became the Holyrood Building Steering Group. It was chaired by Mr Gordon and its objective was to bring together senior officials from different parts of the Scottish Office with varying degrees of involvement in the building project with a view to co-ordinating activities and removing obstacles to progress. After her appointment as Project Sponsor, the Group included Mrs Doig. As well as the Brief it considered matters such as the outline project

---

[231] WS/12/001–007 – Miss Joan O'Connor's Witness Statement and Evidence of Mr Sebastian Tombs on 2 December 2003, Paras 10 and 50 *et seq*
[232] Auditor General for Scotland's Report of September 2000, Para 3.25
[233] SE/7/135-137 - Minute from Mr Paul Grice to PS/Secretary of State, 5 February 1998

timetable, site selection processes and criteria, procurement and management arrangements and planning issues.[234]

5.12 The Consultative Steering Group (CSG) on the Scottish Parliament was set up by Donald Dewar under the chairmanship of Henry McLeish in November 1997, after the referendum. It met for the first time in January 1998 and its membership included representatives of all four major Scottish political parties, as well as of a wide range of civic groups and interests. Its remit included the bringing together of views on and consideration of the operational needs and working methods for the Scottish Parliament. In January 1998 the CSG was invited to comment on the proposals in the latest draft of the Brief for matters such as the shape and size of the chamber and the seating arrangements. Arrangements were thereafter made for the three political party representatives, Alex Salmond for the SNP, Jim Wallace for the Liberal Democrats and Michael Ancram for the Conservatives to be briefed and a mock up of the proposed MSP rooms was constructed at Victoria Quay for inspection.

Further Development of the Brief

5.13 During the course of April 1998 Mr Armstrong finalised the first draft of the entire Brief[235] which he circulated on 1 May 1998.[236] This was a substantial document running to several hundred pages. The Introduction stated its objective was to act as a guide to the Design Team and others involved in the procurement of the Scottish Parliament Building but made it clear that it would be subject to change and that many of the questions it posed might not be answered in finite detail until after MSPs had been elected. It repeated the adopted wording of the White Paper which set out the aspirations for the building and used expressions such as:

> 'The building …must be of such a quality, durability and civic importance as to reflect the Parliament's status and operational needs."
>
> and
>
> "It will be an important symbol for Scotland. It should pay tribute to the country's past achievements and signal its future aspirations…... Quality and value for money are also key considerations'.[237]

5.14 Section 3 of the Brief set out the "Aims and Objectives" for the building and includes references such as:

> 'The … building presents the appointed Design team with a unique opportunity to make a significant contribution to the design of this building which marks a milestone

---

[234] WS/15/001–013 – Mr Alistair Brown's Witness Statement, 6 November 2003

[235] SE/7/180-306 – Relevant extracts from April 1998 draft Building User Brief

[236] SE/7/179 - Minute from Mr William Armstrong, Draft Building User Brief dated April 1998

[237] White Paper - http://www.scotland.gov.uk/government/devolution/scpa-00.asp, Section 10.2 – 10.4

in Scotland's political history. The White paper extract quoted...lays down in outline strategic guidelines which point out the aspirations of the Government and the people of Scotland for this building.'

'The design should embody the image that Scotland has of itself with reference to both its past and future. The building should be vested with the authority and the Scottish peoples' aspirations as a nation.'*

'The architecture should reflect the social and economic culture of the nation as well as producing a building which will be a work of art in its own right. It should reflect the cultural dimensions of the country and be a place for the work of artists and designers in Scotland.'*

'The design should respect its historic surroundings, paying due regard to the significant adjacent buildings of the Palace of Holyrood House, Queensberry House and the Canongate, but at the same time be a building which reflects the culture at the end of the century and the millennium. It will be the first landmark, political building of the 21st Century. It should have a resonance of quality, durability and civic importance of which the Scottish people can be proud.'

'This project represents a wonderful opportunity for the Design Team to produce a landmark building reflecting the aspirations of Scotland as a nation, with a building of quality and value.' [238]

5.15   The terms of the Brief in relation to the expectation of quality, communicated a powerful message to the Design Team as to the client's expectations for the building. Material from the April 1998 version of the Brief was provided to the 12 long listed candidates for the designer selection competition and remained in effect during the early stages of the actual design process.[239] As Mr Brian Stewart, Director, EMBT/RMJM Ltd, put it in his evidence:

"These are stirring words but immensely significant because what it demonstrates was that the client realised the importance of the building as a symbol of political determination. Such high octane rhetoric placed challenging demands on a piece of architecture; requirements which carried its own cost. What was required was not a building imbued with the authority of a modest office building but a structure in which a nation is emblazoned." [240]

---

[238] SE/7/187 - Minute from Mr William Armstrong, Draft Building User Brief dated April 1998. These paragraphs were omitted from November 1998 Building User Brief

[239] RM/1/055-076 - Memorandum of Appointment between the Secretary of State and EMBT/ RMJM, Clause 5.11 specifically required the Architect to take into account in the performance of its duties the information and directions contained within the Brief.

[240] Evidence of Mr Brian Stewart on 11 March 2004 (am), Para 44

Mr Stewart also drew attention to the fact that the Brief provided for a design life of 100 years[241] which is, I understand, approximately double the design life of a standard office block.

Section 3.11 of the "Aims and Objectives" said:

'A budget has been set for the building of the Project of £50 million at current price levels. This should enable the designer to reflect the requirements of the Brief and also to provide quality in construction and design, and value for money.'

This was supplemented by Section 10 which clarified that the £50 million budget was exclusive of VAT and professional fees, that the breakdown was £46.75 million for new building works and £3.25 million for Queensberry House and that demolition costs were not included within the £50 million but that a further £500,000 had been allocated for this.

5.16   In relation to programme, Section 3.14 said:

'It is the aim of the Secretary of State to have the building completed and occupied by the Parliament in the year 2001. To achieve this, the personnel at all levels must make timeous decisions to enable the programme to be achieved.'

This version of the Brief also contained, in Section 11, a master development programme clearly setting out the milestones to be achieved to deliver the construction and fit out of the building for an opening in October 2001. Section 11.4 confirmed that upon the appointment of a Construction Management or Management Contractor the programme would be reviewed "to agree a programme of information and construction to achieve the completion date – July 2001." The Brief also contained various appendices including sections on the roles and activities of the Project Manager, Design Team responsibilities, material on Queensberry House and an independent environmental and site report.

5.17   Over the summer of 1998, during the course of which EMBT/RMJM Ltd were appointed as Project Architect, the Brief was the subject of further comment and refinement as demands for increased space and occupancy continued to come through. On 3 July 1998 Mr Grice, on behalf of the Constitution Group, minuted Mr Armstrong with nine pages of consolidated comments on the April 1998 draft.[242] Demands for increased space were pressing and, as an example, in his letter of 1 October 1998[243] circulating a revised version of the Schedule of Accommodation, Mr Armstrong reported that the number of staff to be employed in connection with the Official Report had increased from 6 to 30 with a requirement for 300m² of space

---

[241] SE/7/366 – 574 - Building User Brief, November 1998, Section 7.4.5
[242] SE/7/307-317 – Minute from Mr Paul Grice to Mr William Armstrong, 3 July 1998
[243] RM/1/077 - Letter from Mr William Armstrong to Mr Brian Stewart, 1 October 1998

rather than 60m², and that in connection with the Public Information Service the number of staff had increased from 4 to 18 with a requirement for 250m² rather than 50m². An issue leading to an increase in area of some 700m² was the decision to provide for three entrances to the building rather than the two originally envisaged in all versions of the Brief.[244] The Design Team had identified at an early stage the need for a third "formal" entrance and had continued to incorporate it into the designs in the light of the RFACS's concerns about the treatment of the foot of the Canongate.[245]

5.18 In October and November 1998 Mr Armstrong issued further versions of the Brief which involved only limited changes from the April 1998 draft. Although arrangements were made for a formal change control procedure to be instituted with effect from November, no steps were taken actually to amend the Brief until June 2000 when Stage D was finally reached. Against the background of the extensive design development which took place over that period, I find this dismaying to say the least. It suggests to me that over that crucial period in the development of the Project, sight was lost of the terms of the Brief. If that is correct, much of the extensive design development over that period was not taking place against the background of the clearly formulated set of client or user requirements, which the Brief should have contained.

Increases in Area

5.19 By early August 1997 Mr Armstrong was putting forward rough draft schedules of accommodation bringing out a net area for the building of 18,000m² net or 22,000m² gross.[246] The gross internal area of a building is defined as its total area measured from the inner face of its exterior walls. The net area represents the area actually available for its primary purposes. The difference between the net and gross areas is referred to as the "balance area" or "circulation space" and comprises space such as stairs, corridors, plant rooms and void areas.

5.20 In the draft circulated by Mr Kinsey on 5 September 1997[247] the net area of the building excluding car parking was to be 13,096m² and the gross area, after allowing 15% for the balance area, was 15,060m². An apparent error was introduced into the calculations from this point in that the percentage balance area should properly have been applied as a proportion of gross area rather than as an addition to the net area. The result of this was that instead of being 15% the balance area actually represented only 13% of the gross area of the building.

---

[244] SE/7/180-306 – Minute from Mr William Armstrong, Draft Building User Brief dated April 1998, Section 4.6
[245] SE/4/100-116 - Paper from Mrs Barbara Doig to Jack McConnell, 26 May 1999
[246] SE/7/18-032 – Minute from Mr William Armstrong to Mr Paul Grice, 6 August 1997
[247] SE/7/084-090 – Minute from Mr Eric Kinsey to Dr John Gibbons and Mr Alistair Brown, 5 September 1997

5.21 In terms of the draft Brief produced in January 1998 and lodged with the House of Commons library, the net area of the building excluding car parking was to be 14,035m² and the gross area, which was intended to allow for a balance area of 20%, was 16,842m². It is not clear why there was this intended change from 15% to 20% but the balance area in fact represented just under 17% of the gross area of the whole building.[248] By 6 February 1998 the gross area of the building was being reported by Mr Armstrong at 17,300m².[249] The drafts of the Brief produced in April 1998 provided for a gross area of 17,400m² [250] and in November 1998 for a gross area of 18,550m², in both cases with an effective balance area of 17% .

5.22 In November 1998 representations were made by the Architect seeking an increase in the balance area.[251] Mr Stewart in his evidence to the Inquiry said that the original estimate was "Absolutely, too optimistic for a public building of this nature."[252] That possibly begs the question as to why the Architect had not made their position in this respect known at an earlier stage against the background that the April 1998 version of the Brief, available at the time of the designer competition, made the position very clear. In March 1999[253] and May 1999,[254] by which time the gross area of the building had increased to 23,000m², Mrs Doig first sought an increase in the construction cost budget from £50 to £60 million. When doing so she confirmed that it was by then accepted against the background of the complexities of the Holyrood site and on the basis of a reappraisal of public buildings, including the Dresden parliament, that a net usable area of only 65% (i.e. a balance area 35%) would be reasonably achievable for a building of this kind. It appears to have been a matter of agreement that the 20% of the net area allowed for circulation was too low and should be increased at an estimated cost, according to Mrs Doig, of a further £5.5 million.[255]

The Shape of the Debating Chamber

5.23 An early draft of the Brief produced in August 1997 suggested for the Chamber that a "circular or semi circular arrangement with the Speaker or First Minister at the focal point would appear to be appropriate".[256]

5.24 Mr Dewar's initial views were set out in a minute of 17 September 1997[257] and were discussed at a meeting of Ministers and officials on 18 September 1997 at which it was agreed that the

---

[248] Evidence of Mr Hugh Fisher, 15 December 2003, Para 486

[249] SE/7/140 – Minute from Mr William Armstrong to Mr Alistair Brown, 6 February 1998

[250] SE/7/084-090 Minute from Mr Eric Kinsey to Dr John Gibbons and Mr Alistair Brown, 5 September 1997

[251] SE/4/040 – Letter from Mr William Armstrong to Mrs Barbara Doig, 25 November 1998

[252] Evidence of Mr Brian Stewart on 11 March 2004 (am), Para 180

[253] SE/4/057-067 - Progress Report from Mrs Barbara Doig to PS/Secretary of State, 23 March 1999

[254] SE/4/100-116 - Paper from Mrs Barbara Doig to Mr Jack McConnell, 26 May 1999

[255] SE/4/057-067 - Progress Report from Mrs Barbara Doig to PS/Secretary of State, 23 March 1999

[256] SE/7/039-083 – Building User Brief (1st Draft) from Mr Eric Kinsey, 20 August 1997, Para 5/10.3

[257] SE/7/098-101 - Minute from Mr Kenneth Thomson to Mr Stewart Gilfillan, 17 September 1997

Chamber should be "horseshoe" shaped and should be "on the small side", while allowing convenient access for the disabled.[258] In the draft Brief produced in November 1997 the Chamber was nevertheless still referred to as "circular or semi-circular".

5.25 At a meeting on 5 February 1998 Mr Dewar confirmed that he wanted a compact Chamber which would generate atmosphere while accepting the need for good accessibility.[259] At the briefing for Messrs Ancram, Salmond & Wallace on 11 February 1998[260] they confirmed their preference for the Chamber to be something closer to a horseshoe than a wide arc and stressed the importance of eye contact between MSPs.

5.26 The November 1998 Brief contained what was then the final word on the shape of the Chamber and said:

> "The arrangement of the Members' seating reflects the role of the Parliament. A horseshoe or semi-circular arrangement with the Presiding Officer at the focal point would appear to be the most appropriate."[261]

Adequacy of the Brief

5.27 The Brief sent out strong messages to the Design Team as to the significance not only of the symbolism of designs for the building but also as to the high quality expected. The messages in relation to programme and, perhaps more significantly, in relation to budget are more muted. With the benefit of hindsight the Brief might well have sent out a more considered message to the Design Team as to the relative significance of cost in the Cost/Quality/Programme triangle.

5.28 It is clear from the fact that it subsequently proved necessary to increase the balance area from some 17% of the gross area of the building to 35% that there was a failure sufficiently to investigate and identify the balance area appropriate for a building of this kind. Recognition of inadequacy of the Brief in this respect is implicit in the acceptance by Donald Dewar in early June 1999 of the revised budget of £62 million predicated on a balance area of 35%.

5.29 It is self evident that the Brief did not anticipate sufficiently the actual requirements of the Parliament once these became apparent following the handover of the Project on 1 June 1999. The November 1998 Brief postulated a requirement for a gross area of 18,550m² for the building, including a 20% balance area but excluding car parking of 3,300m². These figures suggest a gross internal area of at least 21,850m². By the time that Stage D was finally reached in June 2000, after the actual requirements of the Parliament had become

---

[258] SE/7/102-106 - Note from Mr Stewart Gilfillan to PS/Secretary of State, 23 September 1997
[259] SE/7/138-139 – Minute from Mr Paul Grice to PS/Secretary of State, 9 February 1998
[260] SE/7/149 - Minute from Mr Paul Grice to PS/Henry McLeish, 11 February 1998
[261] SE/7/366-574 – Building User Brief, November 1998, Section 5.30.3

established, the gross area had increased to some 30,593m^2.[262] On any view the Brief substantially underestimated the actual requirements of the Parliament as the ultimate client and user of the building.

---

[262] DL/1/008-012 – DLE Timeline Development of Costs, October 1998 – August 2000

Chapter 6

Construction Management

What is Construction Management?

6.1   One of the most significant, if not the most significant, decisions taken during the course of the Project was to adopt construction management as the procurement vehicle for the construction of the Holyrood building. Construction management is one of the relatively new "fast track" methods of construction procurement, developed in the late 1980s. Under traditional contracting, design is substantially completed before the construction work is put out to tender after which a contract is agreed with a contractor to carry out that work, either directly or through sub contractors, increasingly on a fixed price basis. Under construction management design, tendering and construction overlap. The client employs a designer and, separately, a construction manager who is engaged as a fee earning consultant to programme and co-ordinate the design and construction activities. The actual construction work is divided into packages which are sequentially put out to tender and are undertaken by trade contractors who are contracted to the client. Construction management offers the advantage of speed but with the disadvantage of price uncertainty until the last package contract has been let.

Identifying a Contract Strategy

6.2   The Inquiry was assisted with an objective understanding of best practice in the selection of the appropriate procurement vehicle, and by a professional's understanding of construction management, with evidence from Mr Colin Carter of Gardiner & Theobald.[263] Gardiner & Theobald, who are one of the United Kingdom's largest providers of independent professional advice and services to the property and construction sectors, were appointed to give construction expertise to the Auditor General for Scotland and the Holyrood Inquiry in December 2003. I would want to highlight Mr Carter's extensive experience in the construction industry, including his co-authorship of the White Paper, 'Setting New Standards — a Strategy for Procurement by Government'; and his involvement in the publication 'Scrutiny of Construction Procurement by Government'.[264] Mr Carter has had no personal involvement with the Holyrood Project. Mr Carter's evidence was supplemented by slides[265] one of which is reproduced below.

6.3   In connection with the choice of strategy Mr Carter stressed the vital importance of establishing priorities and taking decisions from the start and told the Inquiry that in relation to a project such as Holyrood there were four key areas for consideration:

> **The Client Body**
> In relation to the client body it was necessary to identify its capabilities, resources, culture and profile. Issues to be addressed included its experience, its attitude towards risk, the importance to it of having a fixed price and how good it is at making decisions.
>
> **The Project Team**
> It was important to identify the capabilities and profile of the Project Team including issues such as its experience of different construction methods and the extent to which it is able to work as a collaborative and integrated team, which was considered to be of particular importance in the case of construction management.
>
> **The Objectives and Constraints**
> The constraints of time, quality and cost are traditional considerations for most projects and most clients profess that all three are equally important. It was important to identify whether one was more important than the others and to try and establish at the start what were the true aims and objectives.
>
> **Risk profile**
> A critical consideration was the client's attitude to risk and in particular whether it required a fixed cost before start-up or was content for the final cost to emerge during the course of the Project.

---

[263] Evidence of Mr Colin Carter on 12 February 2004
[264] MS/14/002 - Profile of Mr Colin Carter
[265] MS/14/001–031 - Gardiner & Theobald Presentation on Procurement and Contract Strategies

6.4 Mr Carter's evidence was that for the risk profiles of the various procurement and contract strategies which might have been used for the Holyrood Project there is a spectrum from the low risk PPP/PFI, which is essentially a service delivery, through to construction management where almost all of the risks lie with the client. It can be illustrated as follows:

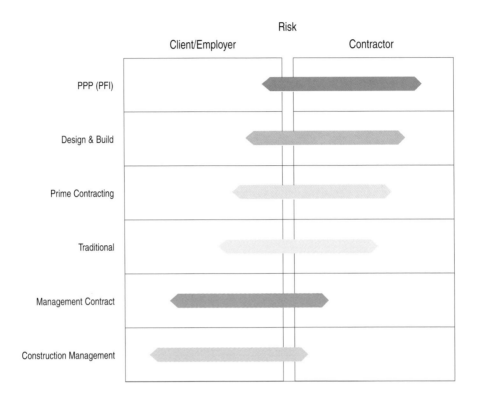

Advantages and Disadvantages of Construction Management

6.5 Focusing in on construction management Mr Carter spoke of what he saw as its key advantages and disadvantages. The former included:

- its relative speed resulting from the possibility of commencing construction before completion of design;
- the possibility of making late changes by the reorganising or redesign of later packages before they are let;
- the control of design; and
- the relative ease with which individual non-performing trade package contractors can be removed.

Crucially however he identified among its many disadvantages:

- the greater client risk;
- the complexity of administering many different trade packages (around 60 in the case of Holyrood);
- the requirement for the client to be informed and decisive;
- the need for a good team and brief;
- the relative difficulty of managing delay and disruption; and

- most important of all, the absence of any overall contractual programme or contract sum.

Perhaps most tellingly in the context of the Holyrood Project Mr Carter said:

"If you are a client who is dependent on having a fixed price before you start, you do not choose to go construction management, because it does not deliver that".[266]

6.6   From his extensive industry experience Mr Carter suggested that for construction management to work effectively it was necessary to have:

1. an experienced and informed client with an understanding of construction and construction processes;
2. an experienced and efficient team with good leadership not forced down the route of just trying to keep the Project going and managing any change;
3. well-defined roles and responsibilities from the start;
4. an architect who can envisage the whole and the detail at the same time, if retrospective change is to be avoided with resultant ripple effect on trade packages;
5. sufficient time up front in planning to foster a "no surprises" culture and to avoid crisis management;
6. a very good construction instruction, approval and change process; and
7. an effective and well-managed risk-management process.

Significantly in the context of the Holyrood Project Mr Carter was of the opinion that it does help to have co-location of the team. He emphasised the importance of getting the team working together in one place.

6.7   Mr Carter's conclusion was:

"It is not easy to use Construction Management well but it is possible if the client and Project Team remain focused on those factors which are most important to achieve success for the client."[267]

6.8   Mr Carter's analysis was a penetrating one and it verges on the embarrassing to conclude, as I do, that virtually none of the key questions were asked. Similarly none of the disadvantages of construction management appear to have been identified and evaluated. If the key questions had been asked and subjected to rigorous assessment, I cannot speculate whether the requirement for an early completion date would have been revisited, enabling a less risky procurement method to be adopted, or whether the construction management route would in fact still have been followed. It is, however, evident that the Scottish Office, while working to publicly declared fixed budgets and being highly "risk averse", was preparing to follow a procurement route for which there could be no fixed budget and a high degree of risk would rest with the client.

---

[266] Evidence of Mr Colin Carter on 12 December 2003, Para 48
[267] MS/14/001–031 - Gardiner & Theobald Presentation on Procurement and Contract Strategies

6.9   In his June 2004 report "Management of the Holyrood Building Project",[268] the Auditor General has undertaken an equally elegant analysis of the risks of construction management and also its advantages. He had covered this ground previously in his September 2000 Report but what he correctly emphasised, more recently, was that under construction management the client retains construction risk: all contracts are placed directly between the client and trade contractors; the client retains interface risk, although managed through the construction manager; and the construction manager is consultant, co-ordinator of the Design Team, manager of the trade contractors, construction adviser to the client, <u>but</u> is not the main contractor.

6.10   Although construction management was relatively new in 1997/1998, published guidance did exist on good project practice – most notably HM Treasury's Guidance Note on Contract Selection Strategy for Major Projects.[269] It listed the advantages and disadvantages very much as Mr Carter did in his evidence to the Inquiry and suggested procurement selection strategies similar to those referred to by him. Mr Wyllie[270] confirmed that Treasury Guidance was available to Government Departments across the UK, was available in his office and, in addition to himself, was probably familiar to Dr Gibbons, Mr Armstrong and Mrs Doig. He was less certain about Mr Gordon and Mr Brown's familiarity with the guidance.[271]

Selection of Construction Management

6.11   There was no detailed consideration of procurement options while the site selection question remained undecided. As discussed in paragraph 2.43 Mr Gordon put up a carefully considered minute on 6 January 1998 in which he considered procurement by the PFI/PPP route as against what he described as a 'conventional procurement' route.[272] He was more concerned to contrast PFI with conventional procurement than to analyse the so-called 'conventional' options. It must be open to question whether there was a sufficiently thorough examination of the range of contract routes available at this stage, although I appreciate that the primary focus at that time was on the selection of a site.

6.12   This, in my view, is the point when the wheels began to fall off the wagon. Ministers had decided unequivocally that for the reasons given a PFI solution should not be pursued and a 'conventional' one should. The primacy of reasoning given for rejecting PFI was that such a course might cause unacceptable delay to the completion of the Parliament building. That was a political judgment Donald Dewar and ministerial colleagues were entitled to make and they

---

[268] Auditor General for Scotland's Report of June 2004, Page 39
[269] SE/5/348–367 - HM Treasury Guidance No 36 Contract Selection for Major Projects, June 1992
[270] Evidence of Mr Alastair Wyllie on 4 November 2003 , Para 445 *et seq*
[271] *ibid*, Para 463 - 466
[272] SE/5/027-34 – Minute from Mr Robert Gordon to PS/Henry McLeish and PS/Secretary of State, 6 January 1998

did so without qualification. After the meeting on 14 January 1998 to consider Mr Gordon's minute, inexplicably Ministers were never again asked to take a decision on the procurement route with senior officials arrogating that responsibility to themselves.

6.13 On 6 January 1998 Mr Hugh Fisher, Partner of Davis, Langdon & Everest, faxed Mr Armstrong a handwritten note saying: "Attached are some notes on Construction Management – hope they are of interest!",[273] which may give an insight into the relative lack of importance placed on this topic at that time. The attachments comprised four pages from CUP Guidance Note 36: Procurement Routes and Guidance Notes on Construction Management [274] and a copy of some notes of a 1996 lecture by a Mr Brian Whitehead (provenance unknown).[275] There is no record of a mature discussion of the contents of these papers.

6.14 After the selection of the Holyrood site, Mr Armstrong minuted Mr Brown on 6 February 1998, advising that the programme largely dictated the adoption of either construction management or management contracting, as traditional contracting would extend programme completion to mid to end 2002. At that time it was envisaged that construction required to be completed by June 2001. Since, in his view, management contracting had been problematic when adopted for the procurement of the Scottish Office building at Victoria Quay, that left only construction management. In Mr Armstrong's view construction management offered some advantages, such as "the early involvement of the contractor with the design team, producing a rational approach to the management of the design information." He expressed the view that the construction management route should be adopted, listing the implications as:

     a. there would be a fee of 1.5% to 1.75% of the construction cost to pay to the Management Contractor (sic);

     b. the cost of preliminaries, site huts etc would be around 8%, which, taken with the fee, equated to the approximately 10% overhead normal in the traditional contract;

     c. although the construction management route would increase fees, it would not increase the overall budget;

     d. it would allow a wider choice of contractors; and

     e. there would be an extra Scottish Office staffing requirement. [276]

6.15 On the evidence which I have heard, while all of these implications are essentially correct, it is surprising that nowhere in this minute did Mr Armstrong address or seek to compare the respective profiles in terms of client risk of construction management and management contracting. Significantly higher risk attaches to the former. While it may have been that the programme was a given factor for Mr Armstrong, and I do not disagree with his view that it

---

[273] DL/1/029 – Faxed Note from Mr Hugh Fisher to Mr William Armstrong, 6 January 1998
[274] DL/1/030-044 - CUP Guidance Note 36 Procurement Routes and Construction Management, 6 January 1998
[275] DL/1/034–044 – Notes by Mr Brian Whitehead on Construction Management, 6 January 1998
[276] SE/5/068-069 – Minute from Mr William Armstrong to Mr Alistair Brown, 6 February 1998

dictated a "fast track" construction method, he might appropriately also have emphasised to Mr Brown, who was not a construction professional, that both construction management and management contracting necessarily entailed very significantly higher client risk than traditional procurement vehicles. Mr Armstrong's advice was poor in this respect and betrayed either a surprising oversight, or at any rate a misunderstanding on his part.

6.16   On 5 March 1998 Mr Brown minuted Mr Armstrong[277] noting that since 6 February he had on two occasions discussed the matter with Dr Gibbons, Mrs Doig and Mr Wyllie and that it had been agreed that traditional contracting was not feasible and that either construction management or management contracting would have to be adopted. It would be helpful, he said, in the three months before a decision had to be taken, to see examples to illustrate the advantages and disadvantages of both methods. He also suggested that it might be helpful to have a presentation from a construction manager on the perceived advantages of the different routes. There is no evidence that any examples were produced, or that his prudent idea of a presentation was followed up.

6.17   The Architect was appointed on 6 July 1998, the contract being silent on the method of procurement, save only that the definition of principal contractor may include "the Construction Management Contractor"(sic). The minute of the first Design Team Meeting on 21 July 1998 attended by Mrs Doig, Dr Gibbons and Mr Armstrong, records that after discussion it was agreed by all parties that "The Scottish Office should follow the construction management process".[278] This, it was said, would allow the client to remain in control of the overall Project. It is not demonstrated how this conclusion was reached, nor that it received the priority consideration it merited. In a three page minute only four lines are given to this vital subject. In evidence Mr Armstrong confirmed that he was still of the view that it was the "only decision possible at that time".[279] Mrs Doig described the choice as being by "pretty unanimous agreement".[280] No consideration appears to have been given to the involvement of Ministers in this decision or even to the possibility of informing them of it. I note that this is in the starkest of contrast to the approach adopted by Mr Gordon in relation to consideration of the possibility of PFI/PPP procurement as described in paragraphs 2.43 and 6.11 where Ministers were fully involved and informed in relation to the decision making process.

6.18   It is clear to me that the implications, particularly as regards risk, of the choice of construction management, which was promoted by Mr Armstrong, were not fully understood. The decision was arrived at principally because it was the only procurement method which could

---

[277] SE/5/071 – Minute from Mr Alistair Brown to Mr William Armstrong, 5 March 1998
[278] SE/5/072-074 - Minutes of Design Team Meeting of 21 July 1998
[279] Evidence of Mr William Armstrong on 3 December 2003, Para 252
[280] Evidence of Mrs Barbara Doig on 4 December 2003, Para 491

accommodate the programme requirements of the political leadership. It must be said, however, that no witness has put forward any suggestion that any other form of construction procurement would have better suited the situation.

6.19   I substantially agree with the thrust of the Auditor General's conclusions in his 2000 report that:

"The Scottish Office chose the construction management procurement route in July 1998 after due professional consideration, including advice from the design team. However, they did not prepare a comprehensive procurement strategy document, and the procurement strategy for the new Parliament was incomplete in that:

There should have been a reasoned analysis supporting the adoption of the construction management route represented by the appointment of Bovis as construction managers in January 1999. Such a strategic consideration of the procurement route could have been best conducted at the beginning of 1998, in conjunction with the evaluation leading to the decision to proceed with an international designer competition for the new Parliament building.

There should have been a systematic assessment of the risks implicit in the chosen procurement route (designer appointment and subsequent construction management) and how best to manage those risks."[281]

6.20   I would emphasise particularly the Auditor General's conclusion that there should have been a comprehensive procurement strategy document. Treasury Guidance[282] at the time recommended a procedure for the evaluation of contract strategies. It suggested that the Project Manager, in consultation with the Project Sponsor should, if appropriate by a numerical scoring system, decide on the relative weighting of the Project objectives such as those of cost, time and quality. It was the Project Manager's responsibility to show the Project Sponsor how different contract strategies satisfy the Project's objectives. The guidance stated:

'The inability of a particular contract strategy to satisfy an important project objective may exclude the strategy from further consideration. If, for example, price certainty is essential prior to commencing construction, management contracting and construction management strategies would be inappropriate.'[283]

---

[281] Auditor General for Scotland's Report of September 2000, Para 3.20
[282] SE/5/348-367 – HM Treasury Guidance No.36 'Contract Strategy Selection for Major Projects', June 1992, Paras 4.1 *et seq*
[283] SE/5/348-367 – HM Treasury Guidance No.36 'Contract Strategy Selection for Major Projects', June 1992, Para 4.5

It also said:

> 'There is unlikely to be a clear-cut "right" or "wrong" contract strategy. Each option will have some disadvantages or an element of risk but some will be better suited than others....'.[284]

6.21 The Guidance is not mandatory but a statement of good professional practice. It recommended that the Project Manager should present a contract strategy report to the Project Sponsor providing details of the options available, the risks associated with those options and after an evaluation of the options it should give a reasoned recommendation of a contract strategy. [285]

6.22 In this regard clear and personal responsibilities were expected from Mr Armstrong as Project Manager and from Mrs Doig as Project Sponsor. Mr Armstrong should have prepared a contact strategy report, and Mrs Doig should have insisted upon being presented with such a report, which would have formed an appropriate basis upon which to seek the views of Ministers. I am of the view that the selection of construction management was the single factor to which most of the misfortunes that have befallen the Project can be attributed. Against that background I am highly critical of the failure of Mr Armstrong and Mrs Doig to ensure that there was an appropriate evaluation of the highly risky contract strategy that was adopted, particularly in view of the choice of Architect.

6.23 In a letter to me dated 25 May 2004 Lord Elder, who had been one of Donald Dewar's Special Advisers until May 1999, and who had earlier given evidence to the Inquiry wrote:

> 'One stark message for the written record is that while there was a careful and clear process as far as site selection was concerned, there is no written record of the decision to adopt 'construction management'. If, as some would argue, this was the biggest single error, along with the decision on the fee structure, it is astonishing that the record is silent and that no Ministerial sign-off occurred.'[286]

6.24 I regard the decision to adopt construction management without advising Ministers of the attendant risks and the inflexible insistence on a rigid programme as among the most flawed decisions in the history of the Project. It beggars belief that Ministers were not asked to approve the proposal to adopt construction management. Nor did they, as Lord Elder correctly points out, have the advantage of Treasury advice.

---

[284] *ibid*, Para 4.6

[285] *ibid*, Para 4.7

[286] CB/5/1071–1074 – Letter from Lord Elder to the Holyrood Inquiry, 25 May 2004, available on the Inquiry website under supplementary information

Chapter 7

Appointment of the Construction Manager

Initial Steps

7.1 When the decision was taken on 21 July 1998 to adopt construction management as the procurement vehicle, it was also decided that the appointment of a Construction Manager would be undertaken "at the earliest opportunity".[287] The role of the Construction Manager is essentially to act as a consultant to secure and manage the services of trade or package contractors, each of whom are contracted directly to the client. The Construction Manager's role does not include the undertaking of any actual construction work on site, but rather the management of others to do that work. It is highly misleading to refer to the Construction Manager as the "builder" or the "contractor". Treasury Guidance[288] emphasised the importance of planning the selection process, and that appointment should be on the basis of value for money and not on lowest price alone.

7.2 European procurement rules applied and DLE drafted the OJEC Notice[289] which appeared in the Official Journal on 12 August 1998. It confirmed that the "restricted" procedure would apply in terms of which prospective tenderers would be subject to a selection process in advance of

---

[287] SE/5/072-074 - Minute of Design Team Meeting of 21 July 1998
[288] SE/5/421-448 - HM Treasury Guidance Note No 3: 'Appointment of Consultants and Contractors', December 1997
[289] SE/5/075-077 - OJEC Notice for Construction Management Services, 13 August 1998

tender invitation. It disclosed a construction cost budget of £50 million and award criteria, as for the Architect, seeking the "economically most advantageous tender in terms of price, quality and other criteria". It indicated a construction period lasting from 1 July 1999 to 29 June 2001, and a deadline for receipt of applications of 11 September 1998, a period of just four weeks from the first appearance of the notice. Pre–Qualification Questionnaires were sent to 29 potential applicants of which 15 were returned by the closing date.[290] A meeting of the Interview Panel was convened on 25 September 1998 to consider the PQQs, which had already been assessed, scored and ranked by Mr McAndie and Mr Jim Fairclough, Secretary to the Interview Panel. After discussion, it was agreed that six would be invited for interview. A programme was set as follows:

'6/7 October 1998	Interviews
30 October 1998	Issue invitations to tender (probably 4)
23 November 1998	Return of tenders
8 December 1998	Post tender interviews
Mid/end December 1998	Appointment made'. [291]

7.3   Prior to the interviews a comprehensive interview evaluation sheet[292] was devised by Mr Armstrong which was available to the panel. Interviews of the six candidates took place as planned on 6 and 7 October 1998 before a panel chaired by Mr Armstrong. The panel included Mr Stewart and Mr Fisher but, significantly, not Mrs Doig or Dr Gibbons. A full minute[293] was taken of that meeting which decided that four candidates including Bovis, Sir Robert McAlpine and two others should be invited to tender. The day before the interview Snr Miralles faxed Mr Armstrong saying: "I think it is important that I'm part of the final selection of 'construction manager'…" and "I know that my presence is not critical but if it is possible I'll be happy to help".[294] Mr Armstrong, in a manuscript note, requested that when arranging final interviews his team should "remember Miralles".

Evaluation of the Tenders

7.4   Invitations to tender were sent out with tenders due for return on 27 November 1998. In an email of 23 November[295] Mr Armstrong advised Mrs Doig that a tender review meeting would be held on 2 December to "decide the recommended Construction Manager", to be followed by a pre-appointment interview on 8 December 1998. Mrs Doig's immediate response by way of

---

[290] SE/5/078 – Minute from Mr Eric Kinsey to Dr John Gibbons and Mrs Barbara Doig, 15 September 1998
[291] SE/5/079-082(R) – Minutes from Mr Jim Fairclough to the Interview Panel, 25 September 1998
[292] SE/5/083–086 – Blank Interview Evaluation Sheets by Mr William Armstrong, September 1998
[293] SE/5/087-092(R) – Note of Construction Management Interviews, 6 and 7 October 1998
[294] SE/5/680-686 - Fax from Snr Enric Miralles to Mr William Armstrong, 13 October 1998
[295] SE/5/093 - Minute from Mr William Armstrong to Mrs Barbara Doig, 23 November 1998

a minute on 23 November 1998[296] was to say that it was "premature to anticipate that there will be a single recommendation" and that "it may be that 2 or 3 of the bidders are in the field and much will depend on the final interview". She said that there "may be interviews with several tenderers" and signalled her intention to be present, along with Dr Gibbons and Snr Miralles.

7.5 At this stage Mr Armstrong's views as to future procedure were beginning, as he put it, to "diverge" from those of Mrs Doig. Mr Armstrong, despite the apparent agreement that there would be a round of post tender interviews on 8 December, told the Inquiry[297] that once the panel had gone through a sifting system and an interview system which produced a number of construction managers considered to be capable of doing the job, all that remained would be to accept the lowest tender received if it was within the budget. Mrs Doig told the Inquiry[298] that at this point she "started to be a little concerned" because the procedure envisaged by Mr Armstrong was not meeting the general framework which she understood to have been set, in terms of which a senior client presence should be involved. Mrs Doig's understanding is supported by the minute of the meeting of the interview panel on 25 September[299] where it records clearly that there would be post tender interviews in which she and Dr Gibbons would be involved.

7.6 The tenders were opened in the presence of Mrs Doig, Mr Armstrong, Mr Kinsey and Mr McAndie on 27 November 1998, and disclosed a range of tenders between £2,784,307.20 and £5,609,616.[300] As well as a percentage fee, the tenders included estimated figures for staff costs and for site organisation costs, both of which fell to be reimbursed. DLE thereafter produced a report[301] which analysed the tenders. The report pointed out that in relation to staff costs Bovis and McAlpine respectively quoted increased figures of £29,000 and £38,000 if the start of work on site was to be May 1999 rather than July 1999, and that Bovis required an additional £500,000 (1% of the anticipated construction cost of £50 million) if a Parent Company Guarantee ("PCG") was to be required, the other tenderers being prepared to provide this at no extra cost. The Bovis staff costs were also to be subject to inflation, which could add £200,000 to the total. For the purposes of their report DLE aggregated all organisational costs across the board at £3 million. The DLE report produced figures which can be summarised appropriately as follows:

---

[296] SE/5/094 – Minute from Mrs Barbara Doig to Mr William Armstrong, 23 November 1998
[297] Evidence of Mr William Armstrong on 3 December 2003, Paras 712 and 713
[298] Evidence of Mrs Barbara Doig on 4 December 2003, Para 193
[299] SE/5/079–081(R) - Minutes from Mr Jim Fairclough to the Interview Panel, 25 September 1998
[300] SE/5/095(R) - Construction Management Confidential Tender Information, 27 November 1998
[301] SE/5/096-102a(R) - DLE Review of Construction Management Tenders, November 1998

Tenderer	£	
Sir Robert McAlpine	Adjusted tender value	4,846,466
Tenderer 2	Adjusted tender value	5,027,156
Tenderer 3	Adjusted tender value	6,136,756
Bovis	Adjusted tender value	5,572,162
	Add estimated inflation	200,000
	Add fee for PCG	500,000
	Total	**6,272,162**

It can be seen that, on the basis of DLE's assessment, Bovis was the highest tenderer. In her evidence Mrs Doig confirmed that there was a guideline figure of £5.5 million.[302]

7.7 A meeting to evaluate the tenders was held on 2 December 1998. The minute[303] records that Mrs Doig and Mr Armstrong attended, as did representatives of EMBT/RMJM Ltd, DLE and Ove Arup. After lengthy debate it was concluded that Tenderer 3 would be dropped on cost grounds, and that Bovis would be dropped on the basis of "cost, the concerns over the 1% charge for a Parent Company Guarantee, and the non-availability of Mr Vic Richardson (their potential Project Director) on a full time basis." Correspondingly, it was "agreed that Sir Robert McAlpine and Tenderer 2 should be interviewed again, with client representation of Dr Gibbons and Mrs Doig present, and members of the previous interview panel would indicate their preferred contractor (sic) before the interviews took place". There were some difficulties in arranging a date for the final interview but it was eventually fixed for 4 January 1999, when Snr Miralles could be present.

Candidates for Final Interview

7.8 After a surprising delay of nearly two weeks, on 15 December 1998 Mrs Doig minuted Mr Armstrong saying:

"... I have been very carefully considering whether as client representative I should accept the recommendation that 2 firms only should be interviewed at the final stage. I have consulted John Gibbons for a wider client cum construction industry perspective and also revisited Mr Fisher's and Mr Alan Tweedie's, Associate, Ove Arup & Partners[304] views (on Bovis). They have confirmed respectively that their initial rejection (of Bovis) was based on interview performance on the day rather than overall confidence in the firm's technical/professional competence and concern about the lead construction manager's availability and long-term commitment to a £50 million project (rather than £200 million).....

---

[302] WS/25/001–021 - Mrs Doig's First Witness Statement, 4 December 2003
[303] SE/5/103-104(R) - Minute of Meeting of 2 December 1998
[304] Mr Alan Tweedie, Associate, Ove Arup & Partners, South Queensferry

I have decided that Bovis should be interviewed on the grounds that the cost position does not in itself rule them out and we are now more fully appraised of their commitment to The Scottish Office as client. In particular their experience at the Museum of Scotland with a challenging design team working under great time and cost pressures has been regarded as very satisfactory".[305]

7.9 In a minute of his own of 15 December 1998 Mr Armstrong demurred, pointing out that the advice that Mrs Doig was receiving was contrary to the views arrived at during the interview and tender process, and that Bovis were £926,000 more expensive than the lowest tenderer, not counting their requirement of 1% for a PCG. [306] He described the "firm decision" made at the tender review meeting, which Mrs Doig had attended, and suggested that her desire to see them again was a waste of time and would "build up false hopes as far as Bovis is concerned".

7.10 Mrs Doig replied repeating her instruction that Bovis should be interviewed and added that she disagreed that it would be a waste of time.[307] She wished to see the successful appointment assessed against other tenderers in terms of value for money, key personnel and their way of working.

7.11 There was confusion in relation to certain aspects of the meeting on 2 December 1998. Mr Armstrong's understanding was that while the outcome of the meeting was no more than a recommendation,[308] EU procurement law and guidance on procurement required acceptance of the lowest tender and that there was no requirement for a further round of interviews. While Treasury Guidance on the appointment of consultants and contractors[309] does not specifically envisage a post tender final interview, I do not read the guidance or understand procurement law to preclude such a step in the process.

7.12 More difficult is the question as to whether the decision to hold final interviews with two tenderers only was one which Mrs Doig was entitled to reopen. Mrs Doig had been present at the meeting on 2 December 1998 but whether her role was that of an observer or a participant is less clear. She described herself as having attended the meeting as an "observer"[310] although it is noted that in the minute of the meeting her name tops the list of attendees; hardly indicative of mere observer status. The position in that respect is not recorded in the minute nor does the minute record any dissent on her part to the decision to proceed to final interviews with two tenderers only. Indeed in evidence Mrs Doig admitted that she had "missed

[305] SE/5/106 - Minute from Mrs Barbara Doig to Mr William Armstrong, 15 December 1998
[306] SE/5/107R - Minute Mr William Armstrong to Mrs Barbara Doig, 15 December 1998
[307] SE/5/108 - Minute from Mrs Barbara Doig to Mr William Armstrong, 16 December 1998
[308] Evidence of Mr William Armstrong on 3 December 2003, Para 811
[309] SE/5/421–448 – HM Treasury Procurement Guidance No.3 'Appointment of Consultants and Contractors', December 1997
[310] Evidence of Mrs Barbara Doig on 4 December 2004, Para 244

a trick" in this respect.[311]   Mr Fisher had not expected Bovis to be further involved.[312]   He remembered Bovis as having been "lacklustre" at their interview in October[313] and found it "a bit surprising"[314] that Mrs Doig had consulted with him about the possibility of reinstating them. In principle he thought that the reinstatement of a candidate at that stage was not "improper, in that the client has the prerogative to make a judgment" and even to "change his or her mind".[315]   Mr Stewart agreed with that view.[316]   In the circumstances, and while there may have been an absence of clarity in relation to the purpose of the meeting of 2 December 1998, I cannot conclude that Mrs Doig was not entitled to revisit its conclusion as to the number of tenderers to participate in the final interviews.

7.13   Where I have greater difficulty is with Mrs Doig's decision to readmit Bovis to the process without also reconsidering the position of Tenderer 3.   As set out in paragraph 7.6, DLE had reported that Bovis was the highest of the four tenderers, after appropriate adjustments to ensure that like was compared with like.   Their analysis of the figures appears to me to be correct.   At the tender review meeting on 2 December Tenderer 3 had been excluded on cost grounds.   Bovis had been excluded not only on cost grounds, including those related to the PCG, but also on account of the non-availability of Mr Richardson.   The tenders of Bovis and of Tenderer 3 both exceeded the guideline of £5.5 million.   Mrs Doig's minute of 15 December 1998 to Mr Armstrong indicated that Bovis' cost position did not in itself rule them out and that they should be probed further on the issue of the PCG and on their personnel.   Her minute did not however suggest that these initial concerns had been resolved.   Rather she chose to proceed on the basis of informal considerations.   She referred in evidence to her "own informal networks"[317] in relation to Bovis' performance on the Museum of Scotland contract.   These included having "got some information from the press"[318] and her awareness of how well Bovis had handled a great many site visits to the Museum of Scotland (designed by signature architects) in the year before its completion and the pressures of a fixed Royal opening date for that building.[319]   She was unable to provide me with any satisfactory reason for her selection of Bovis to be readmitted to the process.   It did not occur to her that there might be legal considerations.[320]   While, as I have found in the preceding paragraph, Mrs Doig was within her rights to revisit the decision of the tender review meeting and to invite a third tenderer to take

---

[311] Evidence of Mrs Barbara Doig on 17 December 2004, Para 359
[312] Evidence of Mr Hugh Fisher on 15 December 2003, Para 860
[313] *ibid*, Para 880
[314] *ibid*, Para 888
[315] Evidence of Mr Hugh Fisher on 15 December 2003, Para 888
[316] Evidence of Mr Brian Stewart on 11 March 2004 (pm), Para 28
[317] Evidence of Mrs Barbara Doig on 4 December 2003, Para 290
[318] *ibid*, Para 399
[319] WS/25/001–021 - Mrs Barbara Doig's First Witness Statement, 4 December 2003
[320] Evidence of Mrs Barbara Doig on 4 December 2003, Paras 309 and 330

part in the final round of interviews, it is my view that such a decision is one which should only have been taken on the basis of a proper evaluation of the comparative positions of both of the two excluded tenderers and on a basis which provided a clear audit trail. In these respects her decision was flawed.

7.14 I am conscious that there have been questions of propriety raised in relation to the circumstances leading to Bovis being invited to final interview. The Inquiry heard evidence from Dr Gibbons in relation to his encounter with the Managing Director of Bovis Europe at the opening of the National Museum of Scotland on 30 November 1998.[321] Dr Gibbons explained that this was a brief social encounter that took place amidst a busy gathering that included the Queen. He rejected any suggestion that this had in any way disposed him favourably towards Bovis. I have no basis on which to reject Dr Gibbons' evidence on this matter and have nothing to suggest there was anything amiss in his relationship with Bovis as a candidate for the construction management contract.

The Selection and Appointment of Bovis

7.15 The final round of interviews took place on 4 January 1999 before a panel chaired by Mr Fisher and including Snr Miralles, Dr Gibbons and Mrs Doig; Mr Armstrong having departed by this time. The proceedings were the subject of a detailed note[322] which discloses that Mr John Anderson, Managing Director of Bovis, said that his company would provide a PCG without any additional charge and it was on this basis that the contract was eventually awarded to Bovis. This had the effect of reducing the Bovis tender by £500,000, which very significantly improved its competitiveness with that of the other four tenderers. I have not been addressed on the legality of allowing such a post tender variation and I refrain from making any comment in relation to the legal implications of the position. It does however appear to me, on elementary considerations of fairness as between competing tenderers, that if one tenderer was effectively permitted to change a very material aspect of the financial basis upon which its tender was submitted that is an opportunity which should have been afforded to the others.

7.16 In all other respects the final interviews on 4 January 1999 appear to me to have been conducted in a way which was thorough, fair, and well documented. In this respect it can be contrasted favourably with the proceedings in the final rounds of the designer selection competition. A comprehensive and transparent evaluation system was adopted from which the completed evaluation forms have been produced to the Inquiry.[323] Of the eleven members of the interview panel, ten completed the evaluation forms, in each case ranking Bovis

---

[321] Evidence of Dr John Gibbons on 3 February 2004, Paras 334 to 351

[322] SE/5/120-125(R) – Note of Construction Management Final Interviews, 4 January 1999

[323] SE/5/083–086 - Evaluation Sheets: Construction Management Appointment, September 1998

significantly ahead of the other two candidates. Out of a maximum of 100, Bovis' average score was 82 whereas that of the next highest was only 65. The note recorded the panel's unanimous view that Bovis had performed by far the best of the final three candidates at interview stage and "although their tender bid was not the lowest one it was crucial that a company that the client and Design team felt comfortable with was selected for this most crucial of roles in the Project."[324]

7.17 It was agreed that, subject to a few financial clarifications to be resolved at a further meeting with DLE, Bovis should be appointed as soon as possible. Following the interviews DLE issued a final tender report[325] which confirmed that the Bovis' PCG was to be provided at no extra cost and that the revised Bovis bid was £5,371,919. On 6 January 1999, following the discussions with DLE, Bovis wrote to Mr McAndie confirming certain points arising from the tender and saying:

> "Our Construction Management Fee is 1.25% to be converted to a lump sum on agreement of the Project Cost Plan." [326]

The copy of that letter produced to the Inquiry bears Mrs Doig's initials confirming that it was received by the Project Team.

7.18 On 7 January 1999 Bovis was informed[327] of the intention of the Scottish Office to enter into a contract and a formal letter of intent was issued on 19 January.[328] The formal legal Memorandum of Agreement subsequently entered into between Bovis and the Scottish Office was, for some reason which was not clarified in evidence, not actually signed until 22 and 25 October 1999. Schedule 1(J) confirmed the fee of 1.25% but failed to make any provision for conversion of that fee to a lump sum on agreement of the Cost Plan. Had the contract reflected the evident willingness of Bovis to convert their fee to a lump sum, the issue of fee capping which arose in 2003 would not have been a problem in relation to Bovis. Further, the conversion of their fee to a lump sum would have served as a powerful incentive to Bovis to apply maximum rigour in relation to cost control. I am aware that in his 2000 Report the Auditor General[329] made the very valid point that it might have been appropriate for the fees of the consultants, including Bovis, to have been tapered so that the percentage fee would reduce as a proportion of construction cost as that cost increases. I agree with that observation although, in the context of Bovis' appointment, it is not as significant as the

---

[324] SE/5/120-125(R) – Note of Construction Management Final Interviews, 4 January 1999
[325] SE/5/109-119 - Report from Mr Hugh Fisher to Mrs Barbara Doig, 7 January 1999
[326] SE/5/273-275 – Letter from Mr Harry Thorburn to Mr Ian McAndie, 6 January 1999
[327] SE/5/126 - Letter from Mr Jim Fairclough to Mr Gordon Ash, 7 January 1999
[328] SE/5/135-136 – Letter from Mrs Barbara Doig to Mr Gordon Ash, 19 January 1999
[329] Auditor General for Scotland's Report of September 2000, Para 3.35

possible conversion to a lump sum upon agreement of the Cost Plan. I did not hear evidence on these points and accordingly I am not in a position to criticise any individual in respect of them. I do however regard this as a significant deficiency in the Bovis contract documentation.

7.19 Both in terms of EU procurement law and in terms of guidance,[330] unsuccessful tenderers should be afforded the opportunity of a debriefing. I heard evidence from Mr David Boyle, Director of Sir Robert McAlpine that his company requested a debrief after the selection process but that no satisfactory response was received to three letters from him dated 7 January 1999,[331] 22 February 1999[332] and 16 April 1999.[333] In her closing submission to me Ms Laura Dunlop QC, appearing for the Scottish Executive, frankly acknowledged that there had been a failure in this respect for which she expressed her regret. I have been informed as to the specific circumstances that led to this administrative oversight and it is very understandable why one individual was not available to conduct a debrief. The system should have allowed for someone else to have taken on the task. It did not and a legal requirement was neglected.

7.20 It is my understanding that, despite the eventual offer of a PCG by Bovis at no additional cost, in the event that offer was not taken up and had still not been taken up as recently as February 2004 when the point was raised in the Finance Committee of the Parliament and when the SPCB recommended that such a PCG should be obtained from Bovis. I understand that this may now have been done. While I recognise that Bovis is a major and reputable company, this is something that should have been done at a much earlier stage.

---

[330] SE/5/421–448 - HM Treasury Guidance No 3: 'Appointment of Consultants and Contractors'
[331] MS/8/003 - Letter from Mr David Boyle to Mr Jim Fairclough, 7 January 1999
[332] MS/8/004 - Letter from Mr David Boyle to Mr Jim Fairclough, 22 February 1999
[333] MS/8/006 - Letter from Mr David Boyle to Mr Jim Fairclough, 16 April 1999

Chapter 8

Project Management - 1998 to 1 June 1999

The Project Management Structure

8.1 After the 9 January 1998 announcement that Holyrood was the preferred site, the second reading of the Scotland Bill became the focus of attention. Securing its passage and preparing the subordinate orders required to bring the new devolution settlement into effect in the spring of 1999 was a major and highly pressured task for Ministers and officials throughout 1998. In parallel a substantial exercise to develop the Parliament's procedures, and ultimately offer it draft standing orders, was established under a Consultative Steering Group chaired by Henry McLeish. In addition the Inquiry learned of the strong Ministerial will and operational need to keep up momentum on the physical preparations for the Parliament including temporary accommodation, services and staffing.

8.2 At the same time as the running of the competition to appoint a designer, the project management arrangements were formalised in early 1998. Mr Armstrong continued as Project Manager and, following a promotion board chaired by Mr Russell, Mrs Doig was appointed Parliament Buildings Project Sponsor in March 1998. Reporting to Mr Gordon, Head of Constitution Group, Mrs Doig did not however assume active Project Sponsor responsibilities for Holyrood until the time of the announcement of the successful Design Team on 6 July 1998.

8.3 Procurement guidance produced by HM Treasury[334] and in force at that time set out a model of good project team organisation and the necessary management and technical abilities of those with responsibility for leading and managing large public sector construction projects.

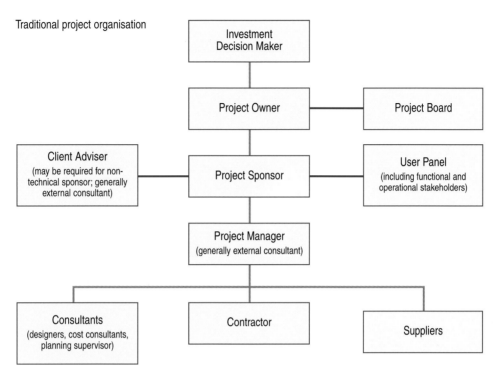

Traditional project organisation

Source: *Essential Requirements for Construction Procurement*, HM Treasury, 1997

8.4 Central figures within this structure are the Project Owner, the Project Manager and the Project Sponsor. The Project Owner for the Holyrood Project effectively sat within a Steering Group of senior civil servants who took strategic decisions on behalf of the client. Mr Brown was the named individual filling the role of Project Owner until December 1998 after which it became Mr Gordon until handover to the SPCB on 1 June 1999. Mr Armstrong was the professional Project Manager responsible for the day to day management of the Project and reported directly to the Project Sponsor. His role was to act as the interface between the Project Sponsor on the 'client' side and the consultants on the 'supply' side. The Project Sponsor was responsible to the Project Owner for the client's interest in the Project. In evidence Mrs Doig described the role rather well:

> "The role of the project sponsor was to act as the client's representative to deliver the Holyrood Building to agreed time, budget and quality."

> "Much of the job involved contractual and reporting relationship management and one analogy is to describe the relationship network as being like a bow-tie with the project sponsor and project manager at the centre, each with their own large networks

---

[334] SE/5/368–398 - HM Treasury Guidance No.1: 'Essential Requirements for Construction Procurement', 1997

respectively of, on the one side clients, and on the other professional appointments and contractors."[335]

8.5 The Project Management structure established by the Scottish Office complied with the Treasury model and, in evidence, the management and technical abilities of the key postholders was explored. In particular, Mrs Doig was questioned in some detail about her career experience and her personal competencies. She accepted that she was not an expert in any of the building or design disciplines but explained that this was not a requirement for a project sponsor. As she saw it:

> "The main role is to understand the client's requirements and to be able to understand sufficient of the technical aspects and all the other external pressures which impact on getting any building through to completion."[336]

8.6 Mrs Doig put great store on the access she had to the technical advice of Dr Gibbons and Mr Wyllie as well as to the experience of her Project Manager, Mr Armstrong. Although Mrs Doig's previous responsibilities in relation to the procurement of Victoria Quay and the refurbishment of St Andrew's House were of a very different nature and complexity to the Holyrood Project, her appointment to the post of Project Sponsor might be justified on the basis of her managerial experience and the technical support her colleagues would be able to offer her. The complexities of this particular project, however, were such that even without the benefit of hindsight it should have been seen that any sponsor appointed should have had greater familiarity with either construction or the sponsorship of major construction projects. I do not underestimate the advantage of having someone who could work within an intricate political environment. Whether an individual with such a full range of skills existed within the Scottish Office at that time I cannot say. However, as Ministers were showing themselves more than willing to become involved, having the pragmatic advice of someone with construction experience to draw upon was more valuable than that of someone with political acumen.

The £50 million Budget – Early Days

8.7 The press release announcing the selection of Holyrood[337] noted that the final costs would depend on the design, the fees negotiated with the successful architect following a competition and the outcome of a competition to select a 'developer'. Parliamentary questions were answered reflecting an estimated construction cost of around £50 million.[338] It is notable that, throughout this period, public announcements invariably focused only on the estimated cost of construction at March 1998 prices without any consistent attempt to quantify the other

---

[335] WS/25/001–021 – Mrs Barbara Doig's First Witness Statement, 4 December 2003
[336] Evidence of Mrs Barbara Doig on 4 December 2003, Para 59
[337] SE/3/011–012 – 'Dewar Opts for New Building in Historic Heart of Edinburgh', 9 January 1998
[338] SE/4/010 - House of Lords Hansard, 4 February 1998

elements of the total cost to the public purse. At that stage no contracts had been entered into with any of the private sector consultants and it would have been inappropriate to disclose publicly an estimate for these costs. Nevertheless, to my mind this early presentational practice had a significant impact subsequently upon the public perception of the escalating cost of the Project.

8.8 The Inquiry heard conflicting evidence as to whether the successful Design Team gave a commitment during their interview that the design concept they were presenting could be constructed within a £50 million budget.[339] The official note of the first meeting of the Design Team on 21 July 1998 suggests that such a commitment was indeed offered (as one would expect during a competitive interview), but of more significance is the fact that the £50 million figure was incorporated into the contract between the Secretary of State and EMBT/RMJM Ltd.[340] The figure was also included in the contracts with RMJM (Scotland) Ltd and Ove Arup.

8.9 Mr Gordon's evidence identified the challenge that working to this budget would pose on both the Design Team and the Project Team:

> "DLE's costings of the indicative offerings of the shortlisted designers suggested that all (or most) would imply buildings that would exceed the budget figure. This was not a major stumbling block at the point of selection since the process was to choose the design team (not the specific design) who would work with the project team, cost consultants (and later the construction managers) to come up with a design which would meet the brief within the budget. It did, however, demonstrate that an early task for the Project Team would be to reinforce to the Design Team the need to stay within budget."[341]

8.10 The note of the first meeting of the Design and Project Teams on 21 July 1998 records that Donald Dewar was aware that the indicative proposals put forward by EMBT/RMJM to the selection panel had been estimated by the cost consultants to be likely to exceed the £50 million construction budget but, at interview, EMBT/RMJM had confirmed that the Project could be delivered within the £50 million budget. The note records that it was clear that the client would not alter the budget and that the scheme must therefore be adapted to the budget.[342]

8.11 Some effort does appear to have been invested by the Project Team in working to bring the early conceptual designs back within budget and, in a letter of 1 September 1998 to Mr

---

[339] Evidence of Sra Benedetta Tagliabue on 29 March 2004, Para 289, Miss Joan O'Connor on 25 November 2003, Para 1002 and Mr Robert Gordon on 16 December, Paras 65-67

[340] RM/1/054-076 – Memorandum of Agreement between the Secretary of State and EMBT/RMJM Ltd, Clause 2.12, 4 November 1998

[341] WS/27/001–008 – Mr Robert Gordon's Second Witness Statement

[342] SE/4/237-239 - Minutes of Design Team Meeting of 21 July 1998

Armstrong, Mr Stewart gave the assurance that 'meeting the budget is at the front of our minds and is a matter that will be addressed as we progress'.[343]

8.12 In his written evidence to the Inquiry Mr Gordon stated:

"I thought at the time that if it eventually became genuinely impossible to meet the Parliament's space requirements with the budget available, it might be necessary to either revisit the budget or the brief but it was not in my view prudent to concede the possibility of increasing the budget well before developed design proposals were available. This would have removed a key control over the cost of the project that the Scottish Office had at the time. I also understood that different approaches to meeting the brief were being produced yielding different cost outcomes in an iterative process involving EMBT and RMJM, DLE and the project team."[344]

8.13 The evidence suggests that at no time before handover did the Project Team succeed in securing a design from the Design Team that could be delivered within budget.[345] The client's increased requirements for space were a significant factor in this situation but I have to question whether £50 million was ever a realistic budget figure and how effective the Project Team were in operating a genuine cost control process.

8.14 In his October report to Mrs Doig, Mr Armstrong stated:

'The Quantity Surveyor has produced a first cost estimate based on draft Stage C… Although the information is inadequate to produce a valid cost plan, all the indications are that the budget of £50m will be exceeded by a significant amount.'[346]

8.15 Although publicly the reported budget remained unchanged, there appeared to be a growing recognition within the Project Team that it was unsustainable. As the design developed over this period DLE reported to Project Management its estimates of construction costs prices as follows:[347]

---

[343] MS/6/009 - Letter from Mr Brian Stewart to Mr William Armstrong, 1 September 1998
[344] WS/27/001–008 – Mr Robert Gordon's Second Witness Statement
[345] DL/1/008-012 - DLE Time Line: Development of Costs, October 1998 to August 2000
[346] SE/4/201–209 – October 1998 Report from Mr William Armstrong to Mrs Barbara Doig
[347] DL/1/008-012 – DLE Time Line: Development of Costs, October 1998 to August 2000

Date	Total (£)	Gross internal area	Comment
23/10/98	58,918,300	21,299m²	At August 1998 prices. All others at March 1998 prices.
02/11/98	74,281,008	22,476m²	Based on EMBT/RMJM Stage C drawings.
16/11/98	68,944,487	21,397m²	This and previous reports include Construction Manager's fees and charges of £5.5 million.
11/02/99	63,397,605	22,905m²	Working document only. This and subsequent reports exclude the Construction Manager's fees and charges.
02/03/99	87,158,356	22,905m²	
12/03/99	88,350,019	23,098m²	Based on EMBT/RMJM Stage C drawings.
26/03/99	88,350,019	23,214m²	
25/05/99	89,200,019	23,214m²	

In his November report to Mrs Doig, Mr Armstrong noted that DLE's estimates were significantly above the official (public) budget figure of £50 million.[348] Asked in evidence whether Snr Miralles had "an awareness of the need to contain his designs within the costs indicated by the client", Mr Fisher replied with his view that "he was less troubled by cost than would have been the case had RMJM been acting in isolation".[349] Pressed as to whether Snr Miralles paid any attention to cost at all, Mr Fisher's succinct response was: "scant".[350]

8.16 There seems to have been growing unease about the direction in which the costings of the indicative design proposals were heading. There does, however, appear to me to have been a reluctance to accept that costs could not be contained by 'cost reducing measures' or to report the deteriorating forecasts to Ministers. In a minute to Mrs Doig, Mr Brown explained the thinking at that time:

> "We could not allow a situation to develop where estimated construction costs ran ahead of budget without our having looked carefully at options for cost reducing measures and discussing these with Finance Group colleagues and with Ministers. In particular, we will have to ensure that there is sufficient time allowed in the programme for accurate cost estimates to be developed and considered fully before we are required to sign up to detailed designs. If necessary, the project timetable will have to slip to make way for this. The Project will build up considerable momentum of its own but we must avoid giving approvals without fully understanding the financial consequences, especially when these are likely to be unpalatable."[351]

---

[348] SE/4/213-221 – November 1998 Report from Mr William Armstrong to Mrs Barbara Doig
[349] Evidence of Mr Hugh Fisher on 15 December, Paras 557 and 558
[350] ibid, Paras 559 and 560
[351] SE/4/212 - Letter from Mr Alistair Brown to Mrs Barbara Doig, 19 November 1998

8.17 Mr Brown's minute was written in response to an indication from Mrs Doig that the construction cost budget would be exceeded by a 'significant amount' and it is evident that Mr Brown anticipated discussions over this with Ministers. Less than a week later Mr Armstrong, reflecting on the Architect's proposed changes, brings out a budget estimate between £69 million and £74 million.[352] In other words, although grave reservations over the budget were being expressed within the Scottish Office as early as November 1998, neither Donald Dewar nor any of his Ministers were being given any warning of impending major cost rises. This makes it all the more surprising that in March 1999 when he was eventually first asked to approve a budget increase he was told it would be "prudent"[353] to lift it from £50 million to £60 million!

8.18 In her evidence to the Inquiry, Mrs Doig felt that it would have been inappropriate to seek a budget increase from Ministers until such time as the design had crystallised and there was greater certainty in the associated cost estimates. As she put it:

> "I certainly would not have felt comfortable going to Ministers one day and saying, "Well, I think I need an extra budget of such-and-such", and then going back the next day and saying, "Oh, no, the design's changed a bit; it's down again, it's up again." That would not be a good use of Ministers' time, and we had to wait and see."[354]

8.19 Mr Thomson spoke in his evidence of the approach generally taken by civil servants in their dealings with Ministers over issues of this kind:

> "If all you can do by going to Ministers is to share your anxiety with them, there is not much point in going to Ministers. You just need to get on with it. When there is a decision point, that is when you go to Ministers."[355]

8.20 Nevertheless, it seems extraordinary that Ministers do not appear to have had any formal indication of the apparent threat to the agreed budget of £50 million during those months of 1998 and early 1999 when officials were evidently well aware of the evolving situation, although Donald Dewar appeared to appreciate that £50 million would only secure Sam Galbraith's 'bog standard building' on a greenfield site. I assume that there were informal contacts with senior officials such as Mr Gordon during which progress with the Project would have been discussed. Mr Thomson suggested that when an approach for an addition to the budget did eventually come forward, Donald Dewar would not have been taken completely by surprise as he would have understood the general direction of the Project from his informal exchanges. Pointedly, however, he also observed that 'like most Ministers on most subjects, he would not have regarded any cost increases as being good news'. However there was no

---

[352] SE/7/578 - Minute from Mr William Armstrong to Mrs Barbara Doig, 25 November 1998
[353] SE/4/057-067 – Paper from Mrs Barbara Doig to PS/Secretary of State, 25 November 1998
[354] Evidence of Mrs Barbara Doig on 4 December 2003, Para 276
[355] Evidence of Mr Kenneth Thomson on 3 February 2004, Para 323

direct evidence of such knowledge. Ministers were briefed in January 1999 that the budget remained at £50 million but, as Lord Elder pointed out in evidence, he was surprised by the extent to which the Project Manager had taken a pretty adverse view as to what was going on in terms of delays and problems with costs but Ministers and special advisers had been unaware of this.[356]

Delivery of Design Information

8.21   A timeline for the Project prepared in March 1998 by Mr Armstrong illustrated that the target for completion of the Holyrood building remained autumn 2001 with a date for the start of construction on site in July 1999. To meet this overall timetable, the programme required the Design Team to deliver outline proposals by September 1998 and the scheme design for approval by March 1999. Although this timetable was developed by Mr Armstrong using his considerable experience of project management, it undoubtedly was driven by the political objective of early completion and occupancy of the Parliament building. It is ironic that throughout his involvement with the Project, Mr Armstrong drove forward a programme that he had devised but which he felt did not incorporate sufficient time for the planning and design phases of the Project.[357]

8.22   The Project Manager made monthly reports to the Project Sponsor during the latter half of 1998 and the Inquiry found this a valuable record both of the events at this time and of the Project Manager's view of the health of the Project. In his August 1998 report, Mr Armstrong notes that the Architect appeared to have made little progress in the time since their appointment in early July and that the Project was currently four weeks behind the programme that he had developed.[358] It was felt that this slippage needed to be recovered if there was not to be disruption to the work of other consultants. This was to be a recurrent theme in his subsequent reports.

8.23   The level of concern even at that early stage was such that Mr Stewart was called to a meeting with Dr Gibbons on 28 August 1998 to agree a 'recovery strategy'.[359] At that meeting RMJM explained the difficulties they had been having communicating with the Barcelona office during the holiday period, the different 'operational characteristics' of the Barcelona and Edinburgh offices and the amount of abortive work that RMJM had undertaken. This does not sound like a joint venture company that had gelled particularly well at that point. Although Mr Michael (Mick) Duncan, Director, EMBT/RMJM Ltd spent some time in Barcelona in an effort to improve communications and the difficulties surrounding a key presentation to Donald Dewar

---

[356] Evidence of Lord Elder on 29 October 2003, Para 132 *et seq*
[357] Evidence of Mr William Armstrong on 2 December 2003, Para 142 *et seq*
[358] SE/4/012–021 - August 1998 Report from Mr William Armstrong to Mrs Barbara Doig
[359] SE/4/195-197 - Letter from Mrs Barbara Doig to Mr Alistair Brown, 15 September 1998

on 16 September 1998 were ironed out, the underlying questions over the ability of the Architect to deliver remained.

8.24 In his October 1998 report,[360] Mr Armstrong recorded that the Architect had presented RIBA Stage C proposals which were overdue, exceeded the briefed area by 3,500m² and did not conform to the Brief in other respects. He also reported that the work of other consultants was being delayed by the Architect's 'lack of progress'. In this apparent fixation with programme, Mr Armstrong appears to be reflecting the clearly-expressed view that the timetable for the Project was tight from the outset and any delay would therefore jeopardise the ability to meet the wishes of Ministers to deliver the Project as early as possible. This urgency does not seem to me to have been echoed by the Project Sponsor who recognised that Snr Miralles "did not work in straight lines" but, instead, would have surges of creative input. She also spoke of the many other ways in which the lead architect was helping the client. I am unconvinced that the value of Snr Miralles' contribution to Edinburgh Festival events and public presentations was as critical as his personal input to the key design work at this crucial stage in the Project.

8.25 Mr Fisher offered a view on the cultural difficulties posed by working with Snr Miralles:

> "It is hard to quantify; a fair degree of irritation and frustration at what one could, at best, describe as Barcelona's lack of understanding as to the importance of time and cost in the UK construction industry."

> "It is merely that there is an entirely different cultural approach to the delivery of buildings between Spain and the United Kingdom. Enric himself had a particular way of designing that was less structured than one might find in a major practice in the United Kingdom, and those cultural differences create operational tensions."[361]

Enric Miralles' Presence in Edinburgh

8.26 At his first interview with the designer selection panel, Enric Miralles proposed to bring a team of architects to Edinburgh and work in Edinburgh himself. However, Dr Gibbons recollected that this commitment had been adjusted at the time of the second interview:

> "At the second interview he qualified that by putting forward the joint venture with an Edinburgh-based firm as an alternative."[362]

8.27 Miss O'Connor's recollection was different:

> "Enric Miralles and Benedetta Tagliabue, either or both committed to being in Edinburgh for the duration of the design phase."[363]

---

[360] SE/4/201–209 – October 1998 Report from Mr William Armstrong to Mrs Barbara Doig
[361] Evidence of Mr Hugh Fisher on 15 December 2003, Paras 207 and 211
[362] Evidence of Dr John Gibbons on 3 February 2003, Paras 130 and 132
[363] Evidence of Miss Joan O'Connor on 29 November 2003, Para 927 and JO/1/099 - Note of Meeting of 6 May 1998

It looks almost certain that such an undertaking was given as it appeared in the Scottish Office news release announcing the result of the competition.[364]

8.28 In evidence we learned that Snr Miralles and Sra Tagliabue visited Edinburgh during August 1998 with their family to gauge how practicable they would find working in the RMJM Edinburgh office. They concluded that they could work more effectively from their own studio in Barcelona:

> "We stayed 12 days that August in Edinburgh … we realised that it was absolutely impossible because we did not have our office with model atelier, with our people."[365]

Snr Joan Callis, Director for the Scottish Parliament Project within EMBT, worked in both the Barcelona and Edinburgh offices throughout the Project and Mr Karl Unglaub moved to the Edinburgh office full-time after Snr Miralles' death in July 2000.

8.29 Mr Armstrong minuted Mrs Doig on 4 December 1998 voicing his concern that the lead architect continued to be based in Barcelona.[366] He warned that the consultants would find it logistically difficult to have two separate bases, that the construction management contract had been tendered on the basis of EMBT/RMJM Ltd working in Edinburgh and that difficulty had already been experienced in getting Enric Miralles to attend meetings in Edinburgh. This final point is borne out in the Auditor General's Report of September 2000:

> 'Between July 1998 and November 1999 the lead architect attended only six of the fifteen meetings (between project management and the Design Team).'[367]

8.30 The two practices had very different cultures and ways of working and found it difficult to adopt a cohesive approach to design issues or resolving problems whilst working in separate locations and communicating mainly via fax. With Enric Miralles insisting on being personally involved in all design issues during these formative stages, there was inevitable delay and disruption caused by his geographical detachment. Although RMJM took steps to better integrate the practices, this was only partially successful. Communication issues have been evident throughout the life of the joint venture company.

Growing Tensions

8.31 The relationship between the Project Manager and the Architect is central to an understanding of this period. Of equal importance is the Project Manager's relationship with his employer. Mr Armstrong was an experienced professional project manager who understood better than

---

[364] SE/3/141-142 - News Release: 'Architect Chosen to Design Scottish Parliament', 6 July 1998
[365] Evidence of Sra Benedetta Tagliabue on 29 March 2004, Para 221
[366] MS/6/041–042 - Minute from Mr William Armstrong to Mrs Barbara Doig, 4 December 1998
[367] Auditor General for Scotland's Report of September 2000, Para 2.28

almost everyone around him how to bring a complex construction project to fruition. He had a structured approach to his work and sought to impose that discipline on the consultants with whom he worked. It is clear from Mr Armstrong's reports that from the outset he was not succeeding in developing a constructive dialogue with (both arms) of the Architect. An exchange under questioning exemplified the communication problem that clearly existed:

> **Mr Campbell QC:** I am trying to find out, Mr Armstrong, how much dialogue there was between the appointed designer, who succeeded in a competition in July 1998, and you, the Project Manager, charged with evolving the brief for the building, which that designer was going to design.
>
> **Mr Armstrong:** Very little.
>
> **Mr Campbell QC:** Looking back on it, do you think that was the right way to go about it?
>
> **Mr Armstrong:** It was not my choice.
>
> **Mr Campbell QC:** That was not what I asked you.
>
> **Mr Armstrong:** I think that is my answer.

8.32 Within the Scottish Office, Mr Armstrong spoke of being "bypassed" and cited an occasion at which he was not present when Snr Miralles met Donald Dewar, Dr Gibbons and others and presented proposals which had not been subjected to technical scrutiny, did not meet the Brief, and extended outwith the site. Mr Armstrong felt that by enabling Snr Miralles to have direct access to Donald Dewar and obtaining agreement at the highest level to proposals not approved by him, he was left having to pick up the pieces.[368] The Inquiry did, however, establish that Mr Armstrong had not been excluded but had been on leave at the time of the presentation.

8.33 Mr Gordon spoke of some concerns he held over Mr Armstrong's approach to resolving his difficulties with the Architect:

> "He was taking a pretty firm line with EMBT/RMJM and was sending them increasingly strong letters. Now I think that has a significant part to play in robust project management, but I was a bit concerned that he did not seem to have a back-up strategy and that the proposition he was making was that we would have to go for the nuclear option of sacking the Design Team, or at least sacking the EMBT part of it if we did not get responses."[369]

8.34 Mr Armstrong's discomfort with the progress being made by the Architect continued into November. The Design Team submitted formally their RIBA Stage C proposal on 2 November 1998 but it was clear that this submission exceed the area in the Brief while omitting some of the requirements of that Brief. The poor level of communication at this time is exemplified by

---

[368] Evidence of Mr William Armstrong on 2 December 2003, Para 181
[369] Evidence of Mr Robert Gordon on 16 December 2003, Para 262

the fact that RMJM and EMBT both submitted separate solutions to the Stage C difficulties to the Project Team; a course of events that exposed tensions between the two arms of the joint venture company. The Inquiry heard how Mr Stewart tried to defuse those tensions through correspondence with Snr Miralles. He explained the rationale of his approach:

> "All that I am trying to say here is …. "Please can you understand that there are enormous pressures on this Project in terms of delivery of design, development of design, and we have acknowledged the programme and we need to try and work to that programme." I think I told him that there are other members of this team — there will be a Construction Manager coming along who will have a contract to deliver certain things and he will. We cannot ignore all of these things. All of these other people have to be considered in the process."[370]

8.35 Whether Snr Miralles fully understood at this time the political environment in which he was expected to work is questionable. He was clearly coming under pressure from the Project Manager and from his business partners in RMJM to work to a schedule in a way that he was unaccustomed to doing. It seems however that he felt strongly that the "gestation" of a project of this type needed time.[371]

8.36 On 6 October 1998, EMBT/RMJM Ltd submitted a claim for payment of a 10% proportion of its total fee which was contractually payable upon completion of RIBA Stage C. The full claim was rejected by Mr Armstrong who authorised only a partial payment in recognition of the work undertaken to that point even though Stage C had not been completed. The payment of fees in instalments was provided for in the contract with the Architect.[372] The full amount was paid on 27 November. Fees were used in this instance by the client as a lever to encourage delivery by the architectural consultants. However, the way in which the issue was handled seems to illustrate the growing tensions in the relationship between Mr Armstrong and the Architect.

8.37 In early December 1998, despite having received further drawings from the architect in response to comments on their RIBA Stage C proposal, Mr Armstrong remained of the view that Stage C had not been achieved. In a damning minute written on 7 December 1998 after he had tendered his resignation he notes that the programme had been delayed by 8 weeks in the 22 weeks since the appointment of the Architect. He saw this as 'quite an accomplishment'. He also noted that 'as long as Miralles insists on making every decision on the design of the building, the joint venture problems will not be resolved and the Project will fall further behind programme'. Finally he commented:

---

[370] Evidence of Mr Brian Stewart on 11 March 2004 (am), Para 298
[371] *ibid*, Para 321
[372] RM/1/076 - Memorandum of Agreement between the Secretary of State and EMBT/RMJM Ltd, Schedule C, Part 5,

107

'There is no indication that Miralles, with a workload of which Holyrood is only a part, can with his limited resources in Barcelona and his desire to take all design decisions, remedy the deficiencies in time, cost and design to meet the programme.'[373]

Resignation of Mr Armstrong

8.38 Mr Armstrong resigned from his position as Project Manager in terms of a letter to Dr Gibbons of 1 December 1998.[374] He had indicated at the time of the appointment of the Architect in July 1998 that, although he had serious misgivings about the appointment, he was prepared to try to make it work. The expectation had been that he would continue until autumn 1999 but Mr Armstrong's experience in those first six months persuaded him that he was not receiving the support necessary to enable him to carry out the job of Project Manager and that his advice was not being listened to.[375]

8.39 In evidence it was heard that Mr Armstrong's resignation was not entirely unexpected and some thought had apparently been given to his effectiveness towards the end of November. Mr Gordon commented on Mr Armstrong's departure in his written evidence:

'I was disappointed, but not surprised, when Bill Armstrong resigned in December 1998. Disappointed because I had worked successfully with Bill previously on Victoria Quay and had greatly admired his commitment, organisation, single mindedness and attention to systems and detail which had served us well in that project; not surprised because as the Holyrood Project developed it became clear that those qualities which carried with them a certain rigidity and inflexibility would not in themselves be enough to develop and sustain a productive relationship with the EMBT/RMJM design team.'[376]

8.40 When asked about the apparent clash of styles, Mrs Doig put things more bluntly:

Mrs Doig: Well, project managers are replaceable.

Mr Campbell QC: But architects are not?

Mrs Doig: The architect in this case was not."[377]

8.41 In a parting salvo to Mrs Doig, Mr Armstrong offered this cautionary advice:

'I have bowed out of the Project Manager's job and shouldn't be offering comment or criticism but, for your own sake and the others involved, a stand must be taken to either bring Miralles to heel, or to accept his inadequacies. He does not believe he

[373] SE/4/044 - Minute from Mr William Armstrong to Mrs Barbara Doig, 7 December 1998
[374] MS/6/043 - Letter from Mr William Armstrong to Dr John Gibbons, 1 December 1998
[375] MS/6/046-071 – Mr William Armstrong's Witness Statement, December 2003
[376] WS/27/001–008 – Mr Robert Gordon's Second Witness Statement
[377] Evidence of Mrs Barbara Doig on 4 December 2003, Paras 311 to 313

has any. The programme will drift, the cost will increase, the design team will make claims, the contractors will make claims, and the project will become a disaster.'[378]

8.42 Surprisingly, Ministers were not informed of the resignation of the Project Manager until his departure was picked up by the media in January 1999. Given Donald Dewar's evident interest in all aspects of the Project, this seems inexplicable.

Budget Increase – Spring 1999

8.43 In January 1999 Mr Martin Mustard, who had been working as a member of the Project Team, was appointed to replace Mr Armstrong as Project Manager; a role which would change substantially with the appointment of a construction manager in that month and with the impending handover to the SPCB.

8.44 In response to an article in the *Architects Journal* about the departure of Mr Armstrong, officials advised Ministers that the Project remained on course for completion in autumn 2001 and that the budget remained at £50 million excluding VAT and fees. This advice was reflected in subsequent answers to Parliamentary Questions. However, with the design continuing to evolve during this period, there was recognition that a detailed cost estimate was required to give the Project Team the tools to impose discipline on costs and programme. DLE submitted their cost estimate on 2 March 1999 and proposed a basic construction cost of £63.4 million, a 10% allowance for contingencies and a further £17 million for risk allowances.[379] This was the first formal DLE cost estimate for nearly 4 months and clearly caused some alarm within the Scottish Office. The absence of estimates seems to illustrate the dearth of design information coming forward over this period and also the lack of adequate joint working between the Architect and the cost consultants. Whether this made any difference to the client is another question. When DLE did submit estimates they were either withheld from Ministers or altered.

8.45 Following a meeting of officials to draw together information on costs, a submission was pulled together and put forward to Ministers by Mrs Doig on 23 March 1999.[380] This set out progress on the Project and informed Ministers of 'the latest cost estimates from our independent cost consultants'. It recommended that it would be 'prudent' to increase the budget from £50 million to £60 million excluding site acquisition, archaeology, demolition, fit-out, VAT, fees and contingency. A figure of £107 million was identified as the total financial provision required (although this figure excluded certain landscaping and road works which would come from other budgets).

---

[378] SE/4/045 – Letter from Mr William Armstrong to Mrs Barbara Doig, 18 December 1998
[379] DL/1/110-112 - DLE Feasibility Estimate, Issue 5, 2 March 1999,
[380] SE/4/057–067 – Progress Report by Mrs Barbara Doig to the Secretary of State, 23 March 1999

8.46 The minute of 23 March 1999 contained the following table:

Cost Estimates – Key Elements	Original 1998 – 03 £ million	Latest Estimate 1998 -03 £ million
Site acquisition, demolition, archaeology	5	5
Construction	50	60
Contingencies (1)	5	6
Fees	10.5	14
VAT	12	14
TOTAL SITE & CONSTRUCTION COST	**82.5**	**99**
Fit-out, loose furniture, IT etc	7.5	7.5
FINANCIAL PROVISION REQUIRED	**90**	**107 (2)**
Landscaping, Roads etc		**5 – 10**
		112 – 117(3)

(1) Construction contingencies included on advice from cost consultants as per normal practice. This is regarded as commercially confidential.
(2) No allowance for landscaping works. Total rounded to nearest million.
(3) Indicative estimated cost range only. See Para 17.

8.47 The reasons given to Ministers for the increase in the cost estimates were threefold. Firstly, the briefed gross area on which the £50 million budget had originally been based had increased from the initial 17,500 to 23,000m² in the latest design proposals. This increase was to accommodate larger numbers of staff in the light of better knowledge of the way the Parliament would operate. Secondly, the design proposals had been unable to match the over optimistic gross/net area proportions in the Brief. Thirdly, the need to incorporate an additional formal entrance to the building had been recognised and imposed additional space demands and therefore cost. Although the submission suggested that savings could reduce the DLE cost estimate from £61.2 million to '£59 or £60 million', it did not at any point indicate to Ministers that DLE had advised that an additional £17 million should be incorporated as a risk allowance.

8.48 The Inquiry heard detailed evidence on the view reached by the Project Team that the risks identified by DLE could be 'managed out' and the decision not to alert Ministers to this aspect of the cost estimates. In his evidence Mr Gordon said:

> "We also had to decide with Ministers what the contingency should be to take account of risks. But at that stage I was not prepared to recommend to Ministers that this additional risk allowance, which included items like the possibility that there would be some delay; the possibility that the basic specification of the building would be higher than the client was asking for; that there would be balustrades; that there would be this, that and the other that was more than we wanted, since it was within the client's control to say, "We do not want these things; we are not going to have that". I am afraid it was pretty much a no-brainer to conclude that these were things that could not be included in the budget as if they were hard items that were going to come to pass, because that would be a totally imprudent use of public money.

… Now it would have been possible to take these figures and put them into notes to Ministers in March and May, but they would only have gone in there with a firm recommendation that no allowance should be made in the budget for the materialisation of these risks because they were not potential costs that were on all fours with those that were included in the core construction costs".[381]

8.49   Similarly, Mrs Doig took the view that it would have been 'irresponsible' to seek an additional budget for risk allowances when to do so would have automatically resulted in fee increases and could have encouraged the Design Team and contractors to overrun. Mr Fisher however expressed his view that had DLE thought that there was a realistic possibility that the identified risks could be managed out by client action, they would not have included those risks in the first place.[382]

8.50   I do not challenge the principle that the Project Team could take a view on whether the risks identified by DLE could be avoided by client action. What I find more difficult to comprehend is why Ministers were not notified within the confidentiality of their exchanges with officials of the reported financial position and the management action taken to address the position. By omitting to inform Ministers of this highly relevant development, a risk was introduced that Ministers would take decisions on the basis of partial or incomplete information and might inadvertently make misleading statements in public or in Parliament. It is evident that DLE were not consulted over the accuracy of the 23 March submission[383] but more surprisingly it does not appear that the Project Team undertook any exploration with them at this time as to the validity of the risks DLE were identifying. Professional advice appears to have been rejected without a proper consideration of that advice or challenge to it.

8.51   By way of illustrating the apparent absence of a thorough understanding within the Scottish Office of the DLE advice, the Inquiry heard evidence that the Scottish Office believed DLE had identified a risk allowance of £5 million for delay caused by the handover of the Project to the Scottish Parliamentary Corporate Body.[384] This issue was also covered in some detail in a letter written by the Permanent Secretary to Donald Dewar in April 2000 to explain the actions of officials at this time.[385] Yet, in examining the precise advice offered by DLE, it was seen that the £5 million allowance referred to 'costs in connection with disruption during construction and delayed construction completion'.[386] DLE dispute that this risk was specifically attached to potential delays at the point of handover of the Project but was of a more general nature.[387] In

---

[381] Evidence of Mr Robert Gordon on 16 December 2003, Paras 423 to 424

[382] Evidence of Mr Hugh Fisher on 15 December 2003, Para 342

[383] Evidence of Mrs Barbara Doig on 17 December 2003, Para 492 and Mr Hugh Fisher on 15 December 2003, Para 314

[384] WS/25/001– 21 – Mrs Barbara Doig's First Witness Statement, 4 December 2003

[385] Auditor General for Scotland's Report of September 2000, Annex B

[386] DL/1/119-122C – Feasibility Estimate from Mr Ian McAndie to Mrs Barbara Doig, 25 May 1999

[387] Evidence of Mr Hugh Fisher on 18 February 2004, Paras 84 *et seq*

correspondence[388] the Scottish Executive have maintained that this issue was discussed with DLE in April 2000 at which time it was clearly understood that the figure related to risk at the time of transfer. The correspondence also indicated that 'the £5 million had been the subject of considerable discussion between the Project Sponsor, the Project Manager and DLE in April and May 1999'. This is not accepted by Mr Fisher of DLE, nor is there documentary evidence to indicate that DLE's position was other than that contained in their cost estimate at the time. The whole episode suggests to me that senior officials did not have a complete understanding of the advice that their professional consultants were offering them.

8.52   Mr Fisher gave evidence that he took some exception to the fact that DLE's estimates of risk had apparently been rejected. He made it clear that if DLE were asked to report it could only do so on the basis of the all inclusive construction cost figure of £89 million at that time and that neither DLE nor Bovis would be party to a Cost Plan based on £62 million. Sir Muir Russell took comfort from the observation in the Auditor General's Report that 'the particular risk items in question did not subsequently materialise'. However, it is not clear to me whether the risks concerning Mr Fisher were the same as the particular risks commented on by the Auditor General. As I read the Auditor General's observations in context, he is referring to those risks identified in Sir Muir Russell's letter of 4 April 2000 to Donald Dewar and not the broader range of risks that concerned Mr Fisher.

8.53   Donald Dewar noted the contents of Mrs Doig's 23 March 1999 submission with some concern and discussed the matter with Mr Gordon and others on 29 March. On the same day EMBT/RMJM Ltd gave a presentation to Donald Dewar of their final design scheme proposals. He was prepared to accept the proposals subject to a review by the client side to ensure that the project brief was being met. He asked for arrangements to be put in hand immediately to assess and if necessary amend budget provision, accepting that the costs of the latest design proposals were being reviewed by DLE and would not be available until May 1999.[389] It was not considered appropriate to make public statements on costs going beyond the Government's existing position until that whole process had been completed. I am sure that this decision was wholly unrelated to the fact that the election campaign for the first Scottish Parliamentary elections on 6 May was getting underway at that time.

8.54   During April and May the review work was undertaken and on 21 May 1999 DLE provided a further cost estimate reflecting the most recent design changes.[390] This estimated a basic building cost of £62.1 million, a contingency/design reserve of £5.2 million and a risk allowance

---

[388] SE/4/568-569 - Letter from Ms Thea Teale to the Holyrood Inquiry, 2 March 2004
[389] SE/4/072-073 - Minute from Mr Kenneth Thomson to Mrs Barbara Doig, 14 April 1998
[390] DL/1/119-122C - Feasibility Estimate from Mr Ian McAndie to Mrs Barbara Doig, 25 May 1999

of £15.8 million within a total construction cost of £89.2 million. In a submission to the newly appointed Finance Minister, Mr Jack McConnell, that was remarkably similar to her earlier submission to Ministers, Mrs Doig recommended an increase in budget from £50 million to £60 million (excluding VAT, fees etc). The submission noted that DLE's latest cost estimate was 'comparable with the feasibility design stage cost estimate of £50 million is £62.2 million (excluding VAT, fees, contingencies, risk allowances, fit-out, loose furniture and artworks, site acquisition etc)'. The table contained within the submission did not identify any sum for risk allowances and suggested that overall financial provision of £107 million would be required (excluding landscaping). Savings of between £1.5 million and £2.5 million were identified to justify bringing the cost estimate down from £62.2 million to a budget proposal of £60 million.[391]

8.55 That recommendation to increase the budget was approved at a meeting attended by Donald Dewar, Jack McConnell and senior officials (including Sir Muir Russell) on 2 June 1999. The note of that meeting records that Ministers considered whether the contingency within the budget was adequate and concluded that to increase it would simply increase the likelihood of spending more.[392] The documentation clearly records that the budget increase both sought and approved was to a construction cost of £60 million. For reasons which were not fully explained to the Inquiry, all concerned seem to have treated the increased budget as £62 million. Mrs Doig explained in evidence that "eventually it came out through the system as £62 million".[393] In the Parliamentary Debate on 17 June 1999, only 15 days later, Donald Dewar confirmed his understanding that the construction cost budget was £62 million and the total budget £109 million.

8.56 It has been suggested that the issue of risk allowances as opposed to contingencies must have been examined at the meeting on 2 June 1999 and it has been speculated that the content of the full DLE cost estimates may have been conveyed to Ministers at this time. I do not however find this supported either in the official record of that meeting or in the written evidence to the Inquiry submitted by Jack McConnell who stated:

> '... neither in the course of the decision being made to increase the budget for the Parliament project from £50 million to £60 million, nor in any subsequent or other discussions, was I shown a report from the cost consultants DLE. The issue of contingencies was discussed in general at the meeting on 2 June, but I was not

---

[391] SE/4/100–116 – Minute from Mrs Barbara Doig to Jack McConnell, 26 May 1999
[392] SE/4/118-119 - Minute from Mr Kenneth Thomson to Mrs Barbara Doig, 15 June 1999
[393] Evidence of Mrs Barbara Doig on 17 December 2003, Para 477

presented then or later with the information that DLE had identified separate potential risks of a further £27 million in their cost report.'[394]

8.57 No evidence has been put before the Inquiry to suggest that Ministers had any knowledge of the true position in relation to the risk allowance identified by DLE. To the contrary it was clear from the evidence of Mrs Doig,[395] Mr Gordon[396] and Sir Muir Russell[397] that a conscious decision had been taken by civil servants that the majority of the risk items identified by DLE could be "managed out" and that it was not in the circumstances necessary or appropriate for Ministers to be informed. When it came to light in March 2000 in Mr John Spencely's report[398] that DLE's estimated costs as at 25 May 1999 had been £89.2 million rather than the £62 million (plus £6 million contingency) reported to Ministers, an explanation was requested by Donald Dewar. That explanation was provided in terms of a letter of 4 April 2000 from Sir Muir Russell, of which a copy forms Annex B to the September 2000 report of the Auditor General for Scotland. The terms of that letter confirm that the Project Team had made the professional judgment not to report DLE's figure. It was put to me by Counsel to the Inquiry in his closing submission that Donald Dewar's "response to the Spencely Report of demanding an explanation from civil servants at the highest level, which subsequently came into the public domain, is inconsistent with any deliberate concealment by him of information provided by those civil servants." I accept that view. Had civil servants in fact drawn the true position in relation to DLE's risk estimates to Ministers' attention I am sure that Sir Muir Russell's letter would have said so. Equally I am sure that a politician as astute as Donald Dewar, had he been aware of the true position, would not have run the political risk of having that awareness pointed out to him in the explanation which he had demanded.

8.58 I should also add that it appears to me that the decision to increase the budget taken on 2 June 1999 had no legal basis. In terms of the Transfer of Property etc. (Scottish Parliamentary Corporate Body) Order 1999[399] all rights and interests in relation to the Parliament had passed to the SPCB on 1 June 1999. From that date the budget was a matter only for the SPCB and the approval of this increase in budget should have been sought from Sir David Steel and his SPCB colleagues, particularly as the increase resulted from significant changes to the brief including an increase in Parliamentary staff numbers, increases in the balance area and a new entrance. I can see that officials might wish to brief Ministers on the increases so that they were content with what was being proposed and as they were cost increases that had arisen

---

[394] MS/25/001-002 - Letter from the First Minister to the Holyrood Inquiry, 23 March 2004
[395] Evidence of Mrs Barbara Doig on 17 December 2003, Para 515 *et seq*; and 12 February 2004, Para 245 *et seq*
[396] Evidence of Mr Robert Gordon on 16 December 2003, Paras 539 and 572
[397] Evidence of Sir Muir Russell on 5 February 2004, Para 217 *et seq*
[398] Mr Spencely's Report, Section 4.2.3 'The basic construction cost' and related table
[399] Transfer of Property etc. (Scottish Parliamentary Corporate Body) Order 1999 (S.I. 1999 No. 1106)

while the Project was still under their stewardship but that does not deflect my concern that Ministers were purporting to take significant decisions in relation to a Project no longer within their remit.

8.59   When Mr Fisher discovered in early July the basis of the £62 million, namely the DLE calculation with risk managed out, he immediately insisted that there should be no tampering with his figures and it was also pointed out that Bovis would have difficulty preparing and publishing a cost plan for other than the true estimated Project value i.e. £89 million and not £62 million. Mrs Doig was present when this was discussed and confirmed that for political reasons a cost plan based on £89 million was inappropriate at that time.[400]

8.60   What is astonishing is that less than a month after Donald Dewar's speech to the Parliament officials knew the independent cost consultants were insisting that their figure was correct but at no time prior to Mr Spencely's Report was this drawn to Donald Dewar's attention. Nor indeed was it raised with Sir David Steel or the SPCB, although Mr Fisher stressed what the risks would be if he were to be questioned by the SPCB.[401]

---

[400] DL/1/196 - DLE File Note of Meeting of 7 July 1999
[401] DL/1/197 - DLE File Note of Meeting of 28 July 1999

Chapter 9

The Project from Handover to February 2000

Health of the Project at Handover

9.1 One of the key questions identified by Mr John Campbell QC, Counsel to the Inquiry in his opening submission was:

> "Whether the Project was handed over by the former Scottish Office to the SPCB in June 1999, in sound health and good condition, within a firm financial structure?"

The question has been the subject of much evidence, strongly held views, and competing submissions. On the one hand it was submitted by counsel appearing for the Scottish Executive that the Project at handover to the SPCB was in good heart and "within weeks of achieving sign-off of Stage D". On the other hand, the solicitor for the SPCB suggested that at the time of handover the Project was not "viable" in cost and programme terms. The question demands an answer.

9.2 I am aware that as at 1 June 1999 design had been in progress since the appointment of the Design Team in the previous summer. Design development had moved towards RIBA Stage D sign off, but that milestone had not yet been reached. Some preliminary work including demolition and archaeology had taken place on the site, but no construction, even in the form of excavation and retention works was due until July 1999.

9.3   A significant complication in the case of Holyrood is that the Scottish Parliament, represented by the SPCB as the ultimate client, only came into existence after the elections in May 1999. Accordingly, prior to that date what the new Parliament would require could only be assessed by Mr Armstrong using his best endeavours, taking into account the views of Ministers and others and the experience of comparable parliaments.

Position with the Project in the Period Leading up to Handover

9.4   A revised building design had been issued by the Architect on 26 March 1999 but not in sufficient time for it to be properly assessed by officials before presentation to the Secretary of State. According to Mr Paul Curran, Senior Project Manager in the Holyrood Project Team, that redesign changed the layout of the buildings in the east part of the site so fundamentally that the "areas and adjacencies" required a fresh review. Stage D was consequently not achieved by the end of March 1999 as planned. As Mr Curran put it, he "had been presented with a completely new design and had to start again". He described the redesign as "very much a Stage C proposal at that time — outline".[402] Mr Curran reported that after 26 March the Project Team experienced difficulties in obtaining amended layout drawings, the reason for which, he thought, was "the refinement of the amended proposal in Barcelona and the link between Edinburgh and Barcelona in producing those drawings".[403] With the object of speeding up progress, a meeting was arranged on 14 April 1999 to review the revised design with Snr Miralles in Barcelona[404] at which a number of outstanding concerns were raised. Messrs Mustard and Curran, together with Edinburgh based members of the Design Team, spent two days going through the plans and "developing Snr Miralles' understanding". Mr Curran told the Inquiry of his impression that Snr Miralles did not fully understand the detailed requirements of the Brief at that time.

9.5   On 25 May 1999 a revised Stage D report was submitted by the Architect. Mr Curran described it as incomplete and "very similar to the previous submission of the Stage D report in March". It is clear from the reports[405] submitted in connection with the Client Project Team meeting on 26 May and from the minute of that meeting[406] that significant design development work was still proceeding. The Project Team's review of the areas and adjacencies had not been concluded, and there were still co-ordination issues to be resolved between the engineers.[407]

---

[402] Evidence of Mr Paul Curran on 17 February 2004, Para 707

[403] ibid, Para 759

[404] SE/4/232-235 - Notes of Meeting held at EMBT/RMJM Offices in Barcelona, 14 April 1999

[405] SE/4/483-505 – Progress Reports for Meeting of 26 May 1998

[406] SE/4/506-512 - Minute of Client Project Team Meeting, 26 May 1999

[407] RM/1/104-106 - EMBT/RMJM Minute of Meeting of 16 July 1999, Para 1.04

9.6 On the evidence before the Inquiry, and leaving aside for the moment considerations as to whether the requirements of the new Parliament had been appropriately anticipated, I accept that the Project at handover was within weeks of formal Stage D approval but only to the extent that the design requirements of the November 1998 Brief were apparently satisfied.[408] However the proper satisfaction of the requirements of RIBA Stage D should have included completion of the Brief and preparation of a cost plan within budget.

9.7 In June 1999, the November 1998 version of the Brief had not been revised, and it did not reflect the many subsequent changes in requirements for the building between these dates. In this respect the Brief was, as at the time of handover, some way from being complete, or indeed useful as a tool for determining design requirements or as an aid to cost projection. Most obviously, the Brief failed to anticipate the requirements of the new Parliament for personnel and space, with the result that the anticipated gross area of the building of some $23,214m^2$ at the time of handover later had to be increased to $30,593m^2$.[409] It was not suggested to the Inquiry that the requirements of the new Parliament, as they came to be articulated, were extravagant or unreasonable.

9.8 Mr Curran, when asked for his view as to the importance of including cost information in a Stage D report, said:

> "I think it is an essential part of the process. Even if you simply read through the Royal Institute of British Architects' requirements for a Stage D proposal, cost information is an essential part of it. It may not be provided by the architect; it may be in this case that the architect has to provide information to others to put together that information. But yes, you would expect a fully costed Stage D proposal."[410]

9.9 In the run up to handover DLE had produced a series of feasibility estimates as follows:

Feasibility Estimates		
2 March 1999	No 5[411]	£87,158,536
12 March 1999	No 6[412]	£88,350,019
26 March 1999	No 7[413]	£88,350,019
25 May 1999	No 8[414]	£89,200,019

Report No 6, subject to the adjustment of the risk figures, informed the first application for a budget increase submitted by Mrs Doig on 23 March 1999.[415] Number 8, similarly adjusted,

---

[408] RM/1/107-108 – Letter from Mr Paul Curran to Mr Brian Stewart, 21 July 1999.
[409] DL/1/009 - DLE Time Line - Development of Costs, October 1998 to August 2000
[410] Evidence of Mr Paul Curran on 17 February 2004, Para 602
[411] DL/1/110-112 – DLE Feasibility Estimate at 2 March 1999
[412] DL/1/113-114 – DLE Feasibility Estimate at 12 March 1999
[413] DL/1/115-118 – DLE Feasibility Estimate (Issue 7) at 26 March 1999
[414] DL/1/120-122C – DLE Feasibility Estimate (Issue 8) at 25 May 1999
[415] SE/4/057-067 - Progress Report from Mrs Barbara Doig to PS/Secretary of State, 23 March 1999

formed the basis for the second application submitted on 26 May 1999[416] which directly resulted in the construction cost budget of £62 million inherited by the SPCB at handover.

9.10 While those involved no doubt genuinely and with the best of intentions believed that the Project was, at the time of handover to the Scottish Parliament, on the threshold of a meaningful Stage D, the evidence before the Inquiry suggested otherwise. It is clear to me that the requirements of Stage D, particularly as regard the Brief and the Cost Plan, were not close to satisfaction at the time of handover. Accordingly, it cannot properly be maintained that the Project was close to a satisfactory Stage D.

9.11 There has been extensive reference in the evidence to "complexity of design" as a factor causing both cost and programme overruns. Witnesses before the Inquiry did not specifically identify this as an issue at the time of handover but many did so at a later stage, particularly in relation to the eastern end of the site. Mr Alan Mack, Project Director, Bovis,[417] Mr Stewart,[418] Linda Fabiani MSP[419] and John Home Robertson MSP[420] all emphasised the complexity of the design.

9.12 As early as August 1998 risk management workshops managed by DLE but involving the participation of all the main players had identified as a risk the prospect that the Miralles concept might not be "affordable". The workshop identified a possible risk exposure of 20/25 (i.e. 80% likely).[421] By March 1999 this risk item was being assessed as having a 25/25 (i.e. 100%) exposure. At that time the risk assessments were not costed. Despite its very high probability, this item was not specifically identified among the risk allowances totalling £15.86 million put forward by DLE in terms of their Feasibility Estimate of 25 May 1999.[422]

9.13 In my opinion, there was a failure at the stage of handover to appreciate sufficiently the extent to which the development of certain aspects of the design, such as the Chamber roof, were leading to a very high degree of complexity. There was also a failure to appreciate adequately the consequences of that complexity. The Architect clearly understood the complexity of the designs and articulated this to the client using all manner of presentation techniques.

---

[416] SE/4/100-116 - Paper from Mrs Barbara Doig to Jack McConnell, 26 May 1999

[417] "The Scottish Parliament Project is unique, has broadened the horizons of design and construction technology and is one of the most complex projects in which Bovis Lend Lease has ever been involved."

[418] "Yes, but this building is very complex. It is unlike anything I've ever worked on before. Professionally, we're used to dealing with budget and programme, but this is exceptional. ....There is an unpredictable element in this building" (SPCB Meeting, June 2003)

[419] "Overall my view is that there was failure by all concerned until too late in the day to appreciate the complications arising from the complexity of the overall design"

[420] "The complexity and development of the design made it inevitable that the Holyrood Project would be expensive, and it would have been surprising if there had not been significant problems in a project of this nature and scale".

[421] DL/2/025 – Paper - Risk Analysis and Management, 21 August 1998

[422] DL/1/119-122C - Feasibility Estimate (Issue 8) at 25 May 1999 from Mr Ian McAndie

However, it is far from clear that the Architect had the budget clearly in mind when producing designs of such complexity. I would have expected Bovis to have appreciated the programme implications. Indeed all who attended risk management workshops should have been on the alert.

9.14 The position in relation to the viability of the Project at handover was most accurately described by Dr Gibbons. In his written statement he said:

'In my view the state of the Project as 'handed over' to the Parliament in June 1999 was viable and could have been delivered to programme within the agreed costs. This would not have been an easy task and I doubt it could have been carried out without some modifications (possibly involving some sacrifice in space and/or quality). These would have been quite normal occurrences in controlling costs and achieving programme targets in any building project.' [423]

9.15 In his oral evidence Dr Gibbons, when asked about viability at handover, said:

"From what we know now, it clearly was not."[424]

9.16 I am bound to conclude that:

1. The Brief was not up to date, and did not reflect the changes made since November 1998.
2. The Brief did not anticipate the requirements of the Parliament with the inevitable result that adherence to it would have produced an unsuitable building.
3. The budgeted construction cost of £62 million was flawed in that:

   a. there was inadequate accounting for risk, and the stated budget bore no relationship to a cost plan;
   b. there had been a failure to fully appreciate the complexity of the design; and
   c. account had not been taken of considerations of blast and security.

In short, the Project was not in a viable and healthy condition when it was handed over to the SPCB on 1 June 1999.

Handover of the Project to the Scottish Parliamentary Corporate Body (SPCB)

9.17 The purpose of the SPCB, as constituted by the Scotland Act 1998, section 23, is "to provide the Parliament, or ensure that the Parliament is provided, with the property, staff and services required for the Parliament's purposes". In terms of the Act and related subordinate legislation[425] all rights and liabilities of the Scottish Office in connection with all of the contracts entered into by it in relation to the Project transferred to the SPCB with effect from 1 June 1999. The SPCB itself had no choice in this and had no legal right to change or vary any of

---

[423] WS/53/001–031 – John Gibbons' Third Witness Statement, Para 6
[424] Evidence of Dr John Gibbons on 6 May 2004, Para 672
[425] The Transfer of Property etc. (Scottish Parliamentary Corporate Body) Order 1999 (S.I. 1999 No. 1106)

the contracts already entered into. It accordingly stepped into the shoes of the former Scottish Office as client for the Project from that date.

9.18   The Act provides that the members of the SPCB are to be the Presiding Officer together with four elected MSPs. The four MSPs initially elected on 19 May 1999 were Robert Brown MSP, Des McNulty MSP, Andrew Welsh MSP and John Young MSP. Des McNulty, upon becoming a Minister in 2002, was replaced by Duncan McNeill MSP. After the 2003 election George Reid succeeded Sir David Steel as Presiding Officer and John Scott replaced John Young. Deputy Presiding Officers can attend, but not vote. Otherwise there have been no changes. The Clerk and Chief Executive to the Parliament has at all times been Mr Grice, who became the Accountable Officer and Project Owner for the Project from the time of handover.

The Project Team

9.19   The Holyrood Project Team transferred over to the Parliament along with responsibility for the Project. Mrs Doig remained in post as Project Sponsor reporting to Mr Grice. Mr Mustard continued as Project Manager assisted by Mr Curran. Dr Gibbons did not transfer to the Parliament but it was arranged informally with the newly-established Scottish Executive that he would continue to be available to the Project Team as Architectural Adviser.

Power of the SPCB to Delegate

9.20   The Scotland Act is very specific about the powers of the SPCB to delegate and provides "The corporation may delegate any of its functions to the Presiding Officer or the Clerk." I am advised that the legal effect of this provision is to preclude delegation by the SPCB to any person or any body other than the Presiding Officer and the Clerk. This restriction on delegation became of significance later in the life of the Project when the Spencely Report recommended the setting up of a "Progressing Group" to assist the SPCB in managing the Project.

Briefing the SPCB

9.21   Mrs Doig was responsible for the preparation of a lengthy briefing paper on the Project which was considered by the SPCB at its first meeting on 8 June 1999. It sounded a number of warnings and set out some lofty aspirations in saying:

> 'The client's core concerns in any major building project involving substantial capital expenditure are that the building is delivered on programme, to budget and to the appropriate level of quality. For most buildings this is a very complex task generally beset by the unexpected. And for a parliament building the complexity is virtually unbounded – the eventual building is a symbol of the parliament itself and the political life that goes on within it, it has to be of great architectural distinction, proper

ambience, and operationally efficient and effective for a wide range of end-users with very different requirements of the accommodation and services. It is part theatre, conference venue, exhibition arena, office, catering outlet, broadcasting studio, school, art gallery. And the client is expected to demonstrate exemplary practices in all aspects of securing the architectural and services appointments, design, including artistic merit and environmental issues, construction and fitting out, financial and project management.' [426]

9.22 This important briefing paper included sections on:

1. **Programme** - it was reported that the building was on schedule for completion by autumn 2001;
2. **Cost** - it was reported that the latest construction cost estimate was £62 million, requiring a total provision of £109 million inclusive of "construction contingencies included on advice from cost consultants as per normal practice" but with no allowance for external landscaping works. It was pointed out that at that stage only cost estimates were available.
3. **Quality** – it quoted passages from the Brief but claimed (incorrectly) that the Brief had been "regularly reviewed throughout the past year as the design process (had) moved on". I have already noted that the draft Brief had not at this stage moved on from the November 1998 draft.
4. **Financial Impact of Cancellation/Postponement** – it pointed out that cancellation could lead to significant cost penalties "in the order of £14 million", the provenance of which figure was not explained, either to the SPCB or to the Inquiry.[427] It indicated that the site had been purchased for "around" £4 million. Mrs Doig postulated that cancellation of the Project would result in a minimum net loss of £10 million. It was also confirmed that any postponement of construction could lead to significant disruption, with "base running costs" continuing to run at £0.5 million per month, and fees continuing to accrue.
5. **Alternative sites to Holyrood** – it was confirmed that Calton Hill represented the only realistic alternative to Holyrood and that the cost differential of £65 million against £50 million continued because of the increase in the briefed area.
6. **Professional and construction appointments** – details of the key appointments were given but without any hint of any previous difficulties with the Design Team.
7. **Procurement route** – it was confirmed that Bovis had been appointed as Construction Managers. The paper gave no information about the implications of construction management for the Project.

9.23 In my opinion this briefing should have alluded to the difficulties that had been experienced with the Design Team and to the fact that the independent professional advice of DLE in relation to the appropriate figure for risk allowances had been disregarded in arriving at the construction cost budget of £62 million. Furthermore, the briefing paper made no attempt to

---

[426] CB/2/001-022 – Paper from the Project Team to the SPCB Paper, 8 June 1999
[427] Evidence of Mrs Barbara Doig on 12 February 2004, Paras 283 *et seq*

impart to the SPCB, none of whom had any significant construction or procurement experience, the risks inevitably involved in construction management as the selected procurement vehicle. In this respect the briefing did not present a balanced picture of the state of the Project as it then stood. The terms of the briefing suggest that the Project Sponsor and Project Management had yet to grasp the potential risks to the Project.

Procedures of the SPCB

9.24 It is important to recognise the huge range of responsibilities thrust upon the SPCB in the early days of the Parliament. Inspection of the early minutes reveal the diversity of those issues which included matters such as finance, MSPs' allowances, broadcasting arrangements, employment and pension arrangements for Parliamentary staff, equal opportunities and smoking policy. While the Project loomed large among these issues, it represented but one of the many calls on the time of the members.

9.25 At the SPCB's first meeting on 8 June 1999 it was agreed:

- 'that any major issues, such as the Holyrood Project, would go to the Parliament "for a decision or a steer"
- that full minutes of its meetings would not be released to MSPs or the public but that an edited summary would be made available which would be "as informative as possible'.

9.26 The fact that only edited summaries of the minutes insofar as they related to the Project were made public was a matter which only emerged during the course of the Inquiry. The thinking appears to have been that the full minutes might contain reference to matters of commercial confidentiality, the wider circulation of which might have given rise to difficulties. That is reasonable enough but MSPs were not informed that they were being given only an edited version. The minutes made available to MSPs and the public were, as Mr Grice described it, subject to a "pretty heavy edit".[428] He agreed that lighter editing could appropriately have been undertaken. The decision of the SPCB to circulate an edited version of its proceedings gave rise to the difficulty described in evidence by John Young. At meetings of his Party group, he found himself, unlike members of other committees, unable to report virtually anything of what went on in the SPCB, causing frustration to his Party leader and others. The practice also frustrated the efforts of MSPs like Margo MacDonald who has from the outset campaigned for information on the Project to be more transparent and accessible to the public. The SPCB's practice of circulating edited minutes continued until June 2000 after which it was discontinued on legal advice.

---

[428] Evidence of Mr Paul Grice on 10 February 2004, Para 583

9.27 It surprised me that the SPCB should have been advised and should have decided to make available to MSPs and the public only a heavily edited version of its minutes, going well beyond the necessary restraints of commercial confidentiality. I consider that the decision to withhold information on the Project from MSPs must to some extent have suppressed informed debate and was evidently a source of frustration. It is difficult to reconcile this practice with the CSG's stated principles of openness and transparency.

9.28 In relation to the handover of the Project to the SPCB, the Auditor General for Scotland in his September 2000 Report said:

> "When the Holyrood Project was added to the responsibilities of the Corporate Body there was uncertainty about how the Corporate Body would undertake their responsibility to oversee progress and implementation of the Project and how often they should meet to do so. It was not until early November 1999 that project management provided the Corporate Body with a report on the project management structure. No decisions were taken at this stage regarding the governance procedures for progressing the Project. None of the members had previous responsibility for or detailed knowledge of the Project. More should have been done to advise members of the SPCB about their proper role, the proper role of officials, and the key features of the project management arrangements."[429]

9.29 Project Management's report on management structure, "The SPCB's client responsibilities for the Holyrood building",[430] was only put before the SPCB on 9 November 1999[431]. It set out comprehensively and for the first time the responsibilities of the SPCB and of the others involved with the Project. Significantly, by referring to Treasury Guidance on Construction Procurement and to Section T of the Scottish Office Finance Manual, the paper drew attention, at least indirectly, to the implications of construction management as a procurement vehicle. At the SPCB meeting on 9 November Dr Gibbons drew particular attention to the resultant limitations on the implementation of substantial changes to the Brief.

9.30 I share the Auditor General's surprise that it was not until November 1999, some six months after it had come into existence and over five months since it assumed legal responsibility for the Project, that the SPCB should have received this briefing. This suggests that both the SPCB and the Project Team had not appreciated the magnitude of the task which the Project represented and the extent to which resource required to be devoted to it.

9.31 In his September 2000 Report the Auditor General further commented:

> 'The Clerk of the Parliament is responsible for all the administrative arrangements associated with the establishment and management of the Parliament. He is also

---

[429] Auditor General for Scotland's Report of September 2000, Para 3.65
[430] CB/2/145A-T - SPCB Paper (HB)(99)7A, 9 November 1999
[431] CB/2/143-145 - Minutes of SPCB Meeting of 9 November 1999

responsible for ensuring that the Corporate Body are properly informed and, where needed, that they receive adequate independent advice on all matters for which they are responsible. As the senior official, he was also owner of the Holyrood Project and responsible for its successful delivery. With hindsight, it may have been advisable to allocate the responsibility for the Holyrood Project to another senior official within the Parliament, so as to safeguard the effective exercise of that role.'[432]

9.32 My overall impression from the evidence was that Mr Grice as the Clerk and Chief Executive was not, during this early period after handover, as personally engaged with the Project in his capacity as Project Owner as I might have expected. While Mr Grice was generally in attendance at SPCB meetings during this period the minutes do not record any significant level of contribution from him. Mr Grice described very fully, and with commendable frankness, the many demands on his own time and the extent to which he was prepared to leave the running of the Project to Mrs Doig and her team.[433] However, as I have noted, the SPCB lacked the legal power to delegate other than to the Clerk. The delegation of responsibility for the Project to another senior official was accordingly not an option open to it beyond section 20(4) which permits the Clerk to authorise another member of staff to exercise functions on his behalf. However, the HPG could never be described as members of his staff.

9.33 In relation to the handover of the Project to the SPCB, the Auditor General was critical of the SPCB when he said:

'At this stage there was a particular need for those accepting responsibility for the Project to have reviewed it, with a degree of independence from the project team, in order to satisfy themselves about its status and health, but there was no such review.'[434]

9.34 While I take the Auditor General's point, I do not think the SPCB is open to any significant criticism on this account. In briefing the SPCB, Project Management had given no hint of anything amiss with the Project. The individual members of the SPCB did not have particular knowledge of construction that might have raised any doubts. Many might have seen the instruction at that stage of an independent report as an indication of an initial lack of confidence in Project Management with which the SPCB was at that time trying to build a working relationship. Perhaps most significantly, a full Parliamentary debate on the Project was to be arranged at an early date. When that debate took place, the Parliament rejected Donald Gorrie's proposal for an independent review. I note that the SPCB in fact gave consideration at its meeting on 29 June 1999 to the possibility of appointing a "facilitator" to provide an external view on the Project, but the possibility was not pursued subsequently.

---

[432] Auditor General for Scotland's Report of September 2000, Para 3.66

[433] Evidence of Mr Paul Grice on 10 February 2004, Para126 *et seq* and WS/22/001-005 Mr Grice's First Witness Statement, Para 7

[434] Auditor General for Scotland's Report of September 2000, Para 3.64

The Parliamentary Debate of 17 June 1999

9.35 On 8 June 1999 against a background of media and political speculation about the future of the Project, a decision was taken by the Scottish Cabinet that time should be found for a debate on a motion to "endorse the Holyrood Project". The minute of this Cabinet meeting, to which the Inquiry had the benefit of access, records that Members of the Executive Parties would be expected to vote in favour of the motion and the matter was actioned to Tom McCabe MSP, the Minister for Parliament. In view of this agreement I am surprised that in the subsequent debate Donald Dewar took issue with Alex Salmond over his decision to whip his Party. Also on 8 June, the SPCB had met to consider Mrs Doig's briefing paper on the Project[435] and had received a verbal report from her. On 9 June 1999 a copy of the briefing paper was circulated to MSPs with a covering minute from Sir David Steel confirming the proposal that the Project was to be the subject of a debate on 17 June 1999.[436] Prior to the debate a briefing for MSPs by the Design Team had been arranged for 15 June 1999.[437] It is recorded that only 27 of the 129 MSPs availed themselves of the opportunity of attending. [438]

9.36 The debate proceeded upon an Executive motion moved by the First Minister:

'That the Parliament endorses the decision to provide its permanent home on the Holyrood site and authorises the Scottish Parliamentary Corporate Body to take forward the Project in accordance with the plans developed by the EMBT/RMJM design team and within the time scale and cost estimates described in the Presiding Officer's note to members of 9 June 1999.'[439]

9.37 An amendment to the motion in the name of Donald Gorrie proposed the setting up of a special committee to work over the summer recess (i) to commission an independent study of the potential sites for the Parliament at Holyrood, Calton Hill/Regent Road and the Mound and (ii) if satisfied that the Holyrood scheme represented the best option, to proceed with it or otherwise to report to the Parliament for a decision as early as possible after the summer recess. The amendment further sought to instruct a pause in the letting of any construction related contracts until the special committee or the Parliament authorised it to do so. [440]

9.38 In moving the motion Donald Dewar gave a history of the Project including the decisions on site selection and the appointment of EMBT/RMJM Ltd as the architects. Arguing strongly against a pause, he described the difficulty in only two months of considering a range of new sites, undertaking feasibility studies and the selection of a new architect. He said there would

---

[435] CB/2/004–023 - Paper from Mrs Barbara Doig to the SPCB, 8 June 1999

[436] CB/2/023A – Paper from Sir David Steel to MSPs, 9 June 1999

[437] Evidence of Sir David Steel on 4 February 2004, Para 346 *et seq* and Dr John Gibbons on 6 May 2004, Para 310

[438] CB/2/025-031 – SPCB Paper from the Project Team, 29 June 1999

[439] S1M-52 – Motion moved by Donald Dewar, Scottish Parliament Holyrood debate, 17 June 1999

[440] S1M-52.1 – Amendment moved by Donald Gorrie, Scottish Parliament Holyrood debate, 17 June 1999

be a major delay, making the Parliament a "laughing stock". He stated that he had received advice that the immediate costs of a two month delay would be around £2 million to £3 million and that there might well be other claims and costs.

9.39   Moving the amendment Donald Gorrie argued, as he did at the Inquiry, that selection of the site should have been and should be a matter for the Parliament itself. He strongly favoured Calton Hill/St Andrew's House for the site and contended that it was essential for the Parliament to have the benefit of independent advice on the options including that of remaining at the Mound. He had serious reservations about the timetable and recommended remaining at the Mound for longer to consider the options of staying there permanently, of going ahead more slowly with Holyrood if some improvements were made, or of going to another site. He considered the cost of any delay to be well worth incurring to enable the options to be evaluated. Donald Gorrie's amendment was defeated by 64 votes to 61 with no abstentions. The substantive motion was approved by 66 votes to 57 with two abstentions, a majority of 9 in favour of endorsing the Project. It is not for me to speculate as to the future of the Project had the result of the vote been different but Alex Salmond has argued strongly, and not without cause, that the new Scottish Parliament should have been fully appraised of all costs beforehand. Transparently, as the Inquiry has revealed, it was not.

Discussion of Costs during the Debate

9.40   The cost of the Project was the not the main focus of the debate. It concentrated on the issues of site selection and the design for the Chamber, although a recurring theme was MSPs' expectations for a building of excellence. In the course of his speech the First Minister said:

> "I will say a word or two about costs. We always said that £50 million was an initial construction cost and that there would be additional costs of VAT, fees and extras. It will be clear to those who bothered to read answers to parliamentary questions......that the final total would be around £80 million or £90 million. ....The information was available and was never hidden. I make it clear that the £109 million that we now hold to—to the best of our ability—includes VAT, fees, site acquisition and preparation, information technology and fit-out. I must make it clear that landscaping into the park and the traffic calming measures, which are a matter for the Executive and City of Edinburgh Council, are not included."[441]

9.41   The evidence of Mr Thomson, the First Minister's Private Secretary was that:

> "For a speech on any parliamentary occasion, the speech would come from the policy officials responsible for that area. Typically with speeches, Mr Dewar would do a lot of work on them himself, and if you read anything in Hansard or the Scottish Parliament Official Report, you see language that is very definitely Donald Dewar rather than civil

---

[441] Donald Dewar's speech, Scottish Parliament Holyrood debate 17 June 1999

servants trying to do it for him. So I imagine that he would have got a submission with a draft in it, and he would then have worked it up himself."[442]

No official's draft was produced to the Inquiry but Mr Thomson's remarks came as no surprise to me.

9.42 The figure of £109 million referred to by the First Minister had been put forward by the Project Team in the briefing to SPCB members which had been circulated to all MSPs. The briefing had included the following table:

Cost Estimates – Key Elements	Original 1998 – 03 £ million	Latest Estimate 1998 -03 £ million
Site acquisition, demolition, archaeology	5	5
Construction	50	62
Fees, VAT, Contingencies [1]	27.5	34
TOTAL SITE & CONSTRUCTION COST	**82.5**	**101**
Fit-out, loose furniture, IT etc	7.5	7.5
FINANCIAL PROVISION REQUIRED	**90**	**109[2]**

(1) Construction contingencies included on advice from cost consultants as per normal practice. This is regarded as commercially confidential.

(2) No allowance for landscaping works external to site. Total rounded to nearest million.[443]

It is significant that the only reference to landscaping is in terms of a footnote. This table had its origins in Mrs Doig's minutes of 23 March 1999[444] and 26 May 1999[445] in which she had sought a budget increase from £50 to £60 million construction cost.

9.43 Donald Dewar was evidently unaware of DLE's detailed advice on risk and I do not believe that he intentionally misled the Parliament in that respect. It is unfortunate, but perhaps not surprising so soon after handover, that the debate was dominated by the site selection issue and failed to address the significant issues in relation to design, budget and procurement method. The debate did not alter the SPCB's mandate nor provide it with any more precise direction or authority as to how it should proceed. It would have been desirable if, as a result of the debate, the Parliament had taken a greater "ownership" of the Project. However, I discern no part of the debate as focusing on that but what discussion there was sent very clear messages to the Design Team about quality. [446]

[442] Evidence of Mr Kenneth Thomson on 3 February 2004, Para 392

[443] CB/2/001-022 - SPCB Paper from the Project Team, 8 June 1999

[444] SE/4/057-067 – Paper from Mrs Barbara Doig to the PS/Secretary of State, 23 March 1999

[445] SE/4/100–116 - Paper from Mrs Barbara Doig to Jack McConnell, 26 May 1999

[446] CB/2/058-060 – SPCB Paper from the Project Team, of 26 July 1999. para 6

Landscaping

9.44　The minutes of 23 March 1999 and 26 May 1999 had both mentioned a possible budget of up to £10 million for landscaping and ancillary works. No breakdown of this figure was given and it was later suggested by the Principal Finance Officer that it may have been "guessed at".[447] At the time of the March minute it was envisaged that the cost of landscaping and related works would form part of the overall budget for the Project which would in due course become the responsibility of the SPCB. By May 1999 some change was envisaged to leave the funding through Historic Scotland and Edinburgh City Council. That is what Donald Dewar's speech appears to suggest.

9.45　Subsequent to this debate the source of the funding for the landscaping was the subject of further consideration within the Scottish Executive.[448] In minutes of 29 October 1999[449] and 4 November 1999[450] it was confirmed by the Principal Finance Officer that Ministers had agreed that the costs relating to work in the Park would be met from Historic Scotland's budget and the costs falling on the City Council would be met from the local government programme. The SPCB would accordingly not be responsible for this expenditure. Thus far the position appeared clear.

9.46　On 6 December 1999, however, Mrs Doig provided an estimate of £11 million for the work, inclusive of fees and VAT, but with no allowance for contingencies.[451] By April 2000 the figure under consideration was £13.5 million, including a contingency allowance, but it later transpired that this covered only the works within Holyrood Park. After further correspondence, agreement was reached in September 2000 on a £14.126 million estimate inclusive of fees, VAT and contingencies.[452] While this estimate covered elements that may not be attributable directly to the Project in the truest sense, it did represent a significant sum that was not explicitly presented as a component of the Holyrood Project costs for a considerable period.

9.47　In Mr Spencely's Report on the Project submitted in March 2000 he made the point that certain costs associated with the Project, including landscaping and the costs of the Project Team, were being met from other budgets.[453] The position in relation to the landscaping costs was taken up by some speakers during the second debate on 5 April 2000. Later in that year it was

---

[447] SE/9/066 - Minute from Dr Collings to Mr Elvidge and Mr Mackenzie, 4 November 1999

[448] SE/9/013 – E-mail from Mr Moore to Mr Howison, 27 July 1999; SE/9/030-032 - Minute from Mr Robert Gordon, 2 August 1999; SE/9/026-029 – Note from Mr Moore, 2 Sept 1999; SE/9/036-040 – Paper from Mr Watkins to Mrs Barbara Doig, 28 September 1999; SE/9/045-047 – Minute from Ms Ure to the Principal Finance Officer, 15 October 1999; SE/9/048 – Note from Mr Henderson to the Principal Finance Officer, 22 October 1999

[449] SE/9/049 – Minute from Mr Collings,29 October 1999

[450] SE/9/051 - Minute from Mr Collings to Mr John Elvidge and Mr MacKenzie, 4 November 1999

[451] SE/9/073 – Letter from Mrs Barbara Doig to Mr John Elvidge, 6 December 1999

[452] SE/9/160 – S1W-9874–Written Answer from Tom McCabe to Maureen Macmillan, 17 February 2004

[453] Mr Spencely's Report, Section 4.6.1 'Costs allocated to other budgets'

identified that the piece of land to be landscaped lying to the south of the main Holyrood site, referred to as the Royal High School Playing Fields, had never been formally transferred from Historic Scotland to the SPCB, yet again revealing the informality with which this major project was being taken forward. Not surprisingly, it was observed that the arrangements in relation to landscaping "had not been as transparent as might have been".[454] On 13 February 2001 a proposal was approved by Ministers[455] to transfer the Royal High School Playing Fields and the budget for landscaping from the Scottish Executive to the SPCB. The transfers of both land and budget were effected on 17 October 2001, and confirmed to Parliament by Sir David Steel on 26 October 2001.[456]

9.48 This is a relatively small part of the ultimate budget but it demonstrates an unacceptable set of switches which must have been, at the least, confusing to MSPs. At the time of the critical debate these costs were not included but by the autumn of 2001 they were. Had I been an MSP alive to constituency concerns about ever-rising costs of the new Parliament, I would have been spitting tacks that yet another £14 million had been slipped under my nose with little or no notice.

History of the Project after the June 1999 Debate

9.49 At the SPCB meeting on 29 June 1999 Mrs Doig presented a paper entitled "Holyrood Building – The Way Ahead on Client/End User Relations". It recorded Sir David Steel's commitment following the debate that the SPCB would "take forward the decision openly with maximum consultation and listening to constructive criticism". The paper proposed a reporting structure which was adopted in terms of which the Project Director was to report monthly on:

- 'Programme
- Finance
- Issues Register – matters such as design development, construction progress, project brief and procurement
- Change Control
- Communications.'[457]

9.50 In June 1999 steps were put in hand by Project Management to prepare a Project Execution Plan, of which a draft was issued by Mr Curran on 24 June 1999.[458] For the client, in terms of Treasury Guidance, the Plan is:

---

[454] SE/9/203-205 – Draft Minute from Mr John Elvidge to the First Minister,13 February 2001

[455] SE/9/194-199 - Minute from Mr John Elvidge to the First Minister, 13 February 2001

[456] SE/9/218 –S1W-19135, Written Answer from Sir David Steel to John Home Robertson, 18 February 2000

[457] CB/2/025-031 - SPCB Paper (99) 21 from the Project Team, 29 June 1999

[458] CB/5/004-005 – Letter from Mr Paul Curran to the Project Team, 24 June 1999 and BV/2/013-054 – Draft Project Execution Plan, June 1999

'the key management document governing the project strategy, organisation, control procedures, responsibilities and, where appropriate, the relationship between the project sponsor and the project manager. It is a formal statement of the user needs, project brief and of the strategy agreed with the project manager for their attainment. The scope... will depend on the size and nature of the project. It is a live management document, regularly updated, to be used by all parties both as a means of communication and as a control and performance measurement tool'. [459]

9.51 Preparation of a client Project Execution Plan is a "key responsibility" of the Project Sponsor[460] who must be satisfied that it represents "a viable and realistic plan for implementing the project and achieving its objectives." The Plan was to complement that issued in May by Bovis for its own management and quality control purposes.[461]

9.52 As highlighted in the September 2000 Report of the Auditor General,[462] there was a failure by Project Management to finalise Mr Curran's draft Plan. Evidence produced to the Inquiry reveals that as late as October 2000 this document was only available in the format of a third draft,[463] and in fact I was unable to ascertain conclusively whether a Plan was ever finalised. I endorse the Auditor General's conclusion that the failure to finalise this key document was a significant shortcoming.

Debating Chamber Redesign

9.53 Mrs Doig's paper[464] highlighted the most pressing issue as that of the Debating Chamber in respect of which some MSPs had expressed reservations at the debate and in the course of presentations by the Design Team. These concerns related particularly to its "flat" configuration and the resultant perceived difficulty in establishing eye contact between MSPs during debate.

9.54 As more fully set out in Chapter 5, the requirements for the Chamber had been set out in the draft of the Building User Brief[465] dated November 1998 which had said "A horseshoe or semi-circular arrangement with the Presiding Officer as the focal point would appear to be the most appropriate". By the time of the handover the configuration of the Chamber had been through a number of evolutions culminating in a "flat" curve of relatively long radius. The configuration

---

[459] SE/5/399–420 – HM Treasury Guidance No. 2 Value for Money in Construction Procurement 1997, Page 414, Para A.5.1
[460] *ibid,* Para A.5.2
[461] CB/5/834-978 – Project Execution Plan from Bovis, 7 May 1999
[462] Auditor General for Scotland's Report of September 2000, Paras 3.38 to 3.39
[463] CB/3/387-451 - Project Execution Plan (3rd Draft), October 2000
[464] CB/2/025-031 - SPCB Paper (99) 21 from the Project Team, 29 June 1999 *supra*
[465] SE/7/366–574 – Building User Brief, Section 5.30.3 from Mr William Armstrong, November 1998

of the Chamber could not be described as a horseshoe or semi circle, and to that extent did not accord with the Brief.

9.55 It was suggested in evidence by Mr Stewart that this was simply the way in which the design had evolved and was a reflection of the "less adversarial" politics envisaged for the Parliament.[466] The EMBT/RMJM presentation at the final stage of the designer selection competition in June 1998 had indicated a "flat" chamber. The outline proposals publicly exhibited in October and the Stage C report approved in November 1998 had clearly indicated such a chamber which had, as Mr Stewart put it, been "approved through presentation and informal discussion with the Secretary of State". Dr Gibbons told the Inquiry that "under what he saw as strong political direction" the proposals agreed by Donald Dewar and contained in the Stage C and the Stage D Report in May 1999 had developed to be more akin to lecture room seating. This was in order to avoid the confrontational seating arrangements of the Westminster Parliament.[467] Sra Tagliabue described the design of the Chamber thus:

> "I think it was also a way to making an elongated chamber, providing a totally different Parliament from the Westminster one. I think it was very much appreciated, because it was really the opposite of the Westminster way of debating".

She also said:

> "I believe that the client liked it, and this remained approved. We never received any indication about the necessity of changing it. It was the Chamber that was decided to be built from September 1998 until June 1999."[468]

9.56 The Chamber as designed prior to handover, even if not in strict conformity with the terms of the Brief, nevertheless appears to have been acceptable to Donald Dewar and the Project Team.

9.57 To address MSPs' concerns, the Project Team had prepared for consideration by the SPCB on 29 June 1999 a proposed revision to the Brief in relation to the Chamber.[469] It was decided at that meeting that it would be appropriate to visit the Flemish Parliament in Brussels and the Tweede Kamer, the lower chamber of the bicameral Netherlands Parliament in The Hague. The SPCB members on the visit preferred the shape of the Tweede Kamer.

9.58 The matter was the subject of some debate with Snr Miralles. As Sir David Steel put it:

> "This was a source of some contention between us and Señor Miralles, and we argued about it quite a lot when we were on those visits. I think I can best explain

---

[466] Evidence of Mr Brian Stewart on 11 March 2004 (pm), Para 36 *et seq*
[467] WS/53/001–031 Dr John Gibbons' Third Witness Statement, Para 9, 6 May 2004
[468] Evidence of Sra Benedetta Tagliabue on 29 March 2004, Para 490
[469] CB/2/025–031 – SPCB Paper from the Project Team, 29 June 1999

how he got into this position by saying that when you see the Flanders Parliament, it is fairly typical of the standard European type of Parliament, where Members do not debate in the Chamber; they come out and speak from a podium at the front, and, indeed, Ministers are at the front alongside the Speaker or the Presiding Officer to answer questions from the Members. That is not what we had in the Scottish Parliament; it was not what was ordered from Mr Miralles, but that was what was in his thinking, and that is what he produced in the first drawings."[470]

9.59 Following the visit Snr Miralles wrote to Sir David Steel on 2 August 1999 suggesting that a pure semi circle might not be the best and proposing the "U" shaped end of an ellipse as the starting point saying that:

'A slight, non symmetrical arrangement of this form inside the actual footprint of the chamber will allow us to solve the disabled access and the location of the VIP balcony.' [471]

9.60 At the SPCB meeting on 6 August 1999 there was tabled a report confirming the preference of the MSPs for the semi-circular shape.[472] Snr Miralles was not at that meeting, following which Dr Gibbons wrote to Mr Stewart on 16 August confirming that the "elliptical chamber layout was strongly preferred."[473] After the Client Project Management meeting on 9 August 1999 it was minuted:

'Regarding Debating Chamber design, MDM (a reference to Mr Mustard) reported "no change of footprint" as confirmed at SPCB meeting on 6/8/99.' [474]

9.61 This was evidently not to Snr Miralles' liking and he indicated[475] that his understanding was that the agreement was no more than to keep the "approximate footprint" and he faxed Dr Gibbons saying: "it is impossible to have the exact footprint. Yes, it would be very similar, but with modifications on its external wall".[476] To this, Dr Gibbons replied, confirming that the Presiding Officer was "emphatic" that there should be no changes to the footprint of the Chamber and that it was "too late" to introduce such changes.

9.62 On 30 August 1999 Mrs Doig convened a meeting of the Client Project Team Principals.[477] At that meeting serious concerns were expressed by Mrs Doig about her perception of lack of coordination within the Design Team. Mr Stewart expressed his clear view that, as matters then stood, Project targets would not be achieved. Stage D had not been achieved and

---

[470] Evidence of Sir David Steel on 4 February 2004, Para 359
[471] CB/5/271-273 - Fax from Snr Miralles to Sir David Steel, 2 August 1999
[472] CB/2/035-039 - Report , SPCB Visit to Flemish and Dutch Parliaments, 22 to 23 July 1999
[473] RM/6/071 – Letter from Dr John Gibbons to Mr Brian Stewart, 16 August 1999
[474] CB/3/010-013(R) - Minute of Client Project Management Group Meeting, 9 August 1999
[475] RM/6/092-093 – Faxed Note from Snr Enric Miralles to Mr Brian Stewart, 24 August 1999
[476] RM/6/094-095 – Fax from Snr Enric Miralles to Dr John Gibbons, 24 August 1999
[477] RM/6/045-047 - Minutes from Mrs Barbara Doig of Client Project Team Principals Meeting, 30 August 1999

possible changes to the footprint and layout of the Debating Chamber and to the shapes and geometry of the Towers exacerbated the problem. It was again repeated that the client had not asked for any change to the existing footprint of the Debating Chamber. Mr Stewart confirmed the difficulty of speaking about the design changes to the Chamber and Towers without first securing confirmation from Snr Miralles.

9.63 Two days after the Principals' meeting Snr Miralles faxed the Project Team saying that the Chamber might have "slight changes on geometry (1 or 2 metres)". [478] This produced a sharp response from Mr Stewart giving his view that Snr Miralles' interpretation of the current situation and general view of the status of the Project did not accord with his and noting that he had not actually been in Edinburgh for "several months".[479] He believed that the present position in relation to cost and programme would be unacceptable to the client and that the introduction of further changes would exacerbate that position. Mr Mustard responded by fax re-emphasising that "on no account should the footprint of the Chamber be changed from that previously presented." [480]

9.64 By 6 September 1999 further drawings, including revisions to the Chamber, had emanated from Barcelona. Mr Duncan responded in acerbic terms expressing his views that the latest drawings ignored the SPCB's instruction to develop the design of the Debating Chamber within the existing footprint and that there was "a real crisis looming on cost, programme and credibility of the team".[481]

9.65 Project Team officials had sufficiently serious concerns about the continuing development of designs involving changes to the layout of the Chamber that they reported them to Sir David Steel who, on 8 September, wrote to both Snr Miralles and Mr Stewart[482] stressing that the development of alternative proposals which had implications for the structural framework would be contrary to the instructions of the SPCB which would be unlikely to accept such late substantive changes. He reminded them that there had been no change to the budget of £62 million.

9.66 On 9 September 1999 Mr John Kinsley, Architect with RMJM, expressed his views to Snr Miralles[483] that the current proposals for revising the setting-out geometry of the Assembly Building not only exacerbated an already significant problem of areas but by changing

---

[478] RM/6/085-086 – Letter from Snr Enric Miralles to Mrs Barbara Doig, 1 September 1999

[479] RM/6/083 – Faxed Note from Mr Brian Stewart to Snr Enric Miralles, 1 September 1999

[480] RM/6/080-081 – Faxed Note from Mr Martin Mustard to Snr Enric Miralles, 3 September 1999

[481] RM/6/073 – Letter from Mr Mick Duncan to Snr Enric Miralles, 7 September 1999

[482] CB/2/713-714 – Letter from Sir David Steel to Snr Miralles and Mr Stewart, 8 September 1999

[483] RM/6/056-057 – Letter from Mr John Kinsley to Snr Enric Miralles, 9 September 1999

previously agreed solutions for escape, circulation and planning issues effectively set the Project back some months and required a re-evaluation of those aspects.

9.67 By this time there were two different designs evolving for the Debating Chamber from Edinburgh and Barcelona. Snr Miralles presented his revised proposal for the whole eastern part of the site which further increased the area and "would require change to the structure design".[484] As he had done in correspondence Snr Miralles disputed that he had made significant changes and maintained that he had improved the design. The minute of the meeting of 14 September 1999 confirmed that "the SPCB was clear that the overriding priority was a solution to the Chamber which did not impact on current cost or programme".

9.68 Sir David Steel wrote to the Design Team on 16 September 1999[485] making clear the concerns of the SPCB at the differences that were apparent between EMBT and RMJM and stating the SPCB's view that design effort had been wasted and time lost arising from work on the Chamber and adjacent spaces carried out on the premise that the footprint of the building could be altered contrary to instructions. His letter formally instructed EMBT/RMJM Ltd to proceed to develop designs on the basis of the drawings submitted on 16 July 1999.

9.69 Design work on the Chamber continued into the autumn but the design priority moved towards the MSP block and Queensberry House, on the basis of an east to west construction plan. On 27 October it was reported that the Assembly building drawings did not contain sufficient detail for Ove Arup to progress further design development.[486] Increasing demands for extra space led to the Design Team being instructed on 17 November 1999[487] to carry out a "feasibility study" to identify a further $2,275m^2$ of extra space. From that time development of the Chamber design was in abeyance pending the outcome of the feasibility study.[488] The outcome of the feasibility study in February 2000 necessitated changes to the geometry of the Assembly building and provided substantial increases in space.

9.70 This analysis is deliberately detailed to demonstrate how over the summer and autumn of 1999, and in relation to the revisions to the design of the Chamber, the constituent parts of EMBT/RMJM Ltd appeared to be operating in a dysfunctional way. Snr Miralles appears to have been primarily motivated by the desire to insist on his design, disregarding the clear instructions from the SPCB and the Project Team to accommodate the required changes to the Chamber within the existing footprint. His joint venture partners seemed to have had a far

[484] CB/2/079A-C - Minutes of SPCB Meeting of 14 September 1999
[485] RM/6/027-028 – Letter from Sir David Steel to Snr Miralles and Mr Stewart, 16 September 1999
[486] CB/3/025A-D - Minutes of Client Project Team / Principals Meeting of 27 October 1999
[487] RM/1/116-120 – Letter from Mrs Barbara Doig to Snr Miralles and Mr Stewart, 17 November 1999
[488] CB/3/054-057 - Minutes of Client Project Management Group Meeting of 10 April 2000.

clearer understanding of these instructions. Much design time was wasted and significant management time was expended on the issue of the Chamber design. It is quite evident to me that Snr Miralles, as "the Principal Person", had failed to appreciate that "instruction" meant just that, and he had failed to work out with RMJM a method of working which was harmonious and productive. In short, the joint venture was a misnomer; in reality the picture discloses two teams, separated by geography, working in quite different ways. The consequence is that the overall performance of the Architect fell below what could reasonably have been expected.

9.71   Overall and because of the extent of the wider redesign which emerged in early 2000 I do not consider that the problems with the shape of the Chamber had a major impact on either cost or programme. However, this time-consuming saga does not reflect well on the progress of the Project. Sir David Steel and others may have been exasperated by Snr Miralles' approach, but in the end they capitulated with only an occasional murmur of dissent.

Increased Space Requirements and Budget

9.72   While the redesign of the Chamber had been identified as perhaps the most pressing problem with the Project in the immediate post handover period, it was far from being the only issue. Leaving aside Queensberry House, which is the subject of Chapter 13, demands for increased space and pressures on programme and budget soon began to emerge. It is outwith the scope of this Inquiry to carry out a minute examination of how these matters developed but it is important to have a general understanding

9.73   Over the relatively short period with which this chapter is concerned design changes resulting mainly from the demands of the new Parliament for additional accommodation were charted by Mr Spencely in his Report, on the basis of DLE's figures, as follows:[489]

	25 May 1999 (i.e. at handover)	30 August 1999	27 September 1999	14 February 2000
Gross area ex car park	23,214	27,329 (+ 4,115)	27,329 (-)	29,579 (+ 2,250)
Car park	3,867	3,792 (- 75)	3,792 (-)	1,731 (- 2,061)
Total gross area	**27,081**	**31,121 (+ 4,040)**	**31,121 (-)**	**31,310 (+ 189)**

All areas expressed as m².

9.74   An issue which was considered during the Inquiry was whether a satisfactory explanation could be found for the increase of approximately 4,000m² identified in August 1999. This was the

---

[489] Mr Spencely's Report, Section 4.2 'The basic construction cost'

subject of comment in the Auditor General's Report[490] in which he said that the Architect had informed the Project Team of this increase "without being able immediately to identify why". Documentary evidence before the Inquiry suggests that this increase in area first came to light on 18 August 1999 in a fax from Mr Duncan to Snr Miralles.[491] Mr Duncan advised that an area check on the latest set of drawings had revealed an increase of $3,815m^2$ since the May 1999 Stage D drawings. Mr Duncan's analysis of the increase was as follows:

Basement	1,693 m^2	"The client has accepted this increase as a consequence of the detailed design of plant space, its integration with complex plan forms and structural constraints and the needs of access for plant replacement. There have also been minor Brief increases (e.g. detention cell) considerable design work and re-planning was carried out in this part of the building to reduce area."
MSP building	581 m^2	"The area increase here is attributable by far the greater part to the need to incorporate full fire fighting cores in the building. There have also been minor increases in Brief area (meeting rooms at garden level)."
Assembly building (above ground)	1,541 m^2	"It would appear that the area increase here has been as a result of design development and meeting net area arrangements. We are currently in the process of undertaking a detailed net and gross comparison to determine where increases have occurred...."

Mr Duncan went on: "Obviously, an area increase of such magnitude will have a considerable impact on cost."

9.75   The 'discovery' of this additional area was reported to the Client Project Management meeting on 23 August 1999 the minute of which recorded:

> 'EMBT/RMJM reported various problems coming to light. There were increases to areas, as a result of the latest EMBT/RMJM revision, in the balance areas of the assembly building and in the public accommodation at the garden level. The total increase was $3,815m^2$ over the previously reported figures. ..The total gross area, excluding the foyer, was now $26,400m^2$. EMBT/RMJM was checking for any areas (that) could be reduced and a response was due on 27/8/99. (Mr Mustard) said there were major cost and budget implications which he would have to discuss with Mrs Doig....'.[492]

9.76   The 'discovery' was the subject of evidence by Mr Grice to the Audit Committee of the Scottish Parliament on 3 October 2000 when he said:

[490] Auditor General for Scotland's Report of September 2000, Para 2.27
[491] RM/4/071-072 – Fax from Mr Mick Duncan to Snr Enric Miralles, 18 August 1999
[492] CB/3/013A-015(R) – Minutes of Client Project Management Group Meeting of 23 August 1999, Item 3.3

"The issue over the 4,000m^2 emerged over the summer—in other words, after we had taken over the Project. It came first from the Design Team—that is, it was not instructed."[493]

In later correspondence with Mr Stewart, Mr Grice clarified what he meant by the expression "not instructed" and said:

'I was referring to the fact that we the client, had not specifically asked for additional space, as we did in November 1999 and which led to the subsequent feasibility study. The origin of and the reasons for the additional space were not therefore clear to me at the time the DLE cost check was produced and, for that reason, the cost check was not regarded as reliable. It did become clear, once the Holyrood Project Team and the Design Team considered the matter in detail, that the additional 4,000m^2 could largely be attributed to the natural evolution of the design, for example, in accommodating plant room etc.'[494]

9.77 Mr Mustard later recorded the disclosure of this additional area as a "bombshell.".[495] A more detailed analysis of the additional 3,815m^2 is to be found in a draft submission prepared by Mr David Miller, of EMBT/RMJM Ltd, on 27 August 1999.[496] If the letter from Mr Duncan and the draft report from Mr Miller are to be relied upon, the bulk of the increase was represented by increased circulation space. This represented a further increase over and above the provision for increased circulation space to a realistic level of some 35%, which was put forward as one of the justifications for the increase in the construction cost budget approved at the time of handover. The issue of the additional 4,000m^2 was discussed at the meeting of Principals on 30 August 1999.[497] Mrs Doig's position at that meeting was to repeat that there had been no changes to the approved area of 23,000m^2.

9.78 That a hitherto unforeseen increase in space of this order of magnitude, representing some 17% of the gross area of the building, excluding the car parking, could have "emerged" as a consequence of the "natural evolution of the design" seems to me to be extraordinary. It has to be strongly suggestive of a disregard by the Architect of the constraints of Brief and budget to which they were supposed to be designing.

9.79 It was agreed at the meeting on 30 August 1999 that the Project Manager, Mr Mustard, was to hold bilateral meetings immediately with the key players to discuss the crucial areas of programme area and costs. He was to report back with options and his recommendations on how to address the problems.[498] Mrs Doig, Dr Gibbons and Mr Mustard met Mr Grice on 7

---

[493] Scottish Parliament Audit Committee Report, 3 October 2000, Column 379

[494] RM/4/130-132 – Letter from Mr Paul Grice to Mr Brian Stewart, 16 November 2000

[495] CB/6/019-023 – Report from Mr Martin Mustard to Mrs Barbara Doig, 26 August 1999

[496] RM/4/081-083 – EMBT/RMJM Draft Submission, 27 August 1999

[497] CB/6/010-018 - Project Team Report from Mr Mustard to Mrs Doig, 17 July 1999 - 24 August 1999

[498] CB/3/015-017 - Minutes of Client Project Team / Principals Meeting, 30 August 1999, Item 14

September 1999 when it was agreed that a Value Engineering exercise would be put in hand. The report of this exercise became available in November 1999 and coincided with a requirement by the Parliament for further space.

9.80   The "budget" inherited by the SPCB was predicated on a construction cost of £62 million at March 1998 prices. As the design developed in the post-handover period, DLE's cost reports produced **construction cost** figures as follows:

Date	Construction Cost
30 August 1999	£115,712,463
27 September 1999	£115,383,697
14 February 2000	£138,495,192

DLE produced their Feasibility Estimate No 9 for the Principals' meeting on 30 August 1999.[499] Taking account of the additional 4,000m² it produced an estimated construction cost of £115.7 million,[500] exceeding the existing £62 million construction cost budget by some 86%. Mr Fisher advised that if the space area could be brought back to 23,000m² there should be a saving of £15 million on that figure. Mrs Doig's position at that meeting was yet again to repeat that there had been no changes to the £62 million budget or to the approved area of 23,000m².

State of the Project in August 1999

9.81   As can be seen from the previous paragraphs, by this time the building was very significantly over area and over budget. Mr Mustard was the author of two papers from that time, both of which are remarkable for the clarity of their insight into the state of the Project at that time. The first was his confidential paper "A Health of the Project Report as at 26 August 1999"[501] which he prepared for the Principals' meeting on 30 August. The second was his Review of the Project produced after the Principals' meeting.

9.82   Mr Mustard's Health of the Project Report revealed his concern at the "us and them" attitude prevailing between the Edinburgh and Barcelona ends of EMBT/RMJM Ltd, instancing the growing habit of the Edinburgh-based staff referring to themselves as "RMJM" and purposely distancing themselves from the work of their Barcelona partners. His opinion was that the architectural service being provided was "not acceptable" and instanced:

- The unexpected requirement for additional space;
- Delay of some 5 months in completion of Stage D, which he regarded as "caused by the Architect" and "only partially due to re-examination of the chamber layout by the SPCB." He noted, correctly in my view, that the failure to complete Stage

---

[499] DL/1/128-131 - DLE Feasibility Estimate from Mr McAndie to Mrs Doig, 30 August 1999
[500] DL/1/008-012 – DLE Timeline: Development of Costs, October 1998 to August 2000
[501] CB/6/019–023 – Report from Mr Martin Mustard to Mrs Barbara Doig, 26 August 1999

D denied the Project a baseline against which to operate an effective change control system;

- Continued failure by EMBT/RMJM to meet design target dates for individual packages; and
- Constant design "tweaking".

9.83 Mr Mustard regarded it as essential that a "full elemental and package cost plan" be established and that the question of budget be addressed and secured. He said that Design Team morale was "non-existent" due, in his opinion, to lack of true leadership and lack of Architect consultation over design development and change. He felt that the role of Project Management was hampered by the fact that Snr Miralles and Mr Stewart had direct access to Dr Gibbons and Mrs Doig, as well as to Sir David Steel, which undermined his own position.

9.84 Recognising that the political situation limited the options in attempting to regain control of the Project he said that "In any other project (he) would be recommending termination of EMBT/RMJM's contract". If that was not an option "then all other measures will merely be damage limitation exercises" but should include:

- 'Getting tough on fees until EMBT/RMJM agree to sign up to programme"
- "Purposely halt(ing) the project whilst cost, programme and management issues (including ...completion date) are fully resolved'.

Mr Mustard expressed his "very serious doubts" as to whether the Project could be delivered within time and cost parameters.

9.85 Mr Mustard's second report was completed after a review process undertaken in conjunction with Mr Curran and Mr William Heigh of the Project Team. Produced on 6 September 1999, the Review examined a number of key areas of the Project and came to some forthright conclusions.[502] It highlighted that the additional 4,000m² of area remained unacceptable and unexplained,[503] that the Stage D report was five months overdue and was having a "severe and direct" impact on the overall construction programme. It also reported the Bovis view that the construction programme was four months delayed against the critical path.

9.86 The Review also drew attention to the fact that DLE's most recent construction cost estimate was in the region of £115 million as compared with their May 1999 estimate of £89 million, both inclusive of risk. The £115 million figure was regarded as "completely unacceptable". It was pointed out that the DLE estimate had not been developed to a detailed cost plan format for each of the buildings, which limited its usefulness for value management purposes. It is noteworthy that the Review takes on the DLE May 1999 figure of £89 million rather than the

---

[502] CB/6/024–039 - Project Review Final Report from Mr Mustard to Mrs Doig, 6 September 1999
[503] *ibid*, Paras 2.2.4 to 2.3- tend to confirm that Mr Miller's paper had not been produced

"budget figure" of £62 million. I cannot avoid the conclusion that the Project Team had never bought into the budget figure of £62 million and always regarded £89 million as a more realistic construction cost figure.

9.87 With regard to procurement, Mr Mustard's Review identified that the Bovis programme dates had "rarely been achieved by the Design Team" and said:

> 'As a result of insufficient design information being made available to Trade Contractors significant costs are now being incurred. This is due to design changes, disruption, standing time and lack of continuity for the initial packages which have been let.'[504]

The Review concluded that the current programme was unachievable and was giving rise to unacceptable levels of risk. (It should be noted that at this time only four of the trade packages having architectural input were programmed to have been released for either construction or tender.)

9.88 In relation to design, the Review noted that the absence of a sufficiently detailed Stage D report, meeting the terms of the Brief, meant that there was no baseline from which to monitor and record change. There were problems with lack of design co-ordination exemplified by the fact that there were two designs for the Chamber circulating within the Design Team, giving rise to obvious confusion. There was a lack of Design Team leadership resulting in a lack of direction and loss of morale caused by the level of abortive work and lack of decisions. Co-operation between Edinburgh and Barcelona remained poor due in part to the fee dispute, and the difficulties were "impacting directly on the Project". The Review highlighted the rift within the architectural joint venture and explored at some length the option of terminating EMBT/RMJM Ltd's contract. A conclusion was reached, however, that the contractual cost, surrender of creative input/understanding, lack of confidence in RMJM alone and negative political reactions militated against doing so.

9.89 In relation to Project Management the Review referred to the considerable confusion within the Design Team on communication routes with the client. Traditionally the Project Manager acts as the focal point for such communications enabling him to "filter the information reaching project sponsor level". In this Project, Mr Mustard felt that a "considerable amount of knowledge on key decisions had been imparted to senior members of the Design Team without the involvement of the Project Manager, resulting in confusion". It was felt by him that there was a general disregard by EMBT/RMJM Ltd for instructions issued by the Project Manager, arising from their direct links to the client.

---

[504] *ibid*, Para 5.3.3

9.90   The Review made a raft of detailed and highly focused recommendations intended to retrieve the gloomy position but concluded with the prescient comment:

> 'The Recommendations set out ....require to be implemented as a matter of urgency. If these measures are not put in place the Project faces considerable delays with time becoming at large, costs spiralling out of control and no guarantees on the quality of the final product'.

9.91   This Review was perceptive; indeed it was a damning indictment of practically everything that was wrong with the Project at that time. The fact that Mr Curran, who was an impressive witness before the Inquiry, was a co-author of the Review lends stature to it. Mr Mustard's work represented the first systematic attempt by Project Management to identify the problems and the steps necessary to resolve them. As I accept that his Review was essentially accurate, the inevitable conclusion has to be that the Project was in danger of running out of control as early as August 1999.

9.92   The factors leading to that conclusion are rooted in the state of the Project at handover exacerbated by subsequent problems with the Chamber and lack of control by the Architect. The budget was seriously out of kilter with such cost estimates as were available and whatever actions were being taken to narrow that gap were subsequently unsuccessful. Mr Mustard regarded the position as recoverable, notwithstanding his damning indictment. I can only conclude that he was hoping against hope as was Mr Spencely some six months later.

The Aftermath of the Project Review

9.93   On 7 September 1999 Mr Mustard met with Mr Grice, Mr Stewart Gilfillan, Financial Controller, Mrs Doig and Dr Gibbons to discuss his report, which resulted in the preparation of an implementation plan dated 8 September 1999 identifying three areas for action as follows:

> **"Budget/Cost Plan**
>
> - Review risks and translate to real costs; establish updated risk profile.
> - Substantiate cost estimate reconciliation with let packages and current overrun.
> - Develop with suitable input from the Design Team detailed cost plans for the MSP building, Queensberry House and the east side of the site to form the basis for the proposed VE exercise.
>
> **Value Engineering**
>
> - A whole site Value Engineering exercise to be carried out to identify savings of £26 million to include identification of the benefits of extending the programme.
>
> **Programme**
>
> - To allow the development of a meaningful programme the SPCB required to take a decision on the required completion date.

- The design programme must be agreed and signed up to by all members of the Design Team".[505]

Subsequent events reveal that this implementation plan did not achieve the anticipated result.

Design Team Issues

9.94 Sir David Steel's letter of 16 September 1999[506] to both Snr Miralles and Mr Stewart about Chamber redesign pointed out that, as the Project moved into its construction phase, there would, as envisaged at the presentation to the designer selection panel, be changes within the joint venture. The lead would transfer from EMBT to RMJM. He made it clear that the current situation could not continue and invited their proposals. Snr Miralles replied confirming that RMJM would have a higher profile during the construction phase, but reminding Sir David Steel that he personally was the "Principal Person" in terms of the Architect's Memorandum of Appointment.[507] He would be personally responsible for decisions affecting the design of the building but he would do his best to prevent the recurrence of differences within the team.

9.95 Mr Stewart responded separately, conveying RMJM's position in relation to the status of the Project. He said:

"I regret to inform you that ... I cannot at this critical point give the assurances you are seeking with regard to achieving the objectives, now or in the future, on the key parameters of programme and budget. ... I am of course very exercised about the present position and agree that the current situation cannot continue. I would welcome the opportunity to consult with your officials on implementation management issues."[508]

9.96 On 23 September 1999[509] Sir David Steel wrote to both expressing his surprise at having received separate replies and his disappointment at the apparent absence of collaboration. Meetings were arranged with EMBT and RMJM to explore how the client's needs could be met following which Snr Miralles and Mr Stewart wrote a joint letter to Sir David Steel on 4 October 1999.[510] The letter stated that agreement had been reached in relation to the division of fees. More importantly, agreement had been reached that Snr Miralles would continue to have overall responsibility for the design and Mr Stewart would have responsibility for execution and delivery. The letter was accompanied by a structure chart[511] and a list of EMBT/RMJM Ltd's

---

[505] DL/4/015-021 – Letter from Mr Ian McAndie to Mr Michael Dallas, 9 September 1999
[506] CB/2/079D-E – Letter from Sir David Steel to Snr Miralles and Mr Stewart, 16 September 1999
[507] CB/2/719- – Letter from Snr Enric Miralles to Sir David Steel, 20 September 1999
[508] CB/2/720 – Letter from Mr Brian Stewart to Sir David Steel, 22 September 1999
[509] CB/2/722 - Letter from Sir David Steel to Mr Stewart and Snr Miralles, 23 September 1999.
[510] CB/2/723-725 – Letter from Snr Miralles and Mr Stewart to Sir David Steel, 4 October 1999
[511] ibid

short term programme actions. At that stage it appeared as though the divisions within the Architectural Team had been resolved.

9.97 The Inquiry had no evidence of further significant divisions until after the death of Snr Miralles in July 2000. To support the view that the team started to work better is the fact that the feasibility study instructed in November 1999 produced relatively quickly a lasting architectural solution to the requirement for additional space. On the other hand design delay remained an issue at this time, as it did throughout the Project.

Reporting of Costs to the SPCB

9.98 At its meeting on 14 September 1999 the SPCB considered a report on the latest position from Mrs Doig. The report referred to the additional $4,000m^2$ and the steps being taken to identify the reasons for this; the fact that there was slippage of 4 months on programme; and the steps being taken to resolve other difficulties with the Project. In relation to cost estimates the report said without further elaboration: "The latest cost estimates and risk allowances …are unacceptable".[512] This was at a time when DLE were reporting a construction cost including risk of £115.7 million.

9.99 The decision to report the costs in these terms without giving a figure was taken at a meeting between Mrs Doig and Mr Grice. When asked about the decision not to give any actual figure to the SPCB Mr Grice said:

> "I had to take a judgment here and the judgment I took was that the SPCB should be left in no doubt that there were significant problems. I took a judgment, and it was my judgment that the £115 million figure was unreliable at that stage."[513]

9.100 This decision was the subject of consideration by the Audit Committee of the Scottish Parliament, to which Mr Grice gave evidence in October 2000. In their subsequent report the Audit Committee concluded:

> 'We disagree with the judgments taken by the Clerk and Chief Executive of the Scottish Parliament, once he became the Accountable Officer, not to inform the SPCB of the Cost Consultants' estimate in August 1999 that construction costs could reach £115 million. The SPCB was entitled to receive all relevant information and it is unacceptable that this information was withheld from that body.'[514]

9.101 In later evidence to the Inquiry Mr Grice accepted the criticism of his judgment:

> "My clear judgment was that I was not prepared to put forward to the Corporate Body figures in which I had no confidence, and so I asked for the Project Sponsor and her

---

[512] CB/2/081-091 – Project Team Progress Report to the SPCB, September 1999, Paper SPCN(HB) (99) 6
[513] Evidence of Mr Paul Grice on 10 February 2004, Para 350
[514] Scottish Parliament Audit Committee - 6th Report 2000 – 'The New Scottish Parliament Building'

team to produce such figures so that I could then report to the Corporate Body. Subsequent to that, both the Audit Committee and the Corporate Body felt that whilst they approved of all the action I took, that I should have reported to them, and I think I have to put my hand up and accept I therefore took the wrong judgment at that point in time." [515]

9.102 Mr Grice cannot avoid the earlier criticism for lack of openness with the SPCB. He may have been right in concluding that the estimate before him was one in which he had no confidence but the consequence of that was that he left the MSPs on the SPCB with a serious under-estimation of likely overall costs. As Sir David Steel indicated in evidence, had the SPCB been provided with DLE's figures at that stage they might have instructed 'the Spencely process' earlier.[516]

9.103 Prior to the next meeting of the SPCB on 28 September, Dr Gibbons and Mrs Doig held several meetings with EMBT/RMJM Ltd in Edinburgh as they tried to establish better internal organisation and management structures. Dr Gibbons and Mrs Doig also considered ways to strengthen the Project Team's internal organisation and the Project Manager's links with all professional appointments. Mr Grice and Mrs Doig briefed the SPCB on 28 September 1999, after which it agreed to increase the frequency of its meetings and requested a critical path plan of when SPCB decisions would be required.[517] [518]

9.104 In the light of that request Mr Grice, Mrs Doig and Dr Gibbons met on 6 October to consider the future arrangements for taking forward the Project, which were set out in a minute from Mr Grice of 7 October 1999.[519] It was agreed at official level that the Project would be steered by the three of them along with Mr Gilfillan. They would meet weekly in advance of the SPCB meeting. In relation to Project Management they agreed that Mr Mustard would report on professional matters to Dr Gibbons, who was to be available to the Project for up to 90% of his time, and that a new person with an architectural background would be brought in to assist Mr Mustard.

9.105 Mr Grice's minute further records Dr Gibbons' report that cordial relations had been established between the two parts of the architectural joint venture and that good progress was expected from them over the coming months. He had assumed a "position of informal arbitrator" and expressed the hope that he would not be required in this capacity too often.

---

[515] Evidence of Mr Paul Grice on 10 February 2004, Para 381
[516] Evidence of Sir David Steel on 4 February 2004, Para 531-534
[517] CB/2/092-093 - Minutes of SPCB Meeting of 28 September 1999
[518] WS/34/001–034 - Mrs Doig's Second Witness Statement, 12 February 2004
[519] CB/5/283 – Minute from Mr Paul Grice to Mrs Doig and Dr Gibbons, 7 October 1999

9.106 At its next meeting at which the Project was considered on 9 November 1999, the SPCB had before it the paper on its own client responsibilities for the Project.[520] It set those out in a coherent format for the first time. The SPCB also had before it a progress report[521] which reported on the position with the Value Engineering exercise and on the emergence of yet further requirements for space. Members expressed their belief that "the building had to be "right" for its purpose, even if that ultimately required the timetable to be extended a little".[522]

Value Engineering

9.107 One of the actions decided upon, following the Project Review in early September 1999, was the carrying out of a Value Engineering exercise. Value Engineering has been defined as follows:

> 'Value engineering is a process usually undertaken at key stages in the development of a project's design to determine whether the major elements of the design provide value in relation to their costs, whether a different approach might offer a better value, and whether the value from the design could be increased within existing costs. To provide an independent fresh view it may be undertaken in conjunction with a team not directly involved in the project.'[523]

9.108 As pointed out by the Auditor General in his September 2000 Report Value Engineering should have been more formally integrated into the process of design.[524] A Value Engineering exercise under the auspices of DLE's Mr Michael Dallas, a specialist in value management, had been arranged provisionally for 4 March 1999 but was cancelled by the Project Team.[525] As Mr Fisher put it in evidence, at that time "the design was moving in a way that was not being influenced by value assessment. In other words, it was too late in the process for the perfect use of the procedure". A workshop did take place on 6 July, the results of which were recorded by DLE.[526] That workshop was ineffective in that none of the agreed actions were in fact implemented as intended before the Design Team meting on 11 August 1999.

9.109 A further "Design and Cost Review Workshop" was arranged for 29 September 1999 to which an invitation was sent out by DLE advising that:

> 'The purpose of the review is to generate graded proposals that could reduce the capital costs of the scheme by up to 25% without reducing quality unacceptably.

---

[520] CB/2/098– 115 – Paper from the Project Team to the SPCB, 9 November 1999
[521] CB/2/116-133 – Progress Report from the Project Team to the SPCB, 9 November 1999
[522] CB/2/143–145 - Minutes of SPCB Meeting of 9 November 1999
[523] Auditor General for Scotland's Report of September 2000, Glossary
[524] Auditor General for Scotland's Report of September 2000, Paras 3.44 and 3.45
[525] DL/4/004 – Fax from Mr Jim Fairclough to the Holyrood Building Project Team, 3 March 1999
[526] DL/4/012–13 - Fax from Mr Michael Dallas to Mr John Kinsley, 4 August 1999

Proposals will be graded to reflect the level of their acceptability to the stakeholders.'[527]

As Mr Fisher put it the declared intention of securing a defined level of saving "makes it very much more a cost-cutting exercise rather than a true value exercise".

9.110 After the workshop Mr McAndie met with Messrs Mustard and Curran on 19 October 1999 and with the Design Team in Barcelona on 20 October 1999 following which he wrote a file note, in which he recorded:

'The elemental cost plan on which the VE was based, i.e. Issue 9A,[528] has been copied to all disciplines. It totals £115 million. I am instructed to tell Enric et al that this figure must reduce to around £62 million for base build cost: - Or the Project may be suspended or cancelled.'[529]

9.111 In relation to this note the following interchange took place between Counsel to the Inquiry and Mr Fisher:

"**Mr Campbell QC:** Just help me to understand that; was that an instruction going out to cut construction costs from £115 million to £62 million?

Mr Fisher: That is certainly how it reads, and it will no doubt be reflective of the message that was conveyed to Mr McAndie at that meeting...... It was, however, a suggestion that provoked considerable ire and irritation amongst the designers, and there was a lot of correspondence between the Architect and the client in relation to the total impossibility of such a move.

Mr Campbell QC: So, was the luckless Mr McAndie the messenger from the client to the designers?

Mr Fisher: In that particular case, he was.

.....

Mr Fisher: I think it is probably an attempt by him to highlight that the client was claiming to be serious about the necessity to reduce costs in this way. It is not one, I think, that was intended to suggest that suspension or cancellation was something that had been seriously considered, because to our knowledge it has not been during the life of the project. Or if it has, we have not been party to those discussions."[530]

9.112 The position of EMBT/RMJM Ltd at this time was expressed in a letter of 20 October 1999[531] to Mrs Doig asserting that the DLE feasibility estimate given to them during the course of the Value Engineering exercise was the first such estimate they had received since inception. This

---

[527] DL/4/015-021 – Letter from Mr Ian McAndie to Mr Michael Dallas, 9 September 1999
[528] DL/1/135 – Letter from Mr Ian McAndie to Mr Brian Stewart, 27 September 1999
[529] DL/4/024 – Mr Ian McAndie's Notes of Meetings on 19 and 20 October
[530] Evidence of Mr Hugh Fisher on 10 February 2004, Paras 582 to 593
[531] DL/4/025 – Letter from EMBT/RMJM to Mrs Barbara Doig, 20 October 1999

was confirmed by Mr Stewart in his evidence.[532] The letter also reported that they had been informed that the budget figure of £62 million was "inviolate" and that they had been instructed to make amendments to design by 3 November to reflect this figure. They said:

'We have to inform you that it is quite impossible to adapt the current project to achieve a reduction of £53,000,000. If a budget of £62,000,000 is to be attained it will be necessary to completely reassess the Brief and the current design in totality. Under the circumstances we do not believe that much of the work executed to date can be retained. We are very disturbed that direction of this nature should come at this time, and in this way particularly in view of the enormity of the impact that this instruction will have on the nature of the Project and on the programme.'

9.113   It is surprising to me that the Architect should claim such apparent astonishment at the news that their design had been costed at £53 million over the budget. Their professional experience should have given them more than an inkling of the likely construction cost of their design as it was developing. Indeed, Mr Duncan wrote on 1 September 1999 pointing out Mr Stewart's opinion at a Project Team meeting that the 'currently declared budget of £62 million was inadequate and...created an extremely serious situation'.[533] Equally, there can be no denying that the client had been making it abundantly clear since their appointment that there was a budget to which the Project had to be delivered. It is not credible that the construction cost figure of £115 million reported by DLE came as a bolt from the blue to the Architect and the client's reaction must have been equally predictable.

9.114   The Value Engineering exercise had identified several hundred recommendations, the vast majority of which could be dealt with by the Project Team. Some of the potential savings requiring a high level decision by the SPCB were discussed at its meetings on 9 November[534] and 16 November 1999[535] and their decisions were communicated by Mrs Doig to the Design Team on 17 November 1999.[536] In February 2000 Mr McAndie produced a paper setting out the actual savings resulting from the exercise.[537] An indication of the items discussed at SPCB level with the DLE assessment of the resultant savings can be tabulated as follows:

[532] WS/42/001–020 – Mr Brian Stewart's First Witness Statement, 11 March 2004, Para 49

[533] RM/6/082 - Letter from Mr Duncan to Mr McGarry, 1 September 1999

[534] CB/2/116–133 - Progress Report from the Project Team to the SPCB, 9 November 1999 and CB/2/143-145 - Minutes of SPCB Meeting of 9 November 1999

[535] CB/2/646-654 – Paper from the Project Team to the SPCB, 16 November 1999 and CB/2/148-149 - Minutes of SPCB Meeting of 16 November 1999

[536] DL/4/035-039 – Letter from Mrs Barbara Doig to Snr Miralles and Mr Stewart, 17 November 1999

[537] DL/4/048-053 - Design and Cost Review from Mr McAndie to Mr Mustard, 10 February 2000

Item	Potential Saving	Decision of the SPCB	Actual Saving[538]
Reduce car parking provision from 129 to 50	£750,000-£1,500,000	Reduce to 65 spaces	£667,000
Convert MSP researcher offices to open plan	£725,000	Remove corridor partitions but ensure flexibility for future reinstatement	£200,000
Review security segregation and reduce lift and stairwell provision in chamber complex	£1,000,000	Agreed to adopt non-segregated approach for public and MSPs in committee room areas thereby removing one staircase and one lift	£1,159,750
Combine press conference facility with another facility	£1,000,000	Press conference room to be retained but to be flexible for other use	-
Delete wash hand basins in MSP rooms	£210,000	Agreed to be deleted	£209,160
Omit fitness suite & changing areas	£170,000	Retain but relocate from MSP block if required	-
Rationalise Bar/lounge/restaurant	In excess of £1m	Maintain existing provision	-
Review of smoking provision	£10,000	Reduce briefed provision to one smoking room in each building	-
Omit nursery provision	£700,000	Retain nursery provision	-
Reduce standard of media accommodation fit out	£235,000	Agreed	£236,140

9.115   In written evidence to the Inquiry Mr Fisher presented a further assessment of the potential and actual savings that had been identified as a result of the Value Engineering exercise. He offered the following figures (all at November 1999 prices):

1. Maximum value of **potential savings** identified at Workshop

   £20,362,600

2. Maximum value of **achievable savings** identified at Workshop

   £13,288,063

3. Value of **savings delivered** (by client decision)

   - Building Works   £ 1,543,567
   - Landscaping   £ 1,204,352
   £ 2,747,919[539]

9.116   In his letter to the Inquiry of 24 May 2004 Mr Dave Ferguson, Audit Adviser to the Scottish Parliament, gave his view that the client had instructed savings of some £13.3 million but

---

[538] *ibid*

[539] MS/15/009A-B - Letter from Mr Hugh Fisher to the Holyrood Inquiry, 25 February 2004

"accepts that these were not completely achieved because of the design feasibility study commissioned subsequently".[540]

9.117 While there may be some uncertainty about the precise extent to which savings were realised as a direct result of the exercise, there can be no doubt that the exercise failed miserably to achieve its stated goal of achieving a £25 million reduction in the construction cost of the Project. The workshop never identified achievable savings of the magnitude required to make a significant impact on the estimated overspend, and when faced with the cold reality of decisions that would have a direct impact upon the quality of the building, the client seems to have taken an approach which did not face up to the reality of their predicament. To some extent the Value Engineering exercise could be interpreted as a knee-jerk reaction to a budgetary crisis. In the event, the exercise rather ran out of steam and it was largely overtaken by the subsequent feasibility study.

Feasibility Study

9.118 Over the summer of 1999 requirements for additional personnel and space had emerged in the light of experience of the new Parliament's actual working arrangements. In terms of a paper submitted to the SPCB's meeting on 9 November 1999[541] it had been identified that extra space was required for an additional 88 Parliament staff and a further 77 Ministerial and Party support staff. Further space was also required for ICT equipment and for mailroom facilities. The identified requirement for additional space was some 2,000m² gross. When the matter again came before the SPCB on 16 November Mr Grice reported that further requests and projections for extra space had surfaced and it was agreed that a contingency element should be added taking the additional space requirement previously identified up to 2,275m² on the basis of a grossed up requirement for net additional space of 1,684.5m². It was regrettable that no-one appears to have been aware that the correct approach would have been to deduct the 35% balance area from the gross figure rather than to add it to the net as both Mrs Doig and Mr Grice had done.[542] To produce an additional net 1,684m² the gross requirement should have been for 2,591m² rather than 2,275m².

9.119 As instructed by the SPCB, Mrs Doig's letter of 17 November to Snr Miralles and Mr Stewart requested them to conduct "feasibility design work to establish how these requirements might be met within the current building line and/or within the site perimeter as defined in the NOPD

---

[540] CB/5/1068–1070 – Letter from Mr Dave Ferguson to the Holyrood Inquiry, 24 May 2004
[541] CB/2/116-133 – Progress Report from the Project Team to the SPCB, 9 November 1999
[542] Evidence of Mr Hugh Fisher on 15 December 2003, para 486 *et seq*

acceptance by the City of Edinburgh Council".[543]   Nothing was said in the letter about the additional fees which would be incurred in carrying out the feasibility study.

9.120   Mr Stewart told the Inquiry that by mid December 1999 the feasibility study was well underway[544] and at meetings with the client in Barcelona on 14 and 15 December 1999, the plan re-organisation was presented and agreed. It involved significant changes, including the re-orientation of the Chamber and towers, and a major change to the circulation arrangements. Previously, the circulation route from the MSP building to the Chamber complex had been through the enfilade on the south side of Queensberry House which had been agreed with Historic Scotland, despite unease at the proposed removal of historic fabric to enlarge existing openings. The new proposal was for this circulation to be through what is now known as the "Foyer" to be built in the former garden area to the south of Queensberry House.

9.121   The feasibility study was refined and was first presented to the SPCB on 1 February 2000[545] when it was noted that the proposals then equated to RIBA Stage C. Mr Stewart confirmed that the study had in fact identified a further 3,000m² of 'suitable' space which allowed for future expansion and took the gross area of the building to 30,800m². While this represented a significant increase he believed it offered a better and more cohesive use of the available area. The SPCB instructed the continued development of the feasibility design and agreed to consider costs at the next meeting at which Holyrood was on the agenda.

[543] RM/1/116-120 – Letter from Mrs Barbara Doig to Snr Miralles and Mr Stewart, 17 November 1999
[544] WS/42/001–020 – Mr Brian Stewart's First Witness Statement, 11 March 2004, Para 51 *et seq*
[545] CB/2/181-183 - Minutes of SPCB Meeting of 1 February 2000

Chapter 10

Early 2000 and the Establishment of the Holyrood Progress Group

Concerns about the SPCB

10.1   In a private letter to Mr Mustard written in December 1999,[546] Mrs Doig expressed her doubts about the SPCB as a client. The SPCB meeting of 1 February 2000 brought her concerns to a head. The Design Team was present. Her briefing for the meeting[547] had included what she considered to be essential background information and advice on whether the emerging proposal met the concerns of statutory authorities, client requirements, key design features, and quality concerns. She had suggested points which SPCB members would wish to consider when viewing the prototype of the external features of the MSP room and had provided detail on design issues on Queensberry House alerting them to the need to consider how the feasibility design treated that building. In preparing for the meeting, she and Mr Grice had recognised the difficulty of obtaining what she described as "a joined up client view" as there was going to be a tour of Queensberry House for SPCB members, the meeting itself, and then a viewing outside the prototype MSP room. Her briefing had indicated that Project Team officials wished to have private time with the SPCB. She must be given credit for her forthright approach and for recognition of the 'knowledge vacuum', into which she saw MSPs as having stepped. In fact she and her colleagues were requested to leave at the same time as the

---

[546] CB/5/026–028 - E-mail from Mrs Barbara Doig to Mr Martin Mustard, 8 December 1999
[547] CB/2/177-180 - Briefing Paper from the Project Team to the SPCB, 1 February 2000

Design Team and were not in attendance when the SPCB decided that the Design Team should continue to develop the feasibility design.[548]

10.2   Mrs Doig was concerned that she and her colleagues had not had the opportunity to provide a private supplementary oral briefing to the SPCB. As Project Sponsor she lacked confidence that the SPCB had made its decisions in the full knowledge and understanding of matters which affected the client position and of the possible cost and programme implications. She discussed the situation with Mr Grice to whom she also wrote formally on 7 February 2000 saying:

> "I am concerned that despite staff's best endeavours to brief the SPCB on the nature of the Body's client responsibilities for the Holyrood building and the issues they must consider about its design and construction, members (both individually - with one or two exceptions – and collectively) are not performing at the level required to obtain what should be Scotland's most prestigious building.
>
> I am unconvinced that the Body understands the importance and elements of its role, the complexity of procuring under considerable media pressure a building with so many external interests, and the implications of its decisions. For the most part members appear unwilling to devote the time required to read the material provided, discus the matter in depth, receive advice and give an appropriate amount of instruction. Individual members' attendance is patchy across meetings and in any single meeting there is a variety of starting and finishing times. Members change their views between meetings and have difficulty recalling factual information and previous presentations and decisions accurately.
>
> Until last week I was hopeful that these matters were resulting in an effective SPCB client input. However, the SPCB meeting on 1 February was unhelpful. This was a very important meeting.
>
> .....
>
> In the event the SPCB did not seriously challenge the Design Team and in the absence of clearly expressed corporate views and decisions left the way open for the Design Team to interpret the meeting's proceedings as total support for their proposals."[549]

10.3   In my opinion, she was correct to be concerned. When her comments were put to Andrew Welsh, in evidence, he responded:

---

[548] CB/2/181-183 - Minutes of SPCB Meeting of 1 February 2000, Para 12
[549] CB/5/055–057 – Minute from Mrs Barbara Doig to Mr Paul Grice, 7 February 2000

"**Mr Welsh:** My response to it is, first of all, that when it comes to issues of not performing to the level, I just thoroughly disagree with her. The level of our decisions were highly dependent on the information on which they were based, and she was one of the primary sources for that information. I think this shows that the situation had been reached that the frustration of the Corporate Body is obviously being mirrored by her frustration.

If she felt that we were not understanding, it was surely her duty as the primary source of information to make sure that we understood. If she thinks we were too thick to understand that, then it was her duty to explain to us where exactly she thought we were going wrong. And, equally, that complaint: she should have had a meeting with the Corporate Body to say that and to clear the air. That never happened."[550]

10.4 This short exchange sums up for me the gulf of misunderstanding, and, I regret to say, mistrust, which quickly grew up between the Project Team and the SPCB. I cannot say whether this was because of personalities or the issues with which they ought to have been concerned. It is easy now to say that Mrs Doig should have done more, but given her rank and status, I doubt that she could have done. She could, however, have enlisted the help of members of the professional team, especially DLE.

10.5 Mrs Doig's opinions were not, however, wholly shared by Mr Grice. Speaking of the 1 February meeting in evidence,[551] he did share her concern that the Project Team had been denied an opportunity to get into the "nitty-gritty" with the SPCB. He accepted that it "was not a well-handled meeting, specifically because Mrs Doig had not been invited to stay behind for a private discussion". What he did not share was her general view that the SPCB was not performing at a sufficient level. He also pointed out that her concerns were to an extent historical and that steps were in hand to improve matters.

10.6 In response to her concerns Mr Grice did arrange for Mrs Doig and Dr Gibbons to attend the SPCB meeting on 8 February 2000[552] at which she was able to check members' views on the Architect's presentation and alert them to potential programme and cost implications. The SPCB again requested a report on the cost and programme implications of the feasibility design. It was noted that the minute of the meeting records that "Actual costs could not be known until the building was completed", hinting at least some awareness of the implications of construction management. I am doubtful, though, that the collective understanding was in any way complete.

---

[550] Evidence of Andrew Welsh on 11 February 2004, Paras 356 to 357
[551] Evidence of Mr Paul Grice on 10 February 2004, Para 72 *et seq*
[552] CB/2/186-187 - Minutes of SPCB Meeting of 8 February 2000

10.7 The minute of the next meeting of the SPCB on 15 February does not record any discussion of costs except to the extent that Mr Grice cautioned that the SPCB "might not be able to sanction the costs associated with elements of the design which they considered to be excessively detailed or poor value for money." In the apparent absence of such discussion it is surprising that the minute also records that the "Corporate Body agreed that the Design Team should be instructed to proceed with the building on the basis of the feasibility study proposals." The minute further recorded that it should be stressed to the Design Team and to Bovis "that their design effort and works programme should be geared towards a fast track delivery with an aim for completion by summer 2002".

10.8 In the course of Sir David Steel's evidence the following exchange about the understanding of the SPCB with regard to costs in the early part of 2000 took place:

"**Mr Campbell QC:** For public consumption, then, at January 2000 ...

Sir David Steel: We are still on £109 million.

Mr Campbell QC: ... You must have known that that was not real.

Sir David Steel: We had been warned that cost increases were in the pipeline. And we knew, of course, from our own decisions — even allowing for the savings — that it was likely that the extra was going to exceed the savings.

Mr Campbell QC: Did you have a sense of by how much or by what sort of percentage?

Sir David Steel: No.

Mr Campbell QC: Not at all?

Sir David Steel: No".[553]

10.9 Notwithstanding these remarks, I have considerable sympathy for the position of Sir David Steel and the SPCB at this time. They had been told that the budget/cost of the new building was £62 million and its gross area was about 23,000m^2. On a 'back of an envelope' calculation increasing the size of the Parliament building to about 30,000m^2 to meet their needs left them comfortably under £100 million, but prior to that most uncomfortable of meetings with Mrs Doig in the spring of 2000, subsequently described as the Dutch Auction meeting, I have found in all that has been presented before the Inquiry that not even the single clang of a warning bell on costs was sounded before that meeting.

10.10 The SPCB had hoped to be in a position by mid February 2000 to report comprehensively to MSPs on the reasons for the increase in the Parliament's space requirements, on Queensberry House, on programme and on the latest estimates of Project costs. Members wished to finalise the terms of a report at the SPCB meeting on 22 February 2000. Prior to that meeting

---

553 Evidence of Sir David Steel on 4 February 2004, Paras 871 to 877

Mrs Doig circulated a further detailed paper which contained a range of cost estimates for the Project.[554] Mrs Doig explained in evidence[555] that in prior discussions with Mr Grice they had agreed that the SPCB had to be given some figures at this stage. She said Mr Grice instructed her to present the best estimates that she could do in the time available. Mrs Doig's paper emphasised that "Cost estimates are simply estimates" and stated that actual costs could not be known until all works were completed and a final figure would also be affected by the construction management procurement route and, in particular, whether programme was met.

10.11 Mrs Doig presented the SPCB with three different approaches, the first of which proceeded by the application of a rate of £3,500 to £4,000 per m^2 to a building of 30-32,000m^2 and produced a construction cost in the range of £105 to £128 million. She reached that figure having "Includ(ed) the original level of risk allowances." That means, as I see it, that she has added back the £27 million most of which had earlier been considered to be capable of being "managed out".[556]

10.12 Mrs Doig's second approach proceeded on the basis of the original budget of £62 million in June 1999, to which she added £7 million in respect of additional costs for Queensberry House and a range of £24.5 to £28 million for an additional 7,000m^2 of space, calculated as above, producing a construction cost in the range £93.5 to £99 million. Adding the same "original" risk allowance of £27 million resulted in a range of £120.5 to £128 million for construction cost.

10.13 Mrs Doig's third approach claimed to represent the outcome of a costing exercise carried out by DLE on 14 February 2000, including the impact of the Value Engineering exercise and the feasibility study, and referred to a cost estimate of £125 million. The report concluded with the statement that further work was required to affirm the detail of DLE's estimate. None of these estimates referred to the cost base of March 1998, nor to the need to make allowance for inflation.

10.14 However unsatisfactory they may now appear to be, these figures produced by Mrs Doig for the meeting on 22 February 2000 gave the SPCB its first indication of the likely level of construction cost for the Project as it then stood. The reaction was one of shock and alarm. In evidence Andrew Welsh described what happened when the SPCB interrogated Mrs Doig on her figures as a "Dutch Auction". In fact members put progressively higher figures of up to £160 million to her and asked if she could guarantee construction cost within that figure. This she could not do. Mrs Doig explained that in her paper she was trying to give a "fair figure" and that her range from £100 million to £150 million was an indication of the "ballpark" the

---

[554] CB/2/197–201 – Paper from the Project Team to the SPCB, 22 February 2000
[555] Evidence of Mrs Barbara Doig on 12 February 2004, Para 401
[556] Auditor General for Scotland's Report of September 2000, Annex B

Project was getting into. She said she was given no opportunity to explain the basis of her estimates. There was an acknowledgment of the impossibility of her position from George Reid, then Deputy Presiding Officer and in attendance at the meeting, that "It was, perhaps, never possible for Mrs Doig, at that point, to produce the sort of information I was asking for."[557] It is clear to me that by this point Mrs Doig no longer enjoyed the confidence of the SPCB.

10.15 The "Dutch Auction" in terms of which guarantees were being sought from Mrs Doig suggests a fundamental failure on the part of the SPCB, even by this time, to understand the nature of construction management under which no "guarantees" are possible. Notwithstanding my earlier expression of sympathy for their position, the SPCB are open to criticism for having failed to take the initiative at a much earlier stage to force the issue on costs; for example by asking for a meeting with their cost consultants, DLE. I sense that the management style of the SPCB was essentially reactive, in that it appears to have relied heavily on the information put before it rather than taking a proactive approach. I have no direct evidence to support such an assertion, but it is open to question whether the members of the SPCB had grasped the detail of Mrs Doig's paper for this pivotal meeting where she pointed out (albeit obliquely) the uncertainties arising from construction management.

10.16 The minute of the SPCB meeting on 22 February 2000[558] blandly recorded that the "meeting noted the implications of the revised cost estimate" and that the SPCB stated its aim for the building to be completed "by the summer of 2002 with occupation as soon as possible thereafter". The minute further recorded that various strategies were discussed for presenting cost figures in the impending report to MSPs to be reflected in a draft for further consideration. The minute conveys none of the sense of crisis engendered by this meeting and of which those present spoke in evidence to the Inquiry.

10.17 Such was the sense of crisis that the members met in private the following day. At that meeting it was agreed that an independent assessment on costs and timetable was required and that this should preferably be available in 3 to 4 weeks time with a view to a Parliamentary Debate. The note of that meeting records:

> 'It was felt by the SPCB that they appeared to lack any cost control and was (sic) in need of an efficient professional project manager to take the scheme forward. They discussed how the "mess" could have happened and what could be done to try and

---

[557] Evidence of George Reid on 2 April 2004, Para 47
[558] CB/2/203-204 - Minutes of SPCB Meeting of 22 February 2000

bring it back on track. They considered there must be a strengthening of the management structure with robust on-going advice.'[559]

10.18   Mr Grice was instructed to take the matter forward and to report back to the SPCB. On 24 February 2000 Sir David Steel made a statement to Parliament confirming the commissioning of an independent report. Mr Grice sought advice from the RIAS and on 25 February the appointment of Mr John Spencely was confirmed.

Mr Spencely's Methodology

10.19   Mr Spencely accepted the invitation from the SPCB to conduct an independent assessment of the Holyrood Project by 27 March 2000. The original terms of reference for the report were agreed with Mr Grice, and later supplemented.

10.20   Mr Spencely informed the Inquiry that the terms of reference were framed to reflect the view that: "The Project appeared to be in difficulty, and the SPCB wanted to know where it stood."[560] The short length of time allowed for completion of the investigation would have been an influencing factor as to how far-reaching the remit was and it would suggest that time was the prime concern.

10.21   With the help of two colleagues, Mr Spencely interviewed members of the Project Team, Enric Miralles, the consultants, Dr Gibbons and Mr Grice. It was agreed with interviewees that information given in confidence would not be personally attributed. Mr Spencely told the Inquiry that he felt that four weeks was sufficient time to fulfil his remit. In effect he completed his report and presented his findings to the SPCB on 24 March 2000, within the four week target. On any view, this was a most significant achievement.

10.22   The Spencely Report was published on 30 March 2000 and MSPs were afforded the opportunity to question Mr Spencely on its content on that date. Although the contents of the Report were central to a debate in Parliament, the report was not examined by any parliamentary Committee. Mr Spencely found that surprising. I agree.

Was a 'Pause' Recommended?

10.23   Within the Spencely Report there is no specific recommendation for a two month pause in the Project to enable a costed design to be achieved. However, in evidence Mr Spencely explained that the eight week pause was implicit within paragraph 5.4 of his Report:

> 'It is clearly imperative that the Brief is frozen now and that the Design Team proceeds immediately to produce a Scheme Design including a cost plan to a Brief

---

[559] CB/2/204A-B – Minutes of SPCB Private Meeting of 23 February 2000
[560] Evidence of Mr John Spencely on 17 February 2004, Para 32

and a budget approved by the client, so that approval may be given to proceed with the Project by 8 June 2000.'[561]

10.24 There has been some uncertainty amongst witnesses as to whether SPCB members were aware that Mr Spencely was recommending a pause. During a discussion of the Report's findings at the SPCB meeting on 28 March, Dr Gibbons advised that: "Detailed design and construction would continue to run in parallel and there was no reason for a pause until 8 June."[562] There is also reference to Mr Spencely recommending one option as: "the cessation of all project activity for a period of three months" in the SPCB's report to Parliament, Paper 99.[563]

10.25 Therefore it would appear that despite the absence of an express recommendation for a pause within the Spencely Report, SPCB members understood that a pause was a possibility, and rejected it on the advice of Dr Gibbons.

10.26 During the debate, MSPs also appeared to understand that a pause was being advised by Mr Spencely. Mike Russell said: "Mr Spencely says that there should be a pause to allow us to get a plan." However, neither the principal motion nor Gordon Jackson's amendment suggested a pause. Donald Gorrie's motion would only have allowed for a pause alongside a reopening of site selection issues. For many MSPs, this was unpalatable.

10.27 Mr Spencely agreed in examination that he had not highlighted the need for a pause in his Report, for example by placing a recommendation to that effect in a list of conclusions. I found his evidence on this point to be somewhat uncertain, but on balance I prefer the view that he was suggesting that a pause would have been beneficial, but that the political imperative of speed intervened to make that a practical impossibility. I am unable to speculate as to whether a pause would indeed have been beneficial.

Reaction of the Consultants

10.28 In evidence, Sir David Steel told of the strong exception to much of the Spencely report expressed by EMBT/RMJM Ltd, Bovis and DLE. These concerns appear to have been voiced at a meeting which the consultants held with Project Management on 27 March. The concerns were not made public and there is no agreed record of their extent. I cannot therefore offer a view on their validity but I recognise the difficult position in which this disagreement must have placed the SPCB. I can speculate that the conflict of opinion between the consultants and Mr Spencely was perhaps reflected in the terms of the motion, which instead of endorsing the report, merely asked the Parliament to note it.

---

[561] Mr Spencely's Report 'Review of the current estimate of time to delivery and occupation', Para 5.4
[562] CB/2/230–232 –Minutes of SPCB Meeting of 28 March 2000
[563] CB/2/660–709 - SPCB Report on the Holyrood Project – Session 1 (2000) SP Paper 99, Para 24

The SPCB Report on Mr Spencely's Investigation

10.29   The SPCB considered Mr Spencely's Report on 28 March 2000[564] and at its meeting of 4 April 2000 authorised Sir David Steel to speak on its behalf in the debate on 5 April. They agreed that the terms of the motion to be debated would ask Parliament simply to note, rather than endorse, all of the findings of the Spencely Report, as apart from the need for parliamentary agreement to continue the Project within a budget of £195 million, SPCB members were unable to unanimously agree its contents. The effect of this decision was that MSPs were not afforded the opportunity of voting on the recommendations in the Spencely Report itself.

10.30   The SPCB's own report to MSPs[565] is unfailingly optimistic about all the aspects of the Project criticised by Spencely. It conveyed no sense of crisis and asserted that the Project could be delivered for a total budget of £195million. It rehearsed the history of the £62 million/£89 million construction cost estimate and the treatment of risk,[566] and variously attributed responsibility to Simpson & Brown and Historic Scotland[567] for issues around Queensberry House. It did not relate the stated budget of £109 million to the estimates being provided by DLE at that time, which showed a construction cost alone of £119.82 million; it dismissed the inclusion of inflation in any overall cost estimate, and apparently adopted Spencely's broad brush estimate of 15 -20% savings on his estimated total cost of £230.86 million[568] without saying whether it had taken advice from the professional teams or the Project Team. I can find no written communication from DLE to the SPCB, nor any evidence in Mr Fisher's testimony which says, in terms, that "cost reductions consistent with a final cost of £195 million can be achieved without reducing the fundamental quality, in line with Mr Spencely's observations."[569]

10.31   However, I believe that I understand at least where the other strand of the figure of £195 million came from, namely a report[570] written after the meeting held in Barcelona on 20 March 2000. That meeting is referred to in the header of Cost Check 11. It reads "This document has been produced to report on the Cost review held in Barcelona on 20 March 2000....This will form the basis of the forthcoming Stage D Cost Plan programmed for mid-June 2000 following Design Stage D being reached at end April 2000 with Structural Stage D being reached at end May 2000. Therefore on the basis of the March Stage D report published by EMBT/RMJM and the Architect's plans received on 11 February 2000 and team discussions in Barcelona on 20 March 2000, the estimate for all construction work being proposed is £119,823,914."

---

[564] CB/2/230-232 – Minutes of SPCB Meeting of 28 March 2000
[565] CB/2/234A-I – Report on the Holyrood Project, SP Paper 99, Session 1, 2000
[566] *ibid*, Para 10
[567] *ibid*, Para 12.2
[568] Report of Mr John Spencely, 'Total Current Budget Requirements', Para 4.5.1
[569] CB/2/234N – Report on the Holyrood Project, SP Paper 99, Para 29
[570] DL/1/169-172 – Letter from Ms Carol Thorburn to Mr Mick Duncan, Feasibility Estimate (Cost Check Issue 11) at 20 March 2000

10.32 If I subtract the "contingency" figures in Cost Check 11 described as "Contingency permitted by client - £5,213,405" and "Design reserve permitted by client - £5,213,405" or £10,426,810 in all, the overall construction cost total of £119,823,914 is reduced to £109,397,104, or, say, £109 million. That is close to the client's target figure of £108,000,000 referred to by Mr Grice in his letter to the consultants of 9 May 2000[571] which is expressed as "excluding contingencies". The difference between £108 and £195 million (i.e. £87 million) is detailed in the tables which comprised Annex 3 to the SPCB's report to MSPs.

The Parliamentary Debate of 5 April 2000

10.33 Following the SPCB's consideration of the Spencely Report a parliamentary debate was held on 5 April 2000. Sir David Steel, on behalf of the SPCB, lodged and spoke to a motion on the Holyrood Project. The text of the motion was as follows:

> "That the Parliament notes:
> a. the attached report of the SPCB on the Holyrood Project (SP Paper 99) together with:
> b. the report by John Spencely attached as Annexe 1;
> c. the photographs incorporated as Annexe 2 which are available from the Scottish Parliament Document Supply Centre;
> d. the revised budget of £195 million set out in Annexe 3."

10.34 An amendment lodged by Gordon Jackson asked the Parliament to direct the SPCB to establish a progress group, to report to it with a remit of finalising the design and completing the Project by the end of 2002 within a budget of £195 million. It remained silent on the other recommendations of the Spencely Report. Donald Gorrie also lodged an amendment proposing that time should be taken to review the Holyrood option, to gather information on costs and design and compare these with similar information for other sites. After a spirited debate Parliament accepted Gordon Jackson's amendment. I have no cause to question the judgment of Mr Spencely, an experienced architect in his own right, but to inexperienced MSPs there was, even at this relatively late stage, no clear comprehension of the consequences of following the construction management route.

Genesis of the Holyrood Progress Group (HPG)

10.35 The resolution passed by the Parliament on 5 April 2000 gave the SPCB a mandate to proceed with the Project and in particular to establish a progress group to work with it to finalise the design and complete the Project by the end of 2002 within a total budget of £195 million. This is in accord with Mr Spencely's recommendation[572] which questioned whether the SPCB had "the time and expertise" to perform the client role on a day to day basis. He did not reflect on

---

[571] DL/1/178-179 –Letter from Mr Paul Grice to Mr Alan Mack, 9 May 2000
[572] Mr Spencely's Report 'Management Recommendations', Para 9.4.2

the SPCB's capability to carry out the task of acting as "the client" in a project of such complexity.

10.36 Asked in evidence whether he had formed a view as to whether the SPCB was in fact able to give the Project enough time, Mr Spencely said he had been "told by them that they could not". His impression was supported by the evidence of George Reid, who at that time attended SPCB meetings in his capacity as Deputy Presiding Officer. He described the SPCB's workload as "absolutely devastating" and said that there "was an infinity of work to be done on top of which there was the building."[573]

10.37 In relation to the functions of his suggested "Progressing Group" Mr Spencely's evidence was as follows:

> "I expected the Progressing Group to operate as the Client – receiving reports and recommendations "upwards" from the Project Sponsor and acting on the latter – to accept, modify or reject; and receiving and sifting requests for variations to the Brief "downwards" from MSPs and Parliamentary staff; all in the light of the Budget and the Programme; and to control Budget expenditure and Programme by making the appropriate management decisions".[574]

10.38 Mr Spencely envisaged a group "... able to pay attention to the documents that they were provided with, and understand them" and in a position to manage with authority and put into effect the client's requirements after crystallising them, but not to micro-manage. He envisaged it saying to "people higher up in the chain", (presumably a reference to MSPs), "No, you cannot have what you want, because we do not have the money or we do not have the time.... The Project Sponsor, without being a member of it would work hand in glove with the Progress Group and would attend all its deliberations, and be the friend of the Progress Group — be its trusted lieutenant."[575]

10.39 The SPCB's paper informed the subsequent debate on 5 April 2000 and said:"...we accept the case for a group which has the time and expertise available to it in taking forward the Project. The SPCB cannot – indeed does not wish - to divest itself of ultimate responsibility for Holyrood. But, we would wish to remit day-to-day responsibility for the Project to a progressing group."[576]

10.40 During the debate Sir David Steel confirmed the SPCB's acceptance of what he described as Mr Spencely's recommendation that "either a professional individual or a progress-chasing group, including professionals, should watch over the project on a day-by-day basis and report

---

[573] Evidence of George Reid on 2 February 2004, Para 19
[574] WS/35/001–004 - Mr John Spencely's Witness Statement, Para 25
[575] Evidence of Mr John Spencely on 17 February 2004, Para 389 et seq
[576] CB/2/660–709 - SPCB Report on the Holyrood Project – Session 1 (2000) SP Paper 99

to us." Donald Gorrie's unsuccessful amendment included approval (of) "the SPCB's proposal for a progressing group to take on day to day responsibility for the project of creating the Parliament's new home". In moving his successful amendment Gordon Jackson said he envisaged that a "project group of suitably qualified professionals will oversee the whole enterprise".

10.41 I have no difficulty in agreeing with Mr Spencely's view that the resources of the SPCB were insufficient to enable it to give the Project the time and attention which it demanded but for which it had to compete with the many other demands of the new Parliament. Against the background of the SPCB's limited powers of delegation, the recommendation to establish a Progressing Committee was a sensible one. Unfortunately, however, in terms of both the debate itself and the papers which informed it, mixed messages were sent out as to the precise role envisaged for the HPG, as it subsequently came to be known. Mr Spencely's Report proposed no more that that the Group should "support" the SPCB in the delivery of the Project. However, in his evidence to the Inquiry he came closer to suggesting that he had in mind a managerial rather than a supportive role. The SPCB's paper stating its wish to "remit day-to-day responsibility" to the Group clearly envisaged a managerial role. Sir David Steel said that the Group should "watch over the project on a day-by-day basis and report to" the SPCB. The final text of Gordon Jackson's amendment envisaged a Group to "work with" the SPCB.

Formation of the HPG

10.42 The HPG met officially for the first time on 28 June 2000.[577] The first Convener was Lewis Macdonald and the first MSP members were Linda Fabiani, Deputy Convener, and Tavish Scott. It had been suggested that George Reid might become the Convener but without the endorsement of the SNP party group he was unable to accept. It had also been envisaged that each of the four main political parties would be represented but the Conservative Party did not nominate a member, after becoming aware that no Minister would be serving on the Group. There have, since its inception, been two changes in the MSP membership of the HPG. In November 2000 Jamie Stone succeeded Tavish Scott and in April 2001 John Home Robertson succeeded Lewis Macdonald as Convener. The two independent members of the HPG were Mr Andrew Wright, Architect, and Mr David Manson, Chartered Quantity Surveyor, both of whom were eminent within their respective professions and whose CVs are set out in their written statements to the Inquiry.[578]

---

[577] CB/4/006–007A - Minutes of HPG Meeting of 28 June 2000
[578] Witness Statements from Mr Andrew Wright (WS/39/001–034) and Mr David Manson (WS/40/001–034)

10.43 The Scottish Executive was asked to nominate a Minister as a member. It was concluded that it would be constitutionally inappropriate for a Minister to be involved on the ground that this might be perceived to blur the SPCB's statutory responsibility for the Project. It was agreed, however, that Mr Gordon, who had previous involvement with the Project as a member of the architectural selection panel and as Project Owner for a period, and Dr Gibbons should both join the HPG in an advisory and non-voting capacity. Although not formally representing the Executive, Mr Gordon did report back to Ministers on the deliberations and decisions of the HPG. His reports over the period from August 2000 to August 2003[579] have been made available to the Inquiry and give valuable insight into the workings of the HPG. To support the HPG, Ms Sarah Davidson, a civil servant on secondment to the Parliament, was appointed as its Secretary.

10.44 To coincide with the setting up of the HPG it was decided and agreed that the Project Sponsor role would be split between a Project Director, and a Financial Controller, Mr Gilfillan. Mrs Doig in fact left the Project Team in May 2000 and the Project Director role was filled on an interim basis by Dr Gibbons pending the appointment of Mr Alan Ezzi as Project Director in November 2000.

10.45 I have to question this arrangement with Dr Gibbons, which to my mind raises substantial issues of governance. I find it difficult to understand that Dr Gibbons could properly act as both the de facto leader of the Holyrood Project Team and sit as a member (even a non-voting member) of the body whose role effectively was to oversee him and his Team. There was no evidence that he abused his position, but it unsettled others and it is another example of the blurred lines of communication that have plagued this Project.

Memorandum of Understanding

10.46 The SPCB had identified at an early stage that a Memorandum of Understanding would be necessary to define not only the HPG's remit but also its relationship with the SPCB and the Parliament. The Memorandum went through various drafts and the final version[580] was approved by the SPCB on 8 June 2000[581] at a meeting attended by prospective members of the HPG.

10.47 A significant legal obstacle to the setting up of the HPG existed in the wording of section 21 of, and Schedule 2 to, the Scotland Act 1998 which constituted the SPCB and defined its powers and which only permitted it to delegate functions to the Presiding Officer or the Clerk. In other words the SPCB had no power to delegate any executive authority to the HPG. This obstacle

---

[579] SE/9/222-388 – Reports from Mr Robert Gordon to Ministers
[580] CB/5/049-054 - Memorandum of Understanding between the SPCB and the HPG, 8 June 2000
[581] CB/2/288F–I – Minute of the SPCB/HPG meeting of 20 June 2000

was circumvented by an ingenious Scheme of Delegation set out in Clause 4 of the Memorandum of Understanding which stated:

'The SPCB has delegated its function to complete the Holyrood project to the Clerk who ....in his day-to-day management of the Project.....will seek the advice and assistance of the HPG and is expected to act on this advice. If, exceptionally the Clerk considers that any advice is inappropriate and should not be implemented, he will refer the matter to the SPCB.'[582]

10.48　The HPG's remit was set out in these terms:

'The HPG is the principal advisory body to both the SPCB and the Clerk in the management of the Holyrood Building Project. It will be a source of political liaison with the Parliament and provide high level authoritative advice on technical, professional and administrative issues relating to the project......it will work with the (SPCB) to fulfil the terms of the resolution of the Parliament, namely to finalise the design to complete the project by the end of 2002 within a budget of £195 million; and to report on progress. In particular its remit will include:

'To advise the Clerk on all issues relating to the progress of the Project

To monitor and report periodically to the SPCB on progress made towards achieving the targets prescribed by the Parliament

To be available for consultation by the Clerk and the SPCB on any aspect of the Project

To promote good communications with MSPs and the public and to optimise presentation of the Project

To make recommendations on matters within its remit

To take formal minutes of its meetings and to inform the SPCB of key decisions / recommendations.'[583]

10.49　While the carefully crafted Memorandum of Understanding emphasised the purely advisory role of the HPG, it is interesting to note that the wording of the minute of the meeting of 8 June is strongly suggestive of a more hands-on managerial role. Paragraph 14 refers to the concern of the SPCB that it should not be taken by surprise by any "decision of the Progress Group". Paragraph 15 said that after stage D "day to day responsibility" would be undertaken by the HPG. Paragraph 17 explained that members of the HPG needed the "reassurance and confidence" of the SPCB to enable it to "sign off any decisions, since responsibility to achieve budget and the timetable target would be with (it)." The use of such language suggests to me that the intention at the time was that the HPG would de facto be a decision making body.

---

[582] CB/5/049-054 - Memorandum of Understanding between the SPCB and the HPG, 8 June 2000
[583] ibid

10.50 Sir David Steel, asked in evidence how deep the HPG could go in problem solving, said: "As far as we were concerned, they were welcome to go as far as they wanted".[584] Mr Grice understood the HPG was "to engage to quite a degree of detail and to engage with big decisions".[585] When asked about the decisions the HPG might take, his response was that they might take "day-to-day decisions on the project; in other words to keep the project moving " and they "would be able to take decisions — allowing the SPCB to focus on the big issues" of cost, programme and the overall quality and concept. He went on "...we had to come up with a mechanism respecting the legal position in the Scotland Act, which effectively — and I say the word carefully — effectively allowed them to make decisions. They made decisions effectively through my delegated authority, and in turn of course the Project Sponsor's position acting under my delegated authority."

10.51 Lewis Macdonald, the first Convener, referred in his written statement to the agreement of the Memorandum as giving the HPG the "green light (it) required in order to take full control of the progress of the Project." He also said:

> "From my point of view as Convener of HPG, it was absolutely essential that we controlled the development of the Project, the decision-making process and communications. HPG was set up to make management of the Project better focused and better understood. Had we not taken the degree of control we did, I believe the effect would have been to increase rather than reduce the potential for confusion and indecision." [586]

10.52 He sought in his oral evidence to qualify his written statement to the effect when he used the phrase "full control of the progress of the Project",[587] it did not imply ownership or executive control. What it did imply was "that the day-to-day progress of the Project in terms of day-to-day management was something on which the Clerk should expect to take our advice as a very clear direction from us to him on behalf of the Parliament." The point was clarified by Lewis Macdonald in two exchanges. The first was as follows:

> "**Mr Campbell QC:** So unless Mr Grice was being given advice which flew in the face of something of which he was aware, either legally or politically or whatever, you would expect him to take your advice and treat it, in effect, as a decision?
>
> **Mr Macdonald:** That is correct." [588]

10.53 The second exchange went:

---

[584] Evidence of Sir David Steel on 4 February 2004, Para 261 *et seq*
[585] Evidence of Mr Paul Grice on 10 February 2004, Para 424
[586] WS/38/001 – 012 - Lewis Macdonald's Witness Statement, 3 March 2004, Para 11
[587] Evidence of Lewis Macdonald on 3 March 2004, Para 65
[588] *ibid*, Para 66

"**Mr Campbell QC:** .. You came into this as a group and you are quite clear in this statement you are taking decisions. All right, you are taking them in the name of the SPCB, but you are taking decisions. Do you accept that you, at the time, assumed, perhaps not instantly, but over time, responsibility so that you actually owned the decisions that were taken; you were taking responsibility for these decisions and having to face up to them if they turned out not to be correct?

Mr Macdonald: We were certainly taking responsibility for the decisions. We felt that was the only correct way to act. However, clearly the purpose of those decisions was to provide the appropriate advice to the Clerk; he in turn being accountable to the SPCB. So in a legal sense, of course, ownership of the decisions, as of the whole Project, continued with the SPCB, but in day-to-day terms, and certainly in terms of our perception of the importance of the decisions we made — our perception and that of everybody, I think, ultimately involved in the Project — was that those were critical decisions and that the HPG had the responsibility for taking those decisions, and decisions taken there would be expected to be put into force." [589]

10.54 Mr Grice gave evidence as to his perception of the role of the HPG[590] during the course of which he confirmed his intention that it should be the body in control. He thought that there had been "a pretty clear line of control and command with the HPG effectively sitting at the top of that in terms of the day-to-day management of the Project." The HPG was there "to monitor cost and programme and to lead the decisions on major issues". His view was that "the clear will of Parliament was that another group should oversee the day-to-day management of the Project". The wording of the Memorandum was to give the HPG as clear a power over that as possible.

10.55 Any doubts as to the day to day management responsibilities being assumed by the HPG were dispelled in terms of the HPG's own newsletter No 1 issued in July 2000 in which it was reported: "As of 20 June 2000, day to day <u>management</u> (my emphasis) of the new Parliament Project has passed to the Holyrood Project Group." [591]

10.56 All this evidence tends to confirm my impression that it was intended from the outset that the HPG would be a <u>de facto</u> decision making body with "hands on" management responsibility. The scheme of delegation set out in the Memorandum of Understanding represented an ingenious solution to the constraints imposed by section 21 of the Scotland Act. At the time this arrangement was set up, no-one was interested in questioning its legality and even now that would appear to be the case. However, to the extent that the HPG assumed a decision making role when under statute decision making power could not be delegated to it, leads me to a conclusion that s. 21 of the Scotland Act might be reviewed as regards the powers of the

---

[589] *ibid*, Para 112 *et seq*
[590] Evidence of Mr Paul Grice on 1 April 2004, Paras 3 to 19
[591] CB/6/186–189 – HPG Newsletter No.1, 1 July 2000

SPCB to delegate. To be fair to him Mr Grice appears to have grasped this. In his evidence he said:

> "Say, for example, (the SPCB) had had a power under the Scotland Act to delegate to other bodies or persons — and that is hypothetical — but in all probability I would have recommended establishing a proper sub-group with proper functional delegated responsibility. That would have been much clearer."[592]

He also said:

> "I think that had the Corporate Body the power to give executive delegation to the Progress Group, I am certain it would have done; and certainly, that would have been my recommendation, but that option was not open to us."

Training for HPG Members

10.57 No formal training was provided for the non professional members of the HPG. They did not, for example, have the benefit of a briefing paper such as that prepared for the assistance of the SPCB at handover in May 1999. The steering brief provided to Lewis Macdonald as Convener was concerned with procedural matters. On the other hand there was available to the HPG material such as the Spencely Report. Linda Fabiani, in her written statement to the Inquiry, said:

> 'The HPG members did not receive any specific training for the task. Although I had the advantage of some familiarity with construction procurement I had no prior familiarity with construction management and there was an immense amount to learn. It inevitably took a matter of some months to get on top of the complexities of the whole project which were so much greater than I had envisaged.'[593]

10.58 Mr Gordon in his evidence said that over the summer of 2000, both the professionals and MSPs, spent time getting themselves up to speed and that "by the autumn of 2000 it had got firmly into stride".[594] This observation has to be treated with some caution, as at the time of the Inquiry at least one member of the HPG had not wholly grasped the range of Bovis' responsibilities as Construction Manager.[595]

---

[592] Evidence of Mr Paul Grice on 10 February 2004, Para 454
[593] MS/22/001-024A - Linda Fabiani's Witness Statement,8 March 2004, Para 5.4
[594] Evidence of Mr Robert Gordon on 23 March 2004, Paras 80 and 92
[595] Evidence of Jamie Stone on 9 March 2004, Para 96 *et seq*

10.59   Mr Wright and Mr Manson, the two independent professional members of the HPG both brought to its deliberations the benefit of their very extensive professional experience. They were notably influential but I continue to find it odd that they were full but non-voting members of the HPG. I would have expected the more conventional arrangement that they, along with Mr Gordon and Dr Gibbons, were "in attendance". If that had been the arrangement, sharply deteriorating relationships with the likes of Mr Ezzi might have been avoided.

Chapter 11

The Holyrood Project - June to December 2000

Progress to Stage D

11.1 An effect of the April 2000 debate was to impose enormous political pressure on those responsible for the Project to achieve formal Stage D sign off as soon as possible. The Stage D report, dated 8 June 2000, was the subject of a minute of 15 June 2000[596] from the interim Project Director, Dr Gibbons, in which he confirmed that the Project Team had submitted the report to careful analysis and invited the SPCB to give approval to it. Dr Gibbons' minute had some caveats. In particular he pointed out that the designs for the Debating Chamber, Committee Towers and Canongate building were not to the necessary level of detail and required development. He also highlighted that the cost estimate from DLE[597] gave a construction cost within the £108 million component of the £195 million budget and that this would require conversion into a Cost Plan as a matter of urgency.

11.2 At the ensuing SPCB meeting on 20 June 2000, which was attended by the prospective MSP members of the HPG as well as Messrs Stewart and Duncan from EMBT/RMJM Ltd and Mr Fisher of DLE, formal approval was given to the Stage D report and for the design to proceed to Stage E. Messrs Wright and Manson had not been formally appointed to the HPG at that

---

[596] CB/2/290-295 – Paper from Dr John Gibbons to the SPCB/HPG, 15 June 2000
[597] DL/1/181-184 – Letter from Mr McAndie to Dr Gibbons, Feasibility Estimate (Cost Check Issue 13) at 8 June 2000

point and were not present. It was perhaps a pity the meeting did not have the benefit particularly of their independent advice at that stage. Mr Wright gave evidence to the Inquiry that he had some subsequent reservations about the Stage D.[598] In the minute of the meeting of 20 June it is recorded that "the Design Team as a whole regarded both the time and cost targets as tight but achievable".[599]

11.3 Two necessary elements of a robust Stage D are to be found in the agreement by all parties of a Cost Plan and in the existence of at least a preliminary structural design by the structural engineers. Neither had been achieved by June 2000.

Stage D – The Cost Plan

11.4 Mr Fisher had reported to the SPCB on 21 March 2000[600] that cost reduction measures discussed at a meeting in Barcelona had brought the construction cost of £125 million down to £108 million. Mr Grice is minuted as having advised the SPCB at that meeting that "based on the construction cost estimate of £108 million, the SPCB could be assured that the entire project could now be delivered at a total cost of under £200 million".[601]

11.5 In relation to the cost estimates being developed at that time, Mr Fisher explained the position in evidence:

> "What is important to understand is that at this stage in the project, the early design work for the west side of the site — the MSP building and Queensberry House — was reasonably advanced; the design work for the east side of the site was embryonic. I should say that that is not unusual, given the way in which the project was being procured, but it did put pressure on the team's capacity to properly assess cost. That being the case — the design being at that stage — the meeting in Barcelona was intended to set cost allowances for a whole range of parts of the building to the east of the site."[602]

11.6 Mr Fisher explained that the object of this costing exercise carried out in Barcelona was to set "acceptable allowances, say for walls, finishes, services, roof — all elements of the building. The team had to agree that it could be built within these allowances and therefore the allowances could then safely be included in the estimates". The meeting in Barcelona had been lengthy and had involved all of the main participants in the Project. To the extent that it resulted in a construction cost estimate within the target of £108 million, the exercise could be regarded as a success. That success was, however, ultimately predicated entirely on the

---

[598] Evidence of Mr Andrew Wright on 4 March 2004, Para 93
[599] CB/2/297 - Minutes of SPCB Meeting of 20 June 2000
[600] CB/2/219-224 – Minutes of SPCB Meeting of 21 March 2000, Para 13
[601] *ibid*, Para 13
[602] Evidence of Mr Hugh Fisher on 18 February 2004, Para 214 *et seq*

ability of the Design Team to complete the design within the relevant cost allowances. As Mr Fisher put it in his evidence:

> "The objective was achieved in that (the) team bought into the provision of a figure of £108 million in line with the client's instruction. The exercise was not successful insofar as the design associated with that exercise was not actually delivered. In other words, the risks that were removed from the estimate to get to £108 million never went away. That was why ... the overall figure shot back up almost immediately after the date that the £195 million was produced."[603]

11.7 The HPG identified at its meeting on 9 August 2000[604] that a Cost Plan should be agreed as a matter of urgency. It may be indicative of the paralysis that affected much of this Project that Dr Gibbons had been saying the same thing two months earlier. At that meeting it decided that the Design Team, the Construction Manager and the Quantity Surveyor should be instructed to agree a cost plan by 31 August to the best of their ability "ring fencing any areas where insufficient information was available to allow full quantification to be made."

11.8 On 28 August DLE delivered the Proof Cost Plan No 14[605] bringing out a construction cost of £108 million at 1998 prices. Mr Manson, to satisfy himself and HPG members of its adequacy, met Mr McAndie of DLE on 7 September 2000. After comment from Mr Manson,[606] Dr Gibbons noted that DLE were lacking design information, for example structural designs for the east basement and superstructure which appeared to be particularly complicated. He emphasised that DLE would require to be proactive to ensure that the £108 million was not exceeded. He identified that due to design delays significant trade packages were being let on a two stage basis in an attempt to keep to programme and that costs would escalate due to inevitable changes at the detailed design stage.

Agreement of the Cost Plan

11.9 There is uncertainty firstly as to the extent to which the Design Team and Bovis can in fact be regarded be regarded as having "bought into" the Cost Plan and secondly as to whether there was sufficient architectural information to form the basis for a valid Cost Plan.

11.10 After production of the Proof Cost Plan 14 on 28 August 2000 there was extensive correspondence between Bovis, DLE and the Project Team with regard to it. Mr Brian McQuade, Director, Bovis Lend Lease (Scotland) Limited wrote to Mr Mustard on 10 October 2000 enclosing a commentary on the Cost Plan together with an annotated copy of the Proof

---

603 Evidence of Mr Hugh Fisher on 18 February 2004, Para 253
604 CB/4/020-022 – Minutes of HPG Meeting of 9 August 2000
605 DL/1/193-195 – Cost Plan from DLE at 28 August 2000
606 CB/4/1153-1155 – Fax from Mr Manson to Dr Gibbons and Ms Davidson, 11 September 2000

Cost Plan.[607] In the letter, and perhaps displaying a lack of confidence in EMBT/RMJM's ability to design to target rates, Mr McQuade said:

> 'We understand that EMBT/RMJM have confirmed they will where necessary carry out any redesign required to achieve the target rates and budgets set for the Trade Packages and we would ask that you obtain their written confirmation on this issue'.

No such written confirmation was ever obtained.

11.11 Mr McQuade asked it to be noted that in particular the East Substructure, Frame and Cladding were of concern to Bovis and that any major Value Engineering exercise on that or any other Trade Package would have an adverse effect on programme. In the commentary headed "Clarifications on DLE Proof Cost Plan 14 Review" it was pointed out that the Cost Plan was based on 1st Quarter 1998 prices with no allowance for inflation and that "Edinburgh is currently the centre of a construction boom" leading to higher tender prices. Attention was also drawn to the fact that the adequacy of the £10.8 million contingency should be reviewed in light of the outcome of the recent Risk Review Meeting. The paper concluded as follows:

> 'The overall cost/m² appears to be adequate. However this is a bespoke building and design has a way of outstripping even the most solid feasibility estimate leaving the client financially exposed.
>
> Because of the varying stages of design development, specifications and lack of detailed build up to the rates the Cost Plan must be viewed as a gross design limit
> .....
> At each design stage, and prior to package tenders being invited, DL&E need to carry out cost checks and estimates to establish whether the package is within the target cost plan. If the forecast is that the scope will exceed the budget then the package will require redesign to keep within budget and maintain programme.'

11.12 This advice was, in my opinion, sound and well-intentioned but there remained the essential incompatibility that if the drive was to early completion, cost was not and could not be containable.

11.13 Although it was also reported at the 15 November meeting of the HPG[608] that Bovis had agreed the cost package plan, other evidence before the Inquiry suggests that any such agreement may have been equivocal to put it no higher. For example in the Bovis written

---

[607] BV/1/626-737 – Proof Cost Plan 14 from Mr Brian McQuade to Mr Mustard, 10 October 2000
[608] CB/4/081-083a Minutes of HPG Meeting of 15 November 2000

submission to the Inquiry on "Stage D: Scheme design" [609] it was said that a weakness was that the information which it contained "did not allow a fully detailed Cost Plan to be developed. Key items were required to be allocated "target sums" for the Design Team to design within, rather than a detailed breakdown with quantities and unit rates."

11.14 On the question as to whether there was agreement to the Cost Plan, I note that the Auditor General in his report of June 2004 considered that there was at best only "qualified agreement".[610] On the evidence before me I am in agreement with that analysis.

Stage D - Adequacy of Design

11.15 With regard to the adequacy of design, Mr Kinsley wrote to DLE on 10 August 2000 expressing his opinion that there had "been sufficient architectural information in place for some time now to allow a good Cost Plan to be prepared." [611] In my view that has to be a questionable assumption particularly with regard to the state of the design at the east end of the site.

11.16 Irrespective of the architectural design an appropriate structural design is a requirement of a valid Stage D. Bovis, in evidence before the Inquiry, and not without cause, suggested that the Stage D report was not a co-ordinated Stage D in that the engineering design information was not a Stage D.[612] Mr David Lewis, Partner at Ove Arup & Partners, when giving evidence said:

> "The second scheme design report did not contain structural or services drawings as the architectural layouts could not be finished in time to use them as templates. We had produced many sketches and designs working with Enric at regular meetings in Barcelona, but much of this advice was not incorporated in the architectural drawings at this stage, and in this respect it was not a coordinated scheme design. This was a concern, as the programme required us to produce tender documents in August, and piling information before that, even though the scheme design had not been fixed." [613]

11.17 Mr Lewis assented to the proposition that the Stage D document was imperfect saying that was "because we did not have time to produce drawings for it" and that the production of drawings might have taken a month. This had been confirmed in a letter from Ms Patricia Johnstone, Associate, Ove Arup & Partners, to Mr Kinsley dated 17 May 2000.[614]

Robustness of Stage D

11.18 Mr Fisher's view was that "it was not a robust Stage D in totality".[615] He said in evidence:

---

[609] BV/1/477-482 – Written Submission from Mr Alan Mack to the Holyrood Inquiry, 10 October 2003

[610] Auditor General for Scotland's Report of June 2004, Paras 2.22 *et seq*

[611] RM/7/080-081 – Letter from Mr John Kinsley to Mr Ian McAndie, 10 August 2000

[612] BV/1/477-482 – Written Submission from Mr Alan Mack to the Holyrood Inquiry, 10 October 2003

[613] Evidence of Mr David Lewis on 7 May 2004, Para 385 *et seq*

[614] OA/1/070 – Letter from Ms Patricia Johnstone to Mr John Kinsley, 17 May 2000

[615] Evidence of Mr Hugh Fisher on 29 March 2004, Para 536

"… the state of the design was very different across the site. So when we produced the cost estimate at that time we were looking at fairly well-developed designs in relation to the MSPs' building and Queensberry House and much more embryonic designs in relation to the east side of the site."[616]

11.19 On the evidence before me I conclude that the Stage D report and the Cost Plan later developed on the basis of it did not provide a robust foundation for the future of the Project. I note that as early as November 2000 DLE were reporting from a risk workshop a nominal design and construction risk exposure, exclusive of inflation, of some £28.7 million,[617] putting the total construction cost significantly well over the Cost Plan 'budget'.

11.20 I noted that Mr Fisher in his written statement[618] put forward a non exhaustive list of the key changes which, with the benefit of 20-20 hindsight, he thought might have most benefited the Project. It struck me as of particular significance that among them he listed:

'Adherence to a logical plan of work (and in particular the opportunity to produce a Cost Plan that reflected a completed Stage D).'

11.21 The practical consequence of the incompleteness, particularly of the engineering design at this stage was explained by Bovis[619] who explained that it resulted in further delay to the design processes for critical trade packages on the east of the site. I am in agreement that this must have been a consequence.

Guaranteed Maximum Price

11.22 Mr Spencely's Report had recommended against any change in the contractual arrangements.[620] His view was that any such change would have had the consequence of considerable delay. He also pointed out that the Project could, in the event of a change of contract, have lost the benefit of Bovis' accumulated expertise.

11.23 Notwithstanding that view, at its second meeting on 4 July 2000 [621] the HPG looked at the possibility of moving to a guaranteed maximum price contract for the remainder of the Project. They were advised by Mr Fisher that the transfer of risk inherent in such a change, with the design of the east end of the site still at a relatively early stage, was likely to add several tens of millions of pounds to the overall cost. The HPG accepted the implications of this advice and decided against pursuing the matter any further.

---

[616] *ibid*, Para 534
[617] DL/2/074-084 - Report from Mr Ian McAndie to Dr John Gibbons, 2 November 2000
[618] MS/15/001-009 – Mr Hugh Fisher's First Witness Statement, 18 February 2004
[619] BV/1/477-482 – Written Submission from Mr Alan Mack to the Holyrood Inquiry, 10 October 2003
[620] Mr Spencely's Report, Section 7 'Review and comparison of the advantages of alternative contractual methods'
[621] CB/4/009-016 - Minutes of HPG Meeting of 4 July 2000

11.24 The HPG's decision on this point and at this time was, in my view, entirely appropriate. Whatever may have been the wisdom of the initial decision to adopt construction management as the procurement vehicle for the Project (and I have already questioned whether it was properly explained), the contractual position in that respect was inherited by both the SPCB and the HPG. The contract with Bovis made no provision for the change of their consultancy role as the Construction Manager to any other role such as that of management contractor or works contractor. While a change in the nature of a contractual relationship, even a fundamental change such as this, might always be a matter for negotiation between the parties there would, quite apart from the cost implications pointed out by Mr Fisher, have been formidable European procurement law difficulties in entering into what would effectively be a new contract without a proper procurement process. Any Guaranteed Maximum Price which might have been secured at that time, either with Bovis or following a fresh and no doubt lengthy procurement process, would inevitably have been very much greater than the £195 million budget set by the Parliament.

The Death of Snr Miralles

11.25 On 17 March 2000 Snr Miralles confided in his wife for the first time[622] that he had been feeling unwell and had arranged to visit a doctor in Barcelona. A scan revealed that he had a large tumour in his brain which was deemed by the Spanish specialist to be inoperable. Almost immediately, he and his family flew to Houston, Texas where on 29 March he underwent surgery to remove the tumour. Initial signs were encouraging and it was believed the operation had been successful although Snr Miralles remained in Houston for some weeks to undergo radiotherapy treatment.

11.26 Mr Stewart had been notified of Snr Miralles's illness on 17 March but, although concerned for him and for the implications for the Project, it is clear that no-one appreciated the full severity of the illness at that stage. Mr Stewart kept in touch with Snr and Sra Miralles in the USA, sharing faxes on his progress and on aspects of the Holyrood Project. On 4 April Mr Stewart and Dr Gibbons personally conveyed the news of Snr Miralles' illness to Donald Dewar. The Inquiry learned that this information was communicated to the Sir David Steel the same day.

11.27 During the debate on 5 April, Sir David Steel reported that Snr Miralles had "lately been quite ill". I am satisfied from the evidence of Sra Tagliabue and Mr Stewart that this was an honourable statement by Sir David Steel based upon everyone's understanding of the nature of Snr Miralles' health at that time, and not an attempt to withhold information from MSPs in advance of a crucial vote. From tapes I have seen, Donald Dewar was clearly uncomfortable

---

[622] Evidence of Sra Benedetta Tagliabue on 29 March 2004, Para 440

about discussing publicly someone else's health but that stemmed from a reticence, of which I can only approve, not from a desire to be evasive.

11.28   Snr Miralles continued to work on the detail of many of his contracts from his Houston base and it was not until the end of May that a further scan revealed that the tumour had not been eradicated. As his health deteriorated, the family returned to Barcelona on 18 June where he continued to undertake treatment. He died on 3 July 2000.

11.29   While the Project had lost its creative and charismatic principal architect the design to his concept should have by this time reached a sufficiently advanced stage for the Project to continue in his absence. His death, however, gave rise to a substantial period of disharmony within the architectural Joint Venture and the only conclusion can be, sadly, that it caused further delay.

11.30   An immediate difficulty that arose was in relation to the replacement of Snr Miralles as principal person to "direct and control ...overall performance by the architect" in terms of Clause 2.2 of the Architect's contract.[623] Within a month of Snr Miralles' death this became the subject of some strongly worded correspondence between Sra Tagliabue and Mr Stewart.[624] On 16 August Lewis Macdonald required to write on behalf of the HPG to the three surviving Directors of EMBT/RMJM Ltd inviting their attendance at its meeting on 23 August to present agreed proposals as to how they intended to co-operate in taking the project forward.[625] Agreement could not be reached before the meeting on a proposal in terms of which all three Directors would assume joint responsibility for the obligations under Clause 2.2. With some difficulty, involving the good offices of Dr Gibbons and after the involvement of lawyers and some further acrimonious correspondence a deal was thrashed out in time for the HPG's meeting on 13 September[626] to which all three Directors put forward an acceptable joint letter[627] in terms of which there was be no replacement of Snr Miralles as 'principal person'. As Mr Gordon reported: "peace has broken out in the Design Team".[628] This led to the anomaly of a conscious decision to leave a deceased person as the 'principal person' for the purposes of the architectural appointment. On one view this was an expedient fudge by the HPG which left the Design Team as something of a rudderless ship. On the other hand Snr Miralles had not been doing much to 'direct and control .. overall performance by the Architect'. He was always a concept designer rather than a manager and it may have made little difference to the practical

---

[623] RM/1/027-052 – Memorandum of Agreement between the Secretary of State and EMBT with RMJM (Scotland) Limited, 24 June 1998
[624] RM/7/066-070 – Letters of 1, 4 and 7 August 2000 and RM/7/074- 076 – Letter of 8 and 11 August 2000
[625] RM/7/083-Letter from Lewis Macdonald to Sra Tagliabue, Mr Stewart and Mr Duncan, 16 August 2000
[626] CB/4/048 – Minutes of HPG Meeting of 13 September 2000, including a chronology of the EMBT/ RMJM correspondence
[627] CB/4/1083-1084 – Letter from Sra Tagliabue, Mr Stewart and Mr Duncan to Lewis Macdonald, 13 September 2000
[628] SE//9/235 – Note from Mr Robert Gordon to the Minister for Parliament, 19 September 2000

arrangements. However, I have a sense that the subsequent problems might have been avoided if a more robust stance had been taken by the HPG at the time.

Cost Reporting to the HPG

11.31 At meetings on 20 September[629] and 15 November 2000[630] it was reported that the Project was on programme and budget. At the first meeting the question was raised with Mr Fisher, apparently for the first time, as to whether the £195 million budget included inflation. He reported his understanding that the £108 million construction cost component of that budget was based on March 1998 prices, in accordance with Government practice. While Mr Fisher hoped the impact of inflation could be absorbed, he sounded warnings that "it would not be easy" and that "it would be giving a hostage to fortune to imply that the Project could be delivered for £98 million at 1998 prices". He clarified that the £10.8 million contingency sum was not designed to cover inflationary pressures. Apart from this possible cloud on the horizon, the news reaching the HPG at this time was basically good news.

The Death of Donald Dewar

11.32 Following an accident, Donald Dewar died suddenly on 11 October 2000. As Mr Stewart put it in evidence his death and that of Snr Miralles earlier in the year left the Holyrood Project bereft of its begetters and prime advocates.[631] Although responsibility for the Project had passed to the SPCB in June 1999 his continuing influence on the Project should not be ignored. As the prime instigator of the Project and having spoken powerfully in its favour at the Parliamentary debates in June 1999 and April 2000 Donald Dewar had a very substantial and continuing personal political investment in the fortunes of the Project.

11.33 I knew Donald Dewar well, having been on the Select Committee on Scottish Affairs early in the 1979 Parliament when he was Chairman of it. I was well aware from at least that time of his commitment to the establishment of a Scottish Parliament. He enjoyed very considerable political influence at Westminster and Scotland which should not be under-estimated. All the comment to me has emphasised that it was his drive and determination that caused the new Parliament Building Project to go forward. That was undoubtedly the case.

11.34 It is more difficult to assess whether he could have or should have asked more searching questions on costs prior to the handover in June 1999. His Special Adviser Lord Elder talked of his unease over the figures being supplied to him[632] but there was no evidence before me that he sought any appraisal of the costs from, for example, the independent cost consultant

---

[629] CB/4/064–066 - Minutes of HPG Meeting of 20 September 2000
[630] CB/4/081-083A - Minutes of HPG Meeting of 15 November 2000
[631] Evidence of Mr Brian Stewart on 22 March 2004 (pm), Para 311
[632] Evidence of Lord Elder on 29 October 2003, Para 132

Mr Fisher of DLE. If he had, it is difficult to believe that there would not have been a searching re-appraisal of the whole Project before handover in June 1999.

11.35 It comes as no surprise that after the revelation by Mr Spencely in 2000 of Mr Fisher's assessment of costs in early 1999 that he contemplated resignation on the basis that he had misled the Scottish Parliament. Donald Dewar was steeped in the Westminster tradition that there is no greater democratic misdemeanour than misleading Parliament and he clearly carried that with him when he became First Minister in the Scottish Parliament. However, there was no evidence whatsoever to suggest that he deliberately or knowingly misled MSPs. He relied on cost figures given to him by senior civil servants. As it turned out, he should not have done so but he did not conceal figures that he knew were a better assessment. In the event he did not resign and in my view was correct not to have done so.

September 2000 Report of the Auditor General for Scotland

11.36 In the summer of 2000 the Auditor General for Scotland undertook an examination of the Project under the Public Finance and Accountability (Scotland) Act 2000, s.23 under which he was empowered to examine the economy, efficiency and effectiveness with which resources have been used. The involvement of the Auditor General was at the request of Andrew Welsh, then convener of the Parliament's Audit Committee. The Report was presented to the Audit Committee on 19 September 2000.[633]

11.37 It would not be appropriate for me to comment in any detail on the conclusions of the Auditor General at that time, but an appreciation of his key findings and recommendations is vital to any proper understanding, not just of the history of the Project to that time, but also of its subsequent history.

11.38 The Auditor General's main findings in his 2000 report were:

- The rise in construction cost estimates from £50 million to £108 million was attributable to two main factors. About half resulted from the 47% increase in the total area of the building. The other main factor was the much greater complexity of design in comparison with the notional concept at the time of the 1997 feasibility studies upon which the original budget was based.[634]

- The programme delay could be attributed largely to difficulties in approving a fixed design due in part to difficulties encountered by the architects in complying with the brief and in part to design change requested by the client.[635]

- The organisation of the project management team reflected good practice with a clear chain of command.[636]

---

[633] September 2000 Report: http://www.audit-scotland.gov.uk/publications/pdf/2000/00g01ag.pdf
[634] Auditor General for Scotland's Report of September 2000, Paras 2.3 to 2.9
[635] *ibid*, Paras 2.20 to 2.34
[636] *ibid*, Para 3.6

- In general terms the appointments of the consultants were properly undertaken although some aspects might have been more systematic and better recorded.

- The use of construction management was innovative in the public sector and, while offering advantages of control, left risk with the client rather than the contractor, raising a question as to whether project management had the appropriate construction management expertise to meet the demands of the Project.[637]

- While the decision to select construction management was taken after due professional consideration, a comprehensive procurement strategy should have been prepared beforehand.[638]

- There should have been a formal project execution plan.[639]

- Value Engineering should have been integrated into the process of design.[640]

- There should have been change control procedures based on a detailed cost plan agreed between all parties at an early stage. It was of concern that there was still no Cost Plan at the time of the Report.[641]

- Cost reporting was deficient:

  - in the absence of an arrangement requiring project management to provide full cost information on a regular and systematic basis;

  - monitoring, particularly before handover, concentrated on construction cost without taking account of fees, VAT and fit out; and

  - although there was a general contingency allowance of 10% of construction costs, there was a departure from good practice in the failure to identify and quantify a separate allowance for the major risks potentially affecting the Project.[642]

- The SPCB should, on taking over the Project, have taken steps to satisfy itself about the status and health of the Project with a degree of independence from project management. An independent review at that time would have been particularly valuable as design was not firmly fixed and the cost consultants were reporting figures significantly higher than budget.[643]

- Mr Grice, as Clerk of the Parliament, was responsible for ensuring that the SPCB was properly informed and that, where needed, they received adequate independent advice. He was also the Project Owner and responsible for its successful delivery. It might have been advisable to allocate responsibility for Holyrood so as to safeguard the effective exercise of each role.[644]

- The establishment of the HPG, with the benefit of independent professional members, should be of assistance to the SPCB in its stewardship of the Project.[645]

11.39   The Auditor General made a number of key recommendations which included:

'A risk analysis should be prepared as soon as practicable to identify all remaining risks to the Project and their potential impact on costs and deadlines and which should be the basis for an action plan to manage those risks.'

---

[637] Auditor General for Scotland's Report of September 2000, Para 3.6 to 3.15
[638] *ibid*, Para 3.20
[639] *ibid*, Para 3.38
[640] *ibid*, Para 3.44 to 3.45
[641] *ibid*, Para 3.40 to 3.43
[642] *ibid*, Para 3.46 to 3.53
[643] *ibid*, Para 3.62 to 3.64
[644] *ibid*, Para 3.66
[645] *ibid*, Para 3.68 to 3.69

'Project management should review the overall cost provision in the light of the risk analysis and ensure that, in accordance with good practice, there is separate allowance for risk in the estimate.'

'Project management, the Design Team and the Construction Manager must agree a Cost Plan taking account of risks and uncertainty to provide an effective basis for managing the remaining stages of the Project.'

'A single authoritative point of contact between the client and project management must be confirmed and through that point must pass all instructions to the Construction Manager and the Design Team.'

11.40   The Auditor General presented his 2000 report at a significant stage in the Holyrood Project; shortly after the establishment of the HPG but (as he recognised was unusual for an audit) before the completion of the Project. As such his report was timely and offered an informed roadmap that could take the Project forward to a successful conclusion which at that stage was envisaged to occur in December 2002. My own investigation has had the benefit of a further three years of activity and the evidence of a number of witnesses not available to the Auditor General from which to draw in reaching my own conclusions about the circumstances that lie behind this beleaguered project. From my own examination I am struck by the perceptiveness of the findings of the Auditor General in 2000 and find it difficult to disagree with his analysis which has proved remarkably durable.

11.41   In my view the recommendations in the Auditor General's report were sound and could have had a significant influence upon the subsequent evolution of the Project. While limitations of time did not permit me to conduct as intensive an examination as I would have wished of the extent to which the report's recommendations were implemented, I have been able to reach some conclusions based upon the evidence before me. I am content that progress was made against almost all of the recommendations but I have to conclude that in almost every case this was either incomplete or fell short of the action I suspect was intended by the Auditor General. What is incontestable is that the Project did not proceed smoothly to the conclusion that was anticipated and many of the shortcomings identified in 2000 have persisted until the present day. I will cover much of this in the remainder of this report.

Scottish Parliament Audit Committee's 6th Report

11.42   The Standing Orders of the Scottish Parliament[646] require the Audit Committee to consider and report on any report laid before the Parliament by the Auditor General for Scotland. The Committee met on seven occasions between September and November 2000 and heard

---

[646] The Scottish Parliament Standing Orders, Rule 6.7

evidence from Sir Muir Russell and Mr Grice as the two accountable officers over the course of the Project. The full text of the Committee's report is available at the Scottish Parliament's website.[647]

11.43   The Committee's main conclusions can be summarised as follows:

- The Committee believed the building to be the most significant in modern Scottish history, posing the challenges to create a building of which to be proud against an imperative that the highest standards of financial management were to be achieved.
- It was unhelpful that a misunderstanding in the public mind had been created about the full costs of this Project . It was unnecessary and wrong not to disclose the estimated full costs once they were available.
- Cost reporting systems were unsystematic and did not adequately reflect the political dimension of this Project leading to important cost information not being provided to the client and, on at least one occasion, to Sir Muir Russell as accountable officer.
- Risk assessment policies which were in operation prior to the agreement of a cost plan were insufficient and at odds with HM Treasury guidance.
- The Committee could not identify conclusively the underlying causes of the increase in construction costs from £62 million to £108 million. It considered that the redesign of the Chamber did not alter the forecast construction costs greatly although it did have a significant impact on programme.
- The Committee did not share Sir Muir Russell's view that the Project, when transferred in June 1999, was clearly sustainable within the budget set.
- There should have been an independent review of the Project in June 1999 which would have provided more positive assurance about the prospects for completion on time and on budget and would have usefully highlighted the remaining risks and uncertainties.
- The Committee disagreed with the judgment taken by Mr Grice not to inform the SPCB of DLE's estimate in August 1999 that construction costs could reach £115 million. It was unacceptable that this information was withheld from the SPCB.
- The Spencely report was a turning point for the Project and there were indicators of improved management now in place. The HPG had added an element of independent scrutiny and political control that was not previously evident.
- Concerns remained about the impact of construction inflation.

11.44   Based on those findings the Committee made a number of recommendations including:

- For future high profile projects it was recommended that accountable officers within the Scottish Administration and other public bodies consider carefully their responsibilities to answer to Ministers and the Parliament for the exercise of their functions. In the interests of good stewardship and public accountability they should, for any major project for which they are accountable, ensure that they are informed and can consider the consequences of the risk of increased costs. Where the consequences may be so great as to undermine confidence in the

---

[647] http://www.scottish.parliament.uk/business/committees/historic/audit/reports-00/aur00-06-01.htm

viability or value for money of the project, the accountable officer should consider informing Ministers, who may then inform the Parliament.

- It was recommended that the Scottish Executive should conduct a review of its policy on fee incentivisation with a view not only to maximising value for money but also achieving best value.

- The Scottish Executive should act to clarify the application of Treasury guidance on risk assessment and tackle the problematic yet critical issue of how risk assessment can be achieved in a robust manner. As part of this review, it was suggested that Ministers might wish to consider guidelines under which accountable officers present monitoring reports to them and recommended that the Scottish Executive consider the issues pertaining to public reporting and overall public expenditure planning. It was considered that the type of questions which needed to be addressed included defining the circumstances where risk assessment figures should - as a matter of course - be reported to the Parliament, and hence made public.

- For future major capital projects it was recommended that the Executive, and other public bodies in Scotland, consider the appointment of independent scrutineers to reinforce project monitoring at critical stages.

All the evidence before me would lead me to conclude that these recommendations were well-founded and I respectfully adopt them.

Health of the Project – December 2000

11.45 On 7 December 2000, shortly after Mr Ezzi took up his position as Project Director, Mr Mustard prepared for his benefit a paper setting out his views on the project culture and dynamics.[648] His main observations were that (1) the main challenge in the Bovis Programme[649] which although "probably achievable", was tight; (2) the relatively poor performance of the Design Team in terms of tender and construction information flow was impacting on budget and (3) the budget and the contingency were under pressure due to design development beyond the Cost Plan agreement. In evidence Mr Ezzi confirmed that he felt Mr Mustard's analysis and observations to be mainly sound.[650] I find myself in agreement with that view. It is not difficult to conclude that by the end of 2000 the Project was in serious trouble despite the best efforts of the HPG and Project Management. As it progressed into 2001 and beyond those difficulties would increase.

---

[648] CB/5/103A-104 – Paper from Mr Martin Mustard to Mr Alan Ezzi, 7 December 2000
[649] *ibid*, Bovis Programme Revision 3 Series – target completion date December 2002
[650] Evidence of Mr Alan Ezzi on 10 March 2004, Para 151

Chapter 12

The Project from Late 2000

The Appointment of Mr Alan Ezzi

12.1   The SPCB had first expressed the view that there was a need for an "efficient professional project manager to take the scheme forward" at its private meeting on 23 February 2000.[651] Although Mr Spencely's Report had not recommended any changes in this area, a review of the Project Sponsor role coinciding with the setting up of the HPG had concluded that the post should be split between a Project Director and a Financial Controller. At its meeting on 18 May the SPCB approved Mr Grice's proposal that an industry professional should be appointed as Project Director.[652] An advertisement[653] for a Project Director was drawn up together with an information pack[654] which proposed a salary of up to £65,000 for "a dynamic individual" with a proven track record of delivering major building projects.

12.2   Both the advertisement and the information pack stated that the appointee was to be the SPCB's representative, acting as the single focal point for day to day management of the Project, "with responsibility for securing the delivery of the new building complex to programme, within budget and to the specified quality." Mr Grice explained in evidence that he

[651] CB/2/204A-B - Letter from Mr Huw Williams to Mr Paul Grice, 24 February 2000
[652] CB/2/743-744 - Minutes of SPCB Meeting of 18 May 2000, Item 1
[653] CB/2/259 - Draft Advertisement for the Holyrood Project Director, 24 May 2000
[654] CB/2/260-265 - Holyrood Project Director post details, 24 May 2000

was looking for someone to perform "a leadership role, using project management, not actually doing the Project managing".[655] Most significantly the minute of the SPCB Meeting of 24 May records Mr Grice having explained "that the Project Director's main responsibility would be the control of the costs of construction which related directly to the £108 million figure."[656]

12.3   There was a good response to the advertisement and following a competitive interview by a panel comprising Mr Grice, Lewis Macdonald and Mr Manson, Mr Ezzi was offered the position. Mr Ezzi was an experienced project manager who had for the previous six years been employed on the project for the construction of the new Royal Infirmary of Edinburgh, latterly as Capital Projects Director. His appointment for a three year fixed term commencing on 13 November 2000 at an undisclosed salary was confirmed in a letter of 5 September 2000.[657] Mr Ezzi was to be entitled to a lump-sum payment equivalent to 10% of his final salary on the successful completion of his contract. It was not until 17 January 2001, over three months after being offered the appointment and some two months after he had actually commenced work, that Mr Ezzi received from Mr Grice a formal letter[658] setting out the terms of the delegation to him and providing him with a detailed job description.[659]

12.4   After accepting the terms of the job description, Mr Ezzi received a paper reviewing the existing management structure from the Parliament's Audit Adviser, Mr Ferguson, on 30 January 2001. This paper detailed the intended structures in place both before and immediately after his appointment[660] and outlined his intended role within the new structure.[661]

12.5   The new organisation chart showed the Project Director as central to the Project, a point which is underlined in the text of Mr Ferguson's letter, where he described the Project Director as *"the key role in the structure."*

---

[655] Evidence of Mr Paul Grice on 1 April 2004, Para 159

[656] CB/2/276 - Minutes of SPCB Meeting of 24 May 2000

[657] MS/17/001-006 – Appointment Letter from Ms Mary Nicol to Mr Alan Ezzi, 5 September 2000

[658] CB/5/105–106 - Letter from Mr Paul Grice to Mr Alan Ezzi, 17 January 2001

[659] CB/5/107-108 – Holyrood Project Director Job Description, 17 January 2001

[660] CB/6/225-228 – Paper from Mr Dave Ferguson to the Project Team, 30 January 2001

[661] *ibid*, Annex B

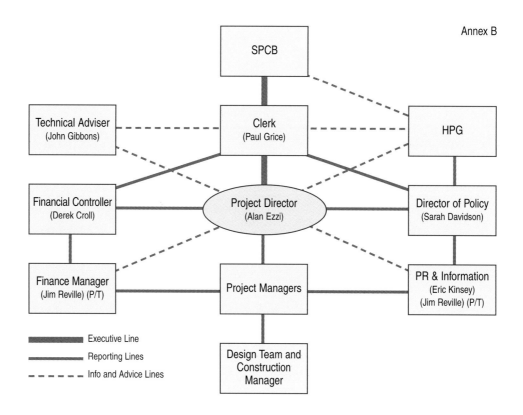

12.6 Furthermore, his role in the decision making process was explained within the letter in the following terms:

"It is essential ... that all executive decisions are channelled through Mr Ezzi and that directions and instructions to the Construction Manager and the Design Team are given only by Mr Ezzi or those at Project Manager level delegated formally by him. The lines of communication should be clarified and understood not only by members of the Project Team but also all consultants and contractors involved in the Project."

12.7 It would be fair to surmise that on receipt of this letter, Mr Ezzi could have realistically expected to be party to all key decisions taken with regard to management of the Project and that all information would flow through him.

Cost Cutting Exercises

12.8 In late 2000 it had emerged that there were problems developing with the trade package for the East Frame, with DLE's pre-tender estimate suggesting that this package alone would exceed the cost plan allowance for this item by £7 million cost. It was recognised that an overrun of this magnitude would put the £108 million construction budget under significant threat and arrangements were made to conduct an exercise to identify site-wide savings.

12.9 At its meeting on 17 January 2001, the HPG endorsed the need for a cost saving exercise to identify savings of up to £2 million, to which it attached 'considerable importance'. Their strength of purpose was diluted by what Mr Ezzi considered to be the 'somewhat ambivalent message'[662] contained in the minutes of that meeting and in the HPG Secretary's report to Mr Grice:

> 'The Design Team should not be encouraged to investigate the possibilities for savings which clearly impact on the brief or on other widely held expectations for the functionality and appearance of the finished building.'[663]

12.10 The HPG Convener, Lewis Macdonald, did not see this as asking the Project Director to pull in different directions. In evidence he explained that the HPG:

> "were asking him to find savings in respect of parts of the Project which would not significantly undermine either the functionality or the appearance or indeed the design quality of the building. ... What we were saying to him was that if there were any respects in which less fundamental parts of the Project could be reduced in scope or reduced in cost, he should report those to us. We had, in other words, set in train a process where we were asking the Project Director to find savings, but we were doing it within the context of the Stage D design and of the overall quality of the final product."[664]

12.11 Mr Ezzi, however, was concerned at the introduction of an essentially subjective factor into project management and the particular hazards that presented themselves when that subjectivity was determined by a diverse committee.

12.12 The meeting of the HPG on 14 February 2001 saw evidence that there was less than ideal collaboration among consultants and between consultants and the Project Team. After a disjointed presentation, the Secretary was forced to write in a letter to Mr Grice:

> 'Members of the Progress Group were unanimous in their view that the meeting .. illustrated the extent to which the Design Team is failing to function in a way that meets the client's needs. Members regard it as unacceptable that the Architect should present a paper to the client including figures to which the cost consultant does not subscribe and equally unacceptable that the cost consultant failed to make his reservations plain to the Project Team at preparatory briefing meetings. The Group recommends that the Project Director should act with their full authority (my emphasis) and support to convey these views to the Design Team in the strongest possible terms.'[665]

12.13 Mr Ezzi's cost-saving proposals were pulled together in the form of a paper for the HPG and were costed by DLE. The proposals covered a range of measures including installing a

---

[662] WS/41/001-015 - Mr Alan Ezzi's Witness Statement, 10 March 2004
[663] CB/4/671-677 - Minutes of HPG Meeting of 17 January 2001 and CB/4/678C-679 – Letter from Ms Davidson to Mr Grice, 19 January 2001
[664] Evidence of Lewis Macdonald on 3 March 2004, Paras 245 to 246
[665] CB/4/732-733 - Letter from Ms Sarah Davidson to Mr Paul Grice, 14 February 2001

supporting pillar under the cantilevered Canongate Building and using alternative materials for the vaulted ceiling of the Public Foyer. It is evident that the Architect was not involved in the preparation of these proposals and the reaction could have been anticipated. Even before the paper could be presented to the Progress Group it evoked a forceful reaction from the Architect who was concerned that the proposals would seriously jeopardise the quality of the building. Writing in support of a critical letter to Lewis Macdonald from Mr Duncan, Sra Tagliabue stated:

> 'Even if it is proved that architecture is not the reason for a particular price increase, the only manner envisaged for cost reduction now is by reducing architectural quality, causing a risk of reaching a paradox of having a cheap building costing a huge amount of money'.[666]

12.14 The majority of the cost-saving proposals did not find favour with the HPG who appear to have been influenced by the lobbying of the Architect and, on this occasion, placed quality ahead of other considerations. Dr Gibbons explained the rationale:

> "Well, the Progress Group thought that was not good at all. On the one hand we are saying, "This building has to stand for a hundred years"; and on the other hand we have a piece of this structure that one member of the Progress Group put his fist through in the room that (it) was being presented to us. In terms of quality of material; yes, there was a reduction in cost, but there was a considerable reduction in the quality of the product as well."[667]

12.15 Interestingly, the SPCB were re-engaged over this matter as it involved a decision to forego potentially significant savings. They gave a strong steer that quality mattered and endorsed the HPG decision to accept some proposals and reject others.

12.16 Mr Ezzi's difficulties continued and the HPG minutes over this period record a growing sense of frustration over the performance of the team as a whole and Mr Ezzi's individual performance in particular. It is evident that relationships between the HPG and others were also strained.[668] In the minutes of the meeting on 25 April it is noted that 'It was suggested that the Project Director was failing to fulfil his declared and expected role in pulling the team together'.[669] The minutes continued:

> 'The Group was conscious of an emerging lack of confidence in the performance of the various members of the Project and Design Teams and in the quality of information presented to them in particular.'[670]

---

[666] CB/4/1090-1091 - Letter from Sra Benedetta Tagliabue to Lewis Macdonald, 5 March 2001
[667] Evidence of Dr John Gibbons on 6 May 2004, Para 242
[668] Evidence of Paul Grice on 1 April 2004, Para 273
[669] MS/17/001-006 – Appointment letter from Ms Mary Nicol to Mr Alan Ezzi, 5 September 2000. The letter required Mr Ezzi to 'co-ordinate and foster teamwork'
[670] CB/4/808-813 - Minutes of HPG Meeting of 25 April 2001

12.17 Mr Grice responded to these concerns by calling a meeting of all the lead consultants. In advance of the meeting Mr Stewart issued what was described in evidence as a trenchant letter to Mr Grice highlighting some of the relationship difficulties that had developed. It is worth considering the terms of that letter carefully:

> 'It is news to no-one that we have struggled to engage DLE sufficiently in the design process and that the dialogue between the cost consultant and Architect, the cost consultant and Construction Manager has tended to be less than close. Nonetheless, however imperfect these relationships may have been in the past, they have in my view reached a perilous state as a result of the approach taken by Mr Ezzi in his role as Project Director. As far as we can tell, his technique appears to be concentrated on separating the members of the team just at the time when we should be pulling closer together; alienating the Project QS from the Design Team when he is most needed in the detailed design process; taking over the business of cost reporting without any reference to the Architect and failing to communicate with speed or accuracy the wishes of the client; a divide and rule approach.'[671]

12.18 The meeting convened by Mr Grice on 1 May 2001 saw an attempt to iron out the difficulties and achieve a more collaborative approach to the Project. It seems evident that key relationships had deteriorated beyond recovery. The Inquiry also learned that around this time Mr Curran, an important member of the Project Management team, had also indicated his intention to resign given the diminution of his role under Mr Ezzi.

12.19 The HPG expressed further concerns over Mr Ezzi's performance in relation to liaison with the Design Team on the Foyer roof. It was reported that Mr Stewart had not returned Mr Ezzi's phonecalls for 2 weeks and was proposing to reduce his personal role with the Project in future. The situation came to a head on 13 June when the Convener, by now John Home Robertson, wrote to Mr Grice in stark terms:

> 'It is our view that very little apparent progress has been made during Mr Ezzi's stewardship of the Project. ... We are not satisfied that he has acquired an adequate understanding of the complexity and sophistication of this Project, defined as it is by its unique history, structure and political context. In particular, we have been increasingly worried by the functional operation of the Design Team which has deteriorated demonstrably in recent months. Given the nature of the problems, we see no possible way in which they can be resolved while the current incumbent remains in post. We do not have confidence in the ability of Mr Ezzi to fulfil the requirements of the job.'[672]

12.20 In such circumstances it was impossible for Mr Ezzi to continue and after a discussion with Mr Grice he tendered his resignation with immediate effect. An undisclosed financial settlement was reached and both parties agreed not to comment upon the circumstances of the

---

[671] RM/7/211-212 - Letter from Mr Brian Stewart to Mr Paul Grice, 30 April 2001
[672] CB/4/1023-1024 - Letter from John Home Robertson to Paul Grice, 13 June 2001

departure. For the purposes of this Inquiry that agreement was waived and I was able to receive candid evidence on the events outlined above.

Loss of Confidence in Mr Ezzi

12.21 Mr Ezzi demonstrably found it difficult to develop a constructive relationship with the Architect, and particularly with Mr Stewart. In evidence he wrote:

> 'I found my own relationships with the architects particularly difficult. I was concerned that the architects in particular were in direct communication with the HPG members and tended to bypass me. John Gibbons maintained an office on site which made it easy for him to be approached directly. This significantly undermined my own authority. My relations with the architects became particularly strained during the period when we were looking at site wide savings and the decision of the HPG not to back up my recommendations further undermined my position. I felt that I had no real personal authority and that the situation was open to exploitation by direct access by the design team to the HPG members.'[673]

12.22 I detect strong echoes here of the difficulties encountered by Mr Armstrong two years earlier, although on the earlier occasion Mr Armstrong's difficulties seem to have concerned the Barcelona end of the joint venture company. Similarly, Mr Ezzi appears to have wrestled with the challenge of imposing a discipline on the Design Team to deliver design information to the agreed programme and to design to a budget rather than simply to a concept.[674] In evidence, Mr Stewart seemed to suggest that his relationship with Mr Ezzi had been largely effective. This was challenged by Mr Grice and, from the evidence I have heard, I have to agree that this was not a particularly harmonious period of the Project's life. Mr Ezzi had been appointed to be a "bruiser" over rising costs but whenever he attempted to fulfil that role he was left without support or had his proposals countermanded.

12.23 Mr Ezzi also grappled largely unsuccessfully with the complexities of working for a political client in the shape of the HPG. There does however seem to have been a failure on the part of the HPG to appreciate the difficulties which their actions placed upon the ability of their Project Director to perform his role. One such instance was the decision to exclude Mr Ezzi from substantive parts of HPG meetings from January 2001 and so make him dependent upon delayed and second hand instructions. As well as the practical difficulties which this imposed, it undoubtedly signalled to the consultants the status in which Mr Ezzi was held and devalued the sense he had of his personal contribution. Mr Stewart identified accurately the position that this peculiar decision generated:

> "It only highlights the point that clearly I am having difficulty getting over, which is the difficulty of Mr Ezzi being on the Holyrood Project Team but not being allowed to

[673] WS/41/001-015 - Mr Alan Ezzi's Witness Statement, 10 March 2004
[674] CB/4/873-879 - Minutes HPG Meeting of 23 May 2000, comments attributed to Mr Robert Gordon

attend Holyrood Progress Group meetings. How is he going to function? He is not carrying the confidence of his client. He is not centre stage; he expected to come in and be the man in control of everything and information would flow through him in the way that the first chart highlights, but he was not faced with that, he was faced with this. He was in an impossible position."[675]

12.24 The decision to exclude the Project Director from parts of HPG meetings was explained curiously as being "to ensure that those carrying executive authority for the Project were not party to the decision-making process of the advisory body, the HPG"![676] It would appear that it was thought that this would lend greater clarity to the process. In fact it achieved exactly the reverse. The line of authority, far from being clarified, was further confused with Mr Ezzi aware that the HPG were taking decisions (described as 'formal recommendations') in private when he was excluded. Mr Ezzi could be excused for being confused.

12.25 Quite apart from the inherent contradiction of a decision-making process of an advisory body, the subsequent Project Director was not excluded from meetings in the same manner as her predecessor. The audit advice to the HPG could evidently be disregarded when convenient.

12.26 Mr Grice spoke of the shared frustrations felt by Mr Ezzi and the HPG:

> "Probably the frustration on their part was that they felt the Project Director was not giving them good enough and clear enough advice. He in turn ... felt that they were perhaps not giving him the latitude to do his job. I think at the heart of it all was a lack of a shared understanding of their role and his role. I do not think that Mr Ezzi ever fully accepted the role given to the HPG by the Parliament. In turn, as the relationship broke down, they lost their trust in the Project Director. And when you lose your trust in somebody you are much less inclined to let them get on and do it; you are more likely to be on top of them. That is the process I observed."[677]

12.27 There does appear to have been a misunderstanding of Mr Ezzi's role and it is evident that this was something that was not adequately communicated to the HPG. In written evidence to the Inquiry Linda Fabiani stated:

> 'I did not see it as Alan's role to bring home the Project on budget and on time at the expense of all else and this may have led to a measure of misunderstanding between Alan and the HPG. The job description provided to him in January 2001 states that his main role 'is to be the SPCB's representative, acting as the single focal point for day to day management of the Parliament's interest in the Project with responsibility for securing the delivery of the new building complex to programme, within budget and to the specified quality'. I now also know, but was unaware at the time, that his contract stipulated an end of contract lump sum of 10% of his final year's salary on

[675] Evidence of Mr Brian Stewart on 22 March 2004 (am), Para 526
[676] CB/4/671-677 - Minutes of HPG Meeting of 17 January 2001
[677] Evidence of Mr Paul Grice on 1 April 2004, Paras 301 to 302

the successful conclusion of the terms of his contract. These details which I now have explain to some extent the attitudes struck by Alan during his appointment.' [678]

12.28 Linda Fabiani expressed her annoyance that her view of Mr Ezzi at the time had been coloured by her lack of awareness of the actual terms of his appointment and the approach that those terms required him to take. She also speculated whether Mr Ezzi had been under any similar misconceptions about the role of the HPG and whether relationships could have been altogether different had these misunderstandings been avoided at the time.[679]

Performance of Mr Ezzi

12.29 Ultimately, Mr Ezzi was unsuccessful because of two factors. Firstly, he was appointed with a strong background as a project manager but did not appear to appreciate the significant behavioural changes that were expected of him in the more strategic role of Project Director. The client did not, however, make the role it envisaged for the incoming Project Director sufficiently clear. In both the public advertisement for the post and in Mr Ezzi's formal letter of appointment the main role of the post-holder was described as 'to be the client's representative, acting as the single focal point for day to day management of the SPCB's interest in the Project, with responsibility for securing the delivery of the new building complex to programme, within budget and to the specified quality'. Against that background it is perhaps understandable that Mr Ezzi felt his most significant responsibility was to manage those around him rather than to relate to the political client.

12.30 Secondly, having failed to win the confidence of the political client, Mr Ezzi was hampered in his ability to perform his role by the lack of clear lines of accountability and the receptiveness of the HPG to alternative advice, guidance and information from other sources. Lewis Macdonald largely confirmed this predicament in evidence:

> "He had come to us and was appointed with a very strong track record as a project manager. I think as a Project Director we were perhaps looking for a development of that role in a more strategic direction. If I was to try and give a summary impression of the period in question it would be that he was clearly very engaged with the Project Management, but with some of the issues around relationships, particularly with consultants but also with ourselves, he perhaps struggled a bit to come to terms with the expectations that we had of the role that he would perform in that respect."[680]

The Appointment of Ms Sarah Davidson

12.31 With the departure of Mr Ezzi, Mr Grice took the view that the health of the Project could be jeopardised if there was a lengthy hiatus before the appointment of a successor. In the face of the growing cost and programme pressures, the SPCB had decided to go back to Parliament

[678] MS/22/001-024A - Linda Fabiani's Witness Statement, 8 March 2004
[679] Evidence of Linda Fabiani on 8 March 2004, Para 450
[680] Evidence of Lewis Macdonald on 3 March 2004, Para 226

for approval of a new approach and a debate had been scheduled for 21 June. Mr Grice was concerned to resolve the issue of the key Project Director post before that debate and, after taking soundings of Dr Gibbons and members of the HPG, he decided to invite the Secretary to the HPG, Ms Davidson, to accept the role. This appointment represented another change in direction in that Ms Davidson was a highly able administrative civil servant but not someone with the construction background of her predecessor. There was some criticism of the appointment at the time and Ms Davidson spoke of her regret that the announcement of her appointment had not made clear the different role she was expected to take from that of Mr Ezzi. Mr Grice explained to the Inquiry why he had sought a strategic Project Director who could manage the political dimension of the Project as well as earn the confidence of the professional consultants:

> "I would argue — and there is plenty of evidence for this — that the level of political and media scrutiny of this Project has been — I cannot find any example of it anywhere in the world. (The type of Project Director I had in mind was) a person who can both ensure that construction takes place and operate in that environment, in other words, that that sort of intensity of pressure does not cause them to collapse or, as I think was the case with previous people, to put that to one side effectively and say, "Right, I am just going to focus on the building of the building." I had Project Managers who could do that; I needed someone who could talk the language of the Project Managers, who could earn their respect and the respect of the key consultants, but who could also be sensitive to, and work with, this political element. That is what I am trying to describe to you. I think that is what makes it unique."[681]

12.32   In terms of her ability to relate to the political client (in the form of the HPG), Ms Davidson's appointment was undoubtedly successful. In evidence members of the HPG praised Ms Davidson's abilities and endorsed her appointment. Mr Wright made the following observation:

> "I think one of Sarah Davidson's real skills was (understanding) the political dimension of the relationships between the Group and the various Committees that existed within the Parliament. There is a very complex web; it is really hard to imagine how someone from outside the system, who is a construction manager — and I use that term advisedly in that sense — or a project manager really could have fulfilled all those roles in writing the necessary papers, say to Finance Committee and the Corporate Body. I think those were done generally — always, in my view — to a very high standard, and had a real grasp of the issues, sometimes much better than even appeared in our own minutes."[682]

12.33   Ms Davidson does not appear to have worked quite so closely with the consultants, drawing upon the team of project managers in the Project Team to manage the operational aspects of the Project. In this respect she represented a return to an organisational structure where the Director/Sponsor acted as the client's representative and the Project Manager oversaw the day

---

[681] Evidence of Mr Paul Grice on 1 April 2004, Para 357
[682] Evidence of Mr Andrew Wright on 4 March 2004, Para 56

to day management of the Project. Using a helpful graphic to illustrate his point, Mr Stewart spoke of a "multi-headed client" in response to whom Ms Davidson spent most of her time looking "upwards".

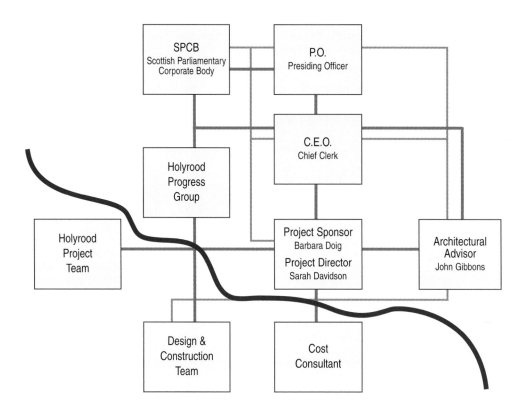

12.34 Mr Stewart spoke of the political interest in the minutiae of the Project which demanded both Ms Davidson's input and required the involvement of the Design Team. Mr Stewart cited as examples the "horrendous" experience of the SPCB selecting the chairs for the Parliament and the distraction of producing a report for an MSP on the specification of oak lamination on what he saw as a "total spurious issue".[683] While recognising this was part of the democratic process, Mr Stewart made the point that it was not possible to respond to these political needs and engage fully with the task of designing and constructing the Parliament building.

12.35 The appointment of Ms Davidson also saw the return of Dr Gibbons to a more prominent position within the Project. Mr Grice recognised that the new Project Director might require access to additional professional advice and so Dr Gibbons was identified as the Client Adviser on design matters. His main role was to act as the interface between the Design Team and the Project Director on technical matters. At that time there was also a strengthening of the role of the Project Managers, with Mr Curran coming to the fore as the Senior Project Manager. In evidence Mr Curran spoke of his 'empowerment' under Ms Davidson and there seems little

---

[683] Evidence of Mr Brian Stewart on 22 March 2004 (am), Paras 277 and 285

doubt that from this point the Project Managers were given more scope to deal with the day-to-day issues with only the occasional reference of decisions to the Project Director for resolution.

The Parliamentary Debate of 21 June 2001

12.36   The parliamentary debate on 21 June 2001 represented another pivotal point in the Holyrood Project's history. The motion passed on that occasion represented recognition by the Parliament for the first time that there were factors exerting an influence on the budget for the Project which meant that it could not be contained within the cap of £195 million agreed in April 2000. As well as requiring the SPCB to report quarterly to the Parliament's Finance Committee, the motion directed the SPCB, through the HPG, to work with the Design and Project Teams to complete the Project without compromising quality. The SPCB and, latterly the HPG, had always been consistent in stating that quality was important but this was the first time that the Parliament resolved explicitly that it must not be compromised.

12.37   Ms Davidson insisted strongly that by removing the cap, carte blanche for costs to rise had not been given to the Project. She spoke to the Inquiry of the motion's implications:

> "So, what was happening in June was a recognition of the fact that the budget that had been compiled at the time of the £195 million had been done on the basis of cost estimates in particular, cost package plan and other known factors. It was simply not going to be possible, however much one might have wished to, to absorb within that total inflation and risk. The fact is that, from then on, we were even more closely focused on the risk register. That meant, .. if anything, the focus on cost control was sharper after this period because we were thinking very hard about the numbers and about how they would turn from risk, as it were, into reality."[684]

12.38   Tellingly, Ms Davidson observed that "under construction management the notion of a cap is somewhat misleading anyway".[685] I have to question whether in approving the £195 million ceiling on costs in April 2000 Parliament fully understood the nature of the Project it was considering or the procurement route that had been selected for it before its inception. Although the HPG gradually developed an understanding of this key facet of construction management as it grappled with the complexities of managing risk and design development, this does not appear to have been shared by other MSPs until a surprisingly late stage. I have to question whether, without that necessary level of understanding, MSPs were well placed to take sound decisions about the direction and financial foundations for the Project. Although briefings and information were available to MSPs routinely and they had the opportunity to question members of the HPG, there is little evidence to suggest that the majority of MSPs had a sound grasp of what was involved. That is not a criticism. I have no evidence that they were encouraged to understand what construction management involved.

---

[684] Evidence of Ms Sarah Davidson on 31 March 2004, Para 332
[685] *ibid*, Para 336

Cost Escalation - The Foyer Roof

12.39 Although cost escalation has been a feature of the Project throughout its life, an examination of the particular circumstances of the Foyer roof (which surfaced as an issue at this time) will serve to illustrate many of the problems and frustrations that bedevilled the Project.[686]

12.40 The foyer had emerged from the decision of Snr Miralles to redesign the 'circulation' route between the MSP building and the Chamber through the courtyard of Queensberry House rather than through Queensberry House itself. It was envisaged that an open covered space would serve as a meeting space for Members and invited guests while also acting as a direct thoroughfare between Members' offices and the public areas of the Parliamentary complex. Difficulties first emerged (as far as the HPG was concerned) in April 2001 when the minutes recorded that:

> 'There was particular concern about the emergence of a problem with the costs of the Foyer roof design which at £3,300/m² compared with an initial cost plan figure of £500/m².' [687]

12.41 The HPG minutes also note:

> 'There was some discussion about how the design could develop so radically from the Stage D design without keeping in line with the allowed cost. .. The Group expressed frustration at the expenditure of design time on proposals which were doomed to fail in terms of cost... Mr Mustard responded by saying that the Architect did not display a clear understanding of the relationship between cost and design control or of what the key design stages meant.'

12.42 The issue had been brought to the HPG's attention following a visit to Barcelona undertaken by Mr Ezzi and Mr McAndie (of DLE). During that visit it became obvious to the visitors that design proposals of such complexity could not have been prepared with a budget of £500/m² in mind. There was apparently no alternative cheaper design to fall back on and the Architect was instructed to prepare one for consideration prior to tender issue. It was Mr Ezzi's evidence that no such alternative proposal was ever received.

12.43 Mr Ezzi suggested that this scrutiny of preliminary design proposals was proof of the design process working. Having been alerted to an emerging problem at a very early stage in the design process, he suggested that DLE and the Project Team had acted quickly to bring it back on course. That may have been their intention but whatever actions were taken at those

---

[686] See also Report of the Auditor General for Scotland 2004, Appendix 2D – Foyer Frame and Glazing
[687] CB/4/808-813 - Minutes of HPG Meeting of 25 April 2001

early stages, they clearly did not succeed in producing a design proposal that could be constructed for anything approaching the original anticipated figure.

12.44   The Foyer roof was the subject of a presentation to the HPG on 23 May 2001. There is a conflict in the evidence as to whether the model produced for this occasion by EMBT had been seen previously by RMJM. Members of the HPG certainly took away the impression that the model had come as a surprise to the Bells Brae members of the partnership. Mr Stewart suggested that it would be naïve to believe that RMJM were not fully aware of what their design partners were preparing. Either way, the HPG detected a dissonance between the two arms of the architectural company and, after the presentation, remained concerned at the anticipated costs of this part of the Project. More robust cost information was sought.

12.45   As an aside, the Inquiry noted that the HPG quizzed the Design Team on very detailed aspects of the Foyer roof design including, for instance, its snow-loading capacity. This does not seem to be the domain of a strategic monitoring body and illustrates the extent to which they had shifted from the principles of their genesis. Mr Ezzi voiced the frustration felt by the Design Team:

> "We spend public money on engaging highly respected architects and probably the most pre-eminent engineers in the world under Ove Arup, and then HPG are questioning whether or not they have included a calculation for snowloading on the roof. Frankly the Design Team thought that it was insulting that they were getting asked these questions. And I have to agree. I think that this is well beyond the remit of a group who are supervising at strategic level."[688]

12.46   The Foyer roof returned to the agenda of the HPG at their meeting on 5 December 2001 when it was reported that an interim contract had been awarded to Mero but they had tendered a figure of £6.1 million. The allowance for this contract had been £1.5 million and the reaction of the HPG was that such an increase was 'intolerable'. Mr Wright spoke of the feelings at the time:

> "It was obvious that there had been considerable design development since the compilation of the Stage D costings of this element and during the second stage of the tender process. The architects were of the view that the original cost allowance had been inadequate. They claimed that the design was unchanged. DLE offered no convincing explanations under examination by HPG as to why these and other costs had drifted upwards. Rather they gave the impression to the Group that there was a degree of inevitability in the outcome which the Group considered unacceptable. In the case of the Foyer roof the Group was aware that the tender must be accepted given that valuable time had been spent already in seeking to reduce the costs through re-design."[689]

---

[688] Evidence of Mr Alan Ezzi on 10 March 2004, Para 527
[689] Evidence of Mr Andrew Wright on 4 March 2004, Para 252

12.47 The HPG's view that the tender for the Foyer roof, which bore no relationship to the Cost Plan allowance, had nevertheless to be accepted to prevent programme slippage is a theme which recurred throughout the evidence. The HPG seemed to be placed in a position where they were required to take decisions at a stage in the process when it was too late to recommend or affect any meaningful change to the outcome. I also heard that the HPG frequently felt that they were "over a barrel" in these situations where cost and programme clashed. Asked why they felt unable to take an alternative course in relation to the Foyer roof, Mr Wright suggested:

> "It was primarily to stick to programme. ... Not to have done so would have a dramatic effect on the rest of the Project. To have done otherwise would have caused significant delay to the Project and the overall completion date as the area occupied by the Foyer was known to be central to maintaining progress on the completion of the external finishes to Queensberry House and the adjoining towers. The situation suggested that the design had been developed in a vacuum; that the two offices of EMBT/RMJM may not have been working closely together; that DLE may not have been monitoring costs as closely as they should have done; and that the episode had not been observed by Project Management." [690]

12.48 I have to conclude that Mr Wright's speculation is an accurate one. The evidence does suggest that levels of communication among key players were extremely poor on occasions, of which the Foyer roof is a prime example. Although I heard evidence of a visit to Barcelona by a member of the DLE team, I am not convinced that there was an appropriate level of interface between the Design Team and the cost consultants on this issue. While my primary criticism is of the Architect, DLE might also have taken a more proactive role in identifying that designs were being developed outwith the Cost Plan and drawing that to the attention of the client. As it was, the HPG inevitably felt bounced into approving actions with significant cost implications in view of the implications on programme (and to an extent on quality) if they were to do otherwise.

12.49 Clearly communication channels were hampered by the fact that the principal work on the Foyer roof took place in Barcelona. Notwithstanding the presence of EMBT staff in Bells Brae, I am tempted to conclude that this design work was not undertaken in a co-ordinated fashion, as it is apparent that the production of the finalised design took almost everyone by surprise. This was wholly unsatisfactory, particularly in respect of such a significant part of the building. I cannot exclude from criticism the Project Team which, against the background of this Project, should by this stage have had an effective monitoring system in place to ensure that such surprises were avoided. Whether this could have been avoided by the strengthening of Project Management I am unclear, but I have found that this incident demonstrates a major failure of management and a loss of control over the process.

---

[690] Evidence of Mr Andrew Wright on 4 March 2004, Paras 254 to 255

Cost Escalation - Kemnay Granite

12.50 The decision was taken to use Kemnay granite on the Parliament building. In November 2000 the HPG recommended that Kemnay granite be procured as part of the cladding package for the complex. In Mr Ezzi's view the use of this material in preference to Portuguese granite would result in additional costs of £520,000 at a time when the bids for the cladding package were already over estimate by around £3 million. Furthermore, uncertainty over the ability of the Kemnay suppliers to provide the quantity and quality of granite to the required timetable would threaten the ability to adhere to the construction programme. It is clear to me that Mr Ezzi in his role as Project Director properly informed the HPG that to proceed with the procurement of Kemnay granite would not represent best value for money and would significantly increase the risk of failing to meet the December 2002 completion date.[691]

12.51 The HPG deferred a decision on the matter but, after establishing that the supply could be assured, opted to incorporate Kemnay granite into the palette of materials. I understand that this decision was taken primarily for aesthetic reasons and as I have indicated I do not wish to offer a view on such matters but it highlights the dilemma facing the Project Director. The HPG took the decision (or at least recommended it) which led directly to an increase in cost at a time when a particular package was already in serious financial difficulty and at a time when the Project Director had been asked to identify potential site-wide financial savings. It suggests to me that even at this stage the client, expressing its will through the HPG, was placing greater store on the issue of aesthetics/quality than on either cost or programme.

Tensions within EMBT/RMJM Ltd

12.52 In the autumn of 2001, friction within the Architect again became an issue of concern to the client. There had been obvious signs of tension between the Directors for some time, such as their very public failure to agree the content of a presentation to the HPG on the Foyer roof.[692] Dr Gibbons attributed the problem to "disagreements over fee issues and the control of design responsibility for the Project".[693] In October the HPG were forced to take action in the interest of achieving 'a sea change in work practices concerning the flow of information to the Construction Manager'.[694] A decision was conveyed to the Architect that Mr Stewart would thereafter be the one point of control in all liaisons with the Project Director. This was not well received in Barcelona where Sra Tagliabue stood her ground as a Director of EMBT/RMJM Ltd. The correspondence between the Directors at this time was available to the Inquiry and is

---

[691] CB/4/1103-1106 - Minute from Mr Alan Ezzi to Mr Paul Grice, 13 December 2000
[692] CB/4/870-872 - Minutes of HPG Meeting of 16 May 2001
[693] WS/53/001-031 - Dr John Gibbons' Third Witness Statement, 6 May 2004
[694] CB/4/923-930 - Minutes of HPG Meeting of 26 September 2001

noteworthy for its forcefulness. I was not convinced by the implication in Mr Stewart's evidence that his relationship with Sra Tagliabue at that time was anything other than tense.

12.53　The HPG met the Directors of EMBT/RMJM Ltd on 13 November 2001 in an effort to resolve the issue. It is clear that there was widespread dissatisfaction within the client team and amongst the consultants at the friction within the Architect, and that it was having an effect on the progress of the Project. The meeting agreed that EMBT/RMJM Ltd would deliver a written management structure for the architectural joint venture. Mr Gordon wrote of the frustrations at the time:

> 'The huge irritation is that there is very little between the design partners but their failure to clarify who is going to do what from here on is wasting a great deal of their and the Project Team's time.'[695]

12.54　To the extreme frustration of all on the client side, two separate versions of a management chart were produced by Mr Stewart and Sra Tagliabue for the meeting of the HPG on 21 November 2001, yet the meeting was unable to secure a resolution. Mr Stewart confessed to Ms Davidson that matters were "descending into chaos"[696] and that litigation was a distinct possibility. Eventually the HPG took decisive action and summoned the protagonists to a further meeting on 26 November 2001 at which the posturing ended and an organisational structure was agreed with Mr Stewart identified as the one point of control. Sra Tagliabue was quick to point out in evidence that notwithstanding the newly proposed organisation structure chart, the chart was qualified with an express declaration that its terms made no difference to the contractual arrangements.[697] She was correct. In my view the chart made no difference, but the evidence suggests that there was an improvement in relationships and working practices after this resolution.

12.55　Mr Stewart insisted to the Inquiry that any disagreement between Directors of the joint venture had no impact upon the delivery of design information and that junior members of the Design Team would probably hardly have known of it.[698] Additionally, Mr Kinsley wrote to the Inquiry insisting that any suggestion that commercial disagreements had affected the delivery of design information could only be 'borne out of ignorance' and that a Project of this complexity could not have been designed by a dysfunctional team.[699] That may be, but I do not find it credible that a disagreement of this significance among directors, going as it does to the very heart of creative responsibility for the Project, did not have any effect upon it.

---

[695] SE/9/298-308 - Minute from Mr Robert Gordon to the Minister for Parliament, 23 November 2001
[696] RM/7/309 - Email from Mr Brian Stewart to Ms Sarah Davidson, 22 November 2001
[697] Evidence of Sra Benedetta Tagliabue on 29 March 2004, Paras 178 to 183
[698] Evidence of Mr Brian Stewart on 22 March 2004 (pm), Para 49
[699] RM/1/247 - Letter from Mr Kinsley to the Holyrood Inquiry, 29 March 2004

12.56   What is beyond dispute is that senior members of the Project Team and the HPG spent a considerable amount of time in an effort to resolve this disagreement. I do not imagine that this investment would have been made if the client did not feel its resolution was crucial to the well-being of the Project. It is evident that through this period the directors of EMBT/RMJM Ltd were unable to resolve their internal disagreements. As a consequence of the HPG's earlier inability to put this difficulty to rest, it had simmered for 15 months largely because the Principal Person issue had not been resolved. The HPG did however eventually take steps to find a solution to the problem. It may be thought that this effort came too late, but I cannot say that the disagreements within the architectural joint venture caused prolongation or material additional cost.

Design Freeze

12.57   The HPG sought to impose a design freeze on the Project in April 2003 and if that had been successful, costs might have been better contained. However, as John Home Robertson and Mr Mack confirmed in evidence[700], design continued to 'creep'. The discipline the HPG sought to impose on the process failed.

Fee Capping

12.58   The consultants' contracts, drawn up by the Scottish Office, had their fees based upon a percentage of the construction cost.[701] This meant that each time the construction cost increased, the consultants' fees increased. This caused the client concern as costs continued to increase and the matter was raised by the Project Sponsor, Mrs Doig, in her report to the SPCB in December 1999.[702] The agreements with each of the consultants were generally very similar and the paper outlined the key aspects of consultant fee arrangements, these included:

> 'Fees are based on a fixed percentage of the Construction Cost without limit; there is no mechanism within the contracts to limit the value of the fee payment or a reducing scale if the contact value increases; and the fees are not related to time and there is no reference to the construction period.'

12.59   The report concluded that there was a clear requirement to control the escalation of fees and provided three methods for consideration. The SPCB were left in little doubt that they had no contractual right to cap fees and nothing appears to have been done at this time.

12.60   During June 2000 discussions commenced between Ove Arup and the Project Team on the possibility of capping their fee based upon the £108 million construction cost estimate at that

---

[700] Evidence of Mr Alan Mack on 2 March 2004, Para 552
[701] Strictly speaking, the Architect's fee was staged to reflect each stage of the Programme of Works being achieved.
[702] CB/5/727–735 - Project Sponsor Report, Appendix 6 'Review of Consultant Fees', December 1999

time. Ove Arup agreed to cap their scale fee on this basis. However, this has not been the final payment made to Ove Arup as an agreement was reached where they continued to be paid for additional services on a "time-charge" basis. I doubt whether such an arrangement does in reality represent a "cap" in the true sense of the word. Furthermore, Arup Security Consulting had a separate fee agreement with the client which was not covered by the capping agreement.[703]

12.61 In his evidence to the Inquiry Mr Curran stated that, although Ove Arup had agreed to a cap, the other consultants were not requested to do so as "At that time there was little appetite within the client organisation to pursue the other consultants to cap their fees."[704] The rationale given was that Ove Arup had undertaken the majority of their work for the client at that stage and were therefore more able to predict their final costs, whereas this was not the case with the other consultants.

12.62 The Project Team in early 2002 began discussions with the Architect on the principle of capping their fees. On 13 March 2002 Mr Stewart wrote to Mr Curran on behalf of EMBT/RMJM Ltd[705] stating that the joint venture company were willing to accept in principle a cap on the scale fee, and requested discussion on this. Although it is clear from the evidence that Mr Stewart seemed willing to move to a capped fee position in 2002, his joint venture partners were less keen and therefore the issue remained unresolved. In evidence to the Inquiry Mr Stewart stated that:

> "RMJM stood ready to discuss sensible fee capping as early as 2002. This conciliatory approach was not one necessarily shared by EMBT."[706]

12.63 The SPCB considered a paper on fees[707] at its meeting of 14 May 2002 which indicated that the Project Team were continuing to negotiate consultants' fees based on the new construction cost of £150 million. There has been little evidence presented to enable me to determine how vigorously this issue was pursued by the Project Team with the various consultants. Mr Curran's minute of 2 October 2003 informed Mr Grice that the Project Team's efforts to cap fees during 2002 were unsuccessful "due to the uncertainty that has surrounded cost and programme."[708] On the instigation of the new Presiding Officer, George Reid, the issue was resolved at a meeting of the SPCB on 10 June 2003 when the consultants "agreed to cap their

---

[703] Evidence of Mr David Lewis on 7 May 2004, Paras 612 to 619
[704] Evidence of Mr Paul Curran on 23 March 2004, Para 607
[705] RM/7/338–339 – Letter from Mr Brian Stewart to Mr Paul Curran, 13 March 2002
[706] WS/42/001–032 - Mr Brian Stewart's Second Witness Statement, 11 March 2004, Para 124
[707] CB/2/488–490 – SPCB Paper on Consultants' Fees 14 May 2002
[708] CB/5/805–807 – Memo from Mr Paul Curran to Mr Paul Grice, 2 October 2003

fees until the end of the Project."[709]   At the meeting Mr Stewart had agreed on behalf of EMBT/RMJM Ltd, as Sra Tagliabue was not present.

12.64   DLE agreed to a fee cap in August 2003.   DLE signed the minute of variation[710] on 26 November 2003 agreeing to a capped fee of £3.885 million excluding VAT.

12.65   Bovis Lend Lease agreed a cap on their staff costs and a construction management fee in August 2003. There is a criticism of Project Management in the Auditor General's June 2004 Report, Section 5.47, that there was the opportunity within the Construction Manager's contract to change to a fixed lump sum and that this should have been done sooner. With that I agree.[711] Bovis agreed to a capped fee of £19.96 million excluding VAT and signed the formal minute of variation on 26 February 2004.[712]

12.66   The capping of the consultants' fees after an announcement of a cost increase of £37.7 million in May 2003 had several repercussions for the Project. It was felt in some quarters that the timing of the announcement implied some relationship between the rise in costs and the consultants' fees.   Mr Stewart felt let down by the client as there had been no acknowledgement of his previous willingness to cap fees. In Mr Wright's view the public nature of the announcement damaged the already fragile relationship between the consultants and the client and led to further antagonism between the directors of EMBT/RMJM Ltd, which it appeared to him almost led to the disintegration of the partnership.

12.67   It is difficult to assess whether the early reliance on a wholly unrealistic budget led first the Scottish Office and then the SPCB to regard consultants' fees as relatively minor or whether there was an unwillingness to raise the issue of fees when it was becoming obvious that costs were escalating as that would highlight the array of problems still unresolved. In any event, as I have narrated, there was a protracted period during which the issue of consultants' fees remained unresolved although overall construction costs clearly had increased. It was only when the present Presiding Officer personally intervened that fee caps were finally established.

---

[709] CB/5/554–555 - Minutes of SPCB Meeting of 10 June 2003
[710] CB/5/818–819 - DLE Minute of Variation from Mr Paul Curran to Mr Paul Grice, 12 January 2004
[711] Auditor General for Scotland's Report of September 2000, Para 3.35
[712] CB/5/809–810 – Bovis Lend Lease Minute of Variation from Mr Ed Parry to Mr Paul Curran, 26 February 2004

Chapter 13

Planning, Queensberry House & the Role of Historic Scotland

The Building, its Symbolism and Condition

13.1 Queensberry House was in a state of disrepair, with very little left of the interiors, when the Scottish Office purchased it from Scottish and Newcastle in early 1998. Dating from before 1640, it was originally an aristocratic townhouse, designed by James Smith, but had changed hands many times since then, had been used for many purposes and had undergone a conversion into army barracks between 1808 and 1810 when a fourth storey was added.

13.2 In his report of 24 November 1997 on the origins and development of Queensberry House,[713] Mr John Hume, then Chief Inspector of Historic Buildings, Historic Scotland, and Consultant to the SPCB, advised that Queensberry House's pre 1808 form could fairly easily be recovered. As Mr Graeme Munro, Chief Executive of Historic Scotland, stated in evidence: "The Secretary of State and the Architect were attracted to the idea of returning Queensberry House as closely as possible to its original form."[714] However, Donald Dewar's overriding concern was that the building should be a working part of the parliamentary

---

[713] MS/7/015–022 - Paper by John Hume: Queensberry House 'Its origin and development', 24 November 1997
[714] Evidence of Mr Graeme Munro on 13 November 2003, Para 329

complex. Mr Hume recommended that any restoration scheme should be preceded by a detailed examination of the fabric of the house.

The NOPD Procedure and the Role of the City of Edinburgh Council

13.3 Civil servants advised Donald Dewar on 18 September 1997,[715] that even though the Scottish Parliament Building was Crown property and therefore exempt from the requirement for planning permission, it would be good practice to follow the procedures contained within Scottish Development Department Circular 21/1984[716] "Crown Land and Crown Development". This required Crown "developers" to submit Notices of Proposed Development (NOPD) and Applications for Planning Permission and/or Listed Building Clearance to the Planning Authority. It also detailed the informal advisory role of Historic Scotland in connection with proposals affecting a listed building. As the process was akin to normal planning procedures advice was given to begin discussions with City of Edinburgh Council as soon as possible, so that the tight timetable could be adhered to.

13.4 The NOPD application was complex, due to the location of Holyrood in a Conservation Area within the UNESCO designated Edinburgh World Heritage Site, the proposal to demolish and restore an existing Category A listed building, and the scarcity of drawn material. Only the architect's drawings were available at the time of application. The Council agreed (unusually) that an Outline NOPD application could be submitted initially, to be followed by a Reserved Matters application containing the required detail.

13.5 The Outline NOPD application was submitted to the Council on 21 April 1998 and agreed by the Planning Committee on 22 July 1998, subject to detailed matters being addressed. Approval did not include Listed Building Consent, which could not be granted as part of an outline application and was therefore postponed until the Reserved Matters application was considered. Historic Scotland's *Memorandum of Guidance on Listed Buildings and Conservation Areas 1998'* specified a period of four months for processing major applications. This case was processed in three months. The need for speed with the application was made plain by Scottish Office officials. As a result the Council did not insist upon an Environmental Impact Assessment being submitted.

13.6 The Reserved Matters Application was duly submitted to the Council on 21 April 1999. Unfortunately it was deficient, due to the lack of an accompanying Traffic Impact Assessment. It was re-submitted twice and was registered on 26 May 1999, so that validation and processing could begin. Details of what was required to be submitted for the

---

[715] SE/2/227–231 – Minute from Mr Affolter to PS/Secretary of State and PS/Henry McLeish, 18 September 1997
[716] Annex A - Closing Submission of Ms Laura Dunlop QC, 26 May 2004

205

application to be adequately assessed had been provided by Council planning officials to the Project Team previously on 25 February 1999.[717] The application was ultimately approved by the Planning Committee on 15 September1999 subject to yet further details being provided on reserved matters. Additional Reserved Matters were imposed, as the Council still required significant detailed design information and developed proposals for Queensberry House before Listed Building Consent could be granted, as well as landscaping details. It was agreed that indicative landscaping proposals were acceptable and that a separate landscaping NOPD application could be submitted at a later date.

13.7 On 5 May 2000 the Design Team lodged an application for an Amendment to the Approved NOPD as a consequence of the Parliament's requirement for an additional 2,275m² of space. It was agreed by the Council on 16 June 2000 subject to concerns being addressed, particularly those relating to Queensberry House. The Council found the proposal to reduce the height of the Belvedere Tower and to remove the majority of the existing floors unacceptable and requested further information following ongoing archaeological investigations. The application was finally agreed by the Planning Committee on 6 September 2000.

13.8 On 1 November 2000[718] the Planning Committee agreed to remit consideration of the Queensberry House details to the Head of Planning, prompted by Mr Richard Emerson, Chief Inspector of Historic Buildings, Historic Scotland. This amendment to Condition 4 of the NOPD application, rather than reserve considerations to the members, helped to accelerate the delivery of the necessary approvals by the Council.

13.9 In written evidence to the Inquiry Mr Ian Spence, Head of Building Quality, City of Edinburgh Council Planning Department, stated that:

> '... all NOPD Applications, with the exception of Landscape Application 00/01992/REM, were dealt with within their 4-month periods despite the complexities involved. That landscape application was time extended by agreement with the architects to allow modification and design development and did not affect the Project programme.'[719]

13.10 It can be seen from the evidence that the planning process continued from 23 April 1998 until 22 August 2001.[720] At the time of handover to the SPCB there were outstanding reserved matters in relation to Queensberry House. As Mr Spence recorded in written

---

[717] WS/44/016–018 - Letter from Ms Gina Bellhouse to Mrs Barbara Doig, 25 February 1999
[718] EC/1/189-196 - Report to City Council Development Quality Sub-Committee, 1 November 2000
[719] WS/44/035-042 – Mr Ian Spence's Witness Statement, 23 March 2004
[720] WS/44/042 *ibid*

evidence to me "Queensberry House assumed extraordinary prominence within the overall proceedings of the NOPD". This has proved to be the case, however, due to the on-going archaeological investigations throughout the building process and the necessary public consultation, which is part of the NOPD process. It would have been highly irregular if full planning permission had been given at an earlier date. In my view the Council acted expeditiously in carrying out its functions and even though there was frustration on the part of the client with the time required to comply with the NOPD process, it did not have a negative impact on either programme or cost.

The Role of Historic Scotland

13.11 SDD Circular 21/1984 "Crown Land and Crown Development - Buildings of Special Architectural or Historical Interest" details Historic Scotland's role as:

'The Department's Inspectorate of Historic Buildings will be pleased to advise informally on what constitutes or affects character and on any other matters in connection with proposals affecting a listed building.'[721]

13.12 Historic Scotland also has the role of mediator in any conflict between the applicant and the planning authority in matters relating to listed buildings.

The Simpson & Brown Report

13.13 As part of the information gathering process on the Holyrood site to assist Donald Dewar in making a decision, it was decided to commission a full condition survey and cost plan of Queensberry House. Mr Brown, Director of Administrative Services, wrote to Simpson & Brown on 17 December 1997[722] inviting them to bid for this piece of work, which was to be completed by 31 December 1997.

13.14 Mr James Simpson, Partner, Simpson & Brown, replied on 19 December 1997,[723] setting out the work they proposed to undertake within what would be six working days. The timescale did not enable them to undertake a full condition survey and they proposed "a systematic visual inspection of the fabric of the building" and "a quick structural appraisal to identify any obvious structural defects". These terms were agreed and work began on Monday 22 December 1997.

13.15 A first draft report was submitted to the Scottish Office on 31 December 1997 and a final report on 5 January 1998.[724] The report concluded that: 'The house was in fundamentally

---

[721] SDD Circular 21/1984, Part IV, Item 26
[722] MS/7/023–025 - Letter from Mr Alistair Brown to Simpson & Brown, 17 December 1997
[723] MS/7/026–029 - Letter from Mr James Simpson to Mr Alistair Brown, 19 December 1997
[724] MS/7/030–074 Simpson & Brown Report: 'Queensberry House', 31 December 1997

sound condition. Only very minor cracking was noted in the masonry and the walls are considered to be essentially sound.' The total cost of restoration was estimated at £6.9 million (inclusive of VAT and fees). The report stated that these findings were based on visual investigation as it had not been possible to open up the fabric of the house and recommended that 'further documentary research and physical investigation should be instructed as a matter of urgency.'

13.16   The Inquiry has heard evidence from Sir David Steel that the SPCB had relied heavily on the finding that the building was fundamentally sound[725] and realised this was not the case when the plaster was later removed once the Project had been handed over to the Parliament. However in a letter to Sir David Steel on 20 December 1999, Mrs Doig wrote:

> 'You will wish to note as officials we have never had a problem with the status or content of the Simpson and Brown 1997 Report. It was prepared in a very short time while Queensberry House was still in the ownership of Scottish and Newcastle. The report was based on visual inspection and non-intrusive survey techniques; this is usual in pre-purchase situations.'[726]

13.17   It seems that the over-riding factor in obtaining a survey and outline cost report on Queensberry House in such a short time was to inform Donald Dewar in time for a site selection decision to be taken and announced on 9 January 1998. The findings could only be based on visual inspection and the recommendation for further investigative works should have been instructed once the building became the property of the Scottish Office to unveil the true nature of the structural soundness of the building before a decision on its retention/restoration was taken. From the evidence provided to me, Sir David Steel's criticism of Simpson & Brown's finding that the building was "fundamentally sound" is misleading when read in the context of the full report and from subsequent advice provided to him by the Project Sponsor at the end of 1999.

Archaeological Studies

13.18   Once the Holyrood site was selected one of the key issues for Historic Scotland was an archaeological investigation of the site and of Queensberry House. Historic Scotland agreed to manage the contract on behalf of the Project Team. The final cost of the archaeological work was projected to be around £850,000.

13.19   On 15 October 1998 Historic Scotland instructed Addyman & Kay to undertake 'a limited programme of opening up, physical investigation and recording over a period of two

---

[725] Evidence of Sir David Steel on 1 April 2004, Para 84
[726] CB/5/292-293 - Memo from Mrs Barbara Doig to PS/Presiding Officer, 20 December 1999

weeks'.[727] Addyman & Kay reported their findings to the Project Team on 30 November 1998. This report has not been presented to me, but it would appear that it was not the full investigation that had been recommended by both Mr Hume and Mr Simpson in their respective reports, and indeed when EMBT/RMJM Ltd requested specific information on the height of the wallheads in January 1999, Addyman & Kay were unable to provide the necessary information.

13.20 On 13 April 1999,[728] Dr Aonghus MacKechnie, Principal Inspector of Historic Monuments, Historic Scotland, met with Mr William Kay, and agreed that Addyman & Kay would undertake a programme of archaeological research. This included the entire removal of the harling of Queensberry House to determine the form and position of the original wallheads.

13.21 Mr Emerson confirmed this proposal in a letter to Mr Kinsley, copied to Mrs Doig, on 19 April 1999.[729] However, it is clear that Mrs Doig viewed this as additional work and questioned the funding and extent of the proposed work on 6 May 1999:

> 'Our understanding from previous discussions with Historic Scotland is that the amount of information which can be revealed by further building archaeology is likely to be limited.'[730]

13.22 The matter was resolved on 22 July 1999 when the client agreed to fund the archaeology and Mr Mustard confirmed that:

> " ... an archaeological study was currently underway to examine the walls under the existing plasterwork."[731]

13.23 In its report to MSPs on the Holyrood Project in 2000, the SPCB stated that in the period June 1999 to February 2000 detailed investigations had found that the structure of Queensberry House was not sound and that:

> "The essential remedial works doubled to £9.4m and an enhanced contingency of £1.4m was required due to the continuing uncertainty on the building condition."[732]

The consequence of this was that more money was spent on making Queensberry House structurally sound than was spent on converting it to usable office accommodation, as confirmed in evidence to me on 10 February 2004 by Mr Grice.[733]

---

[727] WS/24/001–012 – Mr James Simpson's Witness Statement, 17 December 2003
[728] HS/2/060–061 – Mr Aonghus MacKechnie's Minutes of Meeting of 13 April 1999
[729] HS/2/062–063 – Letter from Mr Richard Emerson to Mr John Kinsley, 19 April 1999
[730] HS/2/069–070 – Minute from Mrs Barbara Doig to Mr Richard Emerson, 6 May 1999
[731] HS/2/079-083 – Project Team Note of Meeting of 27 July 1999
[732] CB/2/660–709 - SPCB Report on the Holyrood Project – Session 1 (2000) SP Paper 99, Para 12.3

13.24 It would appear that the archaeological investigations continued as the Project progressed and informed the design and planning process, as can be seen from Ms Davidson's letter to Mr Grice on 4 April 2001:

> "... current design of the wallhead to be altered to take account of new archaeological evidence. Given the point at which the archaeological evidence became available the Group accepts that it would not have been reasonable for the Planning Authority to have anticipated such a development." [734]

13.25 It can be seen from the evidence that the findings of the archaeological study, such as the Belvedere Tower and the reduced height of the wallhead, prolonged the planning process but did not affect the overall programme or costs. However, the discovery that Queensberry House needed extensive structural work seems to have been the major increase in the costs of Queensberry House.

Re-Categorisation of Queensberry House

13.26 Due to the significance of the discoveries during the archaeological investigations undertaken by Addyman & Kay[735] and Mr John Lowrey on Queensberry House, Mr Hume, Chief Inspector of Historic Buildings at the time, decided that Queensberry House be upgraded from Category B to Category A listing and he informed Donald Dewar of his decision in an e-mail on 10 November 1998.[736]

13.27 Mr Munro in evidence to the Inquiry confirmed that the re-categorisation did not require Ministerial consent and outlined the mechanism for upgrading:

> "We do move to list for the first time, or to enhance the listing, if new information comes to hand. In this particular case, John Hume took the view that the previous listing was an "underlisting", if you like, in terms of the historical importance of the building. The new information supported that. I believe that, even without that new information, we would probably have upgraded the listing in any case when we came to do the geographical re-survey." [737]

13.28 Donald Dewar queried the decision to upgrade the listing of Queensberry House at a meeting on 15 March 2000 and was informed by Mr Emerson that:

---

[733] Evidence of Mr Paul Grice on 4 April 2004, Para 4

[734] CB/4/805–807 - Letter from Ms Sarah Davidson to Mr Paul Grice, 4 April 2001

[735] HS/2/026–030 – Addyman & Kay Paper: 'Queensberry House: Scottish Parliament Site', February 1999

[736] HS/1/026 –E-mail from Mr John Hume to PS/Secretary of State, 10 November 1998

[737] Evidence of Mr Graeme Munro on 13 November 2003, Para 246

"... the change in listing did not make any practical difference; he [Mr Emerson] acknowledged that the Planning Committee might take a slightly different view based on the higher listing."[738]

13.29 Objections received by the Council to the plans for Queensberry House during the consultation period from historians and conservationists seem mostly to be based on the false assumption that the client's intention had been for a restoration of the building. It had always been Snr Miralles' intention to retain rather than restore the building, which Historic Scotland had initially agreed with. This is confirmed by Mr Hume in a minute to Mrs Doig on 4 February 1999, when he advocates: "A simple approach to conversion."[739]

13.30 From 1999 onwards Historic Scotland and the conservation lobby pushed for full restoration, and it is clear there is confusion over the original agreement with the Scottish Office. In evidence Mr Hume told the Inquiry:

> "The intention of the listing legislation is not to preserve, it is to manage the process of change in such a way as to respect the character and historic interest of buildings."[740]

Change of Chief Inspector

13.31 Mr Hume was Chief Inspector of Historic Buildings at Historic Scotland until February 1999 when he retired. He was then retained as a consultant by the Holyrood Project Team on matters relating to the adaptation of Queensberry House. From 1997 to February 1999 Mr Hume provided advice on behalf of Historic Scotland to the Project and Design Teams on, among other things, matters affecting listed buildings. He prepared a desk study of the architectural significance of Queensberry House in November 1997, which detailed the history of the building and provided information on the restoration work that Historic Scotland would like to see undertaken.

13.32 Mr Hume, on behalf of Historic Scotland approved some, and agreed a way forward for many of the other proposals for the redevelopment of Queensberry House tabled by EMBT/RMJM Ltd at a meeting with members of the Project Team on 28 January 1999.[741] These included issues that the Architect and the Project Team later maintained were re-opened by Historic Scotland.

13.33 At this meeting the decisions on three of the four key issues were as follows: the use of pantiles for the main roof; further work to determine the height of the Belvedere Tower was

---

[738] HS/2/120–123 – Note of Meeting from PS/First Minister to the Director of Historic Scotland, 15 March 2000

[739] MS/7/114–118 - Minute from Mr John Hume to Mrs Barbara Doig, 4 February 1999

[740] Evidence of Mr John Hume on 13 November 2003, Para 626

[741] HS/2/018–025 - Minutes from Mr David Miller of Meeting of 28 January 1999

to be undertaken; as much retention of the existing flooring as possible was requested, with a decision to be based on the findings of a structural report to be commissioned from Ove Arup. Advice on using the enfilade as the main circulation route had already been provided by Historic Scotland and agreed upon.

13.34 The flooring retention issue was resolved at a meeting on 9 March 1999,[742] after discussion of the Ove Arup findings, when Mr Graham Reed of Historic Scotland agreed to the retention of flooring in identifiable areas only and the removal of all other flooring.

13.35 Mr Emerson became Chief Inspector of Historic Buildings on 1 March 1999. He appointed Dr MacKechnie to represent Historic Scotland on all outstanding detail design issues relating to Queensberry House.

13.36 Dr MacKechnie attended the meeting of 7 July 1999,[743] where EMBT/RMJM Ltd presented the work they had undertaken as a result of Mr Hume's instructions in January. Contrary to the agreement reached at the previous two meetings and the subsequent work undertaken by the Architect, Dr MacKechnie now advised that, in his and Historic Scotland's view, pantiles were not appropriate as a roofing material; the Architect's proposals to remove stonework from the Belvedere Tower were unacceptable; there were serious concerns over the use of the enfilade as a circulation route; and strong objections were raised at the proposal for only two examples of the existing flooring to be retained.

13.37 These were to become the four key issues in relation to Queensberry House throughout the Project. However, it is clear that at the July 1999 meeting the basis of Mr Hume's advice on the treatment of other areas within Queensberry House was subsequently viewed as inappropriate by Historic Scotland, who requested that the Architect revisit these previously agreed issues. Mr Stewart provided a list of these items in evidence to the Inquiry,[744] with which, having examined the evidence, I agree have been re-visited.

13.38 Mr Stewart told the Inquiry that:

> "It became clear that the new regime in Historic Scotland intended to revisit the previously agreed solutions."[745]

It appears from the minutes[746] that advice conflicting with that previously given was being received from Historic Scotland following the change of Chief Inspector. There were

---

[742] HS/2/033–037 - Notes of Meeting of 9 March 1999
[743] RM/1/091-099 - Minutes from Ms Lesley Fisher, 7 July 1999
[744] Evidence of Mr Brian Stewart on 22 March 2004 (pm), Para 36
[745] *ibid*, Para 35

genuinely conflicting opinions amongst conservationists, taken in conjunction with a change of client. To the new client the position can not have appeared clear. Mr Spence said:

'In the case of Queensberry House it was difficult to obtain unequivocal advice due to the range of opinions being made available.'[747]

13.39 The lack of clear direction from Historic Scotland caused the SPCB to feel frustrated in their attempts to make progress, as Mr Grice stated in his evidence to me:

"The general view was that the local authority was trying to get on with its job, but there was some frustration around the SPCB table that Historic Scotland, in their judgment, appeared to be moving the goalposts somewhat, and that made it difficult to make progress with a council in terms of getting Notice of Proposed Development [NOPD] clearance."[748]

13.40 As speed was the priority for the client, this was frustrating. However as Queensberry House was never on the critical path, it did not impact on the overall programme delivery.

13.41 The SPCB had briefly considered opting for Crown immunity. However it was agreed that once the Scottish Office had committed the Project to the NOPD planning process it should be seen through to the end. Officials perceived that an insistence on Crown immunity over such an important project would create a poor impression in the minds of the public.

Roof Covering

13.42 The use of pantiles as the covering for the main roof of Queensberry House was first recommended by Mr Hume in his report submitted to the Scottish Office on 24 November 1997.[749] This recommendation, he said, was based on the Sandby drawings dated between 1745 and 1764. The historical accuracy of this recommendation was disputed in the Addyman & Kay Report, "Evidence for Roofing Materials: An Overview" in February 1999.[750] They found that slate had been the original roof finish for Queensberry House. In light of this report Historic Scotland changed their view and recommended that slate should be used. On 13 April 1999 Donald Dewar resolved the issue in favour of pantiles apparently on aesthetic grounds:

---

[746] HS/2/018-025 – Minutes from Mr David Miller of Meeting of 28 January 1999; HS/2/033–037 – Notes of Meeting of 9 March 1999; RM/1/091–099 – Minutes from Ms Lesley Fisher, 7 July 1999
[747] WS/44/035-042 – Mr Ian Spence's Witness Statement, 23 March 2004
[748] Evidence of Mr Paul Grice on 10 February 2004, Para 56
[749] MS/7/015–022 - Paper by John Hume: Queensberry House 'Its origin and development', 24 November 1997
[750] HS/2/027-030 – Report from Addyman & Kay to Dr Aonghus MacKechnie, February 1999

"...bearing in mind the Design Team's preference and the overall principles being adopted in reusing Queensberry House for parliamentary purposes, pantiles should be adopted as the roofing material."[751]

13.43 Despite Donald Dewar's decision I have heard evidence that Historic Scotland continued to recommend the use of slate until May 2000. Dr Gibbons reported to the SPCB meeting on 9 May 2000:

"... that the architects had received a letter[752] from the Historic Buildings Inspectorate saying they would continue to oppose the use of pantiles as a roofing material."[753]

13.44 The issue was finally resolved in May 2000, when Historic Scotland accepted that pantiles could be used on the roof on aesthetic grounds.

13.45 The issue was clearly kept alive by Historic Scotland from the original advice on 24 November 1997 from Mr Hume until final agreement in the reserved matters NOPD application of 5 May 2000. Despite continued disagreement on this issue, Donald Dewar's decision was not revised and it does not seem to me to have had an impact on either cost or delay.

Flooring

13.46 The Project Team initially considered strengthening the existing flooring[754] in accordance with Historic Scotland's advice.[755] To help inform this decision Ove Arup & Partners were commissioned to undertake a structural assessment of the floors. They concluded in their subsequent report that strengthening the existing floor structures would compromise their ability to cope with increased loadings and accommodate future uses. They recommended that:

"the existing floor structures be recorded and removed in entirety and new floor structures installed."[756]

This was consistent with the security advice that the Design Team were receiving at that time.

---

[751] SE/4/072-072 – E-mail from Mr Kenneth Thomson to Mrs Barbara Doig, 14 April 1999
[752] HS/2/105–116 - Letter from Dr Robin Evetts to Ms Nira Ponniah, January 2000
[753] CB/2/255 - Minutes of SPCB Meeting of 9 May 2000
[754] HS/2/001 –003 – Letter from Mr William Armstrong, 5 November 1998
[755] HS/2/018–025 – Minutes from Mr David Miller of Meeting of 28 January 1999
[756] HS/2/033–037 – Notes on Floor Structure Proposals, 9 March 1999

13.47 A meeting was convened with Mr Reed of Historic Scotland on 9 March 1999 to discuss these findings and to reach agreement on the retention of flooring in identifiable areas only. Mr Reed agreed to:

> "... positively promote the retention of identifiable areas of historic flooring somewhere in the building. Historic Scotland would have no objection to all other areas of flooring being removed." [757]

13.48 The decision made by Mr Reed does not seem to have been adopted by Historic Scotland, who stated at a meeting on 7 July 1999[758] that they strongly objected to the proposal to retain only two examples of existing flooring and minuted citing flooring as one of four on-going areas of concern. At further meetings on 8 October 1999[759] and 25 November 1999[760] Historic Scotland disagreed with the principle of removing floors, requested supporting documentation and raised concerns on conservation grounds.

13.49 Historic Scotland finally agreed to three original floors being retained at a meeting with the Design Team on 6 October 2000.[761]

13.50 Although it is evident from the minutes of meetings between the Design Team and Historic Scotland throughout 1999 and 2000 that the question of floor retention remained contentious, the Inquiry has not heard any evidence to suggest that this adversely affected the timetable or overall costs. It would appear that Mr Hume's original view of retention was not based on historical or structural knowledge of the existing flooring and that the Ove Arup findings were accepted by Mr Reed. Historic Scotland later put the case for as much retention of the original flooring as possible and requested information, which had previously been agreed upon at the meeting of 7 July 1999. When the three areas of retention were finally agreed upon it took just over a year to resolve. This can be viewed as another recurring issue, which the Design Team thought had been resolved prior to handover, but which the SPCB and latterly the HPG had to resolve.

The Belvedere Tower

13.51 The remains of part of a Belvedere Tower were discovered in the autumn of 1998 during the archaeological investigations. The Project Team agreed on 5 November 1998 "that it would have to be retained and expressed in the roof design" [762] and the Architect confirmed at a

---

[757] *ibid*
[758] RM/1/091–099 – Minutes from Ms Lesley Fisher of Meeting of 7 July 1999
[759] RM/3/054-058 – Minutes from Ms Kirsten Spence of Meeting of 8 October 1999
[760] HS/2/095-098 – Notes from Mr David Miller of Meeting of 25 November 1999
[761] RM/3/066–069 – Minutes from Ms Nira Ponniah of Meeting of 6 October 2000
[762] HS/2/001-003 – Letter from Mr William Armstrong, 5 November 1998

meeting on 27 November 1998[763] that they could "see no present difficulties in integrating this into the work". Further work was authorised on 28 January 1999[764] to determine the height of the original Belvedere Tower.

13.52 It was concluded that the original Belvedere Tower would have been visible above the roof level and at a meeting on 7 July 1999 the Architect expressed his concerns over the proposal to retain remnants of the Tower above the roof level. EMBT/RMJM Ltd presented two drawings to Historic Scotland[765] which indicated that some of the original stonework would be removed. Dr MacKechnie, for Historic Scotland, said that this proposal was unacceptable.

13.53 The proposal to reduce the height of the Belvedere Tower was included in the amended NOPD application lodged with the Council on 5 May 2000. The Design Team were subsequently informed by the Council that the proposal to reduce the height was not acceptable and recommended that it either be retained or restored.

13.54 In evidence to the Inquiry Sir David Steel stated that the SPCB were only informed about the Belvedere Tower in August 1999.

> "On 6 August 1999 the Corporate Body was told that the stone remains of a belvedere or outlook tower were situated in the roof space (not mentioned in the survey) and 'that the intention was to keep the Belvedere Tower in situ'."[766]

13.55 It is apparent from minutes that have been presented to me that the Belvedere Tower was known about by the Design Team as early as November 1998. There seems to be some question as to why the SPCB were apparently not aware of its existence once the Project was transferred to them, or of the prior agreement by the Design Team to retain it and incorporate it into the roof design.

13.56 The matter was finally resolved in September 2000 when the SPCB offered to retain the Belvedere: ".. by building up part of the structure which had been lost during the original alterations."[767]

13.57 It would appear that the decision by the Architect in July 1999 to reduce the height of the Belvedere Tower, by removing some of the original stonework, was inconsistent with the previous agreement reached with Historic Scotland in November 1998 that it would be retained.

---

[763] HS/2/004–008a – Minutes from Mr David Miller of Meeting of 27 November 1998
[764] HS/2/018–025 - Minutes from Mr David Miller of Meeting of 28 January 1999
[765] RM/1/091–099 - Minutes from Ms Lesley Fisher of Meeting of 7 July 1999
[766] Evidence of Sir David Steel on 1 April 2004, Paras 116 and 170
[767] Evidence of Mr Graeme Munro on 13 November 2003, Para 566

13.58 Members of the HPG and Sir David Steel have suggested in evidence to me that Historic Scotland were pushing for not just the retention of the Belvedere Tower, but its reconstruction. However, Historic Scotland's evidence has been that there was no change of view from the original decision to retain it, agreed by Mr Hume in November 1998.

13.59 On 25 May 2000 Mr Munro stated that: "There are compelling conservation arguments ... in favour of its reconstruction to its original form"[768] and indicated on 28 September 2000 that "...while Historic Scotland's preference would be to see the belvedere simply rebuilt, the Agency would be content if the SPCB decided simply to strengthen and retain the existing structure."[769] I am bound to conclude that Historic Scotland sought to revisit the issue of the Belvedere Tower with a view to its restoration, as opposed to retention, but ultimately conceded the point and expressed themselves to be content with partial reconstruction.

13.60 The issue of the Belvedere Tower held up the listed building consent according to the evidence of HPG member Mr Wright:

> 'Statutory approvals, critical to the progress of this area of the site were being withheld on the basis that Historic Scotland was seeking the Tower's retention and reconstruction. The approvals were expected to be issued by June 2000, and beyond that there was a risk to programme. They were issued finally in November 2000, and even then they were received only after the intervention of the political members of the group.'[770]

13.61 There was a significant discrepancy between the advice from Historic Scotland and that of Mr Gordon on the potential costs of retaining the Belvedere Tower. In a minute from Mr Gregor Stark, Regional Architect, to Mr Munro on 11 August 2000 he estimated: "... a total estimated cost of the Belvedere at £248,000."[771] However, in a minute from Mr Gordon to Donald Dewar on 1 December 1999 he attaches a potential cost of £1 million to the restoration of the Belvedere.[772] I have received no evidence to support that figure.

13.62 The HPG was informed by Mr Fisher at a meeting on 15 November 2000[773] that "the overall cost of the work on the Belvedere would be in the region of £344,000 including fees and VAT."

---

[768] HS/2/131-132 - Minute from Mr Graeme Munro to PS/SEED, Scottish Executive, 25 May 2000
[769] HS/1/064 – Minute from Ms Sarah Davidson, 28 September 2000
[770] WS/39/001–034 – Mr Andrew Wright's Witness Statement, Para 22
[771] HS/1/055-056 – Minute from Mr Stark to Mr Graeme Munro, 11 August 2000
[772] HS/2/100-101 - Minute from Mr Robert Gordon to Donald Dewar, 1 December 1999
[773] CB/4/081–083a – Minute of HPG Meeting of 15 November 2000

13.63 It is obvious that the issues of retention against restoration and the Architect's plans after handover to demolish part of the existing Belvedere Tower led to unnecessary delays in obtaining listed building consent and added to the cost of the Project. Whilst the costs incurred are minimal when compared with the cost of the Project as a whole, this delay could and should have been avoided. Poor administration, differences of professional view, and changes of personnel are to blame. It was irksome and in some respects irrelevant, but it took up an inordinate amount of time and involvement. Even the Secretary of State was involved in protracted negotiations over a matter which should have been effectively dealt with by the Project Team. Historic Scotland was understandably pernickety, but it might be argued that that is their role. What appears to have gone wrong is that the Project Team placed undue reliance on the opinion of Mr Hume, the former Chief Inspector.

The Enfilade

13.64 The enfilade is a surviving 17th Century architectural feature on the ground floor of Queensberry House consisting of a series of doorways in a straight line along the garden or south front, which at a meeting on 27 November 1998,[774] Historic Scotland had suggested be used as a main circulation route between the Entrance, MSP and Assembly buildings.

13.65 The Architect's drawings for this part of the design were agreed by Mr Hume at a meeting on 28 January 1999,[775] pending more detailed input. Drawings detailing the widening of the enfilade were presented to Historic Scotland at a meeting on 7 July 1999.[776] Dr MacKechnie expressed Historic Scotland's serious concern at this proposal and suggested a number of alternatives. The Architect in turn expressed concern that the alternatives proposed would have a serious impact on programme and cost implications.

13.66 In his evidence to the Inquiry Mr Emerson accepted that Historic Scotland had changed its position on this issue.[777]

13.67 In the event, the Parliament's subsequent requirement for additional space resulted in a major design change to Queensberry House, which included the removal of the circulation space from within the Canongate level of Queensberry House to a new external glazed structure at the original garden level. The garden, previously held as sacrosanct, was given over to the new foyer. This revised design solution resolved the enfilade issue in May 2000.

---

[774] HS/2/004–008a - Minutes from Mr David Miller of Meeting of 27 November 1998
[775] HS/2/018–025 - Minutes from Mr David Miller of Meeting of 28 January 1999
[776] RM/1/091-099 - Minutes from Ms Lesley Fisher of Meeting of 7 July 1999
[777] Evidence of Mr Richard Emerson on 3 March 2004, Para 365

13.68 Although the issue of the enfilade was in contention for almost 2½ years, any delay in receiving planning permission can be attributed to the change in design. Historic Scotland ultimately agreed to building over the garden area, which they had previously asked to be retained. I do not find that the enfilade issue contributed to time or cost delays, although the new foyer resolved upon as a better solution by the Architect contributed significantly to both.

The Wallhead Height

13.69 During the course of the archaeological investigations by Addyman & Kay it was discovered that at some point in its history the wallhead on which the roof rested had been raised. The removal of the harling was discussed by the Project Team in the latter part of 1999, but I have received no documentary evidence of this proposal being implemented by the Project Team at that time. It appears to have been an awkward issue brushed aside. At the 4 April 2001 meeting of the HPG, Mr Kinsley reported that Historic Scotland and the City of Edinburgh Council wanted the wallhead reduced to its original height, which had been 300mm lower.[778]

13.70 The then Secretary, Ms Davidson, advised the Clerk on 4 April 2001 that the design of the wallhead should be altered in line with the new archaeological evidence available:

> "The Holyrood Progress Group therefore recommends that the Design Team be instructed to redesign the wallhead of Queensberry House in line with the archaeological evidence."[779]

This was agreed, even though it meant that some headroom under the roof would be lost.

13.71 The reduction of the wallhead height was estimated at a cost of between £200,000 and £400,000 in January 2001.

13.72 Historic Scotland had identified the investigation of the original height of the wallhead as a priority in April 1999, although it does not appear to have been addressed by the Design Team until January 2001. The SPCB do not appear to have been made aware of this issue at handover, but in any event the resolution of it was left on a back boiler for far too long.

The Spencely Report of March 2000

13.73 In Mr Spencely's analysis of Queensberry House within his Report of March 2000 to the SPCB he concluded that: "the expenditure on Queensberry House, at an estimated £10 - £11 million, is not value for money" and suggested that as most of the architecture would be

---

[778] CB/4/778–783 - Minutes of HPG Meeting of 4 April 2001
[779] CB/4/805–807 - Letter from Ms Sarah Davidson to Mr Paul Grice, 4 April 2001

conjectural, "the same effect could be achieved at lesser cost by building anew from new foundations and I recommend that this be done." In his evidence to me Sir David Steel confirmed that the option of demolishing Queensberry House was discussed but discarded.

Cost of Queensberry House

13.74 In the original cost plan produced by Morham & Brotchie for the Simpson & Brown Report,[780] the total cost of building works was estimated at £6.9 million. The final cost is estimated to be in the region of £14 million including fees. In evidence to me Mr Grice stated that:

> "the Parliament had to meet a much higher bill — indeed approximately double, I think, what the estimate had put in to make Queensberry House fit for use."[781]

13.75 It has proved to be the case that Queensberry House, in terms of cost per square metre, has turned out to be the most expensive part of the entire project. The doubling of the total cost to £14 million is largely attributable to the necessary structural repairs, which are understandable in a building of that age. Nevertheless, the overall cost, when viewed in light of the full cost of the Project currently at £431 million, can be viewed as comparatively minor. As I indicated in my Introduction, it is not part of my remit to comment on the aesthetics of the Project and, in particular, I decline to comment on the aesthetics of the integration into the new Parliament complex of Queensberry House, or the workability of its facilities for MSPs or the Presiding Officer of the day. However, it would appear to me that the insistence that existing features of the building be unaltered in combination with necessary anti-terrorist measures within the interiors does not offer, as Mr Spencely observed, much value for money. Paragraph 15.9 sets out an estimate of overall blast costs. In my view the blast costs specifically related to Queensberry House at just over £2 million has to be regarded as disproportionate. In part that is obviously attributable to the proximity of Queensberry House to the Canongate but if this had been carefully analysed at an early stage, it is an interesting speculation whether a more radical approach to Queensberry House might have been adopted.

Impact on Overall Cost and Programme

13.76 It is clear from the evidence presented to me that the arguments surrounding the treatment of Queensberry House as part of the Holyrood Project were protracted and convictions were strongly held almost from the Project's inception. The time taken to resolve issues was lengthy and hindered by the decision rightly taken to follow the NOPD planning process; the change in Historic Scotland personnel, which resulted in differing advice; the on-going

---

[780] MS/7/072–073 - Simpson & Brown Report - Morham & Brotchie First Outline Cost Plan, 31 December 1997
[781] Evidence of Mr Paul Grice on 10 February 2004, Para 5

archaeological discoveries that informed that advice, and the client's priority of incorporating Queensberry House as a necessary working part of the parliamentary complex, rather than undertaking a full restoration of a Category A listed building.

13.77 There is no doubt that by having to focus on specific recurring themes in relation to Queensberry House, the HPG and the Project Team found it difficult to make progress and that these issues were discussed at the highest level by the First Minister and Presiding Officer to try and find a resolution. Crucially, however, it is to be noted this did not cause any delay to the overall programme, as Queensberry House was never on the critical path. At the same time the costs of Queensberry House have been significantly greater than anticipated at the outset.

Chapter 14

Programming and Design Delay

Factual Background

14.1 In the course of his work in compiling the Brief, Mr Armstrong introduced an initial strategic programme as early as October 1997, subsequently revised in mid March 1998, and again revised in April,[782] June and November 1998.[783] The Brief contained detailed descriptions of, not only the Master Development Programme, but also a Design Programme, to be agreed in consultation with the Design Team, a Procurement Programme, a Construction and Commissioning Programme and a Cost Control Programme. All of these programmes foresaw practical completion in late June 2001. They were devised very much at a strategic level, initially without a site having been selected, and were well developed before the appointment of the Architect in July 1998. They were designed to provide a framework for the Project and Design Teams, and for the Construction Manager. I have no doubt that had he remained in charge, Mr Armstrong would have made every effort to stick to these programmes, or to demand explanations as to why they could not be adhered to.

14.2 By February 1999, as noted elsewhere, accommodation requirements had increased to a gross area (less car parking) of 23,000m^2 and dramatic increases in circulation space had

[782] SE/7/179-306 – Draft Building User Brief (April 1998) from Mr William Armstrong, 1 May 1998
[783] SE/7/324-325 – Minute from Mr William Armstrong to Mrs Barbara Doig, 25 September 1998

been sought. In June 1999 the SPCB became the client body and immediately began to raise issues on the design of the Chamber and to seek additional space. By September 1999 the Chamber design had been revised and the overall estimated area had increased to some 27,000m^2. Construction cost estimates had risen by then to an estimated £115 million or thereby.

14.3 November and December 1999 saw a Value Engineering exercise ostensibly designed to achieve economies in the future course of construction, but which in fact functioned as a cost-cutting exercise. Full details have been supplied by DLE.[784] Stage D – Scheme Design was signed off by the client in June 2000 with overall *estimated* construction costs of £118.8 million, including £11.65 million of Design Risk,[785] within a total budget of £195 million. At that time there was no finalised cost plan, no final structural solution, and much of the east side of the site acknowledged to be still in the early design stages.

14.4 The design process leading up to the sign off of Stage D in June 2000 had taken nearly two years. There was rudimentary compliance with design programming during 1998, as the Architect struggled both internally and with the client to translate the conceptual aspirations which had featured in the competition into the harsh reality of a Scheme Design, achievable at an identifiable price. The requirements of the Brief did not equate with the aspirations of the "new" client after the handover of the Project in June 1999, and a large number of competing demands were made for additional space and different configurations. During 1999, particularly after June, many design changes were required in order to accommodate the expanded requirements of SPCB, and these later included the very substantial revisions to the east side of the site brought about by Snr Miralles' necessary redesign of the Chamber,[786] the addition of the MSP Foyer lying to the south of Queensberry House, and the changes to the configuration of the Committee, Press, and Canongate Towers. Additional accommodation was introduced and some of the basement car parking areas were exchanged for basement accommodation and plant rooms.

Programming and the Construction Manager

14.5 Bovis was appointed as Construction Manager in January 1999 and with the signature of its contract assumed responsibility for master programming for the design, the procurement and the management of the construction of the Project.[787]

---

[784] DL/4/001-054 – DLE Value Management Papers, 1999
[785] CB/2/297 – Minutes of the SPCB Meeting of 20 June 2000
[786] In part to accommodate the client's requirements for disabled access
[787] DL/9/019-069 - Memorandum of Agreement between the SPCB and Bovis, Schedule 2, Paras 1.15, 1.16, 1.17 and 1.18

14.6 The first master programme was issued in January 1999 (Rev 1 series) with a completion date of July 2001. By May 1999 reprogramming had brought the potential completion date to January 2002, but alongside that an accelerated programme was proposed, for completion by September 2001. The latter programme was in turn initially predicated on design being completed and Stage D achieved by May 1999. That did not happen, and the Stage D review process continued, as we have seen, until June 2000. The Inquiry has seen the minutes of the fortnightly Construction Manager's meetings. By issuing reports with the same frequency, my view is that Bovis believed that it was keeping the Design Team and the Project Team appropriately informed as to the likely programming consequences of the design changes as they occurred.

14.7 By May 2000 Bovis had issued comprehensive design, procurement and construction programmes for the MSP building, Queensberry House and the east part of the campus. These programmes contained very little "float" or allowance for overruns, and incorporated a number of assumptions on the amount of lead-in time which was required. Self evidently, the success of these programmes was dependent not only upon the delivery of completed designs to the dates required in the Design Release Schedule, itself incorporated into the larger Tender Event Schedule, but also upon the timeous completion of the tendering and contractor-selection process, and contractor performance.

14.8 Alongside the delivery of designs, the Architect required to make available the drawings for each trade package, so that tendering could proceed as it was planned to do. This necessitated production of drawings to Stage G – Bills of Quantities or Stage H – Tender Action. Bovis was an adviser, not a contractor, and was subjected throughout to significant time pressure by the client. By the time the design Stage D was signed off on 19 June 2000, the design of some packages had reached the much later tender Stage J – Project Planning, but the majority of the drawing information was at Stage C or D only. It is of the nature of construction management that design and construction would be staggered in this way. As a matter of contract, it was for the Construction Manager to 'manage' the interaction of those steps, so that the design process did not find itself significantly out of step with the programming, and *vice-versa*. The Construction Manager is necessarily dependent on the actions and co-operation of others, and in particular the Architect. Conversion of Stage D material into drawings suitable for incorporation into a construction programme comprising between 60 and 70 trade packages is a very significant task for any architect, both in terms of the production of design information and in terms of management of the subsequent tenders and in programming the work.

14.9   The timescales were very short; the amount of design work was very significant; the co-ordination amongst the designers of the building and both engineers was highly complex, and where trade contractors' design was also required, the construction and design timeframes were bound to be stretched to their very limits. In theory, contractor-design ought to shorten the design phase, greater resource being applied to the design process. In practice, the dissemination of design responsibility for the more complex areas of the building meant that time scales were lengthened, as designs by trade contractors had to be approved (and were often rejected) by the Architect before being submitted for approval to the Project Team. Management of all of these variable components was a significant challenge for Bovis. The risk of any deficiencies in that management process fell on the client, and that risk was to programme as well as to cost.

Contractual Responsibilities for Programming

14.10   Bovis' obligations under its contract include:

- Preparation of a strategic development programme; and
- Preparation of a weekly development programme showing all key dates including the package procurement process.[788]

14.11   Bovis has its own management systems for tracking the development of packages. I heard a detailed explanation of the 'Hummingbird' computerised system, which allowed participants in the Project to contribute to the evolution of drawings in a managed way. Overall, Bovis' strategic development programmes are divided by the key elements of the Project, each of which has a detailed design procurement and construction programme. Within the Master Programme trade package tender programmes are then evolved, each having its detailed construction timetable. All of this information is demonstrated in tabular form in the Tender Event Schedule, and the detailed programmes which I have seen. This information has been freely supplied by Bovis.

14.12   I am aware that Mr Steve Briggs, commissioned by the Project Team in early 2002, criticised Bovis for failing to utilise detailed critical path analysis techniques in the preparation of all of its programmes. His report[789] concluded that there was an absence of critical path analysis and "logic links". The report criticised Bovis for failing "to make any significant commitment to programming".[790] Mr Briggs' analysis is a critical review, going to fundamentals such as the use of software, alleging "over-simplicity" and even that the "existing development programme

---

[788] DL/9/019-069 - Memorandum of Agreement between SPCB and Bovis, Schedule 2, Paras 1.16 *et seq*
[789] CB/4/418-439 - Holyrood Project: Programme Review from Mr Steve Briggs, February 2002
[790] CB/4/434 *ibid*, Para 9.1

is of little use...". He criticised the method of measuring progress, and concluded that "the key impediment to completion was the ongoing late release of design information".[791]

14.13 In my view Mr Briggs' highly critical report is to some extent anomalous; although the actual flow of design information was criticised, that criticism was made by Mr Briggs against a series of Bovis programmes which were themselves severely impugned by him, and his report did not, as it appears to me, contain any analysis or review of the design information flow requirements themselves. He called for a review of the system by which design information is programmed. I am bound to say that I am somewhat sceptical of Mr Briggs' conclusion[792] which identifies the "late release of design information" as a "key impediment" to the timely achievement of Programme 5B. That programme was itself described by Mr Briggs as an "...(un) acceptable programme for the completion of the works".[793] In other words, it was curious of him to criticise the Architect for the late delivery of design information if the very programme against which that delivery requirement was being measured was itself unrealistic. However, Mr Briggs was a professionally qualified observer, and he appears to have covered all the salient details, including the Construction Management Agreement.

14.14 Trade Package 2605 (Assembly Frame) was identified by Mr Briggs as the culprit package, and I know from the evidence of Mr Stewart and Mr Lewis that the steel work and structural solution to the Assembly Frame taxed the finest engineering designers in the world, before a solution was achieved. All that being said, I have also to have regard to the very detailed information flow requirements of Bovis, which were clearly articulated at a much earlier date and set out in unmistakable terms,[794] along with the proposed meeting dates to review progress.[795] EMBT/RMJM Ltd signed up to Series 4, revision 4B[796] without qualification, but very detailed letters such as those sent on 14 November 2001[797] and 1 March 2002[798] make it abundantly clear that the Architect was (in the eyes of Bovis) significantly failing to keep up. The second of these letters is an alarming series of detailed complaints, coming as it does from the very experienced Bovis Design Manager, Mr Craig Paterson. I have regard to the fact that TP2605 necessitated no fewer than 1161 Architect's Instructions (AIs). I am satisfied that these were necessary to achieve the final finished product. What I detect is a lack of co-

---

[791] CB/4/421 *ibid*, Para 1.3.6
[792] CB/4/439 *ibid*, Para 10.6
[793] CB/4/435 *ibid*, Para 9.6
[794] BV/1/781-795 – Bovis Programme Review Paper, Key Procurement Dates and Dates of Pre-tender and Construction Meetings
[795] *ibid*
[796] BV/1/798 – Letter from Mr John Kinsley to Mr Alan Mack, 23 March 2001
[797] BV/1/799-804 – Letter from Mr Eddie McGibbon to Mr John Kinsley, 14 November 2001
[798] BV/1/807-810 – Letter from Mr Craig Paterson to Mr John Kinsley, 1 March 2002

ordination and understanding, particularly between EMBT/RMJM Ltd and Bovis, as to the need for and timing of these AIs.

14.15 Oddly, the Project Team did not pass Mr Briggs' report to Bovis. However, I can safely conclude that the gist of Mr Briggs' remarks was indeed made known to Bovis. Mr Curran said in evidence:

> "The report was presented to the Progress Group in February 2002. We then instigated an immediate programme review with Bovis bringing them into the comments that Steve (Mr Briggs) had made trying to get them to embrace and improve upon what was being said here. They recognised a lot of the areas for improvement. They then decided to provide additional planning resources on site. We increased the number of site-based planners from one to three. So, again, this was allowing them to produce better information." [799]

14.16 In her evidence, Ms Davidson explained that, while Bovis was aware of its thrust, the report was not actually given to them.[800] The view was that it had been prepared quickly, that it probably had not identified all "the nuances and subtleties" of what Bovis was doing and that it contained some fairly strong language. She thought the effect of giving it to Bovis would have been that of "throwing a hand grenade into the whole operation." It was considered best that Mr Briggs' expertise should be drawn on by having him work with Bovis, and she thought this proved successful in that, when he reported back in May, substantial progress had been made towards a new programme, Revision 6. As she said:

> "A judgment was taken at that time, effectively, about the best way to keep moving things forward and the best way to influence Bovis' programming. We decided to do that through influence rather than through throwing a report on the table and jumping up and down at them. It was a judgment."

She was in no doubt that in retrospect it was the right judgment.

14.17 It is a matter of judgment whether that was the correct decision, in light of the evident delays which had occurred up to that point. I am bound to be circumspect in reviewing the decisions of professional people who had an intimate acquaintance with the Project, which had by then developed its own unstoppable momentum, but I am not able to resist the impression that there was a cautious approach by Project Management to this difficult subject, which is itself somewhat wreathed in mystery and jargon. Mr Mack had been consistently bullish in reporting to the HPG about the programmes for the Project, but had repeatedly been shown to be over optimistic. It seems to me that more could have been done to inject realism into the programming effort, so as to take proper and full account of the problems which the Construction Manager acknowledged himself to have been facing, and also to force

---

[799] Evidence of Mr Paul Curran on 23 March 2004, Para 394
[800] Evidence of Ms Sarah Davidson on 31 March 2004, Para 249

recognition of the elevated expectations of the new client body, which had by then adopted and endorsed the layman's approach, namely that despite all the evident difficulties it was entitled to know the likely end date, and the likely areas of cost overrun. These are not unreasonable aspirations for a client, and they should not have been in part defeated by such a degree of unwarranted optimism in the programming of the works.

14.18 It was not until 27 March 2002 that Mr Briggs presented himself before the HPG, and he reiterated that design information flow was, in his view, "a recurring theme".[801] Curiously, Mr Mack, who attended the same meeting later, was not asked about Mr Briggs' comments nor shown his report, but the HPG voiced its concerns in private, with Mr Manson stating that he was "extremely doubtful" that completion dates could be met. He was of course correct. By 10 April 2002 Mr Mack's assurances were repeated[802] subject to the caveat that information flow, i.e. drawings, must be maintained, and that there were no changes to design. Mr Wright asked that the new programme should incorporate an indication of where design information was still outstanding, only to be told by Mr Mack that the "only unknown" was in relation to the specialist glazing.[803]

14.19 Programme revisions from Series 3C (July 2000) to Series 7B (February 2004) are fully set out in Exhibit 7[804] of the Auditor General's Report of June 2004. The risk workshops carried out in July 2000 and November 2000 identified potential risks totalling some £51.51 million.[805] Of that figure, a high percentage was for items which were categorised as "highly likely" or "fairly likely" to occur, and to have a potential impact on programme. I observe the contrast between the relatively precise result of this technical risk review, and the constantly ambitious nature of Bovis' reporting of programming.

Delays in the Programme

14.20 I have no doubt that much difficulty was experienced in achieving a flow of design information consistent with the optimistic programmes prepared by Bovis. I am also in no doubt that the design flow was from time to time a source of serious frustration. However, I am far from clear that "design flow" as described to me by Mr Mack, Mr Curran and Ms Davidson was achieved any less quickly than it could ever have been, given the complexity of the designs with which all concerned had to grapple. In consideration of this problem, the tension among time, cost and quality is very well illustrated, in that it is plain that if the time criterion is set too tightly, it is likely to follow that the design flow will fail to meet expectations. In addition if as a result of

---

[801] CB/4/470-476 – Minutes of HPG Meeting of 27 March 2002, Para 22
[802] CB/4/479-485 - Minutes of HPG Meeting of 10 April 2002, Para 20
[803] CB/4/479-485 - Minutes of HPG Meeting of 10 April 2002, Para 21
[804] Auditor General for Scotland's Report of June 2004, Exhibit 7, Page 19
[805] DL/2/074-084 – Draft Risk Review Analysis from Mr McAndie to Dr Gibbons, 2 November 2000

time parameters having been set too tightly, construction cannot proceed in accordance with the programme, then there will clearly be a cost penalty, as has been the case.

14.21 Borrowing again from the Auditor General's June 2004 report, Exhibit 18 [806] shows the slippage in completion of the main parts of the building between September 2000 and the present date. He concluded that the average total delay across the Project was 20 months in a 41 month period. In the result the building has been completed, so far as to allow occupation, in August 2004.

14.22 According to Bovis, the key document against which success or failure of the programming effort should be measured is the Tender Event Schedule.[807] This shows that the main areas of critical delay were TP2205 (Assembly substructure concrete), TP3320 (Foyer frame and glazing), TP3350 (Specialist glazing), TP3525 (Assembly Windows) and TP 2605 (Assembly Frame). A number of these and other packages were awarded with Provisional Sums, significant Trade Contractor design components, or suffered significant variation after the tenders were awarded. Even if tender-issue dates were achieved, the duration of much of the work was prolonged. Design finalisation could not happen if the programme did not allow sufficient time for that design work to be carried out.

14.23 By way of example, TP2605 (Assembly Frame) was originally programmed from November 2000 to December 2001, but in fact stretched from January 2001 until March 2003, and underwent 1800 variations. A significant number of these variations occurred after the original completion date of December 2001. TP3320 (Assembly Foyer Frame and Glazing Stage 2) was originally programmed between November 2001 and April 2002, and suffered 117 variations, taking from August 2001 until April 2004. TP3350 (Assembly Specialist Glazing Stage 1), TP3525 (Assembly Windows) and TP3645 (Assembly Roofing (Stage 2) suffered comparable overruns.[808]

14.24 In coming to a view about why the Project did not meet its estimated completion dates, I have regard to a number of matters. It is well understood that Stage D – Scheme Design in June 2000 was not an entirely settled design. Mr Stewart made the point forcibly[809] that while the extent of client-generated changes may have been reasonable, it was the timing of those changes which caused difficulties with the programme. Architectural instructions given in the course of construction, to maintain quality and achieve design harmony, are properly described as 'design development', but there are many other reasons for the issue of AIs, and on TP2605

---

[806] Auditor General for Scotland's Report of June 2004, Page 38
[807] BV/1/040-044 – Bovis Progress Report No 57 – Tender Event Schedule, 14 July 2003
[808] Auditor General for Scotland's Report of June 2004, Pages 78 to 89
[809] WS/42/001-032 – Mr Brian Stewart's First Witness Statement, March 2004, Para 67

at least 16% had no time or cost implications. 25% were necessitated by the re-allocation of other work into TP2605, and 8% were to take account of changes to work already carried out. Mr Stewart contended[810] that client-driven design change continued throughout the Project, and provided examples, which I accept.[811] In addition, part of the Bovis material[812] lists a very large number of Architect-inspired changes during 2003, right across the Project. I can assume that all of these had client approval, and they ranged from the major, with significant cost implications, to the very minor and those with no cost consequences.

14.25 Differentiating between a 'client-driven change' and a change initiated by the Architect and approved by the client in order to achieve design ambition is beyond the scope of this Inquiry, but in my judgment it does not very much matter. Of 178 Change Request Forms submitted by the client since 29 September 1999, I have been told that 116 were approved at a total cost of only some £600,000.[813] These change requests were costed using the CRFs, but I understand that that costing took no account of any consequential effect on programme, or trade package interfaces. After the approval of Stage D in June 2000, the amount of client-generated change was said to have been relatively minimal. For the client to seek to take credit for 'only' 178 CRFs after Stage D may not disclose the entire picture. When the client seeks to compare this number favourably with the number of Architect-generated changes, and then approves these as they come forward, I have to ask whether it has been fully recognised that a building of this complexity procured using construction management is likely to generate a higher than normal requirement for design changes and consequential Architect's Instructions.

14.26 It is apparent to me from the evidence that the expected design flow failed to keep pace with the programme demanded by the client and proposed by Bovis. Was that failure the sole responsibility of the Architect? Some was, and arose in my view from the indifferent co-ordination and communication between Edinburgh and Barcelona, which was uneven, working well at times but poorly at others. However, the mismatch between design flow and programmed expectations leads me to ask who was really in charge following Stage D in June 2000? Snr Miralles' death in July was bound to have had an adverse effect on the work. It will not do for the client (in whatever manifestation) to simply blame the professional teams, nor for the professional team members to blame one another. I am of the view that it ought to have been more completely understood by the client that high quality design work takes time, and that the programme itself was unrealistic given the complexities of the design especially after Mr Briggs' report in February 2002. Bovis too should have understood that. By the same

---

[810] *ibid*, Para 63 *et seq*
[811] *ibid*, Para 66
[812] BV/1/562 - The Consultant Submission Record or 'CSR Summary'
[813] WS/36/001-035 – Mr Paul Curran's Witness Statement, 17 February 2004, Para 46

token, the Architect should not have signed up to programmes which it could not honour and ought, in my view, to have been more vociferous in relation to the time actually needed to achieve designs which could be programmed accurately. The programme was propelled by the client's obsession with early completion. Irreconcilable objectives were being set. Donald Dewar, the SPCB and later the HPG all wanted to maintain the character and integrity of the Miralles concept for the Parliament. What appears to have been incompletely grasped, if at all, throughout the Project was that if the quality and unique complexity of the building was of overriding importance, the programme and the timing of completion would be affected significantly and extra cost would inevitably occur.

14.27   Having considered all the programming evidence,[814] it is my view that Bovis, in constructing its programmes, probably appreciated as well as anybody the buildability consequences of the highly complex and non-standard designs which were emerging from the Design Team. In my view, its programmes reflected the political imperative for early completion. Bovis reported to the client with a degree of optimism which was often not justified. My criticism is of the way in which timetabling and programme have been reported to the client. Bovis may blame the flow of design information, but no-one has questioned the Architect's ability to find design solutions, nor indeed to design a building of the highest quality; it is only the speed with which those solutions have been delivered that has come in for criticism. Yet the Architect signed up to the Bovis programmes. The Auditor General's assessment was that "the main cause of the slippage is delays in design of a challenging Project delivered against a tight timetable, using an unusual procurement route."[815] I agree.

---

[814] See for example: CB/4/970-974 – HPG minutes of 21 November 2001; CB/4/984-988 - HPG minutes of 5 December 2001. By 17 January 2002 Programme Revision 5B was issued to reflect slippage to TP2605 (Assembly Frame). CB/4/578-583 - HPG minutes of 14 August 2002;CB/4/170-176 - Bovis Report on proposed Strategic Programme Revision 6B Update on 4 April 2003; CB/4/177-182– HPG Minutes of 23 April 2003; and CB/4/1052 – Memo from Ms Judith Proudfoot to Mr Paul Grice, 4 June 2003

[815] Auditor General for Scotland's Report of June 2004, Page 39

Chapter 15

Security Issues

Overview

15.1 The Inquiry heard evidence in camera in relation to matters concerned with security measures as they affect the Holyrood site. As with other aspects of this Inquiry, my primary concern was to investigate events and decisions that may have contributed to increased costs or delay but in doing so the evidence necessarily touched upon aspects of site security. It is not my intention to disclose any information on these matters that could jeopardise the security of the building or the safety of its occupants. The remarks that follow are necessarily a distillation of the main themes to emerge during the course of discussions held with security personnel and the evidence heard in private. Those who attended these evidence sessions will be familiar with the detailed information upon which my conclusions are based and, where there are lessons to be drawn, I trust that those in a position to do so will reflect carefully upon my observations.

15.2 Many factors appear to have impacted upon security considerations; from the geographical location of the site to the complexity of the architectural vision and the palette of materials chosen for its realisation. Security was evidently a consideration from a very early stage and was identified as such in the earliest versions of the Building User Brief in 1998. However, there patently was inadequate recognition of the imposition which security measures would have on the delivery of the Project. It was certainly the view of one witness from the Project Team that the cost and programme implications of security measures had been under-estimated by everyone, including the client. The extent to which additional and unforeseen costs can be attributed to security requirements, however, is certainly considerably less than has been suggested in some quarters. Equally, I am persuaded by the evidence that the events of 11 September 2001 were not the catalyst to a wholesale review of the security requirements on the site nor were they responsible for an escalation in the standards of protection required to meet a previously unforeseen terrorist threat.

Security Requirements

15.3　The Building User Brief of November 1998 contained the security requirements envisaged for the new Parliament building. Of particular relevance were the requirements in relation to 'fabric security'. This would prove to have the greatest impact on the Project in terms of cost and effect upon the construction programme. The security information in the Brief, along with advisory material from the UK Government security services and information specific to the Holyrood site and to Queensberry House, was shared with the Design Team from the outset. Insofar as it reflects security considerations, the Brief and the advisory information from the security services have remained in force throughout the lifetime of the Project.

15.4　From an early stage (indeed it was a consideration of the site selection process) it was recognised that the Holyrood site's proximity to public thoroughfares would impose particular demands. Enhanced security measures have had to be implemented in certain areas of the site to reflect the propinquity of buildings to the perimeter of the site and the requirement that the external look of Queensberry House should not altered substantively. Additional pressures arose from the need to comply with the new Parliament's watchwords of openness, accountability and accessibility and to construct a parliamentary complex where members of the public could have reasonable access to their elected representatives. Of equal significance, however, has been the unique nature of the design and the use of materials within that design. Standardisation is not a feature of the EMBT/RMJM Ltd design and consequently it has not been possible to draw upon experience elsewhere to reach conclusions as to the potential impact of blast on the structure. The Inquiry learned that the bespoke nature of the building and the use of non-traditional blast resistant materials such as natural stone and timber have necessitated an enormous task to develop a design that could be constructed to meet the blast criteria. Rather than designing to a security specification, the nature of the concept meant that a realistic assessment of the detailed security requirements could not be undertaken until the detailed design of the building had commenced. One witness described this approach to the incorporation of security requirements as "iterative". Another spoke of it as being "virtually retrospective" and saw it as "unfortunate" but an approach which had been necessitated by the uniqueness and complexity of the building.[816] Undoubtedly, this process has proved time consuming and it is doubtful if the implications for the programme were adequately considered at any point until the Project was well underway.

Security Consultants

15.5 In March 1999 Arup Security were appointed as security consultants to provide the Design Team with additional expertise on the blast requirements of the building structure and facades. The consultants were required to assist in the development of design solutions that were compliant with the guidelines of the Government security services. The lead consultant with Arup Security, Mr David Hadden, agreed to give evidence to the Inquiry and for his identity to be disclosed. The Inquiry heard detailed (and compelling) evidence on how the consultants' task was fulfilled and I am satisfied as to the thoroughness and professionalism with which this work was undertaken by those involved. In the course of this evidence I learned that, while the extent of the blast testing of components has been comprehensive, there has been no significant failure of those components under test and consequently there was not a requirement for any dramatic redesign in this regard.

Impact of Events of 11 September 2001

15.6 A number of witnesses were questioned as to whether there had been any changes to the security guidance applicable to the building in the aftermath of the events of 11 September 2001. All confirmed the guidelines remained unchanged but that there had been greater attention paid to their implementation than might have been the case earlier. Where relaxation might have been considered in the past, after 11 September 2001 this was no longer permitted. This approach was succinctly if rather clumsily captured in a minute of a meeting in October 2002 where it was noted that "the impact of 9/11 was not to introduce any new measures or guidelines but to make all the measures recommended over the past five years more mandatory." The concept of guidelines being "more mandatory" is one to which all have subscribed and effectively it debunks the myth that enhanced security requirements is a very recent phenomenon.

15.7 As the guidelines on security have remained unchanged at least since the appointment of the Architect in mid-1998, it has to be questioned why the full implications of security measures were not much clearer at the outset. Although it is understandable that the compliance of individual aspects of the design could not be known until such time as that design had developed to a state in which it could be assessed, one would have expected that the

---

[816] Evidence of Dr John Gibbons on 6 May 2004, Para 556

implications of the need to take account of security considerations would have been acknowledged at a much earlier stage than appears to have been the case. An examination of the DLE Risk Register[817] from its inception in August 1998 reveals that it is not until late 2001 that there is any acknowledgement that security considerations could have other than a minimal impact upon design and it is not until May 2002 that this becomes a genuine concern. The earlier cost estimates and ambitious programmes appear to have had a myopic approach to the security issue. I have seen little evidence to suggest that its full implications were foreseen by either the client, the Design Team or their advisers. As I have intimated in paragraph 9.16 the true extent of the implications of security and blast requirements was clearly not appreciated at the time when the Project was handed over by the Scottish Office to the Scottish Parliament.

Costs

15.8   It has been suggested that the full extent of the additional costs attributable to security may have amounted to as much as £100 million. It has also been speculated that the understandable but not fully understood requirements of "security" were a convenient scapegoat for uncomfortable cost rises. In the course of this investigation I have sought to gain an understanding of the true extent of costs attributable to the security measures required for the Parliament building. In doing so, I rest upon the evidence of Mr Fisher who set out, in my view, the clearest expression of these matters that has been presented to me.

15.9   The figures presented by Mr Fisher suggest that a total of £29.11 million is attributable to the changes in design that were necessary to meet the interpretations placed on the anti-blast requirements as they stood.[818] This figure is comprised of two elements. A sum of £17.54 million was identified as the net additional cost of the consequences of the design of anti-blast measures i.e. the cost of the increased specification of materials and components required to meet security requirements over the cost of the equivalent conventional materials. It is arguable that this cost would have been incurred in any event but it is beyond debate that this level of provision should have been identified at a much earlier stage than was the case. The second element in Mr Fisher's total figure is a sum of £11.57 million attributable to the cost of delay associated with blast. This encompasses the consequences of blast-related disruption and includes *inter alia* re-sequencing, re-programming, loss of productivity and the introduction of multiple shift working. Although the evidence on this point was less than conclusive, and in many respects the difficulties echo those faced in relation to non-blast issues, I have to question whether the disruption caused by the need to incorporate blast was managed as

---

[817] The Risk Register is compiled by DLE in consultation with the client, the Design Team and the Construction Manager
[818] Evidence of Mr Hugh Fisher on 29 March 2004, Paras 469 to 482

effectively as it could have been and whether all possible steps were taken to minimise the cost consequentials of this disruption. I am not persuaded that the client was particularly well served in the professional advice it received on how to manage this persistent problem but neither am I convinced that the client's management systems were adequate to retain a sufficient grasp of the true extent of disruption and its cost. It is tempting to suspect that for long periods there was no more than a resigned approach to managing the security issue.

15.10 The evidence has persuaded me that suggestions that the cost of security measures for the Holyrood building could amount to £100 million were wholly inaccurate. While this suggestion appears to have risen initially in the press, it was given some credibility in comments made by Robert Brown to the Finance Committee on 23 September 2003, when he appeared on behalf of the SPCB. While I accept that Mr Brown was speculating in the absence of accurate cost information, I have to reject his subsequent assertion that 'resolution of the bomb blast issue was the biggest single factor affecting both programme and cost" over the last 5 years.[819] As I have sought to demonstrate elsewhere in this Report, that is evidently not the case.

---

[819] Letter from Robert Brown to the Holyrood Inquiry, 6 May 2004, available at the Inquiry website under Supplementary Evidence

Chapter 16

The Holyrood Project from Autumn 2003 Onwards

Introduction

16.1   This section of the Report is included for completeness and offers a factual commentary on the evolution of the Project since the commencement of my investigation in the autumn of 2003. While I have not sought specifically to obtain evidence relating to matters that have occurred after the beginning of my enquiries, I have naturally been made aware of many of the relevant events of this period. I am satisfied, however, that the events that have occurred during the course of my investigation have not made a material difference to the key conclusions that I have drawn and they gave me no grounds to question the direction of my emerging findings. As will be evident from the preceding chapters of this report, the difficulties which have continued to beset the Project in recent months have their origins a considerable time ago. While total costs have regrettably continued to rise and slippage has once again enforced changes to anticipated completion dates, these pressures have not come about through any new factors or changed circumstances. In the end the overall cost of the Project will depend on the resolution of package contractors' final accounts with trade contractors, the extent to which professional fees have been capped, and a host of other matters which are beyond the scope of the Inquiry, and which cannot be ascertained for many months.

16.2 At the time of my appointment in June 2003 the estimated final cost of the Project stood at £373.9 million and construction was forecast to be completed in November 2003. With a three month allowance for fit-out, George Reid anticipated that the Parliament would convene in its new home after the Easter 2004 recess.

Monthly Reporting to the SPCB

16.3 Shortly after my appointment George Reid, on behalf of the SPCB, began reporting monthly rather than quarterly to the Finance Committee in order to keep MSPs fully informed on both the cost and programme of the Project. Those reports have been placed in the public domain and offer a valuable account of the final stages of the Project. In my opinion this was a shrewd, and probably overdue political move, which has served to improve the flow of information and to enhance an understanding of the magnitude of the task of completion of the Project.

16.4 George Reid's Report of August 2003 report gave notice that difficulties in the north lightwell area had led Bovis to propose that the projected completion date be extended to July 2004. The principal reason was stated as being the rate at which the windows in this area were able to be fitted due to the requirements for additional blast proofing. This was having a knock-on effect upon the ability of contractors to work in close proximity in this extremely complex part of the site. It was anticipated that this delay would have cost consequences and these would be reported at a later stage. The programme delay would push occupation of the complex by the Parliament back until after the summer 2004 recess.

16.5 George Reid's September 2003 Report detailed the cost implications of the latest programme delay. It anticipated prolongation costs of £15 million and with VAT, additional site organisation costs and a contingency of £11.8 million for possible disruption the estimated final cost had risen to £401.2 million. A landmark figure had been reached.

16.6 Subsequent reports noted the substantive completion of construction work on the MSP building and on Queensberry House and progress of work on the Chamber and Towers at the east part of the site. In February 2004, though, George Reid reported with some regret that estimated costs had increased once again. Continuing difficulties with the complexities of window installation and some of the cladding had required a reassessment of the programme and, while the overall occupation date remained unchanged, there had been a revision of the estimated cost of achieving what had become a very tight programme. DLE had estimated that the total cost now stood at £430.6 million, including a contingency of £8.4 million. George Reid stated boldly that 'this ought to be the last Holyrood cost increase'.[820]

16.7 Monthly reports since February have not indicated any change either to the estimated final cost or to the anticipated completion date. Over this period, money has moved steadily from reserve allocations or risk allowances to committed costs and it is fair to speculate that the full contingency allocation will be drawn upon.

16.8 The June 2004 report also outlined the arrangements for future financial reporting to the Finance Committee and announced that the HPG would be wound up on 29 September 2004, although with Mr Manson, Mr Wright and Dr Gibbons remaining available to act as advisers to the SPCB thereafter. Saturday 9 October 2004 had been settled as the date of the Royal Opening of the new building, after which only final landscaping work would remain to be undertaken.

New Project Director

16.9 At the end of June 2004, Ms Davidson completed her secondment to the Scottish Parliament and vacated her post as Project Director. The timing of the move prior to the completion of the Project was explained by Mr Grice as being due to the role of the Project Director being largely complete by that stage, as the remaining project-related tasks focused on migration and, thereafter, post-contract management. Ms Davidson was replaced by Mr Curran.

Completion

16.10 Construction work on the site was largely completed during July 2004 and members of the parliamentary staff began to take up occupation of the premises from the beginning of August. As I write this, the Parliament remains on course to resume its business in its new accommodation in early September 2004. I have visited the site on a number of occasions during the course of my investigations and while the terms of my remit have inevitably required me to focus on certain negative aspects of the Project, I acknowledge that a building of considerable impact has been constructed, albeit at great cost to the public purse and years late. I shall make no further aesthetic comment on the design, as that question is not for me.

16.11 The Scottish Parliament, now in its second session has a building that meets the vision that I believe Donald Dewar and his colleagues set for it. I express the hope shared by many that the excellence of the parliamentary activity within the building will reflect the quality of the structure, and that the painful lessons of its procurement are not lost on those privileged to serve there as representatives of the Scottish people.

---

[820] Letter from George Reid to Des McNulty, Convener of the Finance Committee, 24 February 2004

Conclusions and Recommendations

Principal Conclusions

Donald Dewar was determined to provide a site and a building for the new Parliament as soon as possible. The timetable for construction dictated the adoption of a "fast track" procurement method entailing relatively high risk. The decision to adopt construction management was taken without an adequate evaluation or understanding of the extent of risk involved and without being referred to Ministers.

The figure of between £40 and £50 million originally put before the Scottish public was never going to be sufficient to secure the construction of a new Parliament building of original and innovative design.

Whenever there was a conflict between quality and cost, quality was preferred.

Whenever there was a conflict between early completion and cost, completion was preferred without in fact any significant acceleration being achieved.

Not until it was too late to change was there any real appreciation of the complexity of the Architect's evolving design and its inevitable cost.

Tempting as it is to lay all the blame at the door of a deceased wayward Spanish architectural genius, his stylised fashion of working and the strained relationship between his widow and RMJM in Edinburgh, the analysis of the Auditor General is unimpeachable. Costs rose because the client (first the Secretary of State and latterly the Parliament) wanted increases and changes or at least approved of them in one manifestation or another.

Summary of Main Findings

The Incoming Administration

The experience of 1979 may have played some part in the subsequent determination of the incoming Labour administration in 1997 to ensure that its devolution proposals, including a building for the Parliament, were irreversibly established. If he had so chosen, Donald Dewar could have proceeded in a more leisurely fashion with the selection of a site for the Scottish Parliament without putting the Government's devolution proposals in their entirety at risk. (Para 1.2)

There was no reason for any expectation prior to May 1997 that an incoming Labour Government would do other than consider the Old Royal High School building as the preferred home for the proposed Scottish Parliament. (Para 1.11)

The White Paper

The £10 million figure referred to in the White Paper was intended to cover no more than a minimal refurbishment of the Old Royal High School. It would only have been sufficient to provide temporary accommodation for the Scottish Parliament and not a permanent home. By October 1997 it became an irrelevance when it was decided to pursue options involving extensive building work. (Para 2.23)

I am unable to conclude that the decision to adopt conventional funding, rather than resorting to PFI procurement, was wrong and was the cause of the delay and cost which has plagued this Project. (Para 2.51)

Timetable

Donald Dewar did not consider it appropriate to identify only a temporary location and leave the permanent location to the incoming Parliament. Those were matters for his judgment and decisions he was entitled to take at that time. (Para 3.12)

Site Selection

While Donald Dewar was very careful to keep the options open, it is difficult not to conclude that he and his political advisers did not favour the Calton Hill site. (Para 3.29)

There was no evidence before the Inquiry to suggest any covert arrangement between Donald Dewar and Scottish & Newcastle nor that Donald Dewar had reached an early conclusion favouring Holyrood before its candidacy was announced. There was hostility in Edinburgh to the Parliament being located anywhere other than centrally, thus eliminating Leith. Against this background the selection of Holyrood was obvious. (Paras 3.27 & 3.30)

Feasibility Studies

The costings of the feasibility studies were no more than indicative. They did not by themselves provide a meaningful basis for Ministers to reach decisions nor did they represent a sound basis from which to derive a realistic budget for the eventual Parliament building. (Paras 3.23 and 3.31)

Whitehall influence

The Inquiry found no evidence to substantiate the claim that, in selecting the Holyrood site, Donald Dewar was subjected to influence from senior members of the UK Labour Party. (Para 3.39)

Relative merits of sites

It is outwith the remit of the Inquiry to comment on the relative merits of the Holyrood site in comparison with the others under consideration. The evidence before the Inquiry gives no cause to disagree with Mr Spencely's opinion that the delays and cost rises that befell the Project at a later stage were not directly attributable to the Holyrood location. (Para 3.42)

Designer Selection Competition

The press release announcing the competition referred to an early time frame, value for money and quality. That was the architectural equivalent of motherhood and apple pie. Who would not want all these desirable architectural and economic virtues? It appears to me that Scottish Office officials were not slow in understanding their task. What they were to struggle with was where the priority lay: Quality? Cost? Or speed of the completion of the building? As events unfolded it appears to me that they understood their task to be one of trying to achieve early delivery of the new Parliament building, whilst maintaining quality. In my opinion that meant inevitably that whatever lip-service was paid to it, the cost of the building took a back seat. (Para 4.4)

Insufficient inquiry was made of the proposed joint venture between EMBT and RMJM Ltd. It is surprising that the architectural commission for the new Scottish Parliament building was let to a company with a nominal share capital of £100 and only £2 issued and fully paid up. There should have been a rigorous process of due diligence and collateral warranties should have been obtained from both RMJM Ltd and EMBT. (Para 4.33)

None of the finalists adhered to the User Brief or the budget. Consideration should have been given for the contract with the architect to incorporate fee-tapering or other incentive to keep costs down. (Paras 4.40)

I cannot and do not challenge the aesthetic judgement of any of the panel members in their unanimous selection of Enric Miralles. (Para 4.46)

The panel selected a designer, namely Enric Miralles, but the appointment was awarded to EMBT/RMJM (Scotland) Ltd. (Para 4.47)

The so-called budget, which never had any basis in reality, was not at the time of the designer competition set against even the most tentative of cost estimates. (Para 4.49)

Reliance was certainly placed on the assertions by the architectural joint venture at interview that the Project could be delivered within the £50 million budget and adapted to bring about additional cost improvements. It is difficult to see how that assertion could have been given conscientiously or taken seriously, given the embryonic state of the designs. (Para 4.51)

The competition process was in general a sound one. Some parts of the process, such as the evaluation of the Pre Qualification Questionnaires and the visits to the offices of competitors were, however, less systematic than they should have been. There should have been a proper documentary record of the conduct of the competition. (Para 4.52)

Building User Brief

Against the background of the extensive design development which took place from late 1998 to June 2000, no steps were taken to amend the Brief. It suggests to me that over that crucial period in the development of the Project, sight was lost of the terms of the Brief. If that is correct, much of the extensive design development over that period was not taking place against the background of the clearly formulated set of client or user requirements, which the Brief should have contained. (Para 5.18)

The Brief sent out strong messages to the Design Team as to the significance not only of the symbolism of designs for the building but also as to the high quality expected. The messages in relation to programme and, perhaps more significantly, in relation to budget are more muted. With the benefit of hindsight the Brief might well have sent out a more considered message to the Design Team as to the relative significance of cost in the Cost/Quality/Programme triangle. (Para 5.27)

Construction Management

It verges on the embarrassing to conclude, as I do, that virtually none of the key questions about construction management were asked. Similarly none of the disadvantages of construction management appear to have been identified and evaluated. If the key questions had been asked and subjected to rigorous assessment, I cannot speculate whether the requirement for an early completion date would have been revisited, enabling a less risky procurement method to be adopted, or whether the construction management route would in fact still have been followed. It is, however, evident that the Scottish Office, while working to publicly declared fixed budgets and being highly "risk averse", was preparing to follow a procurement route for which there could be no fixed budget and a high degree of risk would rest with the client. (Para 6.8)

Mr Gordon put up a carefully considered minute on 6 January 1998 in which he considered procurement by the PFI/PPP route as against what he described as a 'conventional procurement' route. He was more concerned to contrast PFI with conventional procurement than analyse the so-called 'conventional' options. It must be open to question whether there was a sufficiently thorough examination of the range of contract routes available at this stage, although I appreciate that the primary focus at that time was on the selection of a site. (Para 6.11)

This, in my view, is the point when the wheels began to fall off the wagon. Ministers had decided unequivocally that for the reasons given a PFI solution should not be pursued and a 'conventional' one should. The primacy of reasoning given for rejecting PFI was that such a course might cause unacceptable delay to the completion of the Parliament building. That was a political judgment Donald Dewar and ministerial colleagues were entitled to make and they did so without qualification. After the meeting on 14 January 1998 to consider Mr Gordon's minute, inexplicably Ministers were never again asked to take a decision on the procurement route with senior officials arrogating that responsibility to themselves. (Para 6.12)

Nowhere does Mr Armstrong address or seek to compare the respective profiles in terms of client risk of construction management and management contracting. Significantly higher risk attaches to the former. While it may have been that the programme was a given factor for Mr Armstrong, and I do not disagree with his view that it dictated a "fast track" construction method, he might appropriately also have emphasised to Mr Brown, who was not a construction professional, that both construction management and management contracting necessarily entailed very significantly higher client risk than traditional procurement vehicles. Mr Armstrong's advice was poor in this respect and betrayed either a surprising oversight, or at any rate a misunderstanding on his part. (Para 6.15)

On 5 March 1998 Mr Brown minuted that it had been agreed that traditional contracting was not feasible and that either construction management or management contracting would have to be adopted. It would be helpful, he said, in the three months before a decision had to be taken to see examples to illustrate the advantages and disadvantages of both methods. He also suggested that it might be helpful to have a presentation from a construction manager on the perceived advantages of the different routes. There is no evidence that any examples were produced, or that his prudent idea of a presentation was followed up. (Para 6.16)

No consideration appears to have been given to the involvement of Ministers in the decision to adopt construction management or even to the possibility of informing them of it. I note that this is in the starkest of contrast to the approach adopted by Mr Gordon in relation to consideration of the possibility of PFI/PPP procurement where Ministers were fully involved and informed in relation to the decision making process. (Para 6.17)

The selection of Construction Management was the single factor to which most of the misfortunes that have befallen the Project can be attributed. Against that background I am highly critical of the failure of Mr Armstrong and Mrs Doig to ensure that there was an appropriate evaluation of the highly risky contract strategy that was adopted, particularly in view of the choice of Architect. (Para 6.22)

I regard the decision to adopt construction management without advising Ministers of the attendant risks and the inflexible insistence on a rigid programme as among the most flawed decisions in the history of the Project. It beggars belief that Ministers were not asked to approve the proposal to adopt construction management. Nor did they, as Lord Elder correctly points out, have the advantage of Treasury advice. (Para 6.24)

Appointment of Construction Manager

There was confusion in relation to certain aspects of the meeting to consider the construction manager applications on 2 December 1998. Mr Armstrong's understanding was that, while the outcome of the meeting was no more than a recommendation, EU procurement law and guidance on procurement required acceptance of the lowest tender and that there was no requirement for a further round of interviews. While Treasury Guidance on the appointment of consultants and contractors does not specifically envisage a post tender final interview, I do not read the guidance or understand procurement law to preclude such a step in the process. (Para 7.11)

While there may have been an absence of clarity in relation to the purpose of the meeting of 2 December 1998, I make no criticism of Mrs Doig's decision to revisit its conclusion as to the number of tenderers to participate in the final interviews. (Para 7.12)

Where I have greater difficulty is with Mrs Doig's decision to readmit Bovis to the process without also reconsidering the position of Tenderer 3. DLE had reported that Bovis was the highest of the four tenderers, after appropriate adjustments to ensure that like was compared with like. Their analysis of the figures appears to me to be correct. At the tender review meeting on 2 December Tenderer 3 had been excluded on cost grounds. Bovis had been excluded not only on cost grounds, including those related to the PCG, but also on account of the non-availability of Mr Richardson. The tenders of Bovis and of Tenderer 3 both exceeded the guideline of £5.5 million. Mrs Doig's minute of 15 December 1998 to Mr Armstrong indicated that Bovis' cost position did not in itself rule them out and that they should be probed further on the issue of the PCG and on their personnel. Her minute did not however suggest that these initial concerns had been resolved. Rather she chose to proceed on the basis of informal considerations. She referred in evidence to her "own informal networks" in relation to Bovis' performance on the Museum of Scotland contract. These included having "got some information from the press" and her awareness of how well Bovis had handled a great many site visits to the Museum of Scotland (designed by signature architects) in the year before its completion and the pressures of a fixed Royal opening date for that building. She was unable to provide me with any satisfactory reason for her selection of Bovis to be readmitted to the process. It did not occur to her that there might be legal considerations. While, as I have found in the preceding paragraph, Mrs Doig was within her rights to revisit the decision of the tender review meeting and to invite a third tenderer to take part in the final round of interviews, it is my view that such a decision is one which should only have been taken on the basis of a proper evaluation of the comparative positions of both of the two excluded tenderers and on a basis which provided a clear audit trail. In these respects her decision was flawed. (Para 7.13)

I have no evidence to suggest there was anything amiss in Dr Gibbons' relationship with Bovis as a candidate for the construction management contract. (Para 7.14)

It does however appear to me, on elementary considerations of fairness as between competing tenderers, that if one tenderer was effectively permitted to change a very material aspect of the financial basis upon which its tender was submitted that is an opportunity which should have been afforded to the others. (Para 7.15)

In all other respects the final interviews on 4 January 1999 appear to me to have been conducted in a way which was thorough, fair, and well documented. In this respect it can be contrasted favourably with the proceedings in the final rounds of the designer selection competition. (Para 7.16)

I am aware that in his 2000 Report the Auditor General made the very valid point that it might have been appropriate for the fees of the consultants, including Bovis, to have been tapered so that the percentage fee would reduce as a proportion of construction cost as that cost increases. I agree with that observation although, in the context of Bovis' appointment, it is not as significant as the possible conversion to a lump sum upon agreement of the Cost Plan. (Para 7.18)

Both in terms of EU procurement law and in terms of guidance, unsuccessful tenderers should be afforded the opportunity of a debriefing. I have been informed as to the specific circumstances that led to this administrative oversight in relation to McAlpine and, while I make no criticism of any individual in this respect, I am critical of the system which allowed it to occur and a legal requirement to be neglected. (Para 7.19)

It is my understanding that, despite the eventual offer of a Parent Company Guarantee by Bovis at no additional cost, in the event that offer was not taken up and had still not been taken up as recently as February 2004 when the point was raised in the Finance Committee of the Parliament and when the SPCB recommended that such a PCG should be obtained from Bovis. I understand that this may now have been done. While I recognise that Bovis is a major and reputable company, this is something that should have been done at a much earlier stage. (Para 7.20)

The Project Sponsor

The complexities of this particular project were such that even without the benefit of hindsight it should have been seen that any sponsor appointed should have had greater familiarity than Mrs Doig with either construction or the sponsorship of major construction projects. I do not underestimate the advantage of having someone who could work within an intricate political environment. Whether an individual with such a full range of skills existed within the Scottish Office at that time I cannot say. However, as Ministers were showing themselves more than willing to become involved, having the pragmatic advice of someone with construction experience to draw upon was more valuable than that of someone with political acumen. (Para 8.6)

Adequacy of the Budget

At no time before handover did the Project Team succeed in securing a design from the Design Team that could be delivered within budget. The client's increased requirements for space were a significant factor in this situation but I have to question whether £50 million was ever a realistic budget figure and how effective the Project Team were in operating a genuine cost control process. (Para 8.13)

There seems to have been growing unease about the direction in which the costings of the indicative design proposals were heading. There does, however, appear to me to have been a reluctance to accept that costs could not be contained by 'cost reducing measures' or to report the deteriorating forecasts to Ministers. (Para 8.16)

Reporting to Ministers

Although grave reservations over the budget were being expressed within the Scottish Office as early as November 1998, neither Donald Dewar nor any of his Ministers were being given any warning of impending major cost rises. This makes it all the more surprising that in March 1999 when he was eventually first asked to approve a budget increase he was told it would be "prudent" to lift it from £50 million to £60 million! (Para 8.17)

It seems extraordinary that Ministers do not appear to have had any formal indication of the apparent threat to the agreed budget of £50 million during late 1998 and early 1999 when officials were evidently well aware of the evolving situation. Mr Thomson suggested that when an approach for an addition to the budget did eventually come forward, Donald Dewar would not have been taken completely by surprise as he would have understood the general direction of the Project from his informal exchanges. (Para 8.20)

Timetable

Although the timetable was developed by Mr Armstrong using his considerable experience of project management, it undoubtedly was driven by the political objective of early completion and occupancy of the Parliament building. It is ironic that throughout his involvement with the Project Mr Armstrong drove forward a programme that he had devised but which he felt did not incorporate sufficient time for the planning and design phases of the Project. (Para 8.21)

In his October 1998 Report Mr Armstrong appears to be reflecting the clearly expressed view that the timetable for the Project was tight from the outset and any delay would therefore jeopardise the ability to meet the wishes of Ministers to deliver the Project as early as possible. This urgency does not seem to me to have been echoed by the Project Sponsor who recognised that Enric Miralles "did not work in straight lines" but, instead, would have surges of creative input. She also spoke of the many other ways in which the lead architect was helping the client. I am unconvinced that the value of Snr Miralles' contribution to Edinburgh Festival events and public presentations was as critical as his personal input to the key design work at this crucial stage in the Project. (Para 8.24)

The Architectural Joint Venture

This does not sound like a joint venture company that had gelled particularly well at that point. Although Mr Duncan spent some time in Barcelona in an effort to improve communications and the difficulties surrounding a key presentation to Donald Dewar on 16 September 1998 were ironed out, the underlying questions over the ability of the Architect to deliver remained. (Para 8.23)

The two practices had very different cultures and ways of working and found it difficult to adopt a cohesive approach to design issues or resolving problems whilst working in separate locations and communicating mainly via fax. With Enric Miralles insisting on being personally involved in all design issues during these formative stages, there was inevitable delay and disruption caused by his geographical detachment. Although RMJM took steps to better integrate the practices, this was only partially successful. Communication issues have been evident throughout the life of the joint venture company. (Para 8.30)

The relationship between the Project Manager and the Architect is central. Mr Armstrong was an experienced professional project manager who understood better than almost everyone around him how to bring a complex construction project to fruition. He had a structured approach to his work and sought to impose that discipline on the consultants with whom he worked. It is clear from Mr Armstrong's reports that from the outset he was not succeeding in developing a constructive dialogue with (both arms) of the Architect. (Para 8.31)

The poor level of communication at this time is exemplified by the fact that RMJM and EMBT both submitted separate solutions to the Stage C difficulties to the Project Team; a course of events that exposed tensions between the two arms of the joint venture company. (Para 8.34)

Whether Enric Miralles fully understood at this time the political environment in which he was expected to work is questionable. He was clearly coming under pressure from the Project Manager and from his business partners in RMJM to work to a schedule in a way that he was unaccustomed to doing. It seems however that he felt strongly that the "gestation" of a project of this type needed time. (Para 8.35)

Fees were used by the client as a lever to encourage delivery by the architectural consultants. However, the way in which the issue was handled seems to illustrate the growing tensions in the relationship between Mr Armstrong and the Architect. (Para 8.36)

Resignation of Mr Armstrong

Surprisingly, Ministers were not informed of the resignation of the Project Manager until his departure was picked up by the media in January 1999. Given Donald Dewar's evident interest in all aspects of the Project, this seems inexplicable. (Para 8.42)

Design Information

The absence of estimates seems to illustrate the dearth of design information coming forward over this period and also the lack of adequate joint working between the Architect and the cost consultants. Whether this made any difference to the client is another question. When DLE did submit estimates they were either withheld from Ministers or altered. (Para 8.44)

Reporting Cost Information to Ministers

I do not challenge the principle that the Project Team could take a view on whether the risks identified by DLE could be avoided by client action. What I find more difficult to comprehend is why Ministers were not notified within the confidentiality of their exchanges with officials of the reported financial position and the management action taken to address the position. By omitting to inform Ministers of this highly relevant development, a risk was introduced that Ministers would take decisions on the basis of partial or incomplete information and might inadvertently make misleading statements in public or in Parliament. It is evident that DLE were not consulted over the accuracy of the 23 March submission but more surprisingly it does not appear that the Project Team undertook any exploration with them at this time as to the validity of the risks DLE were identifying. Professional advice appears to have been rejected without a proper consideration of that advice or challenge to it. The whole episode suggests to me that senior officials did not have a complete understanding of the advice that their professional consultants were offering them. (Paras 8.50 & 8.51)

Sir Muir Russell took comfort from the observation in the Auditor General's Report that 'the particular risk items in question did not subsequently materialise'. However, it is not clear to me whether the risks concerning Mr Fisher were the same as the particular risks commented on by the Auditor General. As I read the Auditor General's observations in context, he is referring to those risks identified in Sir Muir Russell's letter of 4 April 2000 to Donald Dewar and not the broader range of risks that concerned Mr Fisher. (Para 8.52)

It has been suggested that the issue of risk allowances as opposed to contingencies must have been examined at the meeting on 2 June 1999 and it has been speculated that the content of the full DLE cost estimates may have been conveyed to Ministers at this time. I do not however find this supported either in the official record of that meeting or in the written evidence to the Inquiry submitted by Jack McConnell. (Para 8.56)

It was clear from the evidence of Mrs Doig, Mr Gordon and Sir Muir Russell that a conscious decision had been taken by civil servants that the majority of the risk items identified by DLE could be "managed out" and that it was not in the circumstances necessary or appropriate for Ministers to be informed. (Para 8.57)

It appears to me that the decision to increase the budget taken on 2 June 1999 had no legal basis. In terms of the Transfer of Property etc. (Scottish Parliamentary Corporate Body) Order 1999 all rights and interests in relation to the Parliament had passed to the SPCB on 1 June 1999. From that date the budget was a matter only for the SPCB and the approval of this increase in budget should have been sought from Sir David Steel and his SPCB colleagues. I can see that officials might wish to brief Ministers on the increases so that they were content with what was being proposed and as they were cost increases that had arisen while the Project was still under their stewardship but that does not deflect my concern that Ministers were purporting to take significant decisions in relation to a Project no longer within their remit. (Para 8.58)

It is astonishing that less than a month after Donald Dewar's speech to the Parliament officials knew the independent cost consultants were insisting that their figure was correct but at no time prior to Mr Spencely's Report was this drawn to Donald Dewar's attention. Nor indeed was it raised with Sir David Steel or the SPCB, although Mr Fisher stressed what the risks would be if he were to be questioned by the SPCB. (Para 8.60)

The Project at Handover

I accept that the Project at handover was within weeks of formal Stage D approval but only to the extent that the design requirements of the November 1998 brief were apparently satisfied. However the proper satisfaction of the requirements of RIBA Stage D should have included completion of the Brief and preparation of a cost plan within budget. (Para 9.6)

It was not suggested to the Inquiry that the requirements of the new Parliament, as they came to be articulated, were extravagant or unreasonable. (Para 9.7)

While those involved no doubt genuinely and with the best of intentions believed that the Project was, at the time of handover to the Scottish Parliament, on the threshold of a meaningful Stage D, the evidence before the Inquiry suggested otherwise. It is clear to me that the requirements of Stage D, particularly as regard the Brief and the Cost Plan, were not close to satisfaction at the time of handover. Accordingly, it cannot properly be maintained that the Project was close to a satisfactory Stage D. (Para 9.10)

In my opinion, there was a failure at the stage of handover to appreciate sufficiently the extent to which the development of certain aspects of the design, such as the Chamber roof, were leading to a very high degree of complexity. There was also a failure to appreciate adequately the consequences of that complexity. The Architect clearly understood the complexity of the designs and articulated this to the client using all manner of presentation techniques. However, it is far from clear that the Architect had the budget clearly in mind when producing designs of such complexity. I would have expected Bovis to have appreciated the programme implications. Indeed all who attended risk management workshops should have been on the alert. (Para 9.13)

I am bound to conclude that:

1. The Brief was not up to date, and did not reflect the changes made since November 1998.
2. The Brief did not anticipate the requirements of the Parliament with the inevitable result that adherence to it would have produced an unsuitable building.
3. The budgeted construction cost of £62 million was flawed in that:

    a there was inadequate accounting for risk, and the stated budget bore no relationship to a cost plan;
    b there had been a failure to fully appreciate the complexity of the design; and
    c account had not been taken of considerations of blast and security.

In short the Project was not in a viable and healthy condition when it was handed over to the SPCB on 1 June 1999. (Para 9.16)

Briefing of the SPCB

In my opinion, the briefing to the SPCB should have alluded to the difficulties that had been experienced with the Design Team and to the fact that the independent professional advice of DLE in relation to the appropriate figure for risk allowances had been disregarded in arriving at the construction cost budget of £62 million. Furthermore, the briefing paper makes no attempt to impart to the SPCB, none of whom had any significant construction or procurement experience, the risks inevitably involved in construction management as the selected procurement vehicle. In this respect the briefing did not present a fair and balanced picture of the state of the Project as it then stood. The terms of the briefing suggest that the Project Sponsor and Project Management were not themselves alert to the potential risks to the Project. (Para 9.23)

SPCB Minutes

It surprised me that the SPCB should have been advised and should have decided to make available to MSPs and the public only a heavily edited version of its minutes, going well beyond the necessary restraints of commercial confidentiality. I consider that the decision to withhold information on the Project from MSPs must to some extent have suppressed informed debate and was evidently a source of frustration. It is difficult to reconcile this practice with the CSG's stated principles of openness and transparency. (Para 9.27)

Clerk and Chief Executive

My overall impression from the evidence was that Mr Grice as the Clerk and Chief Executive was not, during this early period after handover, as personally engaged with the Project in his capacity as Project Owner as might have been expected. While Mr Grice was generally in attendance at SPCB meetings during this period the minutes do not record any significant level of contribution from him. Mr Grice described very fully, and with commendable frankness, the many demands on his own time and the extent to which he was prepared to leave the running of the Project to Mrs Doig and her team. However, I have noted that the SPCB lacked the legal power to delegate other than to the Clerk. The delegation of responsibility for the Project to another senior official was accordingly not an option open to it. However, section 20(4) permits the Clerk to authorise another member of staff to exercise functions on his behalf. However, the HPG could never be described as members of his staff. (Para 9.32)

1999 Parliamentary Debate

It is not for me to speculate as to the future of the Project had the result of the June 1999 vote been different but Alex Salmond has argued strongly, and not without cause, that the new Scottish Parliament should have been fully appraised of all costs beforehand. Transparently, as the Inquiry has revealed, it was not. (Para 9.39)

Donald Dewar was evidently unaware of DLE's detailed advice on risk and I do not believe that he intentionally misled the Parliament in that respect. It is unfortunate, but perhaps not surprising so soon after handover, that the debate was dominated by the site selection issue and failed to address the significant issues in relation to design, budget and procurement method. The debate did not alter the SPCB's mandate nor provide it with any more precise direction or authority as to how it should proceed. It would have been desirable if, as a result of the debate, the Parliament had taken a greater "ownership" of the Project. However, I discern no part of the debate as focusing on that but what discussion there was sent very clear messages to the Design Team about quality. (Para 9.43)

Landscaping

Landscaping is a relatively small part of the ultimate budget but it demonstrates an unacceptable set of switches which must have been, at the least, confusing to MSPs. At the time of the critical debate these costs were not to be included but by the autumn of 2001 they were. Had I been an MSP alive to constituency concerns about ever-rising costs of the new Parliament, I would have been spitting tacks that yet another £14 million had been slipped under my nose with little or no notice. (Para 9.48)

Project Execution Plan

As highlighted in the September 2000 Report of the Auditor General, there was a failure by Project Management to finalise Mr Curran's draft Project Execution Plan. Evidence produced to the Inquiry reveals that as late as October 2000 this document was only available in the format of a third draft, and in fact I was unable to ascertain conclusively whether a Plan was ever finalised. I endorse the Auditor General's conclusion that the failure to finalise this key document was a significant shortcoming. (Para 9.52)

Design of the Chamber

Over the summer and autumn of 1999, and in relation to the revisions to the design of the Chamber the constituent parts of EMBT/RMJM Ltd appeared to be operating in a dysfunctional way. Snr Miralles appears to have been primarily motivated by the desire to insist on his design, disregarding the clear instructions from the SPCB and the Project Team to accommodate the required changes to the Chamber within the existing footprint. In short, the joint venture was a misnomer; in reality the picture discloses two teams, separated by geography, working in quite different ways. The consequence is that the overall performance of the Architect fell below what could reasonably have been expected. (Para 9.70)

Overall and because of the extent of the wider redesign which emerged in early 2000 I do not consider that the problems with the shape of the Chamber had a major impact on either cost or programme. (Para 9.71)

Space Requirements

That a hitherto unforeseen increase in space of this order of magnitude, representing some 17% of the gross area of the building, excluding the car parking, could have "emerged" as a consequence of the "natural evolution of the design" seems to me to be extraordinary. It has to be strongly suggestive of a disregard by the Architect of the constraints of Brief and budget to which they were supposed to be designing. (Para 9.78)

Mr Mustard's Review

It is noteworthy that Mr Mustard's review takes on the DLE May 1999 figure of £89 million rather than the "budget figure" of £62 million. I cannot avoid the conclusion that the Project Team had never bought into the budget figure of £62 million and always regarded £89 million as a more realistic construction cost figure. (Para 9.86)

Mr Mustard's review was perceptive; indeed it was a damning indictment of practically everything that was wrong with the Project at that time. As I accept that his Review was essentially accurate, the inevitable conclusion has to be that the Project was in danger of running out of control as early as August 1999. (Para 9.91)

The factors leading to that conclusion are rooted in the state of the Project at handover exacerbated by subsequent problems with the Chamber and lack of control by the Architect. The budget was seriously out of kilter with such cost estimates as were available and whatever actions were being taken to narrow that gap were subsequently unsuccessful. Mr Mustard regarded the position as recoverable, notwithstanding his damning indictment. I can only conclude that he was hoping against hope as was Mr Spencely some six months later. (Para 9.92)

Subsequent events reveal that the implementation plan did not achieve the anticipated result. (Para 9.93)

Feasibility Study

To support the view that the architectural joint venture started to work better after the Debating Chamber issue is the fact that the feasibility study instructed in November 1999, produced relatively quickly a lasting architectural solution to the requirement for additional space. On the other hand design delay remained an issue at this time, as it did throughout the Project. (Para 9.97)

Project Costs in late 1999

Mr Grice cannot avoid the earlier criticism for lack of openness with the SPCB. He may have been right in concluding that the estimate before him was one in which he had no confidence but the consequence of that was that he left the MSPs on the SPCB with a serious under-estimation of likely overall costs. As Sir David Steel indicated in evidence, had the SPCB been provided with DLE's figures at that stage they might have instructed 'the Spencely process' earlier. (Para 9.102)

It is surprising to me that the Architect should claim such apparent astonishment at the news that their design had been costed at £53 million over the budget. Their professional experience should have given them more than an inkling of the likely construction cost of their design as it was developing. Indeed, Mr Duncan wrote on 1 September 1999 pointing out Mr Stewart's opinion at a Project Team meeting that the 'currently declared budget of £62 million was inadequate and...created an extremely serious situation'. Equally, there can be no denying that the client had been making it abundantly clear since their appointment that there was a budget to which the Project had to be delivered. It is not credible that the construction cost figure of £115 million reported by DLE came as a bolt from the blue to the Architect and the client's reaction must have been equally predictable. (Para 9.113)

Value Engineering Exercise

While there may be some uncertainty about the precise extent to which savings were realised as a direct result of the Value Engineering exercise, there can be no doubt that the exercise failed miserably to achieve its stated goal of achieving a £25 million reduction in the construction cost of the Project. (Para 9.117)

Balance Area

It was regrettable that no-one appears to have been aware that the correct approach would have been to deduct the 35% balance area from the gross figure rather than to add it to the net as both Mrs Doig and Mr Grice had done. To produce an additional net 1,684m² the gross requirement should have been for 2,591m² rather than 2,275m². (Para 9.118)

SPCB and Cost Increases

I have considerable sympathy for Sir David Steel and the SPCB in the latter part of 1999. They had been told that the construction cost budget of the new building was £62 million and that its gross area was 23,000m². On a "back of an envelope" calculation, increasing the size of the Parliament building to about 30,000m² left them comfortably under £100 million but, prior to that most uncomfortable of meetings with Mrs Doig in the spring of 2000, I have found in all that has been presented before the Inquiry that not even the single clang of a warning bell was sounded before that meeting. (Para 10.9)

The "Dutch Auction" in terms of which guarantees were being sought from Mrs Doig suggests a fundamental failure on the part of the SPCB, even by this time, to understand the nature of construction management under which no "guarantees" are possible. Notwithstanding my earlier expression of sympathy for their position, the SPCB are open to criticism for having failed to take the initiative at a much earlier stage to force the issue on costs; for example by asking for a meeting with their cost consultants, DLE. I sense that the management style of the SPCB was essentially reactive, in that it appears to have relied heavily on the information put before it rather than taking a proactive approach. (Para 10.15)

Spencely Report

Mr Spencely agreed in examination that he had not highlighted the need for a pause in his Report, for example by placing a recommendation to that effect in a list of conclusions. I prefer the view that he was suggesting that a pause would have been beneficial, but that the political imperative of speed intervened to make that a practical impossibility. I am unable to speculate as to whether a pause would indeed have been beneficial. (Para 10.27)

Role of Dr Gibbons

I have to question the arrangement with Dr Gibbons, which to my mind raises substantial issues of governance. I find it difficult to understand that Dr Gibbons could properly act as both the de facto leader of the Holyrood Project Team and sit as a member (even a non-voting member) of the body whose role effectively was to oversee him and his Team. There was no evidence that he abused his position, but it unsettled others and it is another example of the blurred lines of communication that have plagued this Project. (Para 10.45)

Role of the HPG

While the carefully crafted Memorandum of Understanding emphasised the purely advisory role of the HPG, it is interesting to note that the wording of the minute of the meeting of 8 June 2000 is strongly suggestive of a more hands-on managerial role. (Para 10.49)

The scheme of delegation set out in the Memorandum of Understanding represented an ingenious solution to the constraints imposed by section 21 of the Scotland Act. At the time this arrangement was set up, no-one was interested in questioning its legality and even now that would appear to be the case. However, to the extent that the HPG assumed a decision making role when under statute decision making power could not be delegated to it, leads me to a conclusion that s. 21 of the Scotland Act might be reviewed as regards the powers of the SPCB to delegate. (Para 10.56)

Stage D

Two necessary elements of a robust Stage D are to be found in the agreement by all parties of a Cost Plan and in the existence of at least a preliminary structural design by the structural engineers. Neither had been achieved by June 2000. (Para 11.3)

The Bovis advice to DLE to check, prior to package tenders being invited, whether a trade package was within the target cost plan was, in my opinion, sound and well-intentioned but there remained the essential incompatibility that if the drive was to early completion, cost was not and could not be containable. (Para 11.12)

On the question as to whether there was agreement to the Cost Plan, I note that the Auditor General in his report of June 2004 considered that there was at best only "qualified agreement". On the evidence before me I am in agreement with that analysis. (Para 11.14)

With regard to the adequacy of design Mr Kinsley wrote to DLE on 10 August 2000 expressing his opinion that there had "been sufficient architectural information in place for some time now to allow a good Cost Plan to be prepared." In my view that has to be a questionable assumption particularly with regard to the state of the design at the east end of the site. (Para 11.15)

On the evidence before me I conclude that the Stage D report and the Cost Plan later developed on the basis of it did not provide a robust foundation for the future of the Project. I note that as early as November 2000 DLE were reporting from a risk workshop a nominal design and construction risk exposure, exclusive of inflation, of some £28.7 million, putting the total construction cost significantly well over the Cost Plan 'budget'. (Para 11.19)

Guaranteed Maximum Price

The HPG's decision not to move to a Guaranteed Maximum Price at this time was, in my view, entirely appropriate. Whatever may have been the wisdom of the initial decision to adopt construction management as the procurement vehicle for the Project (which I have already questioned whether it was properly explained), the contractual position in that respect was inherited by both the SPCB and the HPG. The contract with Bovis made no provision for the change of their consultancy role as the Construction Manager to any other role such as that of management contractor or works contractor. (Para 11.24)

The Architectural Joint Venture

While the Project had lost its creative and charismatic principal architect in Enric Miralles, the design to his concept should have reached a sufficiently advanced stage for the Project to continue in his absence. His death, however, gave rise to a substantial period of disharmony within the architectural Joint Venture and the only conclusion can be, sadly, that it caused further delay. (Para 11.29)

On one view, leaving Snr Miralles as Principal Person was an expedient fudge by the HPG which left the Design Team as something of a rudderless ship. On the other hand Snr Miralles had not been doing much to 'direct and control .. overall performance by the Architect'. He was always a concept designer rather than a manager and it may have made little difference to the practical arrangements. However, I have a sense that the subsequent problems might have been avoided if a more robust stance had been taken by the HPG at the time. (Para 11.30)

Donald Dewar

I knew Donald Dewar well, having been on the Select Committee on Scottish Affairs early in the 1979 Parliament when he was Chairman of it. I was well aware from at least that time of his commitment to the establishment of a Scottish Parliament. He enjoyed very considerable political influence at Westminster and Scotland which should not be under-estimated. All the comment to me has emphasised that it was his drive and determination that caused the new Parliament Building Project to go forward. (Para 11.33)

It is more difficult to assess whether he could have or should have asked more searching questions on costs prior to the handover in June 1999. His Special Adviser Lord Elder talked of his unease over the figures being supplied to him but there was no evidence before me that he sought any appraisal of the costs from, for example, the independent cost consultant Mr Fisher of DLE. (Para 11.34)

It comes as no surprise that Donald Dewar contemplated resignation on the basis that he had misled the Scottish Parliament. Donald Dewar was steeped in the Westminster tradition that there is no greater democratic misdemeanour than misleading Parliament and he clearly carried that with him when he became First Minister in the Scottish Parliament. However, there was no evidence whatsoever to suggest that he deliberately or knowingly misled MSPs. He relied on cost figures given to him by senior civil servants. As it turned out, he should not have done so but he did not conceal figures that he knew were a better assessment. In the event he did not resign and in my view was correct not to have done so. (Para 11.35)

Auditor General's Report – September 2000

What is incontestable is that the Project did not proceed smoothly to the conclusion that was anticipated and many of the shortcomings identified in the Auditor General's 2000 Report have persisted until the present day. (Para 11.41)

It is not difficult to conclude that by the end of 2000 the Project was in serious trouble despite the best efforts of the HPG and Project Management. As it progressed into 2001 and beyond those difficulties would increase. (Para 11.45)

Alan Ezzi

Mr Ezzi appears to have wrestled with the challenge of imposing a discipline on the Design Team to deliver design information to the agreed programme and to design to a budget rather than simply to a concept. Mr Ezzi had been appointed to be a "bruiser" over rising costs but whenever he attempted to fulfil that role he was left without support or had his proposals countermanded. (Para 12.22)

Mr Ezzi grappled largely unsuccessfully with the complexities of working for a political client in the shape of the HPG. There does however seem to have been a failure on the part of the HPG to appreciate the difficulties which their actions placed upon the ability of their Project Director to perform his role. (Para 12.23)

The Budget 'Cap'

Tellingly, Ms Davidson observed that "under construction management the notion of a cap is somewhat misleading anyway". I have to question whether in approving the £195 million ceiling on costs in April 2000 Parliament fully understood the nature of the Project it was considering or the procurement route that had been selected for it before its inception. Although the HPG gradually developed an understanding of this key facet of construction management as it grappled with the complexities of managing risk and design development, this does not appear to have been shared by other MSPs until a surprisingly late stage. (Para 12.38)

The Foyer Roof

Mr Ezzi suggested that this scrutiny of preliminary design proposals for the Foyer roof was proof of the design process working. Having been alerted to an emerging problem at a very early stage in the design process, he suggested that DLE and the Project Team had acted quickly to bring it back on course. That may have been their intention but whatever actions were taken at those early stages, they clearly did not succeed in producing a design proposal that could be constructed for anything approaching the original anticipated figure. (Para 12.43)

The HPG seemed to be placed in a position where it was required to take decisions at a stage in the process when it was too late to recommend or affect any meaningful change to the outcome. (Para 12.47)

The evidence does suggest that levels of communication among key players were extremely poor on occasions, of which the Foyer roof is a prime example. Although I heard evidence of a visit to Barcelona by a member of the DLE team, I am not convinced that there was an appropriate level of interface between the Design Team and the cost consultants on this issue. While my primary criticism is of the Architect, DLE might also have taken a more proactive role in identifying that designs were being developed outwith the Cost Plan and drawing that to the attention of the client. As it was, the HPG inevitably felt bounced into approving actions with significant cost implications in view of the implications on programme (and to an extent on quality) if they were to do otherwise. (Para 12.48)

Clearly communication channels were hampered by the fact that the principal work on the Foyer roof took place in Barcelona. Notwithstanding the presence of EMBT staff in Bells Brae, I am tempted to conclude that this design work was not undertaken in a co-ordinated fashion, as it is apparent that the production of the finalised design took almost everyone by surprise. This was wholly unsatisfactory, particularly in respect of such a significant part of the building. I cannot exclude from criticism the Project Team who did not have an effective monitoring system in place to ensure that such surprises were avoided. Whether this could have been avoided by the strengthening of Project Management as has been suggested I am unclear, but I have found that this incident demonstrates a major failure of management and a loss of control over the process. (Para 12.49)

Kemnay Granite

The consideration of Kemnay granite suggests to me that even at this stage the client, expressing its will through the HPG, was placing greater store on the issue of aesthetics/quality than on either cost or programme. (Para 12.51)

Fee Capping

It is difficult to assess whether the early reliance on a wholly unrealistic budget led first the Scottish Office and then the SPCB to regard consultants' fees as relatively minor or whether there was an unwillingness to raise the issue of fees when it was becoming obvious that costs were escalating as that would highlight the array of problems still unresolved. In any event, there was a protracted period during which the issue of consultants' fees remained unresolved although overall construction costs clearly had increased. It was only when the present Presiding Officer personally intervened that fee caps were finally established. (Para 12.67)

Queensberry House

From the evidence provided to me, Sir David Steel's criticism of Simpson & Brown's finding that the building was "fundamentally sound" is misleading when read in the context of the full report and from subsequent advice provided to him by the Project Sponsor at the end of 1999. (Para 13.17)

Although the question of the amount of floor retention in Queensberry House remained contentious there was no evidence to suggest that this adversely affected the timetable or overall costs. (Para 13.50)

I am bound to conclude that Historic Scotland sought to revisit the issue of the Belvedere Tower with a view to its restoration, as opposed to retention, but ultimately conceded on the point. (Para 13.59)

It is obvious that the issues of retention against restoration and the Architect's plans after handover to demolish part of the existing Belvedere Tower led to unnecessary delays in obtaining listed building consent and added to the cost of the Project. Whilst the costs incurred are minimal when compared with the cost of the Project as a whole, this delay could and should have been avoided. It was irksome and in some respects irrelevant, but it took up an inordinate amount of time and involvement. Even the Secretary of State was involved in protracted negotiations over a matter which should have been effectively dealt with by the Holyrood Project Team. Historic Scotland were understandably pernickety, but it might be argued that that is their role. What appears to have gone wrong is that the HPT placed undue reliance on the opinion of Mr Hume, the former Chief Inspector. (Para 13.63)

I do not find that the enfilade issue contributed to time or cost delays, although the new foyer resolved upon as a better solution by the Architect contributed significantly to both. (Para 13.68)

It has proved to be the case that Queensberry House, in terms of cost per square metre, has turned out to be the most expensive part of the entire Project. Nevertheless, the overall cost, when viewed in light of the full cost of the Project currently at £431m, can be viewed as comparatively minor. (Para 13.75)

It is clear from the evidence presented to me that the arguments surrounding the treatment of Queensberry House as part of the Holyrood Project were protracted and convictions were strongly held almost from the Project's inception. (Para 13.76)

There is no doubt that by having to focus on specific recurring themes in relation to Queensberry House, the HPG and the Project Team found it difficult to make progress and that these issues were discussed at the highest level by the First Minister and Presiding Officer to try and find a resolution. Crucially, however, it is to be noted this did not cause any delay to the overall programme, as Queensberry House was never on the critical path. At the same time the costs of Queensberry House have been significantly greater than anticipated at the outset. (Para 13.77)

Programming

It is a matter of judgment whether the decision of the Project Team not to pass Mr Briggs' report to Bovis was the correct decision, in light of the evident delays which had occurred up to that point. I am bound to be circumspect in reviewing the decisions of professional people who had an intimate acquaintance with the Project, which had by then developed its own unstoppable momentum, but I am not able to resist the impression that there was a cautious approach by Project Management to this difficult subject. (Para 14.17)

I have no doubt that much difficulty was experienced in achieving a flow of design information consistent with the optimistic programmes prepared by Bovis. I am also in no doubt that the design flow was from time to time a source of serious frustration. However, I am far from clear that "design flow" as described to me by Mr Mack, Mr Curran and Ms Davidson was achieved any less quickly than it could ever have been, given the complexity of the designs with which all concerned had to grapple. In consideration of this problem, the tension among time, cost and quality is very well illustrated, in that it is plain that if the time criterion is set too tightly, it is likely to follow that the design flow will fail to meet expectations. In addition, if as a result of time parameters having been set too tightly, construction cannot proceed in accordance with the programme, then there will clearly be a cost penalty, as has been the case. (Para 14.20)

The expected design flow failed to keep pace with the programme demanded by the client and proposed by Bovis. Some such failures were the responsibility of the Architect, and arose in my view from the indifferent co-ordination and communication between Edinburgh and Barcelona, which was uneven, working well at times but poorly at others. It ought to have been more completely understood by the client that high quality design work takes time, and that the programme itself was unrealistic given the complexities of the design, especially after Mr Briggs' report in February 2002. Bovis too should have understood that. By the same token, the Architect should not have signed up to programmes which it could not honour and ought to have been more vociferous in relation to the time needed to achieve designs which could be programmed accurately. The programme was propelled by the client obsession with early completion. It appears not to have been completely grasped throughout the Project that if the quality and unique complexity of the building was of overriding importance, the programme and the timing of completion would be affected significantly and extra cost inevitably occurred. (Para 14.26)

Having considered all the programming evidence, it is my view that Bovis, in constructing its programmes, probably appreciated as well as anybody the buildability consequences of the highly complex and non-standard designs which were emerging from the Design Team. In my view, their programmes reflected the political imperative for early completion. Bovis reported to the client with a degree of optimism which was often not justified. The Auditor General's assessment was that "the main cause of the slippage is delays in design of a challenging Project delivered against a tight timetable, using an unusual procurement route." I agree. (Para 14.27)

Security

Security was evidently a consideration from a very early stage and was identified as such in the earliest versions of the Building User Brief in 1998. The cost and programme implications of security measures had been under-estimated by everyone, including the client. The events of 11 September 2001 were not the catalyst to a wholesale review of the security requirements. (Para 15.2)

Where relaxation might have been considered in the past, after 11 September 2001 this was no longer permitted. This approach was succinctly if rather clumsily captured in a minute of a meeting in October

2002 where it was noted that "the impact of 9/11 was not to introduce any new measures or guidelines but to make all the measures recommended over the past five years more mandatory." (Para 15.6)

The earlier cost estimates and ambitious programmes appear to have had a myopic approach to the security issue. I have seen little evidence to suggest that its full implications were foreseen by either the client, the Design Team or their advisers. (Para 15.7)

It has been suggested that the full extent of the additional costs attributable to security may have amounted to as much as £100 million. It has also been speculated that the understandable but not fully understood requirements of "security" are a convenient scapegoat for uncomfortable cost rises. (Para 15.8)

Mr Fisher suggested a total of £29.11 million. A sum of £17.54 million was identified as the net additional cost of the consequences of the design of anti-blast measures. A second element is a sum of £11.57 million attributable to the cost of delay associated with blast. (Para 15.9)

On the evidence I am persuaded me that suggestions that the cost of security measures for the Holyrood building could amount to £100 million were wholly inaccurate. (Para 15.10)

Recommendations

I do not envisage another Parliament building will be constructed in Scotland in my lifetime or for many years after that and the circumstances of the Holyrood Project might accordingly be regarded as wholly exceptional. However there are a number of recommendations that I might usefully make. Some I am conscious may already have been implemented since the Holyrood Project began or during my Inquiry and I acknowledge that. Where they have been, it may nevertheless be helpful if on the basis of evidence before this Inquiry, I indicate my approval of the changes.

1. Where a competition is held for the selection of a designer, consultant or contractor for a public building project, **I recommend there should be:**

   a) **An orderly evaluation of the Pre-Qualification Questionnaires.**

   b) **A consistency of approach and common membership of those making visits to the offices of candidates.**

   c) **A full and transparent record of all aspects of the competition from start to conclusion.**

2. Where the best design solution is seen to be one of an internationally renowned 'signature' architect linking with a Scottish based practice, **I recommend a full and rigorous evaluation should be undertaken to confirm a compatibility of working cultures and practices.**

3. Construction Management as a procurement route should be used sparingly for any public building project. All risk lies with the client and ultimately the taxpayer. Current Treasury Guidance could not be clearer. It is a procurement route of last resort. **I recommend civil servants or local government officials contemplating construction management for a public project should reflect long and hard on the advantages and disadvantages of such a route and should set before the political leadership a full evaluation of the risks.**

4. The United Kingdom, including Scotland, is a member of the European Union and is bound to observe all the procurement rules from advertisement in the Official Journal through to the de-briefing of unsuccessful candidates. Not all those who appeared before the Inquiry appeared to have a necessary familiarity with these rules. **I recommend that no-one should be put in charge of any public project without a demonstrable appreciation of what is required under EU procurement rules.**

5. **I recommend that where independent professional advisers have been retained, their views should not be filtered by the Civil Service but should be put to Ministers alongside any disagreement officials may have with the judgements expressed by those advisers.**

6. **I recommend that where civil servants are engaged on public projects, governance should be as clear as is now required in the private sector.**

7. As I have expressed in the body of my Report, the lawyers for the Scottish Parliament were ingenious in their side-stepping of the maxim, *delegatus non potest delegare.* If there had been a legal challenge to their solution I would not have been confident that it would have survived. The Clerk and Chief Executive, Mr Paul Grice, nodded an understanding of the problem. Accordingly **I recommend that Section 21 of the Scotland Act 1998 should be amended to give the SPCB wider powers of delegation than exist at present.**

8. After 9/11 and other more recent events, the security and safety of our public buildings has become paramount as much to protect the innocents as those who work within them. I am aware from the evidence heard <u>in camera</u> what steps have been taken to secure the integrity of the Parliament building and the safety of those who occupy it and I am impressed by that without revealing detail. Nevertheless **I recommend that the considerations of the security and safety of public buildings should not be regarded as late 'add ons' to the design but primary integral parts of the User Brief and the assessment of any proposed design.**

9. The previous Presiding Officer, Sir David Steel, expressed in his evidence his frustration and that of other MSPs that the procedures of the Scottish Parliament did not allow for oral questioning of the Presiding Officer. My understanding is that since 13th February 2004 the Standing Orders of the Parliament have been altered to allow such questioning. **If that change had not been made since I embarked on this Inquiry, I would have wanted to recommend the change and, with respect, commend the Scottish Parliament for making it.**

10. The Auditor General for Scotland in his June 2004 Report records at page 27 in relation to the Flour City contract:

> "In September 2002 I informed the Accountable Officer of what I considered then were the key concerns emerging from the work. He accepted that some interim contracts were allowed to continue long after trade contracts should have been finalised and that there were significant delays in obtaining some performance bonds and parent company guarantees. Fortunately, except in the Flour City case, none of the risks implicit in this situation appeared to have crystallised. Following my audit the Accountable Officer took action to ensure that where necessary full contracts, bonds and guarantees were put in place and to prevent similar risks arising again."

> Once again, with respect, I agree with this careful analysis by the Auditor General for Scotland.

In the light of his recommendations I trust this to be an unnecessary recommendation but nevertheless I advise: **Where an architect, consultant or other contractor is comparably employed, on his own account or as part of a joint venture, full contracts, guarantees and bonds should be secured at the outset to prevent risks to the public purse emerging.**

Since early 2004 RMJM Ltd have been offering the necessary undertaking. That should be accepted forthwith but it should not have been incumbent upon them to have taken the initiative.

Annex A - Some Key Dates in the History of the Holyrood Project

1995

30 November	Publication of Report of Scottish Constitutional Convention: 'Scotland's Parliament, Scotland's Right'

1997

1 May	UK General Election
30 May	Donald Dewar visits Old Royal High School
24 July	White Paper 'Scotland's Parliament' published indicating range of costs £10 - £40 million
August to December	Review and appraisal of three short-listed sites
8 December	Holyrood site added to shortlist

1998

9 January	Announcement of selection of Holyrood Site and of competition to appoint designer
3 March	Announcement of Designer Competition Selection Panel
27 March	Announcement of 12 interviewees for Designer Selection Competition
April	Appointment of Davis, Langdon & Everest as Cost Consultants
21 April	Outline Notice of Proposed Development submitted to Edinburgh City Council
7 May	Announcement of 5 shortlisted candidates for designer selection competition
6 July	Announcement of appointment of EMBT in association with RMJM as Architects
21 July	Decision taken to adopt construction management
22 July	Outline Notice of Proposed Development Application approved by City of Edinburgh Council
August to January 1999	Process for selection of construction manager
16 September	EMBT/RMJM Ltd present outline design proposals to Donald Dewar
2 November	Stage C outline design presented by the Design Team
November	Revised Building User Brief issued
December	Departure of Bill Armstrong as Project Manager

1999

4 January	Final interview of shortlisted candidates for Construction Manager appointment
7 January	Appointment of Bovis as Construction Manager
1 June	Handover of responsibility for the Project from the Secretary of State to the Scottish Parliamentary Corporate Body
17 June	First Parliamentary debate – MSPs vote to proceed with Project with a budget of £109 million
July 1999	Demolition works completed and main construction work begins on site

2000

25 February	John Spencely appointed to report on the Holyrood Project costs and programme
24 March	Publication of Mr Spencely's report
5 April	Second Parliamentary debate – MSPs vote to continue with Project subject to cap on costs at £195million and appointment of Progress Group
19 June	Approval of Stage D report by SPCB
28 June	First meeting of Holyrood Progress Group
3 July	Death of Enric Miralles
September	First Report of Auditor General for Scotland into the management of the Holyrood Project
7 October	Death of Donald Dewar
1 November	City of Edinburgh Council Planning Committee remit consideration of Queensberry House Reserved Matters to the Head of Planning
13 November	Appointment of Alan Ezzi as the Holyrood Project Director
December	Audit Committee, 6th Report

2001

January	MSP building topped out
21 June	Third Parliamentary debate – MSPs vote to lift £195 million cap
June	Sarah Davidson replaces Alan Ezzi as Project Director
November	Estimated final cost reported to Finance Committee at £241 million

2002

March	Estimated final cost reported to Finance Committee at £266.4m
October	Estimated final cost reported to Finance Committee at £294.6m

2003

January	Estimated final cost reported to Finance Committee at £323.9 million
May	Election of George Reid as Presiding Officer
June	Appointment of Lord Fraser to undertake independent Inquiry into the Holyrood Building Project
June	Estimated final cost reported to Finance Committee at £375.8 million
September	Estimated final cost reported to Finance Committee at £401 million

2004

February	Estimated final cost reported to Finance Committee at £431 million
June	Publication of Auditor General's Second Report on management of the Project
August	Occupation of building
7 September	Scottish Parliament meets for first time in Holyrood

Annex B – WHO'S WHO

Tom Aitchison	Chief Executive of the City of Edinburgh Council
Wendy Alexander	MSP, former Minister and Special Adviser to Donald Dewar
Anthony Andrew	Civil servant, Chief Estates Officer Head of Land and Property Division
Bill Armstrong	Project Manager, Holyrood Project, 1 November 1997 to 1 December 1998
Gordon Ash	Director, Bovis
Laurence Bain	Director, Bain & Bevington Architects Ltd, formerly Michael Wilford and Partners Ltd
Mark Batho	Civil servant, Head of Division, Finance Group
David Black	Author
Robert Black	Auditor General for Scotland
David Boyle	Director, Sir Robert McAlpine Limited, shortlisted tenderer for construction manager appointment
Steve Briggs	Forensic Programmer, Turner & Townsend
Alistair Brown	Civil servant, Director of Administrative Services 5 May 1997 to November 1999
Robert Brown	MSP and member of the SPCB, 19 May 1999 to present
Bovis	Construction Manager, Holyrood Project Initially Bovis Construction (Scotland) Ltd now Bovis Lend Lease Ltd after change of name on 1 February 2000
Cairn Property Services	Building Control Consultants, Holyrood Project
Joan Callis	Senior Architect, EMBT, Barcelona
John Campbell QC	Counsel to the Inquiry
Colin Carter	Partner, Gardiner & Theobald, Chartered Quantity Surveyors
John Clement	Chartered Surveyor, DM Hall, 1995 – 2001
Paul Curran	Project Manager, Holyrood Project from 17 January 1999 – January 2002 Senior Project Manager – January 2002 – June 2004 Project Director from 21 June 2004
Michael Dallas	Partner, Davis, Langdon & Everest, London
Sarah Davidson	Secretary, HPG, 5 June 2000 to July 2001 Project Director, Holyrood Project Team, July 2001 to June 2004
Davis, Langdon & Everest (DLE)	Quantity Surveyors and Cost Consultants, Holyrood Project
Donald Dewar	Secretary of State for Scotland from 1 May 1997 to 1 July 1999 First Minister from 1 July 1999 until his death on 7 October 2000
DSWR	Cabinet Sub Committee with responsibility for devolution issues in Scotland, Wales and the English regions
Barbara Doig	Civil servant, Head of Parliament Accommodation Division March 1998 to May 1999, Holyrood Project Sponsor, and a Scottish Parliament Director 1 June 1999 to May 2000
Doig & Smith	Quantity Surveyors
Mick Duncan	Director, EMBT/RMJM Ltd
Lord Elder of Kirkcaldy	Special Adviser to Donald Dewar

Richard Emerson	Principal Inspector of Historic Buildings, Historic Scotland, Chief Inspector from 1 March 1999 to date
Dr Robin Evetts	Inspector of Historic Buildings, Historic Scotland
Fergus Ewing	MSP for Inverness East, Nairn & Lochaber
Alan Ezzi	Holyrood Project Director 13 November 2000 - 22 June 2001
Linda Fabiani	MSP for Central Scotland and member of HPG June 2000 – present
Jim Fairclough	Secretary to the Construction Management Services Interview Panel Member of the Holyrood Project Team
Dave Ferguson	Audit Adviser to the Scottish Parliament
Hugh Fisher	Partner, Davis, Langdon & Everest
Lesley Fisher	EMBT/RMJM Limited
Sam Galbraith	Former MP, MSP and Minister
Keith Geddes	Leader of City of Edinburgh Council 1996 to 1999
Dr John Gibbons	Civil servant, Chief Architect to Scottish Office and Architectural Adviser to Project Sponsor and later to SPCB and HPG. Interim Project Director as at July 2000. HPG member.
Stewart Gilfillan	Project Financial Controller
Robert Gordon	Civil servant, Head of the Constitution Group 2 May 1997 – 23 December 1998, Head of Executive Secretariat 23 December 1998 – 1 July 1999 HPG member
Donald Gorrie	MP for West Edinburgh 1997-2001, MSP for Central Scotland
John Graham	Civil servant, Principal Finance Officer May 1997 to May 1998
Paul Grice	Civil servant, Head of Division, Constitution Group Unit, Scottish Office, Clerk and Chief Executive of Scottish Parliament 1 June 1999 – present
David Hadden	Arup Security
William Heigh	Project Manager, Holyrood Project Team
John Henderson	Private Finance Unit, Scottish Office
Sir Russell Hillhouse	Civil servant, Permanent Secretary, Scottish Office from 1 April 1988 to 30 April 1998
Andrew Holmes	Head of Corporate Affairs, Department of City Development, City of Edinburgh District Council, 1996; Director of City Development, City of Edinburgh Council 1999
John Hume	Chief Inspector of Historic Buildings, Historic Scotland until February 1999; from March 1999 Consultant to the Scottish Parliament
Gordon Jackson	MSP for Glasgow Govan
Patricia Johnstone	Associate, Ove Arup & Partners
William Kay	Addyman & Kay
Eric Kinsey	Member of the Holyrood Project Team
John Kinsley	Architect, RMJM, Edinburgh
David Lewis	Partner, Ove Arup & Partners

Isabelle Low	Civil servant responsible for co-ordinating revisions to and publication of the White Paper, 1997
Michael Lugton	Civil servant, Private Secretary to Donald Dewar 1997
Ian McAndie	Partner, Davis, Langdon & Everest, Edinburgh
Tom McCabe	MSP and Minister for Parliament, 1999
Rt Hon Jack McConnell	MSP for Motherwell and Wishaw, First Minister and former Minister for Finance
Lewis Macdonald	MSP for Aberdeen Central, Convener of the HPG June 2000 - 22 March 2001
Margo MacDonald	MSP for the Lothians
Eddie McGibbon	Project Planner, Bovis
Lord Mackay of Drumadoon	Lord Advocate, 1997
Dr Aonghus MacKechnie	Principal Inspector of Historic Monuments, Historic Scotland
Rt Hon Henry McLeish	Former Minister of State, The Scottish Office and Minister for Devolution First Minister October 2000 to November 2001
Professor Andrew MacMillan	Former Head, Mackintosh School of Art, Glasgow; Architectural Consultant, Member of the Designer Selection Panel
Duncan McNeill	MSP, Member of the SPCB, 2002 - present
Des McNulty	MSP, Member of the SPCB, 19 May 1999 to 2002
Brian McQuade	Director, Bovis
Alan Mack	Project Director, Bovis, Holyrood Project
David Manson	Chartered Quantity Surveyor, member of the HPG
David Miller	Architect, EMBT/RMJM Ltd
Rt Hon Eric Milligan	Lord Provost of Edinburgh from 1996 until 2003
Enric Miralles	Architect, Director EMBT/RMJM Ltd until his death on 3 July 2000
Graeme Munro	Chief Executive, Historic Scotland
Martin Mustard	Project Manager, Holyrood Project Team January 1998 – December 2001
Joan O'Connor	Director PMI Ltd (Dublin) Chartered Architect, Member of the Designer Selection Panel
Ove Arup & Partners	Structural Engineers, Holyrood Project
Craig Paterson	Design Manager, Bovis
Brian Peddie	Civil servant, Finance Officer, Scottish Office
Nira Ponniah	Architect, EMBT/RMJM
Charles Prosser	Secretary of Royal Fine Arts Commission.
Judith Proudfoot	Secretary to the HPG July 2001 – June 2004
Graham Reed	Inspector, Historic Scotland
Rt Hon George Reid	MSP for Ochil and Deputy Presiding Officer 1999 – May 2003 Presiding Officer and Chair of the SPCB May 2003 - present
RMJM Ltd	Chartered Architects
RMJM (Scotland) Ltd	Building Services Engineers
John Home Robertson	MSP for East Lothian and Convener of the HPG 22 March 2001 - present
David Rogers	Civil servant, Private Finance Unit

Sir Muir Russell	Civil servant, Head of The Scottish Office Agriculture, Environment and Fisheries Department (SOAEFD) 1995 to May 1998 Permanent Secretary of Scottish Office / Executive 1 May 1998 to 4 July 2003
Alex Salmond	MP for Banff and Buchan, Leader of the Scottish National Party
Tavish Scott	MSP for Shetland and Former member of HPG June – November 2000
Lord Sewel of Gilcomstoun	Parliamentary Under Secretary of State in the Scottish Office, May 1997
James Simpson	Partner, Simpson & Brown, Architects Non-Executive Director, Addyman & Kay
Ian Spence	Development Quality Manager, City Development Department, City of Edinburgh Council
John Spencely	Architect, Author of Report to the SPCB on the Holyrood Project - 24 March 2000
Sir David Steel	MSP for the Lothians and Presiding Officer and Chair of the SPCB June 1999 – May 2003
Gregor Stark	Regional Architect
Brian Stewart	Director, EMBT/RMJM Ltd
Jamie Stone	MSP for Caithness, Sutherland and Easter Ross, Member of the HPG November 2000 - present
Benedetta Tagliabue Miralles	Architect; EMBT; Partner until 3 July 2000 and thereafter sole proprietor
Kenneth Thomson	Civil servant, Former Principal Private Secretary to Donald Dewar
Carol Thorburn	Chartered Surveyor, DLE
Harry Thorburn	Managing Director, Bovis
Sebastian Tombs	Secretary and Chief Executive of the Royal Incorporation of Architects in Scotland
Turner & Townsend	Planning Supervisors and Project Managers
Alan Tweedie	Associate, Ove Arup & Partners, South Queensferry
Karl Unglaub	Architect, EMBT
Jim Wallace	MSP for Orkney and Deputy First Minister
Kirsty Wark	Journalist and Broadcaster, Director Wark Clements Ltd, Member of the Designer Selection Panel
Andrew Welsh	MSP for Angus and member of the SPCB 19 May 1999 to present
Huw Williams	Private Secretary to the Presiding Officer, 1999-2000
Rt Hon Brian Wilson	Former Minister of State, Scottish Office
George Wren	President, Royal Incorporation of Architects in Scotland
Andrew Wright	Architect, member of the HPG
Alastair Wyllie	Civil Servant, Head of Building Division Construction and Building Control Group
John Young	Former MSP and former member of the Scottish Parliamentary Corporate Body 1 June 1999 to May 2003